PHILOSOPHER
AND
PROPHET

SUNY Series in Judaica

Michael Fishbane, Robert Goldenberg,
and Elliot Wolfson, editors

PHILOSOPHER
AND
PROPHET

JUDAH HALEVI, THE *KUZARI*, AND
THE EVOLUTION OF HIS THOUGHT

YOCHANAN SILMAN

translated from the Hebrew by Lenn J. Schramm

State University of New York Press

Publication of this volume was made possible by Bar Ilan University and by the Kunin-Mazor Chair of Philosophy and the Rabbi A Safran Chair.

Published by
State University of New York Press, Albany

© 1995 State University of New York

All rights reserved

Printed in the United States of America

No part of this book may be used or reproduced in any manner whatsoever without written permission. No part of this book may be stored in a retrieval system or transmitted in any form or by any means including electronic, electrostatic, magnetic tape, mechanical, photocopying, recording, or otherwise without prior permission in writing of the publisher.

For information, address State University of New York Press, State University Plaza, Albany, N.Y. 12246

Production by Marilyn P. Semerad
Marketing by Bernadette LaManna

Library of Congress Cataloging-in-Publication Data

Silman, Yochanan.
 [Ben filosof le-navi. English]
 Philosopher and prophet : Judah Halevi, the Kuzari, and the evolution of his thought / Yochanan Silman ; translated from the Hebrew by Lenn J. Schramm.
    p. cm. — (SUNY series in Judaica)
 Includes bibliographical references and index.
 ISBN 0-7914-2461-8. — ISBN 0-7914-2462-6 (pbk.)
   1. Judah, ha-Levi, 12th cent. Kitāb al-ḥujjah.   2. Philosophy, Jewish. 3. Philosophy, Medieval.   I. Title. II. Series.
BM550.J84S5513   1995
181'.06—dc20   94-42398
                                                                      CIP

10 9 8 7 6 5 4 3 2 1

CONTENTS

Preface   vii

Part I The Philosopher's Thought
1   Aristotelian Philosophy in the *Kuzari*   3
2   Divinity and Individuation   15
3   Form and Matter   31
4   Aristotelian Anthropology   51
5   Human Activity   77

Part II Halevi's Earlier Thought
6   Introduction to the Earlier Thought   109
7   The Theology of the Early Thought   119
8   Anthropology in the Earlier Thought   131
9   The Historical Dimension in the Earlier Thought   137
10 The Jewish People, Their Commandments, and Their Uniqueness in the Earlier Thought   143
11 Eretz Israel as the Chosen Land   153
12 An Overview of Halevi's Earlier Thought   159

Part III Halevi's Later Thought
13 Introduction: Unique Features   169
14 Human Experience and the Divine Presence   173

15　God and the World　183

16　The Later Anthropology　227

17　History in the Later Thought　253

18　The Jewish People, Their Commandments, and Their Uniqueness in the Later Thought　275

19　An Overview of Halevi's Later Thought　289

Part IV　The Unity of the *Kuzari*

20　Introduction: The Structure of the Book and Its Unity　311

21　Theology and Anthropology　315

22　Form and Content in the *Kuzari*　331

Appendix: The Giving of the Torah and Commandments as a Process　341

Bibliography　345

Indexes　349

PREFACE

This study aims to shed light on the relations among the main world-views represented in the *Kuzari*. To this end, all the intellectual and philosophical currents found in that work are presented as a single body of thought, whose dialectic unity includes Aristotelian philosophy as well. As we shall see, this unity is woven by tensions inherent to Halevi's philosophical system as well as by this biographical experiences. These tensions derive from the fundamental contrasts between Halevi's thought at the time he wrote the *Kuzari* and the tenets of Aristotelian philosophy, to which he adhered at an earlier period in his life. In the interim, his thought had evolved as he developed various ways to cope with the perceived shortcomings of the latter. According to Halevi, the Aristotelian world-view is an exclusive, faithful, and exhaustive expression of rational knowledge as such. Because he holds that Judaism draws from another unique source, the opposition between Judaism and Aristotelian philosophy is fundamental, not merely a chance expression of transient historical circumstances.

Fundamental contradictions are also to be found in Halevi's own thought at the time of the composition of the *Kuzari*, in the opinions stated by the Rabbi. A large part of the present study is devoted to the attempt to demonstrate that these contradic-

PREFACE

tions reflect defined currents of thought, each of which has a large degree of internal consistency. An analysis of Halevi's thought on key issues, supplemented by external evidence, indicates that these currents express two stages in the evolution of his thought at the time he wrote the *Kuzari*: In the earlier stage, Halevi still adhered to many tenets of Aristotelian philosophy; it is in their spirit that he attempts to interpret the Jewish tradition. Later, though, he broke with many of these tenets and placed the emphasis on the unique experiences of the Jewish people. From this perspective one can see the *Kuzari* as an autobiographical work in which Halevi described the evolution of his thought, marked by vacillation and contradictions, which are expounded in the course of the dialogue that ties the book together. In this study, we shall refer to these two stages as the *earlier thought* and the *later thought*. For Halevi, though, these stages did not have only autobiographical significance; they also represent necessary stages in the spiritual development of man—both the human individual and the human collective. This is why his mature system incorporates the earlier thought, which he himself had already renounced. In the exposition of his earlier thought Halevi is addressing those who are not yet able to identify with the later thought; his goal is to help them make their world-view compatible with Judaism: its commandments and beliefs, the historical destiny of the Jewish people in the present, and its future vocation.[1] As I shall attempt to demonstrate, certain parts and sections of the book can be assigned to one or the other stage. Frequently one can distinguish parts or sections on the basis of formal and literary considerations as well. These signs confirm the basic division of the *Kuzari*.

In the present study we shall examine the main lines that characterize the thought of the Aristotelian philosopher and Halevi's earlier and later thought, while elucidating the dialectic relations among these currents. The first part of this book describes the Philosopher's doctrine; the second part, Halevi's

---

1. Furthermore, Halevi was willing to grant a degree of legitimacy to what he deemed erroneous world-views. See Chapter 19.

earlier thought; and the third part, his later thought. Our identification of the profound contradictions within Halevi's system requires that we consider the unity of the *Kuzari*; this is the topic of the fourth part.

The *Kuzari* and especially Halevi's own thought is replete with hierarchical structures. On the ontological plane, these include the relation between actual existence and potential existence; the relation between great historical events and natural phenomena; the relation between degrees of existence, between nations, countries, seasons, languages, and so on. On the normative plane, we find hierarchical relations between deeds that are pleasing to God and deeds that are not pleasing to God; between action and intention, between action and contemplation; and between the injunctions of reason and Divine commandments. And on the epistemological plane, there are hierarchical relations between different forms of cognition and between opposing world-views.[2]

Hierarchical order is also intrinsic to Aristotelian philosophy. Its acme is the First Cause; its lowest degree, hylic or primordial matter. There are many differences among the various hierarchical structures erected by the different systems expounded in the *Kuzari*. These differences are a faithful mirror of the different meanings given to the ontological poles, to the nature of the relations that evolve between them, and to the ways in which they can be constituted. In this study, an investigation of these differences is the main methodological point of departure for understanding the relations among and within the systems in the *Kuzari*. By considering the essence and source of the "ladder set on the earth and its top reached the heavens," we learn about the nature of the "heavens," the nature of the "earth," and about the meaning of "ascending" the ladder.

We shall examine the differences among hierarchical structures from four angles: (1) their source, (2) their location and

---

2. See J. Schlanger, "La doctrine de la hiérarchie dans le livre du *Kuzari* de Jehuda Halevi (1085–1141)," *Colloque international sur le néoplatonisme, Royaumont, 9–13 juin 1969* (Paris, 1971), pp. 339–353.

PREFACE

scope, (3) the relations among the hierarchical structures, and (4) the relations among the various degrees within each structure and between each of them and the overall hierarchy.

In the last context, particular importance attaches to the possibility of passage from one degree to another, the conditions for such a passage, the role played by the upper degrees vis-à-vis the lower degrees, and the role played by the lower degrees vis-à-vis the higher degrees.

This study is the result of years of research. The first section is based on my doctoral dissertation, "God and Matter in the Light of the Hierarchical Relations in the *Kuzari*," written under the direction of Prof. Shlomo Pines and submitted to the Hebrew University of Jerusalem in 1973. A number of chapters have been added and many important changes made, based on later research. The other three sections of the book, which deal with Halevi's earlier and later thought, reflect conclusions based on recent work, some of which has been published in articles (see bibliography) and has now been integrated, in some fashion or other, into this book.

Jerusalem, May 1994

PART I

THE PHILOSOPHER'S THOUGHT

1

ARISTOTELIAN PHILOSOPHY IN THE *KUZARI*

Aristotelian philosophy plays a central and systematic role in the *Kuzari*. This is not surprising, since Judah Halevi's thought developed through an ongoing dialogue with it. Moreover, he believed that Philosophy (i.e., Aristotelian philosophy),[1] including those of its postulates that he refutes in his book, is an essential component of the process through which both the individual and humanity as a whole work out their relationship with God. Halevi's thought aims to provide appropriate answers to the questions raised by the confrontation with philosophy (1,1 [4]). As we shall see, however, the same questions underlie the progress of his own thought.

In his early period, Halevi still adhered in principle to the fundamental axioms of Aristotelian philosophy. When he

Translator's note: References to the *Kuzari* are given in the form book-paragraph, followed by one or two bracketed page numbers, separated by a slash. The first (and sometimes only) number refers to the Hebrew translation by Ibn Tibbon (the version through which the *Kuzari* has been known and interpreted over the generations), in the Zifroni edition (Jerusalem and Tel Aviv: Schocken, 1967). On rare occasions, where Ibn Tibbon's rendering is problematic, a reference is given to the modern Hebrew translation by Yehudah Even-Shmuel (Tel Aviv: Dvir, 1972), as indicated by the prefixed letters ES.

invoked them he endeavored to synthesize them with concepts derived from Jewish tradition. In his later thought, which is strongly marked by the debate with philosophy, he freed himself from some of these axioms and emphasized the intrinsic virtues of traditional concepts. His quarrel with philosophy does not seek mainly to contradict its assertions, but to undermine its confidence in itself as the absolute expression of intellectual truth, whose practical implications are valid in all contexts. In his later thought, Halevi conceded to philosophy that, in principle, rational thinking can be carried through unambiguously and exhaustively. Aristotle had actually done so; Aristotelian philosophy is the substantive expression of his achievement. Were it not for certain events in which God was revealed to human beings, philosophy would be accepted—and rightly so—as the loftiest religious truth that human beings can conceive by their own power. Philosophy is the fruit of study and careful research (1,62 [29]): "There are differences in the ways of demonstration; some of them are exact, others insufficient; but

---

The page number after the slash refers to what is still the only complete English translation, that by Hartwig Hirschfeld (New York: Schocken, 1964; originally published 1905). Thus 1,1 [5/36] means Part I, §1, p. 5 in Zifroni, p. 36 in Hirschfeld. Unfortunately, Hirschfeld's translation leaves much to be desired, in terms of both readability and accuracy. Isaak Heinemann, in his abridged edition (Oxford: East and West Library, 1947), which is really a revision of Hirschfeld, drastically improved the readability and fidelity to the original of Hirschfeld's text. But Heinemann rarely indicated where he cut material from the beginning, middle, or end of a section, and even joined parts of different sentences into one, silently deleting the end of the first and beginning of the second; this approach makes his version quite unusable for scholarly purposes. Any reader of this book who wants to consult the *Kuzari* in English and see how a particular passage fits into its context has no choice but to use Hirschfeld. Given the problems with his version, however, I have been compelled to revise his translation so extensively (including many silent borrowings from Heinemann) that it would be confusing and pointless to indicate deviations from his text. Thus readers who consult Hirschfeld to locate a passage in context may not always find the text presented here.

1. The terms *philosophy* and *philosopher*, without further qualification, refer throughout to the Aristotelian school, whose main tenets are presented in the first section of Book One of the *Kuzari*. The Philosopher, with a capital *P*—and, similarly, the King and the Rabbi—refer to the three main characters in the book.

THE PHILOSOPHER'S THOUGHT

the ways of the philosophers are the most exact of all" (4,3 [218/199]). Its practitioners have a "refined intuition and clear view" (2,54 [112/116]). Hence philosophers cannot be reproached for their misleading world-view;[2] in fact, they merit reward in the world to come (1,111 [61]).[3] On the other hand, Halevi refused to accept that their positivist assertions are unconditionally valid; they are merely "convincing" (1,2 [10/39]).[4] In particular, he attempted to undermine the foundations of philosophy's answer to the problem of human mortality and death—the answer that gives Aristotelian philosophy its religious significance and turns it into a rival of the historical religions. He carefully avoided any confrontation with the philosophers' trenchant critique of the concept of divinity that lies at the core of revealed religion; this evasion must be understood as an admission that, from the purely theoretical perspective, their criticism is irrefutable.

For Halevi, the dispute with philosophy is not anchored exclusively in historical or biographical circumstances, but in the very essence of man as a rational being. Because the degree of the prophet builds on the degree of the rational man—just as each degree enlarges upon the perfections of those lower than it (1,30–43)[5]—the prophet, as a rational being, must deal with the arguments of philosophy that are necessarily visible on the horizons of his consciousness. Hence Halevi distinguished a philosophical or quasi-philosophical stage in every process

---

2. See 1,63–65; 4,13; 4,16.

3. This contrasts with the opinion of al-Ghazali, who contended that the philosophers, including al-Farabi and Avicenna, were heretics. See al-Ghazali, *Al-Munquid min adalāl*, trans. (into French) F. Jabre (Beirut, 1959), p. 73. Halevi's "liberal" view on this question simply reflects the theory of degrees of reality, on the one hand, and his view of the inferior value of speculative thought, on the other.

4. We must not understand *convincing* here in the narrow sense of the term, equivalent to "proven." Its sense is rather on the order of "adequate" or "plausible," although lacking decisive material proofs. Compare 1,13, where an explicit distinction is made between arguments that are *decisive* and those that are *sufficient*. Compare 1,68; 2,59; 5,2. See also Moscato on 1,68. This is also the opinion of H. A. Wolfson, *Crescas' Critique of Aristotle* (Cambridge, 1929), p. 369.

5. See 1,95 [46]; 2,26 [96/103]; 2,48 [106/111]; 2,50 [108/113].

whereby the individual or nation draws near to its God. Adam should be seen as the first father of philosophy (1,63 [30]), because "he was endowed... with the most perfect soul and with the loftiest intellect that it is possible for a human being to possess" (1,95 [46/64]). Before his first prophetic experience, he too could have only a limited perception of the Deity, that corresponding to the degree of rational understanding—God as Elohim (4,3 [219]).[6] Similarly, the patriarch Abraham, before God was revealed to him in a vision, conceived of Him rationally, by means of speculation. Halevi believed that this conception essentially resembles that of the Philosopher (4,27 [269]). *Sefer Yetzirah* is the literary expression of Abraham's prerevelatory thought (4,37 [270]). Only after his first epiphany did Abraham learn that "no detail of his life escaped God and that He rewarded him instantly for his piety and guided him along the best path, so that he moved forwards or backwards only according to God's will. How should he not despise his former speculations?" (4,17 [247/223]). Similarly, the Jewish people, before their collective experience of the Divine revelation at Sinai, were distinguished among the nations for their philosophical excellence; the other nations learned from them (2,66 [121]).[7] Consequently, the Israelites could not accept the opinion that "God spoke with man, until [Moses] caused them to hear the Ten Commandments" (1,49 [26/50]).

In light of the preceding, the introduction of the Philosopher before the representatives of the revealed religions should be understood as reflecting the idea that philosophical knowledge is prior to the degree of understanding derived from revelation. The philosophical world-view represents the highest stage that can be attained by the pagan. We may plausibly assume that the biography of the Khazar king embodies in miniature the

---

6. Right before this (4,3 [281]), Halevi noted that the philosophers, too, are incapable of surpassing the degree of conception of God expressed by the name *Elohim*, even though in its context they are able to reach the most "precise" idea.

7. See 1,63 [30]; 3,17 [162]. See also D. Neumark, *Essays in Jewish Philosophy* (Cincinnati, 1929), pp. 225ff.

chief stages in the process whereby humanity as a whole aspires to draw nearer to God.[8] The order in which the speakers have their audiences with him parallels the sequence of the historical epochs through which mankind is passing en route to its future full acceptance of Judaism. The Philosopher's appearance before that of the representatives of the revealed religions corresponds to the historical fact of the advent of Greek philosophy before the Torah influenced the nations of the world.

The Philosopher's appearance earlier than the other speakers also hints at the methodological role of philosophical knowledge, which is a necessary precondition for attaining the true religion.[9] Only thanks to the insight he gained from the Philosopher can the king of the Khazars understand the fundamental difficulty of positing the existence of a God who addresses individuals qua individuals: "What could be more erroneous, in the opinion of the philosophers, than the belief that the world was created, and that in six days; or that the Prime Cause spoke with one of the mortals" (1,4 [12/39]).[10] His awareness of this fundamental problem leads the King to the Rabbi and subsequently to Judaism. His recognition of this difficulty engenders

---

8. This aspiration goes back to the pagan era (1,98 [53]; 3,23 [170]; 4,1 [216]). Compare Solomon Ibn Gabirol's *Keter Malkhut*: "For the intention of all is to attain you." See Heinemann, "Philosopher-Poet," p. 202 and n. 8. Most instructive is the analogy between the stages in the integration of the personality of the pious man and the arrangement of the Israelites at Mt. Sinai (3,5 [143]). The analogy rests on the assumption that there is a parallel between the process of spiritual development of the individual and of the human collective.

9. Halevi explicitly describes human history as a process in which philosophical perception plays a positive role in the evolution of humanity (3,54 [112]). See also 4,1–3; 4,15 [246].

10. Here God is intentionally designated by the radically impersonal term *Prime Cause*. This epithet is meant to reiterate the paradox involved in even positing the possibility of "Divine speech." The paradox is even greater when this speech is directed to "one of the mortals" and is thereby an unequivocal expression of a personal relationship. After the Philosopher departs the scene the Khazar king, having been persuaded by the "adequacy" of the Philosopher's remarks, adopts the main points of his view and measures the presentations of the representatives of the three religions against it. See Schweid, *Taʿam ve-haqqashah*, p. 61.

a suspicious and critical attitude toward stories of God's appearing to an individual; hence his strict methodological stipulations for accepting factual and empirical arguments "that God has intercourse with flesh and blood" (1,8 [16/43]). When the representatives of Christianity and Islam confess that they cannot satisfy these demands without relying on the Jewish tradition, the King is compelled to turn to the Rabbi.[11] Is is not only for the non-Jew who is searching for the path to God that awareness of the problem of Divine revelation and a critical attitude toward the assumption of its possibility play an essential role. Prophetic knowledge, too, entails the methodical adoption of a critical and skeptical attitude. According to Halevi, the prophets must assume this attitude even toward their own prophetic experiences. Prophets can comprehend the objective significance of their prophetic experiences only when they juxtapose them with the experiences of other prophets: "The best proof of its truth is the harmony prevailing among the whole of this species regarding those forms. By this I mean all the prophets. For they witnessed things which one described to the other" (4,3 [228/207]).[12] In other words, prophets, too, must satisfy one of the central methodological stipulations that the King sets for verifying the factual and objective status of the revelatory experience—publicness.[13] Furthermore, sensory knowledge, by its very nature, cannot attain the essence of things (4,3 [228/207]). The role of discursive thought is to penetrate to the heart of the revelation and uncover the essence of things. A prophetic experience of revelation that is not subjected to rational criticism leads to an anthropomorphic conception of the Deity. In the words of the King: "If any one were to hear you relate that God

---

11. See 1,4 [12]; 1,9 [16]; 1,109 [58]; 2,54 [112]; 5,21 [328].
12. Compare 4,11 [240].
13. Both the Exodus and Revelation at Sinai involved a public experience "in the presence of great multitudes, who saw indistinctly" (1,8 [16/43]). See also 1,49 [26]; 1,84–87; 4,11 [240]. These crucial events satisfied another methodological criterion: They involved wonders that overturned the natural order, so that "man may recognize that God alone, who created him from nought, is able to do so" (1,8 [16/43]). See also 1,83–86; 1,91 [45]; 2,2 [71]; 5,21 [329].

spoke to your assembled multitude, and wrote tablets for you, etc., he could not be blamed for accusing you of believing in the corporeality of God" (1,88 [42/62]). To this charge the Rabbi replies: "Heaven forbid that we should assume what is impossible or that which reason rejects as being impossible" (1,89 [43/62]).[14] Polytheism, too, has roots in prophetic experiences. These experiences are characterized by a multiplicity of different images; but because all of them are given in immediate experience, they all have equal validity. Prophecy has the capacity to uproot these sources of polytheism by subjecting itself to the light of rational criticism. Such criticism can distinguish the multiplicity and variety of the prophetic images from the single substance that underlies them all (4,3 [228]).[15]

It is a scholarly commonplace that in his youth Halevi was an adherent of the dominant philosophical currents of his age, but that his world-view underwent a sea change before he wrote the *Kuzari*. This opinion is supported by various allusions in the *Kuzari* and in Halevi's poetry.[16] For example, there is the

---

14. See also 1,67 [31]. This is the source of the Rabbi's reservations about a number of talmudic legends (3,73 [211]).

15. A critical attitude toward experience, aware of the problems inherent in the postulate that revelation is possible, is a prerequisite for recognizing authentic revelation. Hence it plays a central role in the debate between Judaism and the other revealed religions. This is how we must understand the Rabbi's remark: "One who accepts [the service in the Tabernacle] with all his heart, without scrutiny or scruple, is superior to the man who scrutinizes and investigates. By contrast, someone who descends from this highest grade to scrutinizing does well to seek a wise reason for these commandments, instead of casting misconstructions and doubts upon them, which leads to corruption" (2,26 [99/106]). The remark is not aimed against Aristotelian philosophy but against the quest to find a rationale for the commandments, a quest that cannot lead to unambiguous conclusions. On this point, compare 2,49. See also Neumark, *Essays*, p. 228; A. Jacobus, "Ha-yaḥas shel sefer ha-kuzari el filosofiya" (The *Kuzari*'s attitude toward philosophy), *Alumah* (1936), pp. 61–62. For a different view see D. Kaufmann, *Geschichte der Attributenlehre in der jüdischen Religions-Philosophie des Mittelalters von Saadja bis Maimuni* (Gotha, 1877), pp. 122ff.

16. See D. Kaufmann, "R. Yehudah Halevi" (trans. from German by A. Zeidman), *Sinai* 9 (1941–1942): 23 and Appendix E [Hebrew]. See also Salo W. Baron, "Yehuda Halevi, An Answer to an Historic Challenge," *Jewish Social Studies* 3 (1941): 259, n. 33; L. Strauss, *Persecution and the Art of*

Rabbi's rhetorical question: "Where is the soul that is strong enough not to be deceived by the view of the natural scientists and astrologers and sorcerers and philosophers and others, and can adopt a belief without having first passed through many stages of heresy?" (5,2 [279/248]). Then there is the decisive argument that only after the Holy Spirit settles on a person do "there vanish all previous doubts of man concerning GOD, and he despises all these syllogistic proofs by means of which men endeavor to attain to knowledge of His dominion and unity" (4,15 [246/222]). In these passages Halevi was relying on his experiences during the period when he was an adherent of philosophy and employed the syllogistic method—which (according to the *Kuzari*) led him into error and skepticism.[17] This scholarly hypothesis is further reinforced by Halevi's overall view of the place of the philosophical stage in the process of man's rapprochement with God. It seems reasonable that Halevi, who found support for his view in the history of mankind, of the Jewish people, and of the patriarch Abraham, also found support for it in his own spiritual biography.[18] A comparison of Halevi's early and later thought reveals his increasing distance from the Aristotelian school.

In his early thought, before the *Kuzari* was written, Halevi seems to have been inclined to Aristotelian philosophy. The Philosopher's discourse in the first section of the book expresses the opinions of that school (or should be understood as a retrospective and critical attempt to uncover the implications that the Aristotelian philosophers themselves attempted to conceal).

Writing (Glencoe, Ill., 1952), p. 109; Shraga Abramson, "Mikhtav R. Yehudah Ha-levi ʿal ʿaliyato le-eretz Yisrael" (A letter by R. Judah Halevi on his aliya to Eretz Israel), *Qiryat Sefer* 29 (1953–1954): 134 and n. 8; Komem, "Poetry and Prophecy."

17. For his opinion on the association between the syllogism in metaphysics and skepticism, see later, Chapter 3, note 6.

18. Isaak Heinemann suggested that Halevi saw the biography of the patriarch Abraham in the mirror of his own life; see Y. Heinemann, "Helekh ha-raʿyonot shel hathalat sefer ha-kuzari" [The current of ideas at the beginning of the *Kuzari*], in Zemora, *R. Yehudah Halevi*, p. 247.

THE PHILOSOPHER'S THOUGHT

In keeping with the Scholastic consensus of his age, and in an attempt to bridge between Jewish tradition and the philosophical world-view, one of the centerpieces of Halevi's thought was a metaphorical interpretation of those ideas derived from the former that are incompatible with the latter. According to this interpretation, those comments interpolated into the Philosopher's discourse that do not seem to play any defined role in his exposition (or any other role in the book) are to be seen as relics of this stage in Halevi's philosophical thought.[19] By the same token, the depiction of philosophy is influenced by Halevi's critical and polemic interests while he was writing the book. Accordingly, Halevi emphasized the radical conclusions of philosophical thought because of his desire to lay bare the dangers it poses for Judaism. It is unlikely that he was aware of all these conclusions in the earlier period when he was still an adherent of philosophy.

A comparison of the philosophy of the *Kuzari* with the various Aristotelian schools known to Halevi indicates that it cannot be identified with any one of them. It differs from those of al-Farabi (875–950), Avicenna (980–1037), and Ibn Bajja (died 1138).[20] The divergences represent not imprecision, but his own original views. Part V of the *Kuzari* must be distinguished from the others sections of the book in this respect. In Part V, Halevi summarized the philosophical views current in his day with the explicit polemic aim of "refuting dangerous and foolish views" (5,1 [278/248]). Here he also summarized Avicenna's psychology (5,12 [292]).[21] By contrast, in the opening section of the *Kuzari* Halevi expounded his own philosophical outlook, a position about which he had reservations by the time he wrote the book. This is the position to which he was referring in his remarks about philosophy in general (without noting explicitly that he is dealing with another philosophy) in

---

19. In the very first section of the book we find metaphorical use of the concepts *creation* and *Divine will*. See also 1,87 [42]; 4,13 [241].
20. This is despite his closeness to the thought of Ibn Bajja. See Pines, "Shi'ite Terms," p. 215.
21. For a different opinion, see H. Davidson, "The Active Intellect."

the first four parts. We shall find that, as a rule, there are contradictions in his description of the philosophical position only when we compare what is attributed to philosophers in the first four parts with what is attributed to them in Part V.

If we assume that the Philosopher's exposition at the beginning of the book reflects the main points of Halevi's own position before the *Kuzari* was written, the book can also be seen as a spiritual autobiography that describes the stages in the development of his thought and the reasons for his passage from stage to stage. The first section of the present volume, which deals with the Philosopher's thought, should be seen as a portrait of Halevi's thought in its first stage, before the composition of the *Kuzari*. The second and third sections of this volume deal with Halevi's thought while he was writing the book: the second with his earlier thought, the third with his later thought.

The first postulate shared by Halevi, the Philosopher, and the representatives of the revealed religions is that, alongside the general and egalitarian relationship that pertains between God and the universe in general, there is also a special relationship between God and some particular entity. Against the background of its milieu, this object appears (or may appear) in terms of its peculiar relationship to God. This is a necessary postulate, both metaphysically, with regard to the relationship between the universe and God, and anthropologically, with regard to the relationship between man and God. From the metaphysical perspective, for both the Philosopher and Halevi God is an agent that explains the existence of the universe—in one sense or another, in its entirety or in one of its aspects. God could not be a factor explaining the existence of the universe were it not for the special relationship between God and the realization of the essence of the universe—its emergence from potentiality to actuality. From the anthropological perspective, the special relationship between the Deity and a particular entity is a necessary postulate of any world-view in which God's existence is a significant factor in the intentional constitution of a way of life for human beings, or at least in their aspirations and expectations. In other words, given the existence of God, the attribution of normative redemptive meaning to human actions entails the fundamental postulate that some situations, things, or deeds are more godlike than others. These situations, things, or deeds are possible poles of attraction for concrete human aspirations. The very possibility of an "ascent," in theological terms, depends on the existence of "higher" and "lower."

A second postulate shared by Halevi and the Philosopher is that human initiative is at least an essential condition for the constitution of the special relationship between God and man.

These postulates occupy a central place in the contest between philosophy and Halevi's later view. The specific meanings ascribed to them by the disputants express different world-views about the essence of these poles of attraction, as well as about their relationship and the conditions in which it is constituted.

Our exposition of the Aristotelian philosophy of the *Kuzari* will begin with the description of the relationship between God and non-Divine reality, that is, the Divine emanation. Next we shall turn to the relationship between the non-Divine and God, followed by a consideration of the essence of God, on the one hand, and the essence of non-Divine reality, on the other. We shall try to understand the Philosopher's anthropology as one manifestation of the relationship between God and non-Divine reality. At the end of the discussion we shall focus on the systematic conclusions concerning the human way of life.

2

DIVINITY AND INDIVIDUATION

1. The Indefinite Nature of Existence Whose Source Is God and the Eternity of the Universe

One of the main principles peculiar to the Aristotelianism of the *Kuzari* is the assumption that the existence of a relationship between God and the non-Divine realm as a whole depends exclusively on the Deity, as the Cause of Causes, whereas the relationship between the Deity and an individual depends upon the essence of the individual, for "there is no niggardliness with God, who allows everyone his due" (5,10 [291/259]). No internal distinctions can be drawn within God's relationship to the non-Divine, which is like light without any specific qualification (4,15 [244/220]). The first expression of this homogeneity is the absence of any Divine intentionality toward the non-Divine: neither on the level of will—"there is no favor or dislike in God, because He is above desire and intention" (1,1 [4/36]); nor on the epistemological level—"in a similar way God is, in the opinion of philosophers, above the knowledge of individuals, because they change with the times; but there is no change in God's knowledge" (ibid. [5/36]; see also 4,3 [218]). Intentionality originates in the tension between an as-yet unfulfilled desire and one that has been realized, between ignorance and knowledge. This tension demands and makes possible a process of change—that is, emergence from potential to actual—and attests to some "deficiency" in the "intending person" (1,1 [5/36]). This deficiency stems from the inferior ontological status of potential, as opposed to actual, being.[1] God's relationship to non-Divine reality is characterized, therefore, as *actual* and *immutable* (4,13 [241/218]).

Existence whose source is God is single and uniform in all possible ways: "Philosophers who speculate on these things conclude that, from *one*, only one can issue" (4,25 [267/238]).[2] This oneness is expressed in uniformity—the lack of articulations between successive moments: "The causes and the things caused are . . . intimately connected with one another; their connection is as eternal as the Prime Cause and has no beginning" (1,1 [7/36]).[3] This leads to the fundamental metaphysical conclusion that God, in His exclusivity, cannot serve as a principle of individuation or source of distinctions, that is, as a sufficient cause of the existence of multiplicity, whether the multiplicity of simultaneous moments or the multiplicity of successive situations.

A corollary of the uniformity and nonarticulation of existence whose source is God is the Philosopher's tenet that the universe is eternal: "Philosophers who, with their refined intuition and clear view, acknowledge a Prime Cause different from and unlike earthly things, are inclined to think that this Prime Cause exercises no influence on the world, and certainly not on individuals, because he is too exalted to know them, much less

---

1. According to Aristotle, what actually exists is ontologically superior to what exists only *in potentia*. This idea has strongly influenced medieval and modern religious thought.

2. In the Philosopher's system we must distinguish between existence that depends on God alone and existence that depends on God plus an additional ontological dimension that is independent of Him—matter. Mutable existence depends on both God and matter. *Existence whose source is God* refers, then, to existence that depends exclusively on the Deity, that is, existence for which God is the necessary and sufficient cause.

3. See also 4,13 [241]; 5,12 [299]. As we shall see later, God's unity is dialectical. On the one hand, it is a unity of reason, thinker, and thought; on the other hand, the thought is personified as an angel, that is, as the first link in the process of emanation.

to make them the basis of a new entity" (2,54 [112/116]). Any new entity cannot escape the particularity of its essence and the particularity of the temporal moment in which it comes into being; but existence whose source is God lacks all internal distinctions and cannot be expressed in any particular and one-time fixity: "Even if philosophers say that He created you, they are speaking in metaphor, because He is the cause of causes in the creation of all creatures, not because this was His intention from the beginning. He never created man" (1,1 [5/36]).[4]

2. Existence Whose Origin Is God as a Plenum

Existence whose origin is God cannot be subdivided, distinguished, or limited, because it is an actual expression of the Deity, with whom "there is no niggardliness" (5,10 [291/259]). This is why the Philosopher rejects the atomic theory,[5] which was accepted by the Kalam and by the Karaite thinkers influenced by it: "Common view and assumption deny the nonexistence of the vacuum, whereas logic rejects its existence. Appearance denies the infinite divisibility of a body, whereas

---

4. See also 4,13. Almost all the schools mentioned in the *Kuzari* agree that one must understand non-Divine existence, at least in a certain sense, as the result of an entity that, by its very essence, can be a principle of order, and as an expression of the Divine emanation. The distinction between the various views is reflected in their different definitions of the same aspect of non-Divine existence, which is understood as an expression of the Divine emanation. The exception is Epicurus, who held "that the universe arose by accident" (5,8 [285/252]).

5. Halevi does not specifically mention the Philosopher in the discussion of atomic theory and the vacuum (see 3,49 [192]); from the context, however, it is clear that the Rabbi is referring to him. The Rabbi asserts that the Philosopher's arguments reflect the unequivocal conclusion of "rational speculation" or "logic," as propounded by Avicenna and in accordance with the Aristotelian tradition. Aristotle identifies space with place. The Rabbi argues that, according to the Philosopher, "the uppermost sphere carries the whole, without place or inclination in its movement" (2,6 [73/87]). Compare Joseph Ibn Sadik, *Sefer ha-ʿolam ha-qatan* (Microcosmos), ed. S. Horovitz (Breslau, 1903), p. 11: "The uppermost sphere does not need a place, since every part of it is the place for every other part."

logic makes it an axiom" (3,49 [192/178]). The Philosopher rejects the fundamental postulates of the atomic theory concerning the unconditional existence of the vacuum and of the atoms within it,[6] because these entail a limitation of Divine activity to make room for the vacuum and require this activity to be concentrated only at the limits of the realization of atomic entities.[7]

Halevi believed that the Philosopher failed to derive the conclusions entailed by his theory of the uniformity of existence whose source is God. This uniformity ought to be expressed in concrete reality as well, as follows:

1. Concrete reality should be infinite in all dimensions, not only in time.
2. Identical laws should govern non-Divine existence at all levels of existence.
3. The distinctions between the various levels should be only relative, within the continuous domain of infinite moments.

Hence Halevi criticized the Philosopher for his inability to back up his argument that the Divine emanations are limited to the spheres down to the lunar sphere and the Active Intellect (4,25 [268/238]). Halevi also asserted that the very idea of emanations has no basis. There is no adequate ontological ex-

---

6. This suggests that the Rabbi, too, rejects the atomic theory and the reality of the vacuum. Cassel, however, identifies the "minute elements that ... defy perception" (1,99 [ES37/71]) with atoms (commentary ad loc.). Moscato, followed by Zifroni, understands this passage differently.

In the Greek philosophical tradition from Leucippus and Democritus on, the postulates of the existence of atoms and the unconditional existence of the vacuum are interrelated. This systematic relationship is problematic for the Kalam school. See S. Pines, *Beiträge zur islamischen Atomenlehre* (Berlin, 1936), pp. 6ff. Abraham Ibn Ezra, too, seems to have accepted the atomic theory while denying the existence of the vacuum; see Efros, *Doctrines*, p. 54, n. 90. In both the *Kuzari* (3,49) and the *Guide of the Perplexed* (1,73, second introduction), however, atomic theory and the vacuum are discussed sequentially.

7. We find a similar argument in Leibniz, *Mathematische Schriften*, ed. Gerhardt (1850–1863), vol. 3, p. 565.

planation for the multiplicity of causes included in the knowledge possessed by Saturnus (the intellect of the sphere of Saturn): "Why did not one thing arise from Saturnus's recognition of what was above, and another thing from his recognition of the first angel, so that there would be four Saturnine emanations?" (ibid.). Halevi argued further that "when Aristotle asserts that he was conscious of his existence, one may consistently expect that a sphere should emanate from him; when he asserts that he recognized the Prime Cause, an angel should emanate" (ibid. [268/239]).[8] This leads to an assault on the theory of qualitatively independent elements: "The element of fire is not distinguished from air, nor the latter from water, nor water from earth, by quantity or strength, but by the form specific to each" (5,4 [282/250]). The Philosopher's basic postulates do not explain our experience; namely, that "we see that the spheres of the elements touch one another, but each preserves its form and particularity" (ibid.). If existence whose origin is God is uniform and undifferentiated, "one [philosopher] might say that the whole sphere is filled up with earthy matter, but . . . one portion is finer than another. Another may assert that it is all fire, but that the lower parts are denser and cooler" (ibid.)— even if we accept the variables of proximity and distance as possible explanations for particularity. Similarly, Halevi criticized the Philosopher's reliance on the factual existence of species, distinguished not only in their accidents but also in their forms; all species "are . . . composed of the four elements . . . [and] are not distinguished by accidental qualities, but by forms that make the substance of one different from the substance of the other. . . . The forms of substances have no quantity" (ibid. [283/251]). Underlying the last two arguments is the difficulty that, according to the Philosopher's theory, it should be possible to base qualitative distinctions in the world on quantitative differences. This problem is also the root of

---

8. These three arguments are derived from al-Ghazali. See Wolfson, "Hallevi on Design"; Davidson, "The Active Intellect."

Halevi's criticism of the Philosopher with regard to the limited number of forms in the world (5,7 [284])[9]—a fact that cannot be explained by the theory of Divine emanations.[10]

For the Philosopher, as noted, existence whose origin is God is a *necessary* expression—both logically and ontologically—of His essence, and these two levels cannot be separated. Halevi, speaking through the King, attacked this position as well: "I would refer my opponent to the uppermost sphere and its mover, and ask him whether or not this is the result of accident" (5,7 [284/252]). Again, "How do we know that if a being becomes conscious of its essence a sphere must arise, and that from the recognition of the Prime Cause an angel must arise?" (4,25 [268/238]). According to Halevi, the process of emanation cannot be understood against the background of the Philosopher's idea that the Divine emanation is rational and necessary.[11] In fact, the Philosopher believes that the twin characterizations of the Divine emanations as both actual existence and totally rational existence are necessarily interdependent, because existence whose source is God is an expression of His essence—which is both actual existence and reason.

As we have seen, existence whose source is God cannot ground an explanation of particularity, according to the Philosopher's method, even if we take into account the multiplicity of essences. In the next four sections we shall address various manifestations of particularity in non-Divine existence.

3. Multiplicity in Non-Divine Existence

Non-Divine existence is characterized by multiplicity, in contrast to the unity of God. As we saw in the previous section, multiplicity—and mutability, too, is a form of multiplicity—

---

9. From the context it is clear that the King's remarks in this section reflect Halevi's own opinion.

10. The Philosopher could have refuted this criticism by adducing the distinction between actual infinity and potential infinity—a distinction frequently made in the Aristotelian tradition.

11. This criticism is directed against the theories of emanations of al-Farabi and Avicenna.

cannot be based on existence whose source is God. In other words, the Divine emanation per se cannot serve as a principle of individuation.

The Divine emanation, as a reality separate from God, entails the postulate of an ontological dimension superadded to Him.[12] The Divine emanation, as a perfect expression of God's self-knowledge, is still not distinct from God Himself. Epistemologically speaking, God's self-knowledge encompasses the totality of His essence. Ontologically, it is identical with Him. "It is therefore also said that actual reason comprehends and is comprehended simultaneously" (5,12 [299/265]).[13]

> The Philosopher's opinion on this subject seems similar to that of *Sefer Yetzirah:* This also demonstrates that the one order is the work of a one-Master, who is God. And although things are multifarious and different from each other, their difference is the result of the difference of their material, which is partly of higher and partly lower order, and of impure or pure character. The giver of forms, designs and order, however, has placed in them all a unique wisdom, and a providence which is in complete harmony with this uniform order, and is visible in the macrocosm, in man, and in the arrangement of the spheres (4,25 [258/231]).[14]

12. In any case one must postulate necessary law, to which even Divine activity is subject.

13. This follows Aristotle (*Metaphysics* 1075^{a}1) "As, then, thought and the object of thought are not different in the case of things that have not matter, they will be the same, i.e., the thinking will be one with the object of its thought" (trans. W. D. Ross, in *Complete Works,* ed. Jonathan Barnes [Princeton, N.J., 1984]). This is also the view expounded by Maimonides in the *Guide of the Perplexed* (1,68) and in the *Mishneh Torah* (*Hilkhot Yesodei Hatorah* 2,10). Halevi also attacked the Philosopher's implicit assumption of the "identity of the unseparated" on the level of "intellectual beings": "In what way does my soul differ from yours, or from the Active Intellect, from other causes and the Prime Cause? Why, also, did not Aristotle's soul become united with that of Plato, either of them knowing the other's belief and innermost thought?" (5,14 [305/271]).

14. See Chapter 3, §5. "The Interrelationship of the Two Ontological Dimensions."

4. Mutability and Potentiality in Non-Divine Existence

The relations between the original and primordial (in the sense of *ante rem*) essences, like the relations among the Platonic ideas, are characterized by their eternal fixity, "reason itself being above time," as is "the deduction of the conclusion" (5,12 [299/265]). Non-Divine existence, however, is subject to perpetual change. Change is a process of emergence from potential to actual; even the sphere revolves because of "the endeavor of the latter to remedy its imperfection, so as to be absolutely exact on all sides. However, because this is not always possible and in all points, it tries to revolve the opposite way" (5,14 [308/273]).[15] Because they *actually* exist, the Divine emanations—including the intellects—cannot be the sole cause of mutable reality, given that all change is a manifestation of potentiality. As noted, change entails the assumption of an ontological dimension superadded to the Deity. It is nevertheless important to distinguish between superlunar and sublunar existence.[16] Potentiality in one realm is not the same as potentiality in the other. Superlunar potentiality produces minimal alteration, in the form of cyclical movement in a fixed and eternal course. Two aspects of this movement are susceptible to full rational understanding: one, its internal laws and necessity; two, its purpose or source—the desire of a rational entity to employ its intellect.

The ontological status of sublunar potentiality, however, is primary and independent of the level of existence that lies above it; by the same token, the concrete manifestations of its potentiality are characterized by contingency and transience. This difference between the two levels of reality goes back to the

---

15. Similarly, the philosophers "concluded that these movements were voluntary rather than necessary or natural" (5,21 [330/292]). These voluntary movements are manifestations of the desire to complete what is lacking, that is, to actualize what is only potential existence.

16. The division of existence into superlunar and sublunar realms derives from Greek tradition, going back to the Pythagoreans (Aristotle, *De Anima* 405). Although it recurs frequently in Platonic cosmology, it acquired its full ontological and moral signification only in the Aristotelian theory of degrees of existence.

ontological distinction between the matter composing the spheres and stars and the matter of the sublunar world, which exists neither *in potentia* nor in actuality (5,2 [280]). Evidently the Philosopher adheres to the view that Halevi ascribed to *Sefer Yetzirah;* namely, that the spheres are made of "pure and lasting matter" (4,25 [262/234]).[17] On this point, too, the Philosopher follows Aristotle: on the level of the spheres, too, one can distinguish matter from form; but the matter of which the spheres are composed—the quintessence—is peculiar to them.

This ontological distinction is based on the unique nature of the source of superlunar potentiality, which is an external ontological expression of dialectical relations within the intellect. The self-knowledge of the intellects finds its ontological expression as possible-existence, as dependence on the existence of God. This ontological condition is in turn the source of the existence and essence of the spheres and stars as material entities[18] whose existence is not entailed by their essence.

5. Individuals and Contingency in the Sublunar Sphere

The distinguishing mark of the sublunar sphere is its multifold individuation, which as a matter of principle can never be fully comprehended. Even though "the forms of substances have no quantity; one horse cannot be less equine than another, nor one man more human than another, because the definitions 'equine' and 'human' are common to each individual horse and man" (5,4 [283/251]), individuals do exist and are distinguished from one another by their accidents: "Accidental qualities . . . distinguish one vine from another, and one palm from another" (ibid.).[19]

---

17. Only the intellects of the spheres are "severed from material substance" (5,21 [330/292]). It is clear from the context that the spheres, inasmuch as they move, are material.

18. See 5,14 [308].

19. By contrast, "The form of the intellect consists in the object conceived" (5,12 [300/266]). "Color and corporeality, as concepts, cannot be subdivided in thought" (ibid.). Accordingly, the chief difference between the superlunar and sublunar realms is that every entity in the former is unique.

Ontologically speaking, accidents do not express essences, which are "the forms of substances" and are not derived from them (epistemologically speaking, accidents are sensory perceptions); nevertheless, they subsist only by virtue of what carries them: "reason maintains that [tangible objects] are borne by a fulcrum" (5,2 [280/249]). As for the fulcrum itself, that is, the material substrate, "our intelligence grasps its meaning only imperfectly, since imperfection is its nature.... It does not really exist, and therefore cannot claim any predicate; although it only exists virtually, its predicate is corporeal" (ibid.).

Because of the fundamental impossibility of pointing to some unifying link that can explain the coincidence of accidents, a material substrate must be posited to account for the relative stability in the existence of isolated accidents and for their coexistence. Since this substrate "carries" all the accidents that can appear in sensory experience, it must itself lack all positive definition; any such definition would impair its function. Thus the nonrational element that causes individual differences and particularizes individual forms is transferred from the level of form to that of matter, that is, to the substrate itself. In sublunar existence, the particular is a partial and incomplete reflection of the form of the species (5,12 [301]).[20]

The "contingent" is another expression of the nonrationality of sublunar existence. As we saw in the previous chapter, it does not derive from the Divine emanation; however, it does serve as

---

20. See 4,17 [247/223], "smallest detail"; see also 2,54 [112] and 4,3 [234] ad fin. Compare 3,19 [164] for Plato's opinion on the relationship between individual and community. In this light we can understand the King's ironic response to the Philosopher's remarks: "What could be more erroneous, in the opinion of the philosophers, than ... that the Prime Cause spoke with one of the mortals—in view of the philosophical doctrine that declares God to be above knowing details" (1,4 [11/39]). Communication between man and God is impossible, because God is the Prime Cause—impersonal being—whereas man is merely a part or detail. God, who is subject to the eternal and necessary laws that are essential to Him as "cause," cannot have intentionality toward an individual, whose ontological marks are transience and contingency.

a legitimate category[21] for explaining natural reality and for describing its inherent multiplicity. It is plausible that the Philosopher holds this opinion,[22] unlike Avicenna. Although he never explicitly states his position on this central issue, we can infer it from the following points.

First, the Philosopher's view of Divine knowledge (1,1) has two facets: (a) God is above the knowledge of "individuals"; consequently (b) "He ... does not know you" (ibid. [5/36]). This Divine "ignorance" is not a result of the fact that things change, but that they "change with the times and there is no change in God's knowledge" (ibid.). On the other hand, God knows and recognizes non-Divine existence that is not "individual."[23] God knows *notions* (5,14 [305/271]), that is, the superlunar world with the changes that characterize it, as well as *essences*—the species and categories of the sublunar world.[24] His

---

21. *Legitimate* here means that the category describes sublunar existence as it truly is and does not merely stem from the limitations of human reason.

22. Wolfson holds otherwise. He does not distinguish between the sublunar and superlunar realms and asserts that the Philosopher's system leaves no place for the contingent in the sublunar world, either ("Hallevi on Design," p. 106). Similarly, Wolfson identifies the philosophers as al-Farabi and Avicenna. Neither of these assertions seems to be correct. This is the source of Wolfson's vacillation in his explanation of the contingency that Halevi explicitly attributed to the philosophers in the discussion of the creation of the four elements (ibid., p. 132).

23. Compare: "Philosophers ..., with their refined intuition and clear view ... are inclined to think that this Prime Cause exercises no influence on the world, and certainly not on individuals, as he is too exalted to know them" (2,54 [112/116]). With this in mind we can understand the Rabbi's argument: "In truth, glory and kingdom do not become visible except to the pious, the pure, and the prophets who teach the heretic that judgment and rule on earth belong to God, who knows every action of man" (4,3 [234/212]). In Halevi's later thought, by contrast, God's dominion and kingdom depend on His knowledge of "every action of man." His providence depends not only on knowledge of changes that correspond to eternal laws, but also on knowledge of contingent change.

24. Hence we must not make God's lack of knowledge depend on the fact that coming into being is necessarily anchored in potentiality nor on the fact that in an eternal universe the number of changes is infinite, so that simultaneous knowledge of all of them would entail the real existence of infinity. Compare Ibn Ezra on Psalm 73:12: "The meaning is that the

knowledge of the mutable does not entail a corresponding alteration in His knowledge. The Divine intellect remains self-identical, and the totality of its contents and nature of its intentionality remain unmodified, since it need not trace the stages of change in sequence. It intuits change "simultaneously" (ibid.), because "the deduction of the conclusion is not dependent on time" (5,12 [299/265]).[25]

Hence we must distinguish between change that is a logically necessary consequence—that is, the emergence of what is latent in the essence of the object of rational knowledge—from contingent change, which does not stem from a prior state of affairs, so that its temporal moment must be viewed as an irreducible component of the event.[26] Only this latter type of change, bound up with "the times," is unknown to God, because knowledge thereof would entail a corresponding change in His knowledge; but "there is no change in God's knowledge" (1,1 [5/36]). In this light we can understand the continuation: "He does not know you, *much less* your intentions and actions, nor does He listen to your prayers or see your movements" (ibid.). This *much less* is out of place with regard to necessary change. It can

---

righteous have true knowledge that there is a God exalted above human knowledge and that in His wisdom He knows the fixed laws; but as for the parts, i.e., individuals, who are changing continually, God does not know them, because they do not endure." See also Ibn Ezra on Psalm 1:6.

25. This is also Avicenna's opinion. See *Avicenna's De Anima*, ed. E. Rahman (London, 1959), p. 217. In the context of this discussion of the Philosopher's view of non-Divine existence, the description of God's intellect is merely an exposition of the conditions that objects must fulfil in order to be objects of His knowledge. On the special nature of the Divine intellect as intuitive, see Chapter 3, §3. "The Imminent Activity of the Deity." This special nature of the Divine intellect and the conditions that the objects of His knowledge must fulfill are interdependent.

26. Nothing can be learned about our present topic from the end of the Ninth Axiom: "In this case . . . His eternal omniscience would be the cause of every existing being just as it is. This agrees with the view of philosophers" (5,18 [314/278]). Clearly the reference is not to the Philosopher who appears at the start of the book (perhaps Avicenna is meant). Alternatively, the words "this agrees with the view of philosophers" may refer to other problems expounded in this section, as Moscato and Cassel hold.

be understood only with regard to contingent change. Intention and actions are doubly contingent.[27]

Second, thus far we have considered only the relationship between the nature of a change and the possibility of God's knowing it. However, just as God's knowledge depends on the nature of the change, so too the nature of the change is determined by God's capacity to know it: God does not know the contingent *because* it is contingent; and it is contingent *because* God is incapable of knowing it. God's knowledge of something entails its eternal existence.

This explains the Philosopher's unambiguous opinion on the immortality of the soul. Here he follows Ibn Bajja, rather than Avicenna: "Thus the soul of the perfect man and that Intellect become One, ... because he becomes united to the other.... He and they, as well as every one who shares their degree, and the Active Intellect, are one thing" (1,1 [8/38]).[28] God does not know the individual qua individual, and a fortiori He does not know the individual's particular and one-time destiny—the particular characterizations that make the individual unique. Hence the existence of the individual is merely contingent and episodic. Individuals are redeemed from incompleteness only when they cast off the qualities that individuate them and merge their intellect with the Active Intellect.

---

27. Perhaps this "much less" alludes to the Philosopher's view of human freedom, a freedom that is bound up with contingency. The question merits further study. Compare: "this Prime Cause exercises no influence on the world, and certainly not on individuals, as he is too exalted to know them, *much less* to make them the basis of a new entity" (2,54 [112/116]). Compare also 3,11 [150/144], where the a fortiori argument is inverted: "God ... penetrates all the secrets of man, *as well as* his actions and words." On human freedom, see Chapter 4, note 2.

28. See also 4,13 [241]; 5,12 [302]. Also, "In what way does my soul differ from yours, or from the Active Intellect?" (5,14 [305/271]). In the last-cited passage Halevi does not criticize the Philosopher's theory of the immortality of the soul as presented at the beginning of the book. Rather, he is reporting the Philosopher's view; namely, that after death souls unite with the Active Intellect, thereby losing their individuality. Halevi's criticism rests on the separate status of souls in this world. Compare the continuation: "either of them knowing the other's belief and innermost thought."

Third, we can now understand the Philosopher's fundamental epistemological postulate; namely, that the empirical encounter with sublunar reality cannot lead to certain knowledge: "The soul does not gain its knowledge empirically. For the results of experience cannot be judged apodictically. No one can assert apodictically that no man can move his ears, just as we may judge that every human being feels; that every one who feels, lives; that every one who lives is a substance; that the whole is larger than a part; and other fundamental truths" (5,12 [301/267]). This passage clearly refers to an ontological distinction between different levels of existence. Reason cannot infer necessary and eternal truth from "experience" (in contradistinction to Halevi's later view, as we shall see), not because reason is limited in some fashion, but because there are inherent irrational elements in concrete experience: "As regards tangible objects, we can perceive [only] their quantity and quality by means of our senses.... Reason answers that quantity and quality are accidents which have no independent existence, but must necessarily have an object to support them. Philosophers call this object *matter*, adding that our intelligence grasps its meaning only imperfectly, since imperfection is its nature" (5,2 [280/249]).

Fourth, the contingency of sublunar reality is expressed in the concrete process whereby primordial matter receives its primary and fundamental particularity. The Philosopher argues that the material substrate acquires the multiplicity of particular forms contingently, as a function of its distance from the source of motion, the uppermost sphere (5,2). The King summarizes this theory as follows: "In the opinion of philosophers, as I see, things arise by accident, since they say that that which happened to be nearest to the sphere became fire, and what was remotest became earth" (5,3 [281/250]).[29]

---

29. According to Wolfson, "Hallevi on Design," pp. 132–133, the conversion of primordial matter into one of the four elements is not contingent, but is entailed by the motion of the spheres. He seems not to have noticed, though, that the distance of any particular portion of the primordial matter from the uppermost sphere is totally contingent. If we read the King's words closely, this is in fact his argument: "they say that that which *happened* to be nearest to the sphere."

Fifth, only in one place did Halevi explicitly consider the determinist view of the sublunar sphere, as part of the discussion of knowledge and free will. There, however, he totally ignored the view of philosophy: "Only a perverse, heretical person would deny the nature of what is possible, making assertions of opinions in which he does not believe" (5,20 [315/279]). Again, "Since events must either be of divine origin or arise out of one of the other classes, and the possibility exists that they are all providential, the people preferred to refer them all to God, because this encourages belief most effectively" (ibid. [319/283]). Thus the determinism expounded in this section is based on Divine decree rather than on some determinism in nature. Here Halevi was referring to views commonly held by Muslim theologians, such as the Ashariya school,[30] as a sequel to the discussion of the Kalam in this section of Part V. Philosophy, as he understands it, does not argue for determinism in the sublunar realm; here the problem of human freedom arises exclusively as a result of the confrontation with views derived from Islamic theology.[31]

In light of the preceding, the nature of the sublunar realm rests on three fundamental axioms:

1. The simultaneous multiplicity manifested in sublunar sensory experience cannot, as a matter of principle, be fully comprehended by reason; that is, it cannot be based on "forms."
2. Likewise, sequential multiplicity—"change"—cannot, as a matter of principle, be fully comprehended by reason; that is, it cannot be based on the logical relationship between premise and conclusion.
3. God knows neither simultaneous multiplicity nor sequential multiplicity.

---

30. See Cassel's commentary on this section.
31. Wolfson believes that the Philosopher's statement that "everything is reduced to the Prime Cause.... The causes and the things caused are, as you see them, intimately connected with one another" (1,1 [6/36]) indicates that he is an advocate of sublunar determinism as well. For in this passage the Philosopher is referring to existence as a whole, including the sublunar sphere. However, the causal chain itself is not a system of necessary and sufficient

The third axiom is based on the first two, as well as on the postulate of God as Intellect. The Philosopher, who accepts the first argument, is forced to accept the second as well. If the individual cannot be based on a rational content, a fortiori change, which incorporates a number of individual moments, cannot be fully grounded on a process of logical inference.[32]

---

conditions, but only of necessary conditions. The characterization of multiplicity in existence, "as you see them," seems to limit the domain of the "everything" that is the subject of the sentence. Primordial matter, which in principle is not seen (5,2 [280]), cannot be "reduced to the Prime Cause."

32. We should make clear that orderly and fixed relationships can also be based on individual moments that are not susceptible to full rational apprehension. Democritus, for example, holds that the random motion of atoms establishes the order of nature. But this order cannot be fully comprehended by reason.

3

FORM AND MATTER

The previous chapter described existence on the phenomenological level. Now we shall deal with the irreducible metaphysical foundations of sublunar existence—God and primordial matter (*materia prima*).

1. The Positive Meaning of Matter

For the Philosopher of the *Kuzari*, primordial matter per se is not a total absence (here he disagrees with Avicenna and the Neoplatonists). Nevertheless, its ontological status can be defined only negatively; that is, it is a unique type of existence to which the categories that apply to concrete existence, in which form and matter are united, do not apply. Primordial matter is neither potential existence nor actual existence. In principle it cannot be apprehended by sensory experience, because, "as regards tangible objects, we can perceive their quantity and quality by means of our senses" and matter "only shows itself clothed in a form" (5,2 [280/249]).[1] The inherent nonrationality of primordial matter rules out any positive definition of its ontological status; hence "our intelligence grasps its meaning only imperfectly" (ibid.).

---

1. This is also Halevi's personal opinion; see 4,3 [225].

These parameters of primordial matter reflect its four functions:

1. It is the substrate of every possible form, in that it has minimum fixity.
2. It serves as the *principium individuationis*, the principle of individuation that determines the unique identity of individuals.
3. It is the source of the difference between existence that is dependent exclusively on the Deity, which is real in every respect, and concrete existence, part of which is only potential existence.
4. It is the source of the ugliness of sublunar existence—its inherent contingency and irrationality.

2. The Function of God

In the Philosopher's system God, like primordial matter, is not an object of immediate experience;[2] in principle the Deity is apprehended only through rational thinking.[3] The place and definition of the Deity in the system are determined by its function—to explain existence.[4] Hence God, in principle, has "no particular name" (4,15 [244/220]).[5] The meaning of the Deity—"His name"—is focused in the name Elohim 'GOD', which is merely a "common noun" (4,1 [217/199]) and derived from *eyaluth* 'force, power' (4,3 [222/202]).[6] From this vantage point,

---

2. 1,87 [41]; 2,54 [112]; 4,5 [235].
3. 1,13 [18]; 4,15 [246]; 4,16 [247]; 4,17 [247].
4. It is true that, for the Philosopher, the Deity also has a meaning that is not functional, which expresses God as in principle unknowable to the rational mind. See Chapter 4, §5, "The Contemplative Relationship to God."
5. So too 4,3. In Halevi's later thought, however, the "special qualification," the private, "definite proper name" (4,3 [218/200]) of the Deity, depends on His presence in immediate experience and the *unique nature* of His intrinsic simultaneity—"in one sudden flash" (4,5 [235/213])—and its exclusive attachment to a particular and unique subject. See Chapter 4, §3, "The Philosophical Theory of Prophecy."
6. Halevi believed that the Philosopher's God, apprehended through rational thought and analogy, and a being that fulfills a function, necessarily

Halevi considers the Aristotelian concept of God to be essentially pagan (4,3).

There are two aspects to these specific functions of God. First, the formal aspect of existence, as one and unified, and as actual, reflects the Divine Emanation in its most general nature; in His relationship to it, God is "the Cause of causes in the creation of all creatures" (1,1 [5/36]). Hence the philosopher emphasizes the primacy of God as "Prime Cause" (ibid.), His unity (4,25 [254/228], 4,27), and His ontological status as an "actual cause" (4,13 [241/218]).[7]

Second, the formal aspect of concrete existence, which is expressed in the rational order inherent in existence as an ordered *multiplicity* of particular and distinct individuals, reflects the Divine Emanations in their *real individuation* in the multiplicity of things. From this point of view God is "the spirit, soul, intellect, and life of the world" (4,3 [230/209]). He is the very *essence* of existence, its formal aspect.[8] The hierarchical order that ranks concrete existence on the ontological, epistemologi-

---

lacks a clear and unambiguous definition: "Had it not been for this experience, [Adam] would have been satisfied with the name GOD [*Elohim*]; he would not have perceived what God was, whether He is one or many, whether He knows individuals or not" (4,3 [219/200]). See also 1,13; 1,20; 2,48; 3,17; 4,13; 4,15; 4,25; 4,27; 5,14. Hence the skepticism that the philosopher attributes to his particular view of "divine influences." According to Halevi, this also explains the disagreements among philosophers on these matters. Furthermore, "no people ... were reconciled *to any law without a visible image* on which they could depend" (1,97 [50/67]; emphasis mine).

7. From this perspective, the assertion that "the Divine Influence grudges nothing" (5,10 [291/258]) should be seen only as a reflection of God as cause. God, as a real genetic cause, is necessarily the guarantor of the inexhaustible eternity of the Divine Emanations.

8. Compare Spinoza, *Ethics* 1,25, and Corollary. Typical, from this perspective, is the parallel between man and the universe: "Philosophers compared the world to a great man, and man to a small world. If this be so, God being the spirit, soul, intellect, and life of the world ... " (4,3 [230/209]). God relates to the world in the same way as the rational soul relates to man, who is an amalgam of body, soul, and intellect. Compare Ibn Ezra on Daniel 12:7. We also read: "imagination can give him no other form than that of the noblest human being, who arranges order and harmony for the rest of mankind, in the same systematic way as God has done for the universe" (ibid.

cal, and ethical scales—both in the static sense of order, that is, the demarcation of boundaries and the classification of individuals in defined species, and in its dynamic sense, as constituting processes—is manifested also in the ranking of God Himself. In this context we can understand what Halevi writes: "We take . . . no heed of the words of philosophers who divide the divine world into degrees . . . and called these 'intellects,' 'angels,' 'secondary causes,' or other names. The nethermost degree, nearest to us, is the Active Intelligence, of which they taught that it guided the nether world. The next is the Hylic Intellect, then comes the soul . . ." (5,21 [329/291]).[9]

Concrete existence, which is the union of form and matter, is ontologically dependent on the Deity. Like Avicenna, but unlike Aristotle, the Philosopher does not accept form and the union of matter and form that constitutes existence as irreducible ontological givens; instead, he derives them from God. In his opinion, God is the only explanation for the formal and rational aspect of existence: "everything is reduced to the Prime Cause" (1,1 [6/36]). God, in His functional association with the rational aspect of concrete existence, is: (a) intellect (5,14 [305])

[231/209]). Or again: "They [the philosophers] recommend good . . . in order to resemble the Creator who arranged everything so perfectly" (4,19 [249/225]); compare further 1,12.

Two points bear noting: (1) the resemblance between the Deity and the greatest of human beings (this similarity is also expressed in the importance accorded to the pious, who strive to resemble the Active Intellect (1,1); see Chapter 5, §3, "The Rationality and Universality of Rules of Conduct"); and (2) the emphasis on similarity against the background of the hierarchical order that characterizes the political order that "emerges" from the greatest of human beings. See Moscato on 1,1, *incipit* משתמש בהם. The philosopher's resemblance to God has ontological significance and leads to the doctrine that the soul survives after being separated from the body. See further Chapter 4, §2, "The Goal as the Actualization of Human Potential." With regard to the epistemological realm, see the same chapter, §5, "The Contemplative Relationship to God."

9. From this perspective there is no qualitative difference between the first rung on the hierarchical ladder and subsequent rungs, including "the faculties of each [human] organ" (5,21 [330/292]). Compare also 5,12, where the emphasis is on the continuous nature of the hierarchy of existence.

or the "the intellect... of the world" (4,3 [230/209]);[10] (b) essence that necessarily exists: "the existence of God is identical with His essence" (4,25 [265/236]);[11] and (c) "actual cause" (4,13 [241/218]).

The first characterization derives from God's unique function as the cause of the rationality inherent in existence; the other two stem from His ontological pre-eminence and irreducibility as "Prime Cause." God's perfection (1,1 [5])—an attribute that plays a central role in the Philosopher's system—is merely an expression of the fact that God's essence is absolutely an actual existence. This is not absolute infinity, but the maximum actualization of God's particular essence, as manifested in (a), (b), and (c) above.[12]

10. See also 5,21 [330], as well as the opinion of the Masters of the Kalam (5,18, Eighth Axiom [314]).

11. Halevi attributes this view to *Sefer Yetzirah*, but it is also the opinion held by the Philosopher, following al-Farabi and Avicenna.

12. To use the terminology of Spinoza, for the Philosopher of the *Kuzari* God is "infinite in His kind" and not "infinite absolutely"; see *Ethics*, Part 1, Definition 6. Spinoza's a priori ontological proof leads him to define God as perfect in the sense of totality or as absolutely infinite. For the Philosopher of the *Kuzari*, however, as for Avicenna, God's essential necessary existence does not entail deriving all existence from it. This is the starting point for the Rabbi's fundamental argument: "It would be a defect in him if we were able to grasp [His nature]" (5,21 [329/291]). Any attempt to derive God's essence from His works, a posteriori, must, as a matter of principle, relate to a deficient Deity. Moscato interprets this passage differently (ad loc., *incipit* היה זה חסרון בו). But my interpretation is supported by the Rabbi's opinion that only "the meaning of 'GOD' [Elohim] can be grasped by way of speculation, since a Guide and Manager of the world is inferred by Reason" (4,15 [246/222]). "The meaning of 'the LORD' [Adonai], however, cannot be grasped by speculative thought" (ibid.; see also 5,14 [308]). The Philosopher would agree with the Rabbi's conclusion that it is fundamentally impossible for some other being to know God, in a full and absolute manner. This stems from the principle of the identity of the intellect and the intelligible, which requires that any mind that has perfect knowledge of God identify with Him totally. Compare Saadia Gaon, *The Book of Beliefs and Opinions*, trans. Samuel Rosenblatt (New Haven, Conn., 1948), Introductory Treatise, III, where research and analysis are held to be essential for created beings to acquire knowledge. See a similar argument in Joseph Albo, *Sefer ha-ʿiqqarim, The Book of Principles*, trans. I. Husik (Philadelphia, 1929), 2,30: "As the wise man said when asked if he knew the essence of God:

3. The Immanent Activity of the Deity

According to the Philosopher, God's activity is a necessary expression of His essence as *actual* intellect. However, unlike the "material or passive intellect" (5,10 [291/258]), which "cannot . . . be obtained except by devoting one's life to research and continual reflection" (4,19 [249/224]), actual reason is a unity manifested in the identity of the intellect, the perceiver (the intellectually cognizing subject), and the perceived (the intellectually cognized object).[13] This identity is not peculiar to the Divine intellect, but is the property of every intellect insofar as it is actual reason (5,12 [299]),[14] including human reason, to the extent that it succeeds in uniting with the Active Intellect (1,1 [37]).[15]

'If I knew Him, I would be Him.'" This is the source of the distinction between God in Himself and God as an object of the positive knowledge of a non-Divine intellect.

According to Ibn Gabirol, the fundamental impossibility of comprehending the essence of God is bound up precisely with His infinitude, because "the infinite cannot be encompassed by knowledge" (*Fons Vitae* 1,5 [Latin trans. Johanne Hispano and Dominico Gundissalino, ed. C. L. Bäumker, Münster, 1892–1895]) and is not a direct result of the identity between intellect, perceiver, and perceived. (In this, Ibn Gabirol agrees with Descartes and Leibniz.) The differences on this point between Ibn Gabirol and the Philosopher are rooted in the antithetical foundations of their doctrines: For the Aristotelian philosopher, God as intellect is given to be fully known; whereas for Ibn Gabirol, influenced by Neoplatonism, God cannot be identified with intellect. See Natan Rotenstreich, *Al teḥumah shel ha-filosofiyah* (The scope of philosophy) (Jerusalem, 1969), p. 37. Rotenstreich agrees with Moscato's interpretation of Halevi's argument (5,21 [329]). In light of what we have said, the view he attributes to Halevi is to be found in Ibn Gabirol. See Chapter 4, n. 45.

13. The terms in parentheses are those used by Shlomo Pines in his translation of the *Guide of the Perplexed*. See note 15.

14. Again, "The causes and the things caused are . . . intimately connected with one another; their connection is as eternal as the Prime Cause" (1,1 [6/36]); here the original Arabic (*talāzimat, talāzimaha*) refers to an essential link that cannot be dissolved. Hence this "intimate connection" must be understood as a partial identity between the perceiving intellect and the perceived object and as primordial, because, for actual intellects, perception is not a process.

15. See also 5,14 and Chapter 4, §4, "The Goal as a Supreme Value." Compare also the *Guide of the Perplexed*, trans. Shlomo Pines (Chicago, 1963),

Thus activity characterizes not only the mind of God, but all other intellects as well, to the extent that they are actual. Actual intellects, too, inasmuch as they perceive, are "causes" (1,1 [7]) or "secondary causes" (5,21 [330]), resembling God, who by His very essence is the "Prime Cause."[16] In this fashion the "Divine world" is divided into levels (ibid.).

Nevertheless, there is a fundamental difference between the Divine intellect and all other intellects. The identity of the Divine intellect with what it perceives is also the ontological identity of the objects of its perception and the objects themselves: "The form of the intellect consists in the object conceived" (5,12 [300/266]).[17] The identity of all other minds with what they perceive is also an identity of perceiver and perceived; but in this case there is no absolute ontological identity of the objects of perception and the objects themselves, because that would abolish these intellects' separate existence from God. If non-Divine minds perceived themselves as they truly are, that is, as the source of their existence (God as He is to Himself), they would be identical with God, by virtue of the identity between the perceiving intellect and what it perceives.

1,68: "It is accordingly also clear that the numerical unity of the intellect, the intellectually cognizing subject, and the intellectually cognized object, does not hold good with reference to the creator only, but also with reference to every intellect." The comparison between the Active Intellect and potential intellect—the type of intellect that characterizes man as a rational being—constitutes the background for Halevi's criticism of the Philosopher's doctrine of union with the Active Intellect. The difference between potential intellect and actual intellect—accepted by the Philosopher—cannot be eliminated, according to the Rabbi; hence such an intimate connection is impossible (5,14).

16. This is the starting point of the Rabbi's criticism of the Philosopher's view: "Why did this emanation cease? Did the Prime Cause become impotent?"; "When Aristotle asserts that he was conscious of his existence, one may consistently expect that a sphere should emanate from him" (4,25 [268/238]). That is, the Rabbi criticizes the Philosopher's basic assumption about the relationship between the epistemological and ontological planes, from the perspectives of both emanating and emanated.

17. This identity, which exists in the mind of God, is bound up with the essence of God as the Cause of causes: the perceived objects, as they are in themselves, as effects, are "necessarily included" in the cause.

In other words, in the Philosopher's system, only God is a totally "authentic" existence; only with regard to Him is there perfect identity between existence "for its own sake" and existence "in itself." This is the source of His simple unity. By contrast, the separate existence of other intellects involves an inherent internal opposition: between their being an object of knowledge "for its own sake" and their essence in itself. The separate existence of the non-Divine intellects entails their "alienation" from themselves. This self-alienation is the hallmark of non-Divine intellects. Their aspiration for greater self-awareness leads only to knowledge of their ignorance. This is the difference between God and the actual intellects that emanate from Him. Ontologically, God's self-perception is manifested in the emanation of the first intellect, which is necessarily "one" (4,25 [267/238]). The self-perception of each intellect is manifested ontologically in the emanation of a multiplicity: sphere, soul, and angel (ibid.; 5,21 [330]). This multiplicity is rooted in a multiplicity of distinctions that are essential for the perception of the emanated intellect: Insofar as the intellect successfully apprehends its cause, it resembles its cause and gives rise to an angel; insofar as the intellect perceives itself when it discerns the difference between itself and its cause,[18] a sphere emanates from it. The material substance of the sphere and its rotation manifest its "deficiency" as well as it desire for "perfection": The sphere "endeavors . . . to remedy its imperfection, so as to be absolutely exact on all sides" (5,14 [308/273]). Clearly this difference is merely an expression of the difference between the limited self-knowledge of the intellects that are emanations of God and the perfect self-knowledge of God Himself. It in no way cancels what God and the intellects have in common, both in their essence and their functions. What is more, this difference between God and the intellects that emanate from Him appears precisely against the backdrop of what they have in common. From this perspective the philosophers called

---

18. See the commentary on the *Kuzari* by Yisrael Halevy, *Oẓar Neḥmad*, ad loc. According to Davidson, "The Active Intellect," p. 358, the influence of al-Ghazali is evident in Halevi's presentation of the doctrine of emanations.

"these intellects gods, or angels, or secondary causes" (5,21 [330/292]) and said that the Active Intellect is of the "divine nature" (1,1 [7/36]).

There are two facets to the activity of actual intellects: (1) contemplative-reflective activity, and (2) productive activity. The contemplative activity of actual intellects is manifested in their reflexivity. In intellects that are Divine emanations, this activity takes place in the broad ontological context of the source of the existence of the particular intellect. Such a relationship to its cause is a metaphysically necessary condition for the hierarchical order that characterizes non-Divine existence on all levels. Spontaneous reflection by the emanated intellect, which necessarily includes its relationship to its causes, is manifested in recognition of the ontological and ethical primacy of the causes, because of the identity between intellect, perceiver, and perceived, which exists only when an intellect perceives its own essence—the ground of its existence—its causes. This recognition is an essential expression of the ontological and ethical perfection of the emanated minds as actual intellects.

The reflexivity of the intellect's relation to itself is thus its goal. The goal of God's activity is self-knowledge, whereas the goal of the activity of other intellects is to know both themselves and their causes. Because God is the Prime Cause, however, knowledge of His essence is necessarily included in the self-knowledge of every intellect. This explains God's place in the system; namely, as the pole sought by existence, in its rational aspect, as its final cause—in order to know and thereby to be like Him. In other words, according to the Philosopher of the *Kuzari*, as for Aristotle, God is self-sufficient; the goal of His activity is identical with His activity, with His very essence. For non-Divine existence, however, God is the pole to which it aspires, out of its infinite desire to be like God and to be united with Him.

Superlunar objects move in a direction that perfectly reflects the desire of intellects to know their causes and to resemble them, and first and foremost to be like the cause of causes—God. In the sublunar sphere, however, the way in which objects move and change depends (to the extent that they are rational) on the essence of each individual. Like Aristotle, the Philosopher believes that, at least in the organic realm, the evolution of the individual expresses an immanent aspiration (conscious or not), "a wisdom implanted in it" (5,10 [289/257]) to actualize the peculiar essential form that is potentially immanent in it: "Every soul instinctively uses its faculties according to their nature" (ibid. [290/258]). "The nature of the soul, in the comprehensive and generic sense, is defined by the examination of its actions as issuing from the forms adhering to matter, but not from matter, inasmuch as it is matter only, and without form. A knife, for instance, does not cut inasmuch as it is a substance, but inasmuch as it has the form of a knife" (5,12 [292/259]). Below the lunar sphere, as above it, there is an aspiration to realize the innate potential form. This aspiration is rooted in form—in the rational aspect of existence.[19]

To sum up, the main points of the Philosopher's position with regard to the teleological order of existence are as follows:

1. The goal is identical with maximum realization.
2. The goal is located in the rational plane of existence—in intellects or forms.
3. For intellectual beings, actualization of the goal depends on an act of intellection.
4. For actual intellects, the content of the goal, as a situation of actual being, is manifested by their perception of the cause of their existence; for forms (including "passive" intellects), however, the goal is the maximum realization of each essential form.
5. On every level of existence, the goal is in the realm of causes and not of effects.
6. Hence, to the extent that the goal causes the aspiration and effort to realize it, the aspiration and effort are directed "upward," toward the causes, and not "downward," toward the effects.

---

19. Nevertheless, the aspiration of actual intellects is not a process, whereas the aspiration of all other forms is necessarily a process.

This leads to fundamental conclusions about the possible relationship between every actual intellect (including God) and all existence that is not the cause of its own existence and whose intellection does not entail self-perception by an actual intellect, as well as about the meaning, for human beings, of the existence of God and the existence of actual intellects (including the Active Intellect).[20] Because an actual intellect cannot intentionally relate to any existence that is not its cause, we cannot explain the hierarchical ordering of existence—an ordering that entails the existence of "special relationships"—by the existence of God or of any particular actual intellect. The ordering principle (which, ontologically speaking, explains the special relationship) must be rooted in what is ordered: Its relationship with other orders of the hierarchy[21] and its particular essence, as it is in itself, highlight its uniqueness. This emphasis on the particularity of the element of the hierarchy is a necessary and sufficient cause for the constitution of the "special relationship" that obtains between it and God or between it and some actual intellect.

Our conclusion that the "special relationship" depends on the ordered element itself applies on all levels of existence. In superlunar existence, the place of each entity (mind, soul, or sphere) in the hierarchy depends on its specific place in the "logical space"—on its meaning in the intellection of the intellects.[22] In sublunar existence, the place of an element depends on its location in physical space (5,2; 5,10) or on its specific essence, its "combinations" or "mixtures" (5,10 [288/256]). This "special relationship" accounts for the normative weight of each element. This is how the ontological hierarchy, which expresses the objective order of non-Divine existence, acquires its normative significance.[23]

20. We shall deal with the conclusions concerning man in the next chapter.
21. In this way, primordial matter assumes the form of a particular element as a function of its proximity to or distance from the lunar sphere.
22. 5,14; 5,20; 5,21.
23. This principle about the relationship between the normative and ontological planes runs through the philosophical tradition until Hume and Kant. The *ought* reflects a demand and realization of the potential inherent in the real and corresponds to the natural aspiration to emerge from potential to actual.

4. Divine Productivity

The activity of actual intellects, in addition to its immanent manifestation, is productive. The Divine intellect is not only a final cause, as Aristotle thought, but also a cause for the existence of the non-Divine realm, inasmuch as the latter is rational—that is, forms are impressed on it. Because the existence apprehended by sensory experience is always a union of matter and form, everything in it, "as you see," "is reduced to the Prime Cause" (1,1 [6/36]).

From this perspective, the existence of God guarantees the actualization of what is potential. God, by virtue of His essence as a "real cause," prefers actualization over non-actualization.[24] This preference in no way manifests any Divine intention whatsoever. God's intention is located exclusively in intellection of His own essence. The relationship is only an external ontological consequence of the activity of the Active Intellect within itself: "Everything is reduced to the Prime Cause—not to a Will proceeding from it, but to an Emanation . . . " (ibid.).

The fundamental postulate of the Philosopher of the *Kuzari* (following al-Farabi and Avicenna) concerning the ontological significance of the contemplative activity of the Divine intellect makes it possible to accept the Aristotelian characterization of God as both sufficient for Himself and sufficient in Himself, as well as the Neoplatonic characterization of God as the cause of causes and source of all emanations. These do not contradict each other; in fact, they are in some measure interdependent.

Divine productivity is directly expressed only in the existence of the first intellect: "Philosophers speculating on these things arrive at the conclusion that from *one* only one can issue. They conjectured an angel, standing near to God, and having emanated from the Prime Cause" (4,25 [267/238]). This productivity is merely an external projection of God's reflection on

---

24. This applies to actual intellects, too: Every actual intellect plays this role for whatever emanates from it. But God and actual intellects are not an explanation for the concrete individuation of whatever emanates from them.

Himself from Himself. For other intellects in the superlunar world and for forms in the sublunar world, Divine productivity requires mediation.

Let us now turn to the concrete manifestations of indirect Divine productivity in the sublunar world. The factor that mediates between the sublunar and superlunar worlds is the Active Intellect, the last in the sequence of emanated intellects: "This is the degree of the Active Intellect, namely, that angel whose degree is below the angel who is connected with the sphere of the moon" (1,1 [8/37]).[25] Located on "the nethermost step of seraphic beings" (ibid.) or intellects, it occupies "the nethermost degree, nearest to us... and guides the nether world" (5,21 [330/292]). The activity of the Active Intellect, like that of the upper intellects, expresses its essence as an actual intellect. It apprehends itself and the intellects that lie above it—the intellects that are the source of its existence. The productivity of the Active Intellect is no more than an external projection, a by-product of its immanent activity.

Just as the intrinsic function of the Deity, vis-à-vis the totality of existence, has two sides, there are also two sides to the function of the Active Intellect vis-à-vis sublunar existence. First, with regard to the origin of the formal aspect of actual existence in the sublunar world, the Active Intellect is a genetic cause, as the source of the forms—the "form-giving Intelligence" (5,4 [283/251]; 5,10 [288])—and also the "secondary cause" (5,21 [330/292]).[26] Second, with regard to the essence of the formal aspect of concrete existence in the sublunar world, in its concrete manifestations as the forms of objects, the Active Intellect is the "spiritual" (1,1 [10]) or "universal intellect" (5,12

---

25. In 1,87, the Philosopher identifies the Active Intellect as the "Holy Spirit" or the Angel Gabriel. In this identification and his location of the Active Intellect "below the angel who is connected with the sphere of the moon" the Philosopher is relying on the opinions of al-Farabi and Avicenna. See Efros, *Doctrines*, p. 186.

26. The Philosopher agrees with Avicenna rather than with al-Farabi, who restricts the influence of the Active Intellect to rational beings only. See ibid., p. 187, n. 9.

[298/265]),[27] with regard both to its individuation and ranking in the hierarchy of defined realms and its distribution into the processes characteristic of this level (5,10 [288/256]).[28] For this reason, the rational soul retains the fundamental possibility of attaining "scientific" knowledge (5,12 [301]) and uniting with the Active Intellect.

The productivity of the Active Intellect, however, unlike that of the upper intellects, depends on the conditions that exist in the sublunar world—conditions that reflect a "stubborn" reality. This is a different existence, that of the material element, and cannot be nullified. Only sublunar existence is a manifestation of the reciprocal relations between the Divine emanation and matter: The Divine emanation finds expression in the rational and formal aspect of the world—the aspect that, epistemologically, can be fully known by reason. Matter, for its part,

---

27. Note that these characterizations of the Active Intellect as "spiritual" and "universal" appear in the context of the description of union with the Active Intellect, motivated by a desire to highlight the common denominator of the human mind and the Active Intellect—a common denominator that makes this union possible.

28. This is how we should understand the King: "We are misled by these names and we are persuaded to add an associate to God, if we say that Nature is wise and active, that perhaps Nature even creates..." (1,76 [34/55]). Compare: "This seed, then, according to a wisdom implanted in it, pursues a similar course. Philosophers call this nature, or rather powers that guard the preservation of the species" (5,10 [289/257]). Compare also the place of nature in the general ontological hierarchy and its ranking in the hierarchy after the soul: 5,12; 5,21. According to this, the King's "error" with "these names" is a reflection of his superficial philosophical education (something emphasized in this very passage—1,72 [33]). The cultivated Philosopher, however, is aware of these consequences of the doctrine. It is no chance that the Rabbi deviates from Aristotle in his definition of the concept "nature" (see Cassel ad loc.): Nature is divine in that it is "the beginning and primary cause through which a thing either moves or rests, not by accident, but by virtue of its inherent essence" (1,73 [33/55]). "Contingent" existence does not express God, but the material aspect of existence, because "color and corporeality, as concepts, cannot be subdivided in thought" (5,12 [330/266]). For philosophers, the homonymity of the concepts *God* and *nature* expresses two sides of the same coin: "I gave you the example of the creation of the plant and animal...[as] a work of God, called nature by philosophers" (3,23 [171/162]). Compare 1,80; 1,81.

gives the world its nonrational aspect—the aspect that can never be fully known.

5. The Interrelationship of the Two Ontological Dimensions

Here we encounter the fundamental problem of the interrelationship of the two mutually independent ontological dimensions: How is such a relationship possible? The dualism of the Philosopher of the *Kuzari*, reflected in the polarization of the totality of existence into two elements that are mutually estranged, in both source and essence, raises the problem of how the two poles can have any relationship—when it is this relationship that constitutes the single concrete world.[29] What is more, the relationship must explain the individuation of the multiplicity of concrete existence. The Divine emanation and primordial matter, in and of themselves, lack all individuation; how can their relationship be the source of multiplicity? The Philosopher, it is true, does not refer to this problem directly; but we can indicate two lines of thought that hint at an attempt to deal with it. First, although primordial matter per se is absolutely devoid of form, the Philosopher will allow it some minimal order, in that it is extensive, occupies space, and various and defined regions can be discerned within it. The distinction among regions is a function of their proximity to the lunar sphere (5,2–4).[30]

---

29. In the context of the system as a whole, this problem parallels that of the Platonic relationship between the ideas and the sensory world or that of the Kantian schematism. For Kant, though, the problem is epistemological, whereas here it is metaphysical.

30. Both Avicenna and al-Ghazali do not see extension as a manifestation of the essence of primordial matter. Hence they make two distinctions. First, they distinguish primordial matter, which lacks the form of corporeality, from secondary matter, which is already imprinted with this form and as such can serve as the substrate for the forms of the four elements. Second, they distinguish corporeal form from the forms of the four elements. Although they disagree when it comes to defining corporeal form, they agree that its source, like that of the other forms, is the "Giver of forms" rather than matter. The Philosopher of the *Kuzari* totally ignores these distinctions. Perhaps we may conclude, then, that he believes that matter per se is

The second line of thought is that actual intellects are ontologically productive. Because it is a consequence of their very action as intellects, this productivity is necessary and eternal (5,10 [291/259]). This provides our point of departure for bridging between the Divine emanation and matter: matter, possessed of only minimal form, is exposed to the mechanical influence of the spheres, which are also material objects; it is also ready to accept forms from the "Giver of forms," the Active Intellect. This minimal order that characterizes matter regulates the undifferentiated influence of the spheres and distinguishes among the four elements. These distinctions are the initial basis for the emergence of concrete multiplicity in sensory experience. Even after its various elementary forms have been determined, however, concrete multiplicity, especially in the organic realm, requires the Active Intellect, because the finer the mixture of the elements, "the nobler is the form in which the Divine wisdom manifests itself in a higher degree" (5,10 [289/256]). God's infinite productivity guarantees the emanation of the forms when there is an opportunity for it to occur—when there is an object with the capacity to merge with these forms.

The emergence of a situation that enables some form to be received by matter depends either on that matter's proximity to the spheres or on a process of change that expresses emergence from potential to actual—an expression of the inherent "aspiration" of the individual to self-realization, because a potential

---

essentially extensive, but does not consider this extension to be form. Accordingly the very first changes that take place in primordial matter are ascribed to an order that permits relations of proximity and distance. These changes, deriving from the motion of the sphere, are directly manifested in the application of the forms of the four elements. The unique ontological status of extension, as a manifestation of an order that is nevertheless not a *form*, is also expressed in the ontological status of primordial matter as matter that is neither potential nor actual (see 5,2). If this interpretation is correct, the Philosopher of the *Kuzari* anticipates Crescas's view of the essence of matter. See Moscato ad loc. See also A. Hyman, "Aristotle's 'First Matter' and Avicenna's and Averroes' 'Corporeal Form,'" in *H. A. Wolfson Jubilee*, vol. 1 (Jerusalem, 1965), pp. 385–406; H. A. Wolfson, *Crescas' Critique of Aristotle* (Cambridge, 1929), pp. 579–590 and 598–602; Efros, *Doctrines*, pp. 30–38.

THE PHILOSOPHER'S THOUGHT

form is already innate in it. From this latter vantage point, the form latent in the individual is the final cause (the necessary but not sufficient condition) that prepares it for a renewed encounter with the Divine Influence. But the proximity of matter to the spheres, as well as the emergence from potential to actual, depends on the "responsiveness" of matter—a "responsiveness" that is no more than a successful chance.[31]

The utter indifference of primordial matter to assuming a form and the partial indifference of an individual object, inasmuch as it is material, to assuming a new form are reflected in the nature of matter's "responsiveness" to assuming a new form or indeed any form whatsoever.

First, primordial matter's "responsiveness" to assuming a form is not an essential property of matter, but only a consequence of a chance proximity to the lunar sphere. As such it is necessarily limited and incomplete: limited by the boundaries of the realm where primordial matter and the lunar sphere meet, and incomplete because of the intensivity of the influence associated with this encounter. The two are interdependent: that is, the unmediated encounter between primordial matter and the lunar sphere is expressed in the optimum degree of intensivity associated with this encounter. "The first process was that the air near the moon sphere became hot, because it was nearest to the periphery. It thus became an etherial fire, called *elementary fire* by natural philosophers, having neither color nor combustion, and being a fine, delicate, and light substance. It is called the fire sphere" (5,2 [281/250]).[32] As stated, one of the most conspicuous manifestations of this limitation and incomplete-

---

31. Because the Philosopher denies the existence of the vacuum, the successful chance lies in the realm of primordial matter and not in its common boundary with the lunar sphere.

32. The unmediated encounter itself, a necessary condition for the process, is not itself a process. It is clear that this view of the limited and incomplete nature of primordial matter reflects the stance of the Philosopher rather than that of "some people" (ibid.), who advocate the doctrine of a "created world," although not ex nihilo creation, according to which the divine will is manifested in "all parts of the primordial." This view expresses their belief that God has a will.

ness in the Philosopher's system is the contingency of sublunar existence.[33]

Second, the "responsiveness" of the concrete thing, the individual object, as a form impressed on matter, and its willingness to assume a different or more developed form necessarily find expression in a process. Despite the innate aspiration of the form, the indifference of matter requires that the object be prepared to receive a new form through a gradual and continuous process, until the new and more developed form is attained: "These perfections exist only in the form of latent powers that require instruction and training to become active, bringing to light this capacity in all its completeness or with its deficiencies and innumerable grades" (1,1 [7/37]).

The change that characterizes non-Divine existence at all levels (along with its associated potentiality) is always a manifestation of the tension between the poles: in superlunar existence, the tension is between the Divine and "Pure Matter" (as an external manifestation of logical relations); in sublunar existence, it is between the formal and material aspects of existence. The ultimate ontological elements of existence, as they are in themselves, in their purity—that is, God and primordial matter—allow neither process nor potential. What they share is that they are not potential: God is actual; primordial matter is neither potential nor actual.

Primordial matter's *responsiveness* to the Divine influence, expressed in a process, is the source of the three aspects of sublunar existence: (1) multiplicity (process entails the existence of multiplicity); (2) the fixed order among the moments of the process, an order in which each "earlier" moment is a necessary (but not sufficient) cause for the very existence of the "later" moment; (3) the fixed order as a *hierarchical* order—a "later" moment in the process is ontologically and axiologically superior to an "earlier" moment.

---

33. This limitation and incompleteness can be associated with the possibility of positing human freedom of decision.

With regard to the *incompleteness* of the responsiveness, however, multiplicity and hierarchical order are manifested not only in the distinction among different moments in the process itself, but also in the distinction between degrees of intensity of the potentials available to some object, as the possible ultimate boundary in the process of its realization. "Every individual on earth has its completing causes" (1,1 [7/36]). That is, potentiality, as the necessary ontological condition for the possibility of change, determines also the ultimate limit of change and is accordingly divided among the various stages of the process; and the two, potentiality and change, are interdependent.

These two aspects of potentiality are reflected in sensory reality, both in the existence of empirical multiplicity and in the various meanings of the hierarchical order that characterizes this existence: (1) As divided among the various stages of process, potentiality is manifested in the existence of multiplicity and in the existence of a hierarchical order among the stages of the process.[34] (2) As setting the ultimate limits to the process, potentiality is manifested in the ranking of all existence on an all-inclusive hierarchical scale.[35] This hierarchy appears in the ranking of the species, in the sublunar realm, and in the ranking of the entities, in the superlunar realm.

34. 1,1; 5,10. From this perspective, potentiality is the exclusive distinguishing feature of sublunar reality.
35. 1,1; 5,2; 5,12; 5,21.

4

ARISTOTELIAN ANTHROPOLOGY

The previous chapters have focused on the metaphysics propounded by the Philosopher of the *Kuzari*. Now we shall concentrate on its significance for human beings, with regard to both its theoretical assumptions and its practical conclusions. We shall deal with his anthropology only as it relates to his general metaphysics. The way of life that human beings should adopt in order to realize their ultimate goal as rational beings depends on the nature of that goal. First, then, we shall consider the goal that human beings ought to pursue and only then the way of life that leads to it.

For the purposes of our discussion, three different senses of *goal* must be distinguished:

1. Goal in the sense of *final cause*—the pole that ought to give direction to a change or process.
2. Goal as a *state of perfection*—a state in which what is realized fully exhausts the possible.
3. Goal as *absolute rationale*—as *supreme value*.

1. The Final Cause of Human Existence

The goal of an object is to attain the most intense relationship with God by realizing its own inherent potential. This goal is realized by virtue of the final cause inherent in the object: "Every soul instinctively uses its faculties according to their nature" (5,10 [290/258]).

The ultimate goal, as final cause, is anchored in the meaning of the existence of God for each object, and not necessarily for human beings. True, only human beings, who are rational, have the possibility of choosing God as a goal and steering the process of emergence from potentiality to actuality through which they draw nearer to God. In this respect human beings, who remain in a state of potentiality, differ from superlunar objects and intellects, which already exist in actuality and realize their goal in the present. Rational man is also different from other sublunar objects. Although they, like man, are engaged in a process of emergence from potentiality to actuality, the direction of the process is imposed upon them by the nature of their inherent potentiality; but no direction of process and change is imposed upon human beings, who can always choose some other goal.[1]

The unique status of human beings vis-à-vis their goal—vis-à-vis God—stems from their unique position on the ladder of existing entities, since man is the only entity that combines two different elements of existence: intellect, which is located near the lunar sphere and above it, on the ontological scale of objects; and the four material elements, which are found in the sublunar realm. Human beings, as creatures participating in both worlds, can sever their connection with one of them: they can commune with the Active Intellect and sunder their minds from their sublunar bodies; or, paying no attention to their potential intellect, they can cleave to their bodies and ignore their minds.[2]

---

1. There is no need to associate this argument about the unique relationship between objects and their goal with any particular assumption about human freedom, although, as stated, it is plausible that the Philosopher of the *Kuzari* believes that man chooses out of *freedom to*.

2. Man's status, like that of every other entity, is determined neither by his predisposition nor by his efforts, but by the actual position that he manages to attain. From this point of view, if we could imagine (though as a matter of principle we cannot) that human beings might realize their goal without knowledge of their duties, it would not detract from their value.

THE PHILOSOPHER'S THOUGHT

In other words, for intellects—including the human intellect—the final cause, with regard to its content, is identical with the goal in the sense of *ultimate rationale*; the ultimate rationale is the ground for the activity of the intellect, and this ground itself is the cause of its specific activity as intellect.[3] The specific potential of rational human beings is the "passive intellect." This potential is manifested in the special character of "natural" change—consciousness and intentionality (5,10 [291/258]).[4]

Thus for human beings, and them alone, knowledge of God's existence has *practical* significance. Knowledge of God's existence is accompanied by the demand to take steps to attain Him: "so that your intellect may become active, not passive" (1,1 [9/38]).[5] For human beings, this demand is called, "allusively and approximately," the *divine will* (ibid.). The Philosopher sees himself duty-bound to realize his goal; from this perspective his relationship to his goal has something in common with the belief held by all the revealed religions that the "divine will" is the will of one who justly makes a demand. The Philosopher begins his discourse, at the beginning of the book,

---

(The comparison with Kantian ethics is fascinating, but this is not the place to consider it.) By definition, actual intellects actively intuit by virtue of *freedom from*—as a manifestation of their own intrinsic spontaneous activity. The motions of the spheres are "independent" (5,21 [330/292]), and they do not act out of *freedom to*. Man's specific freedom as *freedom to* is a manifestation of his inferiority, of the fact that he has a body. Philosophers who manage to unite with the Active Intellect "lose" their freedom, in the sense of *freedom to*. They always choose the good, "as if [all their organs] were the organs of the Active Intellect" (1,1 [8/37]). The Rabbi agrees with the Philosopher that true freedom is conditioned not by the circumstances that operate on the will but by its concrete content and realization.

3. Compare the intention underlying action "from duty" as opposed to action "in accordance with duty" in Kant's ethics. For Kant, too, this intentionality itself serves as a "motive" (*Triebfeder*) for the determination of the will.

4. See also 4,19; 5,12.

5. For God, there is absolute identity between *ought* and *is*. For the superlunar intellects, *ought* is not identical with *is*, but *what is* is identical with *what can be achieved*. For the human mind (and all other forms in sublunar existence), not only is *ought* not identical with *is*, *what is* is not identical with *what can be achieved*.

with a third-person recitation describing "his belief." After he has identified man's goal—communion or merger with the Active Intellect—with the divine will, he addresses imperative demands to the king: "endeavor to reach it and . . . keep to the just way" (ibid.).[6] The extent to which perfection is attained determines the essence of individual entities—their place in the overall hierarchy of existence; hence for human beings, as for all other segments of existence, the specific place of individuals in the hierarchy is determined by the individuals themselves, and not through an intentional intervention by the "causes."[7] This means that the relationship between human beings and the causes is similar to that between the other intellects and their causes. The unique nature of human potentiality, however, determines not only how human beings relate to the goal, but also the content of the goal itself.

2. The Goal as the Actualization of Human Potential

The goal of superlunar intellects is inherent in them, and the same holds for the human intellect: Reason attains its goal by

---

6. Note that what the Philosopher has to say in Part I is a reply to the King's question rather than a systematic or didactic exposition of his doctrine. For what Halevi considered to be the appropriate method for teaching philosophy, see 5,2. In his remarks at the beginning of the book, the Philosopher relates chiefly to the King's dream. Accordingly he starts by demonstrating that God does not have a will, in the common acceptation of this term, so that there are no intentions that are pleasing to God or actions displeasing to Him. After he has explained to the King the goal-oriented and hierarchical order of non-Divine existence and emphasized the status of rational beings in this order, however, he permits himself a metaphorical application to God of the term *will*. The identification of man's goal with the performance of God's will is the methodological link between the Philosopher's metaphysical presentation and practical suggestion. He concludes by explaining the legitimate sense of deeds and intentions that are "pleasing" to God.

7. Ibn Bajja's position on this critical issue is far from clear; in places he seems to imply that sometimes the human intellect communes with the Active Intellect thanks to God's active assistance. Clearly this view assumes a God who is intrinsically able to serve as a principle of individuation—a God with the capacity to relate to objects. See A. Altmann, "Ibn Bajja on Man's Ultimate Felicity," in *H. A. Wolfson Jubilee*, vol. 1 (Jerusalem, 1965), pp. 47–87.

knowing itself and its cause. Thereby it also realizes itself: It causes itself to emerge from potential to actual by actually intuiting the intelligible objects that are potentially within itself. Aristotle's self-perception and perception of his Prime Cause are similar to the superlunar intellects' intuition of themselves and of their causes (4,25 [268]). The human intellect's self-perception, like that of all other actual intellects, is bound up with knowledge of its causes and is manifested, ontologically, in union with these causes.

Unlike the partial union between superlunar intellects and their causes—a communion that does not annul their individual existence (i.e., the distance between themselves and their causes[8]) and does not alter their place in the ontological hierarchy—the union of the "perfect" human intellect[9] with the Active Intellect means its full identification with the Active Intellect[10] and the consequent abrogation of its individual existence. In fact, the two are interdependent: It is precisely man's existence as an individual, who changes in time, that redeems him from his individuality. But even if his intellect is perfect and allows him to unite with the Active Intellect, "a complete connection is . . . impossible, unless all physical powers are subdued. It is the body alone that prevents this connection. As soon as the intellectual soul is separated from it, it becomes perfect, connected with what renders it immune to injury, and united with the noble substance that is styled the higher knowledge" (5,12 [302/268]).[11] Unlike the factual and ephemeral link between the

---

8. See Chapter 3, §3, "The Immanent Activity of the Deity."

9. The "perfect" intellect is that of philosophers (1,1). Survival of the intellect is the lot of philosophers alone (ibid.; see also 1,110 and 5,14).

10. 1,1; 4,13; 5,10, 5,12. According to al-Farabi and Avicenna, the human intellect always remains inferior to the Active Intellect; but the Philosopher of the *Kuzari* tends to the view of Ibn Bajja. See Davidson, "The Active Intellect," p. 364.

11. See also 4,19. On this point, too, the Philosopher seems to follow Ibn Bajja. See Altmann, "Ibn Bajja"; Davidson, "The Active Intellect," p. 365 and n. 4. Abraham Ibn Ezra evidently held the same view; see his long commentary on Ex. 33:21 and short commentary on Ex. 33:22. The Philosopher argues for union with the Active Intellect (1,1) while man is still alive; but this passage seems to refer to only a partial union.

human body and mind, the link between enduring pure matter and the superlunar intellects is logical and permanent. This contrast underlies the difference between the human mind, which can achieve absolute union with the Active Intellect, and the superlunar intellects, which cannot attain full union with their causes.

Partial union with the Active Intellect—the sort that can take place while a philosopher is still alive—is reflected by a metamorphosis in the essence of the human intellect itself. Whereas the acquisition of knowledge by potential intellects depends on a process of "instruction" (1,1 [9/38]), on "careful rational thinking" (5,12 [299/265]), the intellect, to the extent that it is already Active Intellect, "conceives spontaneously and conceives itself as often as it desires" (ibid.).[12] Its "deduction of the conclusion *is not dependent on time*" (ibid.) and it perceives "simultaneously" (5,14 [305/271]). When it unites with the Active Intellect, the human intellect is exempt from having to use "logical conclusions and meditation, escaping such necessity by inspiration and revelation. This special distinction is styled sanctity, or holy spirit" (5,12 [300/266]).[13] A mind that unites with the Active Intellect changes from a discursive to an intuitive intellect; its process of intellection no longer takes place in the temporal continuum; instead, it occupies a single and indivisible moment. This is because of the ontological identity of

---

12. According to Halevi himself, though, intuitive knowledge does not depend upon perfection of the intellect: "The soul with which [Adam] was endowed was perfect; his intellect was the loftiest that a human being can possess. Beyond this he was fitted with divine power of such high rank that it brought him into connection with divine and spiritual beings and enabled him, with slight reflection, to comprehend the great truths without instruction" (1,95 [46/64]). The prophet sees "in one sudden flash" (4,5 [235/213]); what is more, "a religion of divine origin arises suddenly" (1,81 [38/58]). These unique events are focused in a single moment of the temporal continuum.

13. This is a quotation from Avicenna's *Psychology;* see H. A. Wolfson, "Hallevi and Maimonides on Prophecy," *Jewish Quarterly Review* 32 (1941–1942): 349, n. 20; Cassel, p. 27, n. 3. The burden is removed by inspiration and by revelation (or prophecy), and not as Moscato interprets this passage.

observing and observed mind that characterizes actual intellect—an identity represented, epistemologically, by the mind's capacity to observe its objects while observing itself, such that its self-perception is the perception of its objects: "Actual reason is nothing but the abstract of objects conceived, potentially existing in reason itself [and rendered actual by the same]. It is therefore also said that actual reason comprehends and is comprehended simultaneously" (ibid. [299/265]). Now the characteristic discursiveness of the activity of potential intellect derives exclusively from the fact that the mind "learns" about external objects. This is why it requires the mediation of the senses (ibid.) and the appearance of objects as given in experience.

This sensory mediation between object and mind—as a result of which the initial datum is not directly grasped by the mind—entails a process of progressive abstraction within the latter; that is, a process of analysis followed by one of synthesis: "We shall then find that these forms have some attributes in common, but that they differ in others.... The soul divides or combines the forms. It then combines them by means of syllogisms" (5,12 [298/264]).[14] The mind's dependence on experience of external objects explains the irreducibility of the primary epistemological datum and thus the mind's dependence on concrete circumstances (ibid.). In other words, the discursive process whereby the mind acquires knowledge is not an expression of its essence per se[15] but of its concrete status in the sublunar world—a world marked by the tension between form and matter, both for the mind as potential intellect and for the forms as potential objects of knowledge. Potential intellect emerges into actuality only by extracting the forms that are imprinted on matter. In this, human reason and the emanation of forms by the Active Intellect operate in opposite directions. Because an actual intellect perceives its object independent of any particular reality outside itself, its self-perception is the perception of objects

14. 1,87 [60]. See also Efros, *Doctrines*, p. 193.
15. See Chapter 3, §3, "The Immanent Activity of the Deity." On the concept of *necessity*, see H. A. Wolfson, "The Classification of Sciences," *Hebrew Union College Jubilee Volume* (1925), p. 268.

as they truly are. From this perspective, to the extent that the philosopher's mind perceives itself, its objects of knowledge are "obtained by way of divine inspiration" (ibid. [297/263]). Hence "the power of intellect conceives *spontaneously* and conceives *itself as often as it desires.*" That is, the perceiving intellect, because it perceives of its *own* accord and perceives its *own* self—independent of external reality—perceives when it wishes, because "the deduction of the conclusion is not dependent on time, reason itself being above time" (5,12 [299/265]). Intuitive cognition liberates the mind from the *necessity* that is part of the mode of perception of the passive intellect, but it still reflects the systematic order that prevails among the objects of perception. The very possibility of intuitive knowledge stems from the necessary rational relations among the objects of perception. The resemblance to the Active Intellect must be expressed in *faith* (Arabic *iʿtiqād*) (1,1 [10])—faith that has a systematic rational grounding and reflects the relations found in reality itself.[16]

3. The Philosophical Theory of Prophecy

The preceding sheds light on the Philosopher's theory of prophecy. According to the Philosopher, the prophet is merely a human being who has attained full union with the Active Intellect (5,12 [299]). *Prophecy* is simply another term for intellectual intuition or the special capacity associated with the mode of perception of actual intellects. The term highlights two aspects of this intuition: (1) the active nature of the union—the union is not only a state of actual knowledge, but also an openness to additional direct and immediate knowledge, "as often as it desires" (this openness is itself a manifestation of the partial union that alone is possible while human beings are still alive); and (2) the special place occupied in perception by actual intellects by the pole

---

16. See Efros, *Doctrines*, pp. 86–87; idem, *Terms*, s.v. *emunah*; Moscato 1,1, *incipit* האמונות והדתות: "What the Philosopher says at the end of the section indicates that what he believes as a result of his syllogisms is also called 'faith.'"

with which the union takes place—the causes. Actual intellects perceive effects from causes, "for our belief in the correctness of opinions is not regulated by instruction ... The rational soul comes into connection with the divine emanation" (5,12 [302/268]).[17] The Philosopher of the *Kuzari*, unlike Avicenna, does not distinguish between prophecy as ʾ*ilhām* and prophecy as *waḥy*.[18] According to the Philosopher, *waḥy* too is a manifestation only of the state of the intellect. Union with the "universal reason" (ibid. [300/266]) is the only condition for the intellect's attaining the level of both "inspiration" and "prophecy"[19] (ibid.).[20] If the imagination (or fancy) nevertheless plays a role in prophecy, this role is merely to explain certain phenomena in prophecy—phenomena that are not necessarily intrinsic to it or an inseparable part thereof (1,87 [61]). What is more, none of these is in any way superior to union with the Active Intellect: "then you will reach your goal, namely, union with this Spiritual, or rather Active, Intellect. Maybe he will communicate with you or teach you the knowledge of what is hidden through

---

17. Again, "The Law [is] of human origin, *and only later on supported by divine inspiration*" (1,87 [40/60]); "prophecy did not (as philosophers assume) burst forth in a pure soul, become united with the Active Intellect (also termed Holy Spirit or Gabriel) and then assist and inspire the prophet [in the context, Moses]" (ibid. [61]).

18. Wolfson, "The Classification," n. 23.

19. Arabic: *biʾ lilhām waʾ lwaḥy*.

20. The mention of the two degrees of prophecy, with no distinction indicated, even though they are quite distinct—in both the Islamic theological tradition and philosophy as well as for Halevi himself (see 5,12, where he summarizes Avicenna's psychology)—indicates that the Philosopher sees no need for or at least attributes no fundamental importance to this distinction (see *Encyclopedia of Islam*, s.v. *ilhām*; Efros, *Doctrines*, p. 193). The Philosopher also holds that there is no distinction between the degrees of prophecy with regard to their social or political function. The full vocation of philosopher-prophets is to realize themselves, not to perform some function in the realm of society and politics. Hence from this perspective, too, the imaginative faculty, as a capacity whereby prophets "translate" intellectual truth into terms that can be understood by the masses, has no significance—unlike the view of al-Farabi. Compare Ibn Ezra's etymology of *navi* 'prophet' (long commentary on Ex. 7:1). See also Shlomo Pines's introduction to his English translation of *The Guide of the Perplexed*, p. lxxxix.

true dreams and positive visions" (1,1 [10/39]). That is, the supreme goal attainable by human beings, and imposed on them as a duty, is only to *seek* union with the Active Intellect. On the other hand, there is no way to guarantee that a person will have prophetic visions. Having such visions is merely a successful chance—a legitimate *possibility* only, not a goal sought after.[21] There are two reasons for this: On the one hand, prophetic visions are not a necessary result of the union of actual intellects with the Active Intellect. On the other hand, the imaginative faculty per se lacks the capacity to be a source for intentional perceptions; the "someone" who speaks "with him" in a dream and is "heard" is none other than the Creator: "and afterwards pretended that *God* had spoken *in him*" (1,87 [42/61]).[22] When philosophers, waking, review their dream visions (only, of course, if the dream is a "true" one—a dream that also reflects the activity of the intellect), they are purifying the dream of its fanciful and sensory content and physical images, such that the "someone" of the dream is interpreted as being the Creator, or "the Cause of causes in the creation of all creatures" (1,1 [5/36]). The dream speech—the speech "with him" that depends on the existence of "someone," a "you" speaking to "me," face to face and with knowledge of its interlocutor—rests on speech "in him": "he only heard the words in fancy, but not with his ears; ... he saw him in his thought, but not with his eyes" (1,87 [42/61]).[23] That is, in dreams, too, the ultimate source of truth is union with

---

21. I. Husik, *A History of Medieval Jewish Philosophy* (New York, 1969), p. 165, thinks otherwise.

22. On the other hand, according to the Rabbi: "The people prepared and became fitted to [the degree of prophecy] and even to hear the words of God face to face" (1,87 [41/60]).

23. Compare the Philosopher's doctrine of the abstraction of forms from sensory matter, which serves as a condition for converting potential into actual intellect (5,12). Compare also *Guide of the Perplexed*, 1,65; 2,29 and the commentary on the *Guide* by Shem Tov ibn Joseph Ibn Shem Tov, *Shem Tov* (ad loc.). See also Maimonides' reply to R. Hisdai Halevi, *Iggerot ha-Rambam* (Letters of Maimonides) (Leipzig, 1859). The problem of Divine speech is associated with the problem of the meaning of Divine intentionality and with the problem of appraising the language of the Bible (similar to the problem of the language of the Koran in Muslim thought). See also Ibn Ezra on Gen. 1:3; and the supercommentaries *Yahel Or* (ad loc.), §151; *Qarnei Or*, §59. See also Chapter 5, note 29.

the Active Intellect: "he is able to grasp all metaphysical problems with the abstract intellect alone, without the *support* of anything that can be conceived or seen" (4,5 [235/213]).[24]

The Philosopher's view that the fancy can be a source only of images and not of adequate knowledge entails a conclusion based on his two fundamental positions. One concerns the essence of the metaphysical truths whose knowledge by human beings grounds their communion with God (ibid.). In his opinion, such matters, by their very nature, are intelligible and can be known only by the mind. Fancy can invent only plastic images, "forms," and not "subjects in their true essence" (4,3 [226/206]). "The faculties of perception and imagination can neither judge nor decide; they can only picture an object" (5,12 [296/262]). It follows that "the faculties of perception acquire something only relative to the object as perceived," whereas "the intellectual faculties conceive the conceived object itself" (ibid. [299/265]).[25] The second basic principle is that appropriate knowledge is possible only as an expression of the ontological identity between the intellect, intellection, and the intelligible object.

---

24. Compare what the King says: "What could be more erroneous, in the opinion of the philosophers, than the belief... that the Prime Cause spoke with mortals?" (1,4 [11/39]). The King explicitly extracts the methodological conclusion from the Philosopher's principled position. The identification of the Divine being who spoke in the dream with the "Prime Cause" entails subjective explanations for the personal relationship manifested by the deity who speaks with human beings—explanations that immediately nullify the theological value of the dream. But the King himself (1,95 [53]) insists on the fundamental and ontological importance of the concrete dream, associated with vision and the Divine word, of which he has personal experience. Compare also 1,8 [16/43], where the King points out to the Muslim scholar the grave problem posed by the assumption that "God has intercourse with man." See also 1,9, where the Muslim endeavors to prove that God did in fact speak with Moses. See also 1,49 and 1,99; and compare Ibn Ezra's short commentary on Ex. 43:23.

25. Compare Ibn Ezra's short commentary on Ex. 33:23 and the supercommentary *Zafenat Paneaḥ* ad loc. Halevi and the Philosopher agree on this characterization of the imagination. Halevi also agrees with the Philosopher's view of the fundamental parallel between the faculties of knowledge and the essence of known objects. The King concludes that "should anyone hear you relate that God spoke with your assembled multitude, wrote tablets for you, etc., he could not be blamed for accusing you of

Just as this identity depends on the ontological essence of perceived reality, it also depends on the nature of perception itself: if objects must be perceived, cognition must be perceptive. Of course, the imaginative faculty cannot be identical with the object imagined, even when the image is true (that is, an accurate reflection of the external object), because imagination lacks the capacity to attain essences (5,12). It follows that imagination is among the powers that "perish with their organs; only the rational faculty endures" (ibid. [296/263]). According to the Philosopher, revelation, in the traditional sense of the historical religions (that is, a process in which prophesying subjects receive truths that are *external* to them, conveyed by words spoken to the prophets by God), is impossible—not only because "speech with" is impossible, but also because such revelation, which would be intrinsically external to the subject and not the result of its own self-perception, is epistemologically inferior. True prophecy must be a manifestation of "speaking *in*."[26] What is more, any linguistic expression, because it is necessarily bound up with speech, is irrelevant to the perceived truth. Nevertheless, the Philosopher is willing to entertain the possibility that "perhaps the Active Intellect will communicate with you or teach you knowledge of what is hidden through true dreams and positive visions" (1,1 [10/39]). He explains knowledge of the future as a manifestation of the knowledge of causes "as often as it desires"—a cognitive faculty pertaining to actual intellect. Foreknowledge of future events is clearly limited to knowledge of effects, in the same sense that God and the upper intellects know effects.[27] Likewise, "true dreams" and "positive visions" can be explained as a manifestation of the autonomous activity of actual intellect—its union with the Active Intellect, expressed by the persistence of its activity independent of the state of the

---

holding a materialistic theory" (1,38 [32/62]). Halevi basically concurs (ibid. 89), except that he holds that one must distinguish between God as He is for Himself and the deity who appears in the realm of human experience.

26. See below, note 31.
27. See Chapter 2, §5, "Existence Whose Origin Is God as a Plenum."

body; "the activity of the body is limited, but not that of the soul" (5,12 [301/267]).[28]

In summary, the Philosopher tries to offer a plausible solution for the ancillary phenomena associated with prophecy, such as are recounted at length in the traditions of the historical religions. Although he does not question the veracity of the traditions, the Philosopher does reject their explanations of these phenomena.[29] He accepts the traditions on the basis of his own explanation of these phenomena, in the context of his overall view that perfection is the goal. Accordingly, prophecy is a manifestation of the perfection that human beings can attain while alive. Hence the prophets spoken of by the religious traditions must have been philosophers, and the ancillary phenomena associated with their careers are merely possible phenomena.

Halevi criticizes the philosophical theory of prophecy on two fronts: (1) He attacks the theory itself, denying that it is possible for an individual rational human intellect to unite with the Active Intellect. As we have seen, this possibility underlies the Philosopher's theory of prophecy, his views on the survival of the intellect after death, and his entire epistemology. (2) Relying on historical experience, Halevi seeks to demonstrate

---

28. The intensivity of the activity of the mind that unites with the Active Intellect has other manifestations as well (1,1). See Chapter 3, §3, "The Immanent Activity of the Deity." Halevi disputes the assumption that actual intellect perceives even when the philosopher is asleep: "why is not a philosopher conscious of himself when he is asleep?" (5,14 [306/271]). His argument is based on the Philosopher's own postulate that any perception by actual intellect is self-perception. He thus contends that the mind's self-perception necessarily entails self-consciousness. The idea of the continuous activity of actual intellect, with the corollary that forgetting is impossible, is shared by the Philosopher of the *Kuzari* (5,12; 5,14) and Ibn Bajja, for similar reasons. This is also the opinion of Maimonides (*Guide of the Perplexed*, 1,62). See also A. Z. Berman, "Ibn Bajja ve-ha-Rambam" (Ibn Bajja and Maimonides), (doctoral dissertation, Hebrew University of Jerusalem, 1961), p. 28.

29. Nevertheless, the Philosopher is unwilling to accept the King's dream as a true dream—not only because of its content but also because his school holds that true dreams, like all the other ancillary phenomena of prophecy, depend on union with the Active Intellect, a degree the King has not yet attained.

two things: first, the prophets were not philosophers; second, some phenomena associated with prophecy cannot be explained by the Philosopher's approach. Indeed, the Philosopher's doctrine quite rules out wonders and portents (1,42 [23]; see also 2,54 [112]; 4,3 [218]).[30]

4. The Goal as a Supreme Value

In light of this, the goal of rational beings, as of intellects, lies in the domain of intellect itself: On the one hand, the mind perceives of its own accord and from within itself; on the other hand, it actualizes itself by perceiving itself, and this actualization constitutes its specific normative value.

"The acme of human success is speculative science and the conception by reason and thought of all intelligible matters. This is transformed into actual intellect, then into emanating intellect, through which it draws near to the Active Intellect" (4,19 [248/224]). Again, for the Philosopher, "the real benefit is to be found only in the cognizance of the true nature of things, through which man becomes akin to the Active Intellect" (4,13 [241/218]). For the human intellect, as for all intellects (including God), the material goal, as the supreme rationale and supreme value, is identical with the ontological goal—perfection. For man, as a *rational being,* this state of affairs finds expression in union with the Active Intellect, "not in order to receive favor from the Prime Cause or to divert its wrath, but solely to become like the Active Intellect" (1,1 [9/38]).

True, the process of cognition involves a subjective sense of "enjoyment" (3,1 [141/136]); when "a man's intellect is in conjunction with the [Active Intellect], this is called his paradise and everlasting life" (5,10 [292/259]). Nevertheless, according to the Philosopher, nothing in this "enjoyment" and "paradise" can constitute an ultimate rationale and supreme value. The

---

30. On this question, the position of the Philosopher runs counter to Avicenna's. See Shlomo Pines in his introduction to his English translation of the *Guide of the Perplexed,* p. xciv.

happiness associated with the process of union, and with union itself, is only the emotional state of one who has "the necessary learning to be absorbed in it" (3,1 [141/136]). We can learn about the Philosopher's view from his failure to mention happiness in those sections that describe the goal as he understands it. With regard to the state of human perfection, the idea of happiness appears, as an aside, only in these two passages. The philosopher's "happiness" is a subjective resonance of being in a state of both ontological and ethical contentment. "Happiness" is an expression of the satisfaction that follows confirmation of a given state. God is free of any positive or negative desire, because "a desire intimates a want in the person who feels it" (1,1 [5/36]). "The motive powers"—"to obtain what is desired" or "to repel what is undesirable" (5,12 [295/262])—stem exclusively from the "want" of living beings who depend on their environment. In this respect, the perfect human being resembles God.[31]

5. The Contemplative Relationship to God

Even though realization of the intellect is the goal, contemplation of God does not have an unlimited value. For the Philosopher, "the real benefit is to be found only in the cognizance of the true nature of things, through which man becomes akin to the Active Intellect" (4,13 [241/218]). The Rabbi rejects this idea: "The philosopher seeks God only that he may be able to describe Him accurately, as he would describe the earth.... [For him,] ignorance of God would be no more injurious than [is the] ignorance concerning the earth [of] those who think it is flat" (ibid.). According to the Philosopher, the appropriate

---

31. On this point, the Philosopher champions the view of Ibn Bajja; see Berman, pp. 14 and 28; see also Moshe Narboni, "Bi'ur kavvanat Abu-Bakr ben al-Sayag, be-hanhaggat ha-mitboded ve-hu ḥeleq medinah" (Commentary on Ibn Bajja's ascetic rule), ed. David Herzog, *Qoveẓ ʿal yad* 11 (1896), p. 12. Compare 4,4 and 4,5. See also Ibn Ezra on Deut. 6:5—"With all your heart and all your soul": "The heart is knowledge and a designation for the perceiving spirit."

attitude toward God—toward knowledge of God—has a finite value, comparable in principle to the value of knowing other intelligible objects; as the Rabbi puts it, philosophers "consider Divine worship to be only a refinement of conduct and confession of truth; they extol Him above all other beings, just as the sun is to be extolled above all other visible things. They consider the denial of God only as a sign of a low standard of the soul, which acquiesces in untruth" (4,15 [246/222]). Or, as the Philosopher states *in propria persona,* the endeavor to become like the Active Intellect is "accompanied by the veneration of the Prime Cause" (1,1 [9/38]); but knowledge of the Prime Cause is of finite value, given that the supreme value and the purpose of all this effort is "to become like the Active Intellect" (ibid. [10/38]).[32] The Philosopher's ascription of an intrinsic ethical value to the proper attitude toward God would seem to be incompatible with his general theory of man's goal. Understanding this view in the overall context of his doctrine (we

32. Compare also: "Rational law demands justice and recognition of God's bounty" (2,48 [106/112]); "be he believer or free-thinker [Arabic: *zanādiqa*], it does not concern him, if he is a philosopher" (4,13 [241/218]). Again, "consider that many among the nations incline towards heresy [Arabic: *al-zandaqa*]" (4,23 [252/227]). The reference seems to be to an adherent of a religion other than official Islam, Christianity, and Judaism (see *Encyclopedia of Islam,* s.v. *zindīq*). Sometimes this term refers to an individual who is not meticulous in observance of the practical commandments. See Y. Goldziher, *Harẓaʾot ʿal ha-Islam* (Lectures on Islam) (Jerusalem, 1951), p. 117 and n. 7, p. 128 and n. 5. That this is its meaning can also be inferred from what follows: "His axiom is that: 'God will do no good, neither will He do evil' " (4,13 [241/218]). Similarly, the Rabbi speaks of "the heretics [*al-zanādiqa*] who followed the view of the Greek philosopher Epicurus, namely, that all things are the outcome of accidents, since no settled purpose is ever discernible in them. His school is called that of the Hedonists, because they held the opinion that pleasure is the desired aim and absolute good" (5,20 [320/283]). This also is implied by the context in 4,23. Again, "the prophets . . . impart the conviction to the heretic [*al-zandīq*] that judgment and rule on earth belong to God" (4,3 [234/212]; see also 1,84). Compare Ibn Ezra on Deut. 21:20, where we have a similar use of the term *heretic.* Compare further: "We must not take it amiss that Aristotle thinks lightly of the observance of religious laws, since he doubts whether God has any cognizance of them" (4,16 [247/223]; and 4,19). In any case, the term is not to be understood as referring to one who denies the existence of God.

must distinguish between the Philosopher's views and Halevi's assessment of them) is a precondition for understanding his theory of man's goal, including the significance for man of God's existence. The Philosopher's unwillingness to accord infinite value to the contemplative attitude toward the deity must not be seen as a consequence of the intellectual nature of this attitude. We cannot sunder the essence of the intellect and its mode of activity—perception—from its supreme goal: to know "the true nature of things"; that is, "to become akin to the Active Intellect" (4,13 [241/218]). For the Philosopher, supreme value adheres to *union* with the Active Intellect. Furthermore, the ontological and epistemological planes are inseparable, because even if the subjectively supreme rationale belongs only to the epistemological plane (where knowledge of God is one truth among many and has no absolute primacy), it is only one manifestation of a deficiency on the epistemological plane itself. Cognition, if perfect, also includes knowledge of knowledge; that is, knowledge of the ontological significance of knowledge—which is union. The ontological significance of cognition is merely a manifestation of its essence, because union is with the intelligible object inasmuch as it is intelligible.[33] Nor should we

33. We cannot accept the argument of Julius Guttmann, *Philosophies of Judaism*, trans. David W. Silverman (Garden City, N.Y., 1966), p. 141: "As an historical account, this characterization of philosophy is decidedly one-sided. Halevi's Aristotelian opponents were far from thinking of God only as an object of knowledge. In fact, Halevi himself attributes to them the opposite tendency of endeavoring to attain communion with God through knowledge, thereby substituting a kind of pseudo religion for the true religion." Halevi, characterizing the Philosopher's view of the limited value of knowledge of God, emphasized the ontological significance of intellectual perception in his theory of union with the Active Intellect. Nor can one accept without refinement Guttmann's idea (ibid.) that for the Philosopher, according to Halevi, "God is merely an object of knowledge towards which he adopts the same theoretical attitude as he does towards other objects of knowledge." The intellect does indeed aspire to knowledge of existence, but this knowledge itself relates to "existing objects" only as "intelligible objects"; that is, only as causes (because the totality of intelligible objects is identical with the Active Intellect, and so on). From this perspective, the Cause of causes naturally has fundamental importance. Guttmann supposes that, both methodologically and

attribute the unwillingness to see union as a goal in its own right to the "frailty" of the intellectual mode of relationship. According to the Philosopher, not only is the intellect the cause of its own activity, it also has the power to awaken an emotional resonance—fear and love (4,4; 4,5).[34] Furthermore, when a man's intellect unites with the Active Intellect, this union finds expression in "all his organs" (1,1 [8/37]). The power of intellect led the philosophers to "renounce wealth, rank, and the pleasure of children, in order not to be distracted from study" (4,19 [249/224]), and to reject the pleasures of the world (5,14).[35]

Hence it is Halevi who asserts that, for psychological reasons, the intellectual relationship by itself, without an ontological one, lacks the intensity required to lead concrete human beings to a comprehensive attachment to God. This is the starting point of his critique of the Philosopher's view on this issue: "This is a doctrine of philosophers. We see that the human soul shows fear whenever it meets with anything terrible, but not at the mere report of such a thing. It is likewise attracted by a beautiful form which strikes the eye, but not so much by one that is only spoken of" (4,5 [235/213]). Again, "You will not reject everything that has been said concerning such verses as 'He beholds the likeness of the Lord' (Num. 12:8). . . . These passages are referring to the awe of God that is implanted in the

---

systematically, the Philosopher appears in the *Kuzari* only as a debating partner for Halevi. The present work, however, rests on the assumption that the Philosopher of the *Kuzari* is none other than Halevi in one period of his intellectual development. Hence the Rabbi's description of the Philosopher's world view has the status of a confession. The description of the Philosopher's position in the present volume must always be understand as a description of his position as reflected in the mirror of Halevi.

34. Compare the role of emotional resonance in the Philosopher's system with that of respect for the law in Kantian ethics. The King, in his critical question (4,4), seems inclined to a view close to that of Maimonides. Maimonides, too, believes that there is a type of awe that is peculiar to those who unite with the Active Intellect, by virtue of their union. See *Guide of the Perplexed*, 3,52. See also Shimon Rawidowicz, *Iyyunim be-maḥshevet Yisrael* (Studies in Jewish thought) 1 (Jerusalem, 1969), p. 322.

35. See also 3,1.

human soul" (4,3 [234/212]).³⁶ In other words, the Rabbi is explicitly criticizing the Philosopher for reasons external to the system. According to the Rabbi, experience teaches us that an intellectual relationship to God—like an intellectual relationship to any other object—cannot motivate the emergence of relations that are not intellectual.³⁷ Halevi also offers a "psychological" explanation for the intrinsic normative weight that the Philosopher's doctrine attributes to the correct relationship to God. According to Halevi, the Philosopher's view is really a secondary reflection, on the theoretical plane, of an existential and psychological constellation that is part of the Philosopher's personality. The Philosopher by his very nature cannot have an immediate relationship with God and cannot attain "prophetic vision" (5,14 [307/272]). The Philosopher's relationship to God is necessarily mediated: The primary datum is empirical reality, the existence of the world; the intellect teaches us that there is "a Guide and Manager of the world" (4,15 [246/222]).³⁸ The relationship with God that comes through syllogistic reasoning or analogy is incomplete. Its incompleteness is expressed, on the emotional plane, by a psychological incapacity to "perish for the

36. See also 1,109 and 2,72.
37. Nevertheless, for the Rabbi, too, the intellectual relationship is expressed by a voluntary intentionality. The Rabbi also seems to agree with the King's remark that a philosopher "yearns for God all his life" (1,110 [61/78]); see also 3,1. We must distinguish between the Philosopher's evaluation of the contemplative relationship toward God and his evaluation of the life that a philosopher should lead. The latter includes an obligation for "worshipping and blessing" God (1,1 [10/38]; 2,48; 3,21). This is what the King means when he says: "Speculation makes veneration a duty only as long as it entails no harm, nor causes pain for its own sake" (4,16 [227/223]). Any veneration that is liable to be associated with pain and harm is necessarily manifested in actions that have public significance. In addition, veneration also entails "speech," "language," and "deed" (1,1 [10/38]); compare 5,14; see also Chapter 5, note 21. Nevertheless, the Rabbi does not argue that the Philosopher is not prepared to suffer *because* of his contemplative attitude to God.
38. As we shall see, Halevi found a correlation between the level of one who relates to God and the mode of his knowledge of God, on the one hand, and the psychological significance of the relationship to God, the ethical value of the relationship, and the image of God as a pole of relationship, on the other.

sake of his love of God" (ibid.) and, on the theoretical level, in the view that the relationship with God does not have an infinite value, because "we draw near to GOD [*Elohim*] through speculation" (4,16 [247/223]) and because "the meaning of GOD [*Elohim*] can be grasped by speculation" (4,15 [246/222]). Hence "the philosophers . . . consider Divine worship to be only a refinement of conduct and confession of truth; they extol Him above all other beings, just as the sun is to be extolled above all other visible things" (ibid.). By contrast, those who have the natural ability to relate to God with their entire personalities, by "tasting and seeing" (4,16 [247/223]),[39] are willing to give their lives for their love of God (4,15; 4,16). The Philosopher would reject the validity of these psychological explanations that undermine the absolute reliability of theoretical views produced by reason. The irreducible ontological status of the intellectual dimension of existence, on the one hand, and the ontological essence of actual human intellect—its position in the overall hierarchy of intellects—on the other hand, guarantee the fundamental independence of actual intellect when it perceives existence that is not intellect.[40] In light of the preceding, it is clear that the Philosopher's view that the relationship to God has only finite value does not reflect the intellectual nature of that relationship.

According to the Philosopher, one must distinguish between the significance for rational beings of the Active Intellect

---

39. See also 1,109 and 4,5.

40. For similar ontological reasons we must understand the Philosopher's opinion that the perception of a philosopher, endowed with an actual intellect, is in principle exempt from the possibility of error and sin: "His organs— I mean the limbs of such a person—serve only the most perfect purposes, at the most appropriate time, and in the best condition" (1,1 [8/37]). As we shall see in the next chapter, this is the root of his authoritative stand. This is also the source of the relationship that pertains, according to the Philosopher, between philosophizing and sensation, on the one hand, and a world-view, on the other. His basic position on the autonomy of intellectual activity also grounds his view of the relationship between thinking and doing and between body and soul. On the other hand, Halevi's psychological criticism is only one expression of his fundamental belief that the human intellect depends on domains that transcend reason—a polar antithesis to the Philosopher's position. This basic opposition has many implications for many issues.

and the significance for them of God, who is the Cause of causes. This distinction is a particular expression of the general ontological principle concerning the status of God. In the previous chapter we saw that in the sublunar realm the relationship to God, as Cause of causes, requires mediation by the Active Intellect. There are two sides to this mediation: One is positive—the Active Intellect makes possible the relationship between rational beings and the higher world; the other is negative—the mediation limits this relationship. Because the intellect of rational beings, which is a form that emanates from the Active Intellect, can have no more potential than its cause, and the Active Intellect itself has only a limited perception of the Cause of causes, the ontological significance of perception by rational beings lies in their union with the Active Intellect, not in their union with God as Cause of causes.

It follows, then, that the goal (the state of perfection, the supreme rationale, the highest value) of rational beings must be union with the Active Intellect, which is "the nethermost degree, nearest to us ... about which the philosophers taught that it guides the nether world" (5,21 [230/292]). The Active Intellect perceives God as the Cause of causes, but this perception is incomplete; accordingly, the human intellect can attain only incomplete knowledge of God, as the Cause of causes, as entailed by existence, as an actual cause, and so on. When it perceives these truths about God, the human intellect unites with the Active Intellect, just as it unites with it when it perceives other truths. "Veneration of the Prime Cause" (1,1 [9/38]) is only a means "to become like the Active Intellect in finding the truth" (ibid. [10/38]). The correct attitude toward God is only a *means* for union with the Active Intellect; as such, its value is limited: "The real benefit for the philosopher is to be found only in the cognizance of the true nature of things, through which man becomes akin to the Active Intellect" (4,13 [241/218]). But incomplete knowledge of God is "no more injurious than [is the] ignorance concerning the earth [of] those who think it is flat" (ibid.). Nor is the correct relationship to God, in and of itself, a necessary condition for union with the Active

Intellect. According to the Philosopher, rational beings can attain some degree of union with the Active Intellect even when they are ignorant of God, for, ontologically speaking, "the denial of God [is] only a sign of a low standard of the soul, which acquiesces in untruth" (4,15 [246/222]).[41]

It seems plausible, then, that, for the Philosopher, the survival of the intellect after death does not depend on the correct attitude toward God, but is rather an expression of union with the Active Intellect: "If a man's intellect is in conjunction with the [Active Intellect], this is called his paradise and everlasting life" (5,10 [292/259]). Because union with the Active Intellect does not depend on a correct relationship with God, neither does the survival of the intellect after death.[42]

6. The Twofold Meaning of God as Intelligible

Materially speaking, there are two facets to the incomplete perception of God, as Cause of causes, by rational beings. On the one hand, God is only one entity among many—one cause among many causes, even though God is ontologically exceptional by virtue of His "magnitude" compared to other entities. His very presence in the same hierarchical scale with other entities attests

---

41. As we have already seen, the identity between the intellect that perceives and the perceived object is manifested on two planes. For the mind itself, the perceived object is the content of knowledge, which exists in the mind; the mind is conscious of it and identifies with it as such. On another plane—that shared by the intellect and existence as it really is—the perceived object is the ontological reality of which the intellect is conscious. The intellect that "acquiesces in falsehood" identifies with its deceptive perceived object—according to the first rather than the second sense—whence its ontological inferiority. Compare the meaning of sensory and imaginary knowledge.

42. We can learn this from 5,14, even though in that section the Rabbi is arguing against Avicenna and not against the Philosopher. A proof of this is provided by the debate about the survival of the soul. Throughout the attempt to give possible answers to the rhetorical question, "what are the limits of metaphysical knowledge by means of which the human soul is separated from the body without perishing?" (5,14 [306/271]), the Rabbi never considers the possibility that, according to the Philosopher, the survival of the soul depends on knowledge of God.

to His similarity to them and to what they have in common. The ontological principle that determines the place of each particular entity in the overall hierarchy of existence—the principle that determines the "magnitude" of each particular entity as compared to another entity—is the extent to which it is a cause.[43] The "magnitude" of God vis-à-vis "all other beings" is the same as that of the sun vis-à-vis "all other visible things" (4,15 [246/223]). Accordingly, God, as the Cause of causes, stands at the pinnacle of the hierarchy of existence, *primus inter pares*, while the sun, as the cause of visibility, stands above all "visible" existence.[44]

Second, the characterization of God as Prime Cause leads the Philosopher to conclude that this ontological primacy reflects precisely the difference between the existence of God, as sublime, and other entities: philosophers "acknowledge a Prime Cause different from earthly things" (2,54 [112/116]). The Rabbi himself recommends "the attributes of sublimity and holiness commented upon by philosophers" as an appropriate intention during recitation of the benediction on the "sanctification of the Name" (3,17 [162/155]).[45]

We see, then, that the contradictory characterizations of God as one entity among many and as "sublime" reflect the two

---

43. See Chapter 3, §3, "The Immanent Activity of the Deity."

44. Compare 2,53 [111/115], where the sun is described as standing "next to God as the cause of being." See also *Guide of the Perplexed* 1,36.

45. Compare: "HOLY expresses the notion that He is high above any attribute of created beings" (4,3 [222/203]). We must distinguish between the concept the *wholly other*, as used by Rudolf Otto, *The Idea of the Holy*, trans. John W. Harvey (London, 1950), Chapter 5, and the term *sublime*. According to the Philosopher of the *Kuzari*, God—even in the negative sense, as He is Himself and for Himself—is not the "wholly other." The deity is a particular: as intellect, as actual existence, as necessary existence, and so on; whereas "God" as the wholly other is not particular in any aspect. *Sublime* is therefore to be understood as referring to the deity in the context of the infinite difference between the deity and other things. But the meaning of this difference itself, even though it cannot be conceptually exhausted by non-Divine existence, is bound up with the fact that the deity and other entities *do have* something in common. On the other hand, some passages reflecting Halevi's later thought suggest that God, as the ineffable Name, is indeed wholly other.

meanings of *God* in the philosopher's system, for human beings and for God Himself. The King is referring to both characterizations of God in his answer: "How could this compel me, when I am not sure whether the justice of the Indian people is natural and they have no king at all, or due to their king, or both?" (1,20 [19/45]). The view that "the justice of the Indian people is natural and they have no king" is championed by the pagan King. According to this view, the sense of the cosmic order is innate in the powers or divinities that fill it.[46] The view

---

46. Although in the Hebrew versions of both Ibn Tibbon and Even-Shmuel the King entertains the possibility that they have no king at all, Hirschfeld's rendering is "natural and not dependent on their king." This is more in keeping with the Rabbi's question (1,19), which does not allow the answer that there is no king of India; the question is, does the Khazar king feel an obligation to revere the king of India? That is, the question refers to how the Khazar king relates to the king of India, not to the existence of the latter monarch. The Khazar king must accept the existence of the king of India as a given, just as he assumes the existence of an ideal order in the kingdom of India. The point of the question is the relationship between these two assumptions. Moscato interprets the passage differently; but he too is unsure that the King really means to doubt the existence of the Indian ruler. Compare 2,6; 2,54; 4,1; 4,3. According to Halevi, one must distinguish between the pagan and atheist world views: The pagan believes that the cosmic order is of the essence of the existence of the universe, whereas the Epicurean believes "that the universe arose by accident" (5,8 [285/252]). In other words, the Epicurean contends that the cosmic order can be explained by the random arrangement of a chaotic reality. Halevi rejects the latter view for philosophical and rationalist reasons. The order impressed upon the world attests in and of itself to the existence of a governing and ordering Deity (4,15). According to Halevi, the "original" pagans believed in a single and transcendental Deity. See 1,79; see also 1,73; 3,17. According to the pagans, the direct origin of the cosmic order lies in (relatively) autonomous "beings" (1,69). God is the source of this order only indirectly, through the medium of those beings. Accordingly, God should be worshipped through the mediation of those beings. The Rabbi holds that this explains the suspicion of the Israelites and of Pharaoh's magicians when they heard Moses' assertion that God had spoken with him (1,49; 1,87; see also 3,73). This is also Ibn Ezra's view of paganism; see his short commentary on Ex. 20. See also S. Pines, "Note sur la doctrine de la prophétie et la réhabilitation de la matière dans le Kuzari," *Mélanges de philosophie et de littérature juives* 1–2 (1956–1957): 253–260. See further Chapter 16, note 4.

THE PHILOSOPHER'S THOUGHT

that "the justice of the Indian people is due to their king" is upheld by the adherents of the monotheistic religions.[47] Finally, the view that the righteousness of the Indians is "due to both" is championed by the Philosopher: God, on the one hand, is *primus inter pares*—immanent in the world—and in this respect "the justice of the Indian people is natural"; on the other hand, He is transcendent, and "the justice of the Indian people is due to their king."[48]

God, as available to positive perception by philosophers, through syllogism, and as immanent in the sublunar world, cannot be perceived as transcendent. Any thought about the Divine by a human intellect necessarily starts from non-Divine existence—from the universe.[49] From this vantage point, God can be perceived only as performing certain functions in the tangible world (that is, as relating to the world) or as one cause among many, such that He has something in common with other entities and other causes. However, this positive perception of God is inseparable from knowledge of its fundamental limitations: the intellect that perceives God as first among equals is at the same time perceiving itself and its own limits. The

---

47. See especially: "I should also acknowledge that his dominion and his word had touched me" (1,22 [19/46]). This phrasing relates to the parable in §21, where the Khazar king is totally passive and the initiative is taken by the Indian monarch. Hence the King's question: "Then your belief is confined to yourselves?" (1,26 [20/47]). That is, because it is God alone who takes the initiative, and the Divine initiative—God's address to human beings—is a condition for worship of God, that is, for human beings to respond to God's initiative (see 1,25), one who has not had "communion" with God cannot worship Him.

48. Compare Aristotle, *Metaphysics* 1075^{a}11: "We must consider also in which of two ways the nature of the universe contains the good or the highest good, whether as something definite and by itself, or as the order of the parts. Probably in both ways, as an army does" (trans. W. D. Ross, in *Complete Works*, ed. Jonathan Barnes [Princeton, N.J., 1984]). Aristotle is a proponent of the latter view; see also Plato, *Laws* 898–899; see also Chapter 3, note 28.

49. The superlunar intellects, too, perceive God as the Cause of causes from this starting point, i.e., from the perspective of their own—non-Divine—existence.

intellect's recognition that its knowledge of God is incomplete leads to its characterization of God as transcendent.[50]

This was acknowledged by Socrates,[51] the outstanding philosophical truth-teller: " 'Citizens, I do not contest your doctrine of God; I say only that I do not penetrate so far; I understand only the doctrine of man'" (4,13 [242/218]).[52] Nevertheless, knowledge of God as unknown—as transcendent—cannot be a focus for union by any non-Divine intellect, because knowledge of ignorance does not cancel out the ignorance itself.

50. The possibility of being aware of ignorance—knowing God as unknown, as transcendent—is entailed by His description as "necessary existence." Even though one can infer necessary existence from possible existence, they are absolutely different.

51. 3,1.

52. See also 5,14. Compare Plato, *Apology* 20. The negative aspect of knowledge of God—knowledge of ignorance—is important for understanding Halevi's idea that the philosopher can learn from the prophet, an idea that takes the Philosopher's own doctrine into account: "As Socrates said: 'O my people, I do not deny your knowledge of the gods, but I confess that I do not understand it. As for me, I am wise only in human matters.' Philosophers justify their recourse to speculation by the absence of prophecy and divine light" (5,14 [307/272]). See also 4,13; 4,27. When the Jewish people entered upon the stage of history, however, when "the community was at last considered sufficiently pure for the light to dwell on it, to be worthy of seeing miracles," a cause was created to direct "the hearts. All who came after these philosophers could not detach themselves from their principles, so that today the whole civilized world acknowledges that God is eternal and the world created" (2,54 [112/116]).

5

HUMAN ACTIVITY

1. Introduction: Goal and Activity

The Philosopher's doctrine about the specific goal of man rests on postulates derived from his general doctrine of the intellects and from his idea of the dualism of sublunar existence. Accordingly, there are two facets to his theory of this goal:

1. Man's goal, which is to perceive, does not lead the human intellect to intentionally overstep its purview. The telos of rational beings reflects only the rank of human intellect in the overall hierarchy of intellects.
2. Even though man's goal is not determined by the concrete conditions of sublunar reality, realization of the goal nevertheless requires that these conditions be taken into account. Because it exists in the sublunar sphere, the human intellect is condemned to actualization under the sign of the ontological tension, characteristic of this level of existence, between matter and form. The goal appeals to the human intellect, demanding accomplishment; and this accomplishment depends on realization of its potential, which in turn depends on the consolidation of an appropriate constellation of natural circumstances. In the kingdom of the intellects, the human intellect has a unique ontological

status: it is part and parcel of a reality that is neither purely intellectual nor purely physical. Because of this special status, the human intellect is endowed with the capacity—as intellect—for intentional activity; but as part of a reality that is not only intellect, the human intellect must adapt the conditions of its existence to its own particular goal.

In parallel, the Philosopher's doctrine of activity also has two facets:

1. From the axiological perspective, any particular human deed has no inherent absolute value. A particular human deed, whether considered with regard to its association with the intellect—as an effect—or considered with regard to its association with a realm that is not exclusively intellect—as a cause—cannot be considered to be exclusive. This idea is pivotal, because it is the crux of the dispute between the Philosopher and the king of the Khazars. The King does not accept the Philosopher's position, chiefly because he believes that "there must ... be a way of acting that is pleasing in itself and not only through the medium of intentions" (1,2 [11/39]). Clearly the King's rejection of the Philosopher's view represents a basic principle shared by the advocates of the monotheistic religions and of the pagan creeds.[1]

2. On the ontological plane, the essential activity of the human intellect, that is, its reflective introspection, is manifested in a productive emergence beyond itself, that is, in

---

1. See also 1,98; 2,46. In the *Kuzari*, the King has the role of the ideal spokesman for the world-view of those who, even though not adherents of one of the monotheistic religions, are seeking that lifestyle that is pleasing to God. From what the angel says in his dream—"your way of thinking is pleasing to God, but not your way of acting"—the King learned that there *are* particular deeds that are pleasing to God, pleasing in themselves and "not through the medium of intentions" (1,2 [11/39]). The angel's criticism of the King's deeds rests on the fundamental postulate that there are certain deeds that are intrinsically pleasing to God. The different definitions of the content of these deeds offered by the various historical religions constitute the foundation for the differences among the religions and the wars waged by their adherents (1,2).

a concrete human deed. An act of perception or cognition by God and the superlunar intellects produces an emanation. The productivity of the Active Intellect is manifested in the formal aspect—in the proper order of the sublunar sphere; but the productivity of the perfect human intellect, which unites with the Active Intellect, is manifested "only ... in the most perfect purposes, at the most appropriate time, and in the best condition, as though its organs were the organs of the Active Intellect" (1,1 [8/37]).[2] According to the Philosopher, just "as God has arranged order and harmony ... for the universe," so too "the noblest human being ... arranges order and harmony for the rest of mankind, in the same systematic way" (4,3 [231/209]). Because the Philosopher's actions are an (external) reflection of his ontological status,[3] human beings should "adhere to the way of the righteous, as regards character and action, because this will help you effect truth, gain instruction, and become like this Active Intellect" (1,1 [9/38]).[4] This is why the Rabbi says that philosophers "recommend good and dissuade from evil in the most admirable manner, ... in order to resemble the Creator who arranged everything so perfectly" (4,19 [249/225]).

With regard to the concrete conditions affecting the human intellect, then, the intrinsic ethical weight of any human deed is determined by its contribution, in a given situation, to

2. For the Philosopher, the Socratic postulate that there is a link between knowledge of the good and performance of the good is a conclusion of his doctrine of union with the Active Intellect.
3. See Chapter 3, note 8.
4. Compare *Guide of the Perplexed* 1,72. Just as the philosopher "draws nearer" to the deity, ontologically speaking, when he unites with the Active Intellect, so too human beings of a lower degree draw nearer to union with the Active Intellect when they cleave to the way of the righteous. In this context we should also note the impersonal nature of the relationship between righteous persons and those who draw nearer to them: the cleaving is not to righteous individuals but to "their way." Just as the Philosopher tends not to address the King in the second person, so too he does not speak in the first person, unlike the representatives of Christianity, Islam, and Judaism.

realizing the goal. The value of human action as a means is associated with the absence of obligatory material and universal rules of conduct. True, rules of conduct are laid down in the spirit of general principles, which are based on ontological and epistemological postulates of the Philosopher's doctrine;[5] however, given that the natural conditions in which human beings find themselves are not within the realm of the intellect, it is impossible to set rules of conduct that are appropriate to every concrete situation.

It is no accident that the King chooses holy wars to represent and exemplify the internal significance of deeds that are intrinsically pleasing—deeds that are the essential hallmark of the revealed religions (1,2 [11]). These wars, by their very nature, entail a belief that actions pleasing to God "in and of themselves" cannot be replaced by others, that human beings' right to exist depends on their doing what is pleasing to God, and consequently that the heretic is doomed to destruction. Hence the act of annihilating heretics, as an act that is intrinsically pleasing to God, leads to deeds that entail a willingness to give up one's life.[6]

It is in character that the Philosopher avoids recommending any particular religion[7] (as a preferred state religion) for a king upon whom fortune has shined and whose subjects rely

---

5. "The consequence of this will be contentment, humility, meekness, and every other praiseworthy inclination" (1,1 [9/38]). "In sum, seek purity of heart" (ibid.). See also 2,46; 2,47; 3,7. This contradicts Moscato's interpretation of 4,19, *incipit* אלא בעת הצורך.

6. See also Chapter 4, §5, "The Contemplative Relationship to God."

7. In ideal conditions, the Philosopher prefers an invented religion, in which the philosopher-king retains maximum sovereignty, even to the "religion of the philosophers" itself. See §7, "Predisposition and the Meaning of an Act." Despite what Strauss says (*Persecution and the Art of Writing* [Glencoe, Ill., 1952], pp. 116ff.), the view of the Philosopher of the *Kuzari* is closer to that of Plato in the *Republic* than in the *Laws*. Still, Strauss is probably right with regard to the preference for the religion of philosophers in a state where the king's rule is limited; that is, in a state where the subjects do not rely on the religion invented by the king or, according to another version, do not rely on the king himself.

upon him (1,1).⁸ The Philosopher prefers that such a king invent a religion, so as to preserve maximum freedom with regard to particular concrete laws. This also explains the need to cleave to the "way of the righteous" (1,1).⁹ As we shall see later, the Philosopher's view of the value of action as a means has several consequences.

2. The Validity of Rules of Conduct as Conditional

According to the Philosopher, then, there are no rules of conduct that are valid in all possible circumstances. Nevertheless, he champions their relative validity in a given situation. The philosopher who unites with the Active Intellect does not have to observe Divine laws: "be he believer or free-thinker, they do not concern him" (4,13 [241/218]).[10] For example, the renegade talmudic sage Elisha ben Abuya "repudiated practice, having perceived the intellects; he said: 'Human actions are but means and instruments to attain spiritual rank. I have attained it and do not need to bother about religious actions'" (3,65 [207/190]). Aristotle, too, "thinks lightly of the observance of religious laws" (4,16 [247/223]) or the "divine law" (4,17 [248/224])—that is, ritual commandments that, according to the adherents of the historical religions, derive from God's will and are "of divine origin" (1,81 [38/58]). Divine laws are nonrational;

---

8. See also 2,49, where we read of man's capacity for inventing a religion. There the reference is to a religion contrived by and for an individual, whereas in 1,1 the concept has distinct political overtones.

9. Compare Aristotle, *Nicomachean Ethics* 1095ª2 : "Hence a young man is not a proper hearer of lecturers on political science" (trans. W. D. Ross, rev. J. O. Urmson, in *Complete Works of Aristotle*, ed. Jonathan Barnes [Princeton N.J., 1984]). In consequence, it is important that this subject be taught by sages who have experience in the practical realm (ibid., 1143ᵇ11). This seems to be the starting point for how the Philosopher would explain the historical facts cited by Halévi in his criticisms of the Philosopher: (1) There is no general agreement among the philosophers as to "one action" (1,13 [18/45]); and (2) "some doctrines can be established by arguments which are only partially satisfactory and still much less capable of being proved" (ibid.).

10. See Chapter 4, note 31.

their validity depends on the belief that God knows whether they are observed.[11] By contrast, philosophers endeavor to observe the "laws of reason."[12]

According to the Philosopher, were the King to adopt the appropriate lifestyle he would discover, through his own efforts, the specific rules of conduct that are pertinent to the particular circumstances in which he finds himself and that would lead him to "purity of soul" or "purity of heart" (1,1 [38]). The King, who is just setting out on his journey to discover his goal, must first attain "purity of heart,"[13] which depends on human self-control.[14] Human beings attain self-control, says the Philosopher, through a defined way of life in accordance with rules, which include the "divine laws" and rituals.[15] When the King discovers his real purpose, he will learn that there are no rules of conduct appropriate to every possible situation. The King summarizes the Philosopher's position: "The only one who becomes a pious man is one who does not care in which way he

---

11. See 4,13; 4,17. Here and elsewhere Cassel renders the Hebrew *nimmusim* 'laws' as "*göttliche* Gebote"; in general, throughout the *Kuzari* the term *nimmus* 'law' means Divine law or religion; see 1,79; 1,109; 2,20. We must distinguish between "law"/"divine law" and "laws of reason." Although the latter, too, "may be overridden in times of need" (4,19 [249/225]), their conditional validity is subject to fixed principles (1,1). The "laws of reason" are determined by man as a rational being (1,1; 1,81; 4,19; 5,14) and are a manifestation of "the intellectual power that distinguishes man above all living beings" (1,35 [22/47]). The concern for conduct according to the "laws of reason" reflects the "resemblance to the creator who arranged everything so perfectly" (4,19 [249/225]). On the ambiguity of the Hebrew term *nimmus*, which takes over the ambiguity of the original Arabic term *al-nāmūs*, see H. A. Wolfson, "Additional Notes to the Article on the Classification of Sciences," *Hebrew Union College Annual* 3 (1926): 374.

12. See 1,1; see also 4,19.

13. Here the Philosopher's remarks are directed not to actual philosophers but to human beings who are taking their first steps; this is why he demands that the King's deeds also include those ordained by Divine laws. On the other hand, the conduct of Elisha ben Abuya corresponds to that required of the real philosopher, who, like Aristotle, disdains ritual commandments. Here I part company with Strauss, *Persecution and the Art of Writing*, p. 115.

14. 5,10; 5,12. Compare 3,3–5.

15. 1,1; 2,60; 3,1.

approaches God, whether through Judaism or Christianity, or in a way that he himself contrives" (2,49 [107/112]). On the one hand, individuals can draw closer to the right way through religion; but this can be "through Judaism or Christianity, or in a way that he himself contrives." Unlike philosophers, who are sovereign over individual and particular rules of conduct, nonphilosophers must accept a defined system of beliefs and opinions in order to assume the burden of particular rules of conduct (including "divine laws"). These beliefs and opinions, like general rules of conduct, are dictated by those authorized to do so.[16]

The nature of the action ordained for human beings depends not only on their degree, but also on the circumstances of their lives: The case of those who find themselves in a given framework of law, religion, or way of life is not the same as the case of those who are outside those contexts; nor is the case of a king whose subjects accept a religion he has devised like that of a king whose subjects reject the faith he has fashioned (1,1).[17] Hence human beings are duty-bound to venerate God only in a situation where this "entails no harm, nor causes pain for its own sake" (4,16 [227/223]).[18] Even deeds that are incompatible

---

16. 1,1; 1,81; 4,19; 5,14. Compare also 2,48. On the purpose, principle, and scope of the philosopher's political activity as legislator and on the special nature of the path whereby the political order is constituted see Strauss, *Persecution and the Art of Writing*, p. 68.

17. Evidently we must also distinguish a philosopher-king from a philosopher who is not a king and can withdraw from worldly affairs (3,1; 4,19). In any case, even the withdrawal from "wealth, rank, and the pleasure of children" (4,19 [248/224]) does not prevent the philosopher from teaching the good and warning against evil. Similarly, it is philosophers who lay down the "laws of reason" (5,14).

18. See Chapter 4, note 37. The duty to venerate God is a means to become like Him: "venerate . . . the Prime Cause" (1,1 [9/38]) "in order . . . to become similar to this Active Intellect" (ibid.). This is why the King demands that his subjects venerate God (ibid; see also 3,21 and 4,19). However, this veneration also indicates that the resemblance has been achieved. Resemblance to God by perceiving Him as "greater than other beings" is bound up with recognizing that one ought to "extol Him" (4,15 [246/222]). From the perspective that union with God is a means and goal, philosophers "consider Divine worship to be only a refinement of conduct and confession of truth" (ibid.).

with the "laws of reason" may be sometimes be appropriate (4,19 [249]). According to the Philosopher, the so-called laws of reason are merely conventions[19] laid down by the philosophers; consequently their validity is necessarily conditional (ibid.).

3. The Rationality and Universality of Rules of Conduct

One expression of the status ascribed to action by the Philosopher's system is the inherent rational content of rules of conduct. This rationality determines the extent to which these rules are valid. To the degree that their content can be justified rationally, they are valid in more situations. Most rational are principles, less rational are "laws of reason," and still less rational are the prescriptions that regulate religious rituals. These last can accordingly be modified with relative facility. Philosophers need not observe them; in ideal conditions a king may even invent a totally new religion. Insofar as they are rational, rules of conduct can in principle be understood by the human intellect. According to the Philosopher, they are "of human origin" (1,81 [38/58]); this alone gives them obligatory force (ibid. 87 [40/60]).

The rationality of the intrinsically correct act is a necessary corollary of its place in the Philosopher's system, whether we examine the act as an external manifestation of the actual attainment of the goal or only as a means for attaining the goal. When an act is considered in the former sense, its essential link to actual intellect that communes with the Active Intellect is a warrant of its quality and of its fitness to serve as an ideal to be emulated (1,1). When a deed is considered as a means, however, this status determines both its particularity and the criteria for possible criticism. The idea that the human intellect can discover appropriate rules of conduct necessarily follows both from the Philosopher's doctrine that the intellect achieves its goal independent of any outside agencies and from his view of the essence of God—a God who is not a principle of hierarchical order.

---

19. For the meaning of this term, see Strauss, *Persecution and the Art of Writing*, pp. 119–120.

THE PHILOSOPHER'S THOUGHT

The Philosopher's basic notion that rules of conduct, including those that are only conditional, are inherently rational ipso facto guarantees their universal validity. It is typical that the Philosopher, unlike the angel in the King's dream, speaks mainly in the third person; because he speaks by virtue of his intellect alone—by virtue of the perspective he shares with rational beings who hear his doctrine—a philosopher cannot address any particular concrete individual. The very act of speaking to an individual recognizes a particular personality as a pole that ought to be addressed. In this context there is a far-reaching analogy between God's influence on heavenly beings, the manner in which the Active Intellect influences sublunar existence, and the way a philosopher influences his own human environment. This analogy stems from the fundamentally identical ontological relations that obtain between the various intellects and their levels.

The universal validity of religion becomes problematic precisely in the context of Judaism, Christianity, and Islam, which rest on belief in revelation. Revelation as such is an expression of a preference—a preference for the human being and nation to which it was granted. The representatives of Islam and Christianity intentionally emphasize the universality of their religions (1,4; 1,5). Hence the King concludes that were he preferred by the "king of India" and were the latter's kingdom and word to "touch" him personally, he would be "beholden to him" (1,21 [19/46]).[20] Following this line of thought, the King concludes

---

20. We should probably understand "I should also acknowledge that his dominion and his word had touched me" (1,22 [19/46]) according to the interpretations of Moscato and Cassel rather than that of Zifroni. Leaving aside methodological considerations, in Zifroni's interpretation the King fails to answer the question posed by the Rabbi in §21. Moscato also emphasizes the relationship between messenger and preference alluded to in this section: "The allusion here is that the giving of the Torah to Israel, in the manner he mentioned, made plain to them that the King exists and directs all reality by way of volition, and furthermore that his providence is focused more on them than on others because his glory became attached to them in particular." The use of the king of India in the parable evidently reflects the Rabbi's belief that India is an exemplary state. See Ibn Ezra, short commentary on Ex. 23:20, and the supercommentary *Qarnei Or*, 28.

that "your belief is confined to yourselves" (1,26 [20/47]). The Rabbi agrees with him on this point: "The Torah is binding because He led us out of Egypt and remained attached to us. For we are the pick of mankind" (1,27 [21/47]). The Jews' acceptance of the burden of the Divine law depends on His attachment to them, and this in turn depends on His preference for them as "the pick of mankind."[21] On the other hand, the Philosopher totally ignores the possibility that the universal validity of his world-view is a problematic topic that requires explicit consideration.

4. The Philosopher and Rules of Conduct

Nevertheless, the fact that rules of conduct are transparent to reason and can, in principle, be understood by human beings says nothing about whether the latter succeed in actualizing this potentiality. In the Philosopher's thought, the "democratic" view that all rational beings are in principle capable of comprehending the rules of conduct cohabits with the "aristocratic" view that there are an infinite number of intermediate levels separating "an individual with perfect causes who becomes perfect" from "another with imperfect causes who remains imperfect" (1,1 [7/36]).

According to the Philosopher, knowledge of the rules of conduct, like the perception of truth in general, is a spontaneous activity of the human intellect working alone, with no outside help from an omnipotent deity. This idea underlies both the "democratic" and "aristocratic" views. Precisely the fact that there is no assistance from an omnipotent deity rules out the possibility of blurring or eliminating differences between individuals.[22] Human beings, according to the Philosopher, are abandoned to their fate precisely because they hold their destiny in their own hands.

---

21. Given that this is Halevi's view of Judaism, we can understand various emphases in the presentation by the Christian scholar.
22. We should again stress that, according to the Philosopher, such external assistance is impossible not only because of the nature of God but also because of the nature of the goal as knowledge.

They must make do with achieving the optimum level feasible within the limits of their potential. Hence there is an essential link between the most excellent persons and rational rules of conduct: "rational religions of human origin" begin precisely from "distinguished personalities" (1,80-81 [37/58]).[23]

However, the reliance of nonphilosophers on the judgment and verdicts of philosophers, as well as their need to "adhere to the ways of the righteous," does not stem only from the special relationship between philosophers and the rational rules of conduct, but also from the absence of particular and invariant rules of conduct. A philosopher who comes to know the principles of conduct can also determine the applicability of abstract general principles to concrete situations and choose among alternative rules of conduct. Thus the status of the philosopher as both legislator and judge results from the gap between the laws that define appropriate activity and the need to apply them in given situations, as well as from the fundamental incapacity of the masses to attain appropriate knowledge of general principles.

5. The Philosopher as Mediator, and Ontological Dichotomy

The tension that informs the philosopher's influence on nonphilosophers and on the political state is another manifestation of the basic ontological tension between the formal and material dimensions of sublunar reality. Like the latter tension, which is reflected in matter's partial and incomplete response to form, so too the masses—the king's subjects—must take account of and compromise with the philosopher's influence (even in ideal conditions, when the philosopher is a king). True, the constitution of the social order is an expression of mankind's

---

23. Compare: "By these means all evil suspicion was removed from the people, lest they believe that prophecy is only the privilege of the few who claimed to possess it" (4,11 [240/217]). See also 1,87. The passages quoted in the body of the text are spoken by the King and the Rabbi, but it is clear that the Philosopher shares their view. He himself emphasizes the role of legislator assumed by a king when he adopts the philosophical way of life (1,1).

potential; but the potentiality of rational beings contains no guarantee of emergence from potential to actual.[24] Thus the Philosopher counsels the King to consider the extent to which his subjects are willing to accept some existing creed when he chooses a state religion (1,1). The King begins with the assumption that "all religions start, no doubt, from single individuals who support one another in upholding the faith which it pleased God should be promulgated. Their number increases continually and they grow more powerful, either by their own virtue or through the assistance of a king who compels the multitude to adopt that particular creed" (1,80 [37/58]).[25] The Rabbi agrees with him in principle: "It is only rational religion of human origin that spreads in this way" (1,81 [38/58]).[26]

If so, Halevi and the Philosopher agree that the gradual process whereby a king's influence has an effect and the need for compulsion actually express two things: the limited ability of the king/philosopher and the disposition of the passive and influenced side to resist change. Given their agreement, we can understand the Rabbi's comment that "a law of divine origin," which is rooted in the word of God,[27] has no need, by its very

---

24. This is not only because appropriate "external" conditions are absent or because of external disturbances. Compare the status of human freedom in the Philosopher's doctrine.

25. The process by which Judaism spread in the Khazar kingdom is described at the beginning of Part 2: "They ... returned to their country, eager to learn the Jewish law. They kept their conversion secret, however, until *they found an opportunity of disclosing the fact gradually to a few of their special degree. When their number had increased* they made their belief public and *overcame* the rest of the Khazars, and converted them to the law of the Jews" (2,1 [66/82]). It is typical that, for "the rest of the Khazars," that is, those not of "their special degree," conversion to Judaism requires compulsion, just as a king may "compel the multitudes" (1,80 [37/58]). Thus the Jewish law was accepted by Gentile nations, including the Khazars, whether by compulsion or voluntarily, without their having had any direct or indirect experience of prophetic vision (1,100).

26. See also 1,13; 2,48; 4,19.

27. The Divine law (1,81) is mentioned on purpose, to establish a link with the Creation. According to Halevi, the Divine law is meant to emphasize God's absolute sovereignty over all creation. This sovereignty has many manifestations and implies both nonreliance on means and the capacity to instigate innovation and novelty suddenly, rather than through a process. Compare 1,89.

essence, to make an effort in order to exert an influence. The created universe cannot resist the Creator. Hence "the law of Divine origin," unlike "laws of human origin," "arises suddenly . . . similar to the creation of the world" (ibid.).

6. The Source of the Ethnological Manifestations of Order

The Philosopher explains other systems characteristic of various realms of human existence in the same vein as the constitution of the social order. Their establishment, too, depends on an appropriate "procedure." In the discussions of the source and existence of languages and of customs common to all mankind, such as the decimal system and the seven-day week, three alternative hypotheses are offered. One is that these systems express the inherent potential of rational beings only. According to this thesis, the origin and survival of the rational order of these systems cannot spring from a chance arrangement of simple entities of less-developed form, nor from the influence of the "Giver of forms"—the Active Intellect. Even though the Philosopher's opinion is not made very explicit in the passages, close analysis and comparison with the discussion of the social order allows us to state that the Philosopher is a proponent of this thesis.

According to the Philosopher, even language is not a necessary outcome of any particular situation: just as language cannot be based on prelinguistic naturalistic foundations, neither can it be based on man's essence as percipient. On the one hand, an analysis of the complex structures of language discloses only meaningful elements—elements in which the intrinsic order of language is already inherent: "Languages undoubtedly had a beginning, which originated in a conventional manner. Evidence of this is found in their composition from nouns, verbs, and particles. They originated from sounds derived from the organs of speech" (1,54 [27/51]).[28] On the other hand, concrete language

---

28. For this reason, the Epicurean theory of the origin of human language is rejected. The argument is clearly polemic; it is directed against Epicurean philosophy and is in accordance with its own doctrine. The Epicurean philosopher does not accept the fundamental axiom of the Aristotelian

has a nonrational stratum alongside the rational one, expressed in the arbitrary determination of a particular set of symbols. Hence language is a preeminent manifestation of innovation. It is a human invention—a "contrivance" (1,55) born by chance in some generation. Because the existence of particular languages is the result of contrivance and convention only, languages say nothing about the essence of things. Nor is there any reason to prefer one language over another. Hence the Philosopher counsels the King not to be "concerned about the forms ... or the word or language you use in prayer" (1,1 [10/38]).[29] However, the phenomenon of language is not explained by positing an act of invention that constitutes an arbitrary but

---

philosopher that a rational order per se cannot emerge as the result of chance from an irrational material reality. Epicurus believed that "the universe arose by accident" (5,8 [285/252]) and "that all things are the outcome of accidents, since no settled purpose is ever discernible in them" (5,20 [320/283]). Against this view that language is the fruit of chance, the King argues that one might also expect the Epicurean philosopher to propose an atomic theory of language. This, the King believes, is impossible, because language cannot be reduced to chance or to compounds of meaningless primary elements. From this perspective, according to the Philosopher, who is an Aristotelian, Epicurus too should have acknowledged that the order manifested in language is unlike that found in the world. According to the Philosopher, though, the actual rational order cannot be based only on an irrational reality, in human existence as well as in nature. See also H. A. Wolfson, "The Veracity of Scripture in Philo, Hallevi, Maimonides and Spinoza," *Alexander Marx Jubilee Volume* (New York, 1950), pp. 603–630.

29. Halevi accepts the Philosopher's contention that languages are indeed a matter of contrivance and convention and hence the fruit of a process that goes back to a particular moment: in a particular generation, in an act of decision, etc., and by the consent of the many—the subsequent generations—to the original one-time and chance decision. He also acknowledges the Philosopher's view as to the source of the law of reason. Unlike the Philosopher, however, Halevi believed that the necessary consent depends on the existence of a "natural language," which includes the allusions and gestures that reflect the essence of the symbolized objects (4,25); this language is the Hebrew language, "created and instituted by God" (2,72 [125]).

With regard to the origin of languages, Maimonides in the *Guide of the Perplexed* (2,30) agrees with the Philosopher of the *Kuzari*. In his treatise on medicine (*Pirqei Moshe*, included as Appendix B to *Mikhtevei ha-Rambam* [Letters of Maimonides], ed. and trans. into Hebrew J. Kapah [Jerusalem, 1972]), however, Maimonides tends to the opinion of Galen concerning

THE PHILOSOPHER'S THOUGHT

at the same time meaningful set of symbols. Language, by its very nature, is rooted in the public domain; hence, one must posit, in addition to the one-time act of invention, the process of consent by the multitude (1,54; 1,56).[30]

The Philosopher's thought about the origin and essence of language is of great importance. His view of the relationship between intellect and language determines the place of the latter in the various levels of existence. In polar contrast to the Rabbi, the Philosopher believes that language and dialogue have no place in the superlunar spheres: neither between the intellects themselves[31] nor between the heavenly intellects and the human intellect.[32] Hence the human intellect and its essential manifestation, perception, are preconditions for the development of

---

the influence of climate on the development of languages. Accordingly, Maimonides argues for the superiority of languages that originated in the temperate zone. In that work, though, he ascribes no special preference to Hebrew; what is more, he states that Hebrew and Arabic are a single tongue, and that Syriac is its close cousin. For the Rabbi's opinion, see 2,68.

30. The institution of a contrived religion by a philosopher-king also depends on the consent of his subjects (1,1 [10/38]).

31. Emanation, by its very essence, does not entail dialogue. Emanation is accompanied by introspection on the part of the intellect—self-perception. Halevi believes, however, that Hebrew is the language "in which God spoke to Adam and Eve" (2,68 [122/124]); in addition, "Moses invited only *his* people and those of his own tongue to accept his law" (1,101 [56/73]). Halevi agrees with the author of *Sefer Yetzirah* that "in the nature of God ... *S'fār* [= number], *Sippūr* [= language], and *Sēfer* [= writing] are a unity" (4,25 [255/229]), whereas for the Philosopher there is a unity of intellect and intelligible objects. The unity of *S'fār*, *Sippūr*, and *Sēfer* leads to an emphasis on the importance of the existence of language. Accordingly, Halevi goes on to stress the special value of Hebrew: "This shows the excellence of the 'holy tongue' as well as the reason why the angels employed it in preference to any other" (ibid. [256/229]). The Hebrew language, "created and instituted by God," is superior thanks to the "subtle elements calculated to promote understanding, and to take the place of the above aids [tone of voice and gestures] to speech. These are the accents with which the holy text is read" (2,72 [125/126]). Halevi believes that there is also a need for a public revelation—that at Mount Sinai—to ground any material speech by God (1,87; 1,89).

32. This is the origin of the Philosopher's theory of prophecy.

language and precede it in time. Language, as the product of contrivance and convention in some generation, is necessarily rooted in prelinguistic rational activity.[33] The Philosopher holds that there can be thought that does not entail linguistic elements (4,5).[34] It stands to reason that precisely this thought expresses the pure activity of the intellect, as this takes place among the heavenly intellects.[35]

According to the Philosopher, the customs shared by all humanity, namely, the decimal system and the seven-day week, also go back to a "common beginning, agreement, and convention" (1,57 [28/51]). For "what instinct induced them to keep to the number ten?" (1,59 [28/52]).[36] In general terms there seems to be no difference between the discussion of these customs and that of language. The emphasis there on the public as a condition for agreement about fixed customs alludes to the Philosopher's difficulty in explaining an order accepted by all mankind, that "the people of China could agree with those of the western islands" (1,57 [28/51]). The Philosopher does not have to deal with this problem with regard to language.[37]

---

33. From this we can conclude that, for the Philosopher, human beings as rational individuals precede human beings as involved in dialogue, both logically and temporarily. Accordingly, as we have already seen, law, which permits social life, must be viewed as the result of consent.

34. According to the King, however, as well as the Rabbi, "thinking is like narrating" (4,6 [236/214]). This leads to the discursiveness of concrete human thought (ibid.).

35. This leads to the fundamental distinction between the intuitive intellectual activity (a sudden event) of actual intellect and the discursive intellectual activity (a process enduring in time) of potential intellect. See Chapter 4, §2, "The Goal as the Actualization of Human Potential." Compare also Maimonides, *Millot ha-higgayon* (Treatise on logic), ed. Israel Efros (New York, 1938), Chapter 14, where a distinction is made between "internal speech" and "external speech."

36. Compare: "*Sefer Yetzirah* is constructed on the mystery of *ten units*, equally acknowledged in east and west, but neither from natural causes nor rational conviction" (4,27 [270/240]).

37. In Arabic philosophy, the assumption that underlies the common proofs that the world was created is that an order whose constitution does not proceed from the essence of the ordered realm is necessarily determined by a being that is rational and volitional. See H. Davidson, "Arguments from

One can observe the ambivalence of the ordered systems typical of human existence while analyzing the meanings of the key terms used in these discussions: *consent* and *contrivance*. On the one hand, both are rooted in intention and creation, which characterize man as rational; from this perspective they are reflected in the rational stratum that is typical of these systems inasmuch as they are ordered and meaningful. On the other hand, these concepts are rooted in the human capacity to have an arbitrary preference for one possibility out of many, even when all options are equal in and of themselves. This preference is reflected in the nonrational stratum of language.[38] From the latter perspective, consent and contrivance are expressed in the nonrational stratum that is another facet of the ordered systems of human existence.

This ambivalence, which is essential to the ordered systems of human existence, is a consequence of the place that this existence occupies in the sublunar world.[39] As we have already seen, all of sublunar existence is marked by the meeting of ontological dimensions that are intrinsically alien to each other. The Philosopher agrees with the Epicurean view that

---

the Concept of Particularization in Arabic Philosophy," *Philosophy East and West* 18 (1968): 299–314. The Philosopher of the *Kuzari*, too, accepts this postulate in principle, but holds that such an order exists only on the plane of human existence. On that plane, the background of the Philosopher's explanation of order is the essence of human beings as possessing both intellect and volition.

38. Consent depends, by its very nature, on the existence of poles that are not predisposed to any fixed and obligatory interrelation. Consent that is confirmation of unchanging relations is quite untenable, like the vanity of contriving an order that is already inherent in reality.

39. Evidently this analogy between order in human existence and in sublunar existence in general is already implicit in the Rabbi's initial remarks, in the parable about the king of India (1,19–20). The content of the parable was not chosen by accident. One can understand the Philosopher's view that the justice of the Indian people is due both to their nature and to their king as referring to the ambiguity that constitutes the various ordered systems of sublunar reality, including the human realm, and also as alluding to the nature of the relationship between the two facets: the emanation of the Active Intellect in the sublunar world and the influence of the philosopher in the human world, on the one hand, and the response by the recipient of the emanation or influence, on the other.

disharmony precedes harmony (at least logically).[40] Unlike Epicurus, however, the Philosopher believes that, in the sublunar world, the transition from disharmony to harmony depends on the spontaneous dynamics of the rational dimension, through the eternal activity of the form-giving Active Intellect. In human existence, though, this transition depends on the act of contrivance and the process of consent, which take place in some generation and constitute the conditions for linguistic relationships as well as the political order and common customs. Halevi rejects both views; he believes that the harmony in nature and in human society is preordained by the Creator and precedes disharmony. In addition, harmony is a logical precondition and prior in time to consent and contrivances. In the realm of language, for example, Hebrew is the language "in which God spoke to Adam and Eve" (2,68 [122/124]).

7. Predisposition and the Meaning of an Act

Another expression of the ontological tension between matter and form, on the plane of human existence, can be seen in the Philosopher's notion of the actual content of the intention that should accompany a deed. This notion is bound up with his doctrine that a deed is a means.

The Philosopher of the *Kuzari*, more than he is interested in clarifying the rules of behavior, endeavors to discover the intentions that should occupy the background of human activity. In his opinion, philosophers must intentionally distance themselves from their deeds. They must act with a measure of disinterestedness, both in their intellectual assessments and in their feelings about the success of their actions. The Philosopher tells the King: "If you have reached such disposition of belief, do not be concerned about the

---

40. This idea has many implications. See N. W. De Witt, *Epicurus and His Philosophy* (Minneapolis, 1964), p. 129.

forms of your humility" (1,1 [10/38]).[41] The Philosopher, in polar antithesis to what the angel says in the King's dream, tells the monarch to "strive after purity of soul" (ibid.). That is, intention has an unlimited value, whereas deeds always have only a conditional and limited value; the value of an intention does not depend on its outcome. According to the Philosopher, deeds acquire whatever positive value they have from the intention that spawned them: "In sum, seek purity of heart in whatever way you can, provided you have acquired the totality of knowledge in its real essence" (ibid.). To which the King responds: "Your speech is convincing, yet it does not correspond to what I am seeking. I already know that my soul is pure and that my actions are directed to gain God's favor. To all this I received the answer that this way of acting does not find favor, though the intention does. There must be a way of acting, pleasing in itself, and not through the medium of intention" (1,2 [10/39]).

We should distinguish the Philosopher's mental predisposition toward action and its consequences from the way his activity really occurs. An act must be performed in accordance with rules (even if relative ones): "His organs—I mean the limbs of such a person—serve only the most perfect purposes, at the most appropriate time, and in the best condition" (1,1 [8/37]). In the same passage where philosophers are said to "recommend good and dissuade from evil in the most admirable manner" (4,19 [249/225]), we also read that the philosopher "need not care what he does." Even while acting to improve the world,

---

41. Just as the Philosopher ascribes no importance to the existential situation expressed by a problematic dialogue—the dream—so too he rejects the existential situation that spawned the dream—the "zealousness" (the state of his soul) that accompanies the King's service in the pagan temple (1,1). Compare 2,49. One must distinguish between the Philosopher's relativism, expressed in the *content* of particular rules of conduct, and his indifference about deeds, which is expressed in his *subjective attitude* toward action and therefore to the rules of conduct that govern its occurrence. We must not infer relativism (in this sense) from indifference, nor indifference from relativism.

philosophers reject the world. Similarly, the "divine laws" do not concern any philosopher, whether "believer or Epicurean" (4,13 [241/218]).[42]

Here, as on the issue of man's proper attitude toward God, Halevi proposed a psychological explanation for the philosopher's role. A philosopher, argued Halevi, has no trouble coming to terms with the absence of fixed rules of conduct for realizing the goal, not because there is no objective need for them (as the Philosopher believes), but because a philosopher's intellectual mode of relationship is psychologically incompatible with the possibility of their existence. A philosopher's exclusively intellectual attitude toward God cannot serve as a basis for an emotional or psychological willingness to withstanding the difficulties associated with obeying fixed rules of conduct—rules that are mandatory in all possible concrete conditions.[43] In other words, Halevi asserts that the philosopher's fundamental relativism actually expresses an opportunism that stems from an insufficient motivation. According to Halevi, motivation, which makes the will vigorously defend its decisions, even in borderline situations, is associated with love and fear of God (4,15–17); but nothing in the relationship between God and the human intellect represents an appropriate background for the evolution of such "feelings." Halevi supports the last assumption from two perspectives: (1) from the Divine pole, the Philosopher sees no place for any reward for deeds (other than the consequences of the deeds themselves), whereas, according to Halevi, love and fear depend on reward and punishment (4,16–19 [247]); and (2) from the human pole, the Philosopher sees no place for any sensible presence of God, whereas, according to Halevi, love and fear depend precisely on this sensible appearance.[44]

42. For the meaning of *Epicurean*, see Chapter 4, note 32. Clearly a philosopher is not required, in every situation, to be either a righteous man or an Epicurean; but he is called upon to be indifferent to his actions, even when external stringency is invested in their performance—even when the philosopher is "a righteous person." See also 5,14 [309/273].

43. 4,15; 4,16; 4,17; 4,19.

44. See also 4,15. On the other hand, there is 4,17 [247/223]: "God commanded Abraham to leave off his speculative researches...and to

8. Asceticism as the Philosopher's Way of Life

The systematic function of action in the Philosopher's doctrine—on the axiological plane, as a means, and on the ontological plane, as an expression of the fundamental tension between form and matter—is evident in the description of the philosopher's way of life. On the one hand, a philosopher relates to existence that is not intellect through both contemplation and action; on the other hand, this relation, particularly that expressed in action, is marked by the suspicion that it might become a goal instead of serving as a means. Philosophers are concerned that their actions not drag them to involuntary involvement in worldly affairs, which would be a descent with no possibility for ascent. Their way of life is designed to ward off the danger of such an involvement and descent by means of a withdrawal from worldly affairs: "The highest human success consists in theoretical knowledge.... This cannot be obtained, however, except by devoting one's life to research and continual reflection, which is incompatible with worldly occupations. For this reason [philosophers] renounce wealth, rank, and the pleasure of children, in order not to be distracted from study" (4,19 [248/224]). This renunciation entails limiting economic ambition ("wealth"), reining in aspirations for social and political advancement ("rank"), and forgoing hopes connected with family life ("children").

Although the philosopher follows an ascetic way of life, it must be distinguished from the life of the anchorite, "who desires to retire into ascetic solitude" (3,1 [140/136]). The asceticism of philosophers is an internal manifestation of their "love of solitude" (ibid. [140/135]), of their genuine love of the "learning necessary to be absorbed in the divine light and enjoy it" (ibid. [141/136]), and of their recoiling from activities that can

---

devote himself to the service of Him who he had tasted, as it is written: 'Taste and see that the Lord is good' (Ps. 34:9)." Indirectly, it is clear that for Halevi, one who has not "tasted"—a philosopher—is not able *to cleave to the worship of God*; this parallels point (2) in the text. Compare 1,109 and 4,15.

yield no intellectual profit (ibid.). On the other hand, the anchorite, who has withdrawn "not because he enjoys his seclusion" (ibid.), resembles someone who has put himself in prison: The walls press in upon the prisoner and do not express his essence—his authentic feelings. The prisoner's willingness to immure himself[45] immeasurably exacerbates the antithesis between the prisoner as a human being and the circumstances in which he finds himself. Necessarily split within himself, he "disdains life out of disgust for his prison and pain. . . . Thus he remains night and day, while his soul urges him to exert its inherent powers of seeing, hearing, speaking, moving, eating, cohabitation, gain, house-managing, helping the poor, and upholding religion with money in case of need" (ibid. [140/136]). The anchorite hungers for the world but loathes his life. This is not the case with philosophers, who "reject the world" (5,14 [309/279]) but nevertheless "enjoy" their lives (3,1 [141/136]).

Therefore the asceticism of philosophers does not result from an acceptance of some set of rules. According to the Philosopher (as well as Halevi), their disposition toward asceticism grows out of their unified personality. This description of their way of life is compatible with his view of the appropriate relation to action—indifference—as well as with his view concerning the relativism of rules of conduct.

Despite the substantial differences between philosopher and anchorite as to the concrete meaning and importance of their asceticism, they agree that an ascetic life is to be preferred over involvement in the affairs of the world, and for a similar reason: Both believe that the life of this world is incompatible with their aspiration to achieve the goal intended for man qua man.[46] Of course, from the philosopher's vantage point, the ideal of the ascetic life should not be seen as merely an expression of the desire "not to be distracted from study" (4,19 [249/224]). Rather,

---

45. The lack of authenticity is alluded to in the very act of decision as well as in the description of the anchorite state as imprisonment.

46. Compare 4,19. Ibn Bajja, too, concluded that the solitary life is preferable. For his influence on the opinion of the Philosopher of the *Kuzari*, see H. Davidson, "The Active Intellect."

THE PHILOSOPHER'S THOUGHT

this ideal, just as it is rooted in the ontological dualism of sublunar existence, is also anchored in the meaning for philosophers of the Active Intellect, namely, a pole to which they cleave and which they strive to resemble.[47]

A philosopher's distaste for involvement with nonintellectual existence involves more than just his relations with his milieu. When he unites with the Active Intellect, a philosopher's apathy extends also to "the decay of his body or his organs" (1,1 [8/38]).[48] Furthermore, and parallel to the burdens associated with worldly affairs, which lead the philosopher to love a life of solitude, "the burden of the body" leads him to "loathing and disgust for all physical faculties" (5,12 [302/268]).[49] According to the Philosopher, the association of body and intellect prevents, ontologically, union between the human intellect and the Active Intellect. This is a consequence of the ontological alienation between body and intellect.[50]

The philosophers' distaste for overinvolvement with an existence that is irrelevant to the human objective is expressed in their attitude toward the social and political spheres as well. In the inevitable confrontation between the deed as a means and as an expression of attaining the goal—union with God—they explicitly prefer the deed as means and no more. When it comes to the active life that aims at amending the world, philosophers

---

47. In the context of the Philosopher's doctrine as a whole, the opposition between the affairs of the world and contemplative action, too, is based on the ontological polarization of reality into two mutually alien dimensions.

48. See also 4,14.

49. Hence it is not enough to restrain sensory appetites. Philosophers do not restrain the body per se, including "all physical powers" (5,12 [302/268]), but feel "loathing and disgust" for it (ibid.; compare 1,115). Such loathing and disgust are not associated with the effort to abstain from physical pleasures, because it is all the same to philosophers, even Epicureans. Similarly, the Philosopher is not an advocate of the doctrine of the golden mean, mentioned in 3,3ff. See also Strauss, *Persecution and the Art of Writing*, p. 127.

50. See Chapter 4, §2, "The Goal as the Actualization of Human Potential." Compare S. Pines, "Note sur la doctrine de la prophétie et la réhabilitation de la matière dans le *Kuzari*," *Mélanges de philosophie et de littérature juives* 1–2 (1956–1957): 253–260.

attach no positive value to improving the world, despite the fact that in improving the world an actor resembles the Active Intellect.[51]

A philosopher aspires to unite with the Active Intellect by means of mental action. In sublunar reality, such cogitation is necessarily associated with deeds as means. As happenings in the sublunar sphere, deeds influence the course of events. This influence necessarily amends the world, so that the human intellect resembles the Active Intellect: "To the perfect person there adheres a light of divine nature, called Active Intellect; his Passive Intellect cleaves so closely to it that it considers itself to be one with the Active Intellect. His organs—I mean the limbs of such a person—serve only the most perfect purposes" (1,1 [7/37]). Although philosophers of the degree "of Socrates and those who were like him" (3,1 [140/136]) may a posteriori renounce the advantages of solitude, their real intention in this renunciation—given that even then they "desire only the society of disciples" (ibid. [140/135])—is to "stimulate their research and retentiveness, just as one who is bent on making money would surround himself only with persons with whom he could do lucrative business" (ibid. [140/136]).[52] Hence even though philosophers have no intention of doing good to others, in the final analysis that is precisely what they do.

---

51. Yet, according to 4,19 [249/225], philosophers "recommend good and dissuade from evil in the most admirable manner, ... in order to resemble the Creator." Moscato (ad loc., *incipit* אבל צוו על השוב) resolved this contradiction with difficulty. For the doctrine as a whole, the contradiction reflects a more fundamental problem. On the one hand, the Active Intellect is the Giver of forms, and the philosopher, as legislator and ruler, does indeed resemble the Active Intellect. On the other hand, there is no intentionality in the Active Intellect's form-giving; from this perspective, on the level of intention and predisposition, the philosopher's resemblance to the Active Intellect is expressed by an intentional focus on reflection.

52. On this question the Philosopher tends to the view of Ibn Bajja rather than that of al-Farabi; see E. I. J. Rosenthal, "The Place of Politics in the Philosophy of Ibn Bajja," *Islamic Culture* 25 (1951): 187–211.

9. Overview: Ontological Dichotomy and Human Existence

A philosopher's qualified and ambiguous attitude toward the various spheres of action is anchored in the very essence of the human intellect. The human intellect participates in the common ontological rhythm shared by all intellects. For the human intellect, as for all other intellects, a reflective introspection precedes its productive expansion. But the human intellect differs from other intellects because its introspection in the act of cognition necessarily involves an escape from the surrounding world. Both thematically and temporally, this escape, with all its manifestations and stages, precedes the productive expansion of the human intellect, as expressed in the a posteriori significance of human action aimed at amending the world. To summarize this chapter, we shall attempt to highlight the main points of this rhythm while clarifying the relation between the ontological and human planes.

The very essence of the intellects constitutes the ground bass of this rhythm. The shared essence of the intellects is the ontological condition for the full unity of the realm of intellects: On the one hand, God, despite His place in the hierarchy of intellects, is one among them. On the other hand, the common essence of all intellects is the ontological background for the intrinsic uniqueness of the realm of intellects as wholly other—Divine—than the ontological dimension that is not intellect; that is, matter. This polarization of existence—both existence as a whole and human existence itself—into two ontological dimensions underlies the problematic nature of the Philosopher's system. In existence as the All, the underlying dualism is of intellect and matter. In human existence, however, it is the dualism of intellect and body, of intellect versus the interestedness of life in the world, of the individual possessed of a perfect intellect vis-à-vis the many who lack such perfection. Halevi focused more on the possibility of bridging between these two ontological dimensions, on the level of the All and especially on the level of human existence, than on discovering the truth about these dimensions themselves.[53]

In light of this, the special role that the Philosopher allots to human action is particularly prominent. On the one hand, human action—as a manifestation of an intention that is anchored in the intellect but produces results in a dimension of reality that is not exclusively intellect (but also with regard to its specific content)—is a bridge between the ontological dimensions; on the other hand, this bridge reflects the essence of these estranged ontological dimensions.

From this latter perspective we can understand the Philosopher's basic position—which, as already noted, is the chief bone of contention between the Philosopher of the *Kuzari* and Halevi's later thought. The Philosopher believes that there is no act "pleasing in itself" (1,2 [11/39]) and that any deed that can be recommended is necessarily pleasing "through the medium of intention" (ibid.). Before we consider this position, however, we should review the three main aspects of the distinction between an act that is "pleasing in itself" and one that is pleasing "through the medium of intention":

1. Their source—whereas acts that are pleasing in themselves depend on "Divine ordinance" (1,98 [53/70]), acts pleasing through the medium of intention are of "human origin" (1,81 [38/58]; 1,87 [50/60]).[54]
2. Their location—whereas the positive value of an act that is pleasing in itself depends chiefly on its emergence from intention to implementation, the positive value of an act pleasing through intention depends on the content of the intention.[55]

---

53. In a certain sense, the particular interest in the possibility of bridging is typical of the specific theological interest shared by Halevi and the Philosopher of the *Kuzari*.

54. For various reasons, Halevi associated acts that are pleasing in themselves with Divine revelation.

55. According to Halevi, this point was not clear to the High Priest Aaron. This is how he explained the latter's role in the sin of the golden calf (1,97 [51]). On the other hand, the Lord made trial of Abraham "in order

THE PHILOSOPHER'S THOUGHT

3. Their validity—whereas acts that are pleasing in themselves cannot be replaced by other acts (at least not by human beings), the philosopher, who knows the "reasons" that underlie the deeds, can replace acts that are pleasing through intention with other equally pleasing acts.

These distinctions between acts pleasing in themselves and acts pleasing through intention should be seen as three aspects of a single fundamental and essential difference: Recognition of the value of acts pleasing in themselves reflects recognition of the unconditional positive value of nonintellectual existence, whether or not this is identified with the Divine will. Recognition of the positive value of existence (any existence) that is not intellect is expressed in the aspects enumerated above. On the other hand, recognition of the positive value of acts pleasing through intention rests on the assumption that only intellectual existence has unconditional status. The Philosopher of the *Kuzari*, who rejects the positive value of acts pleasing in themselves, locates the goal in the intellect, and there alone.

Returning now to the association between the Philosopher's ontological and anthropological thought, let us try to discover his position in the central dispute concerning the value of acts pleasing in themselves and the possibility of revelation—an event in which God commands or teaches. The Philosopher's theology has no room for acts pleasing in themselves. Such acts must begin with God; but a deity who is not a principle that can explain an intentional relationship that focuses on a particular subject at a particular moment cannot be the cause for any beginning, not even a "beginning" for the laws of action.[56]

---

to render his theoretical obedience practical" (5,20 [319/282]). Compare Ibn Ezra on Gen. 22:1. The Rabbi leaves the King to go to the Land of Israel, out of his recognition that "actions must be perfect to claim reward" (5,27 [333/295]). From this perspective the end of the book returns to its start: by emigrating to the Land of Israel—and "no function can be perfect except there" (5,23 [341/293])—the Rabbi physically implements the angel's demand of the King at the beginning of the book.

56. It is no accident that the angel in the King's dream, as well as the King himself (1,2), refers to God as the Creator. The Philosopher, for his part, begins by pointing out that this is an error. The deity defined as

Furthermore, because the Philosopher's anthropology has no room for acts pleasing in themselves, and because acts, to the extent that they have a positive value, are necessarily pleasing through intention, there is no justification for Divine revelation; hence it cannot be attributed to a rational deity.

Still, the association between the act of revelation and acts that are pleasing in themselves cannot explain all the essential aspects of the Philosopher's view of such deeds.[57] Nor can it explain other facets of his anthropology.[58] Furthermore, this association expresses fundamental ontological postulates. The Philosopher's views that Divine revelation is impossible, that acts pleasing in themselves have no value, and that the goal is focused in the intellect have a single root: all exemplify the essence of the two ontological dimensions of existence—intellect and matter. For the same reason that God does not reveal Himself of His own initiative to any entity outside Himself, the human intellect, too, does not go beyond itself to realize its goal. The reason for this derives from the ontological similarity of the Divine and human intellects and from the arrangement of existence as a whole into two ontological dimensions whose essential alienation persists even when they come together, concretely, in the sublunar sphere.[59] The human intellect that, according to the Philosopher, stands opposite a deity who has no intention-

---

Creator can begin a new initiative: to appear to human beings and disclose which acts are pleasing to Him. God as Creator is involved with creation, and this is the source of acts that are pleasing in themselves. Compare Strauss, *Persecution and the Art of Writing*, p. 113.

57. This association explains neither the Philosopher's view of the importance of intention (2) nor his view of the fundamental possibility of replacing one deed by another (3).

58. Clearly nothing in this association can provide a foundation for the Philosopher's theory of teleology or for the asceticism and indifference he evinces toward action.

59. When the King dismisses the Philosopher, he stresses that he is doing so because "between the Divine power and the non-Divine souls there are secret relations that are not identical with those you have mentioned, O Philosopher" (1,4 [12/40]). This explicitly alludes to the essential parallel between the characterization of the poles God and man, a parallel that also determines the relationship between them, as the King notes at the beginning of the section. See also 4,1.

ality toward it as an individual can find religious significance in God only against the background of the redeeming ontological essence of the relationship to Him. But not only is this relationship located in the realm of the intellect itself, whence it entails no fundamental excursion beyond its own province,[60] such an excursion would be an ontological expression of the remoteness of the human intellect from union with the Active Intellect and would prevent its attainment.

The closure of the human intellect in itself, expressed in the negation of any interest in external reality as possessing intrinsic value, also negates the intrinsic value of any individual human entity. Thus, as we have seen, philosophers of the rank of Socrates teach their disciples only as a means to "stimulate their research and retentiveness" (3,1 [140/136]). The human intellect, confronting a deity that has no proper name—a deity that by virtue of its essence as intellect relates to existence only inasmuch as the latter is perceived—unites with that deity by escaping the individuality that is foreign to its essence as intellect. The individual qua individual is not perceived; as perceived, it is not individual.[61] Just as the release from individuality entails the negation of any interest in the body and its characteristic preoccupations, so too it entails the negation of interest in the individuality of the other.

---

60. Hence the human intellect's partial independence from external reality (including language) is a particular projection of the general relationship between intellect and matter. It follows that an act is only a means for changing the face of reality so that there will be no impediments to achieving the goal.

61. Halevi and the Philosopher agree about the link between the individual and the irrational. Halevi, too, believed that God "sustains and guides all living creatures with a wisdom our intellect cannot grasp in detail, but only in a general way" (3,11 [154/148]); see also 3,43. Hence, according to the Rabbi, Divine revelation about actions is required to teach human beings the specific and detailed measures of its general rules, which in principle could be acquired by the human intellect on its own. The Philosopher, following the same line of argument, arrives at the fundamental ontological inferiority of act to cogitation and at the importance of the philosopher as the living judge who can apply the principles of rational conduct to concrete situations.

In light of the above, the Philosopher would agree with Halevi that his view of man is inseparable from his view of God. The very fact that philosophers "only cultivate the intellect" (1,3 [11/39]) exempts them from any need for external manifestations of intention. On the other hand, the Philosopher would totally reject Halevi's attempt to reduce his theory of man to some psychological explanation; that is, to the psychological significance of his notion of the essence of God.

From this vantage point the Philosopher rejects the possibility of ranking the ontological elements as they are ranked in the King's dream. The Philosopher expounds to the King the ontological nullity of the dream. Hence he relates not only to the King's repeated dream, but also to the very possibility of dreams; that is, to God's having a relationship with human beings as individuals. In the course of rejecting this possibility he naturally dismisses the angel's message as well, both because the words cannot have been spoken and because their content is null. The very idea that "your intention is pleasing to God, but not your way of acting" rests on the assumption that there exists a deity who goes beyond His own sphere—that God takes an interest in existence outside Himself—and also on the assumption that there exists a subject in a sphere of existence where action has meaning. As we have seen, the Philosopher rejects both of these assumptions.

PART II

HALEVI'S EARLIER THOUGHT

6

INTRODUCTION TO THE EARLIER THOUGHT

1. The Philosopher's Thought versus Judah Halevi's Thought

Judah Halevi's thought in the *Kuzari* gradually distances itself from Aristotelian philosophy. There are various reasons for this movement. Some—historical events and personal experience—have nothing to do with philosophy; others are internal developments in his doctrines that lead to immanent criticism of basic axioms of Aristotelian philosophy. Halevi's thought shows an acute awareness of the meaning of the historical events of his age, such as the Reconquista, the Murabti invasions, and the Crusades, including the Crusader conquest of Jerusalem in 1099.[1] These fateful events worsened the situation of the Jews, imperiled their future, and underscored the problems associated with the unique historical destiny of the Jewish people. They reawakened the trenchant questions about the meaning of Jewish

---

1. An outstanding manifestation of his acute sensitivity to current events appears at the very beginning of the book, in the concise description of holy wars and their presentation as an integral part of the relations among the revealed religions—religions that emphasize the importance of the specificity of human deeds (1,3).

history, in both past and present, and gave added urgency to the issue of the future existence of the Jewish people. In the background were the interreligious polemics, given new momentum by the ongoing holy wars, as well as internal Jewish uncertainties. Pious individuals were duty-bound to be ready to answer the question of the Tempter, who has the power to make us despair: " 'Can these bones live?' (Ezek. 37:3)—our traces being thoroughly destroyed and our memory wiped out" (3,11 [156/150]).²

The destiny of the Jewish people is linked to the meaning of the uniqueness of the Jewish experience, in all its elements. The significance of this destiny, its sense and justification, as well as the future of the Jewish people, depend upon the meaning of this uniqueness. Aristotelian philosophy rules out the existence of a unique nation, for reasons both theological (the impossibility of a Divine act that could establish absolute uniqueness) and anthropological (the location of the human essence exclusively on the intellectual plane, which by its very nature is universal). The Philosopher accordingly counsels trimming one's religious sails to the prevailing wind (1,1; 2,49). It hardly need be said that in the situation of the Jewish people at this time, his advice was tantamount to preaching conversion. From this perspective philosophy (if only for its own reasons) allies itself with Christianity and Islam and calls into question the value of Judaism's continued existence.³

---

2. This question appears in Part III, which evidently reflects Halevi's earlier thought, as well as in his later thought (4,20–21). The reference to Satan or the Tempter reflects the extraordinary importance of the question. See also the ambiguous meaning of the word *she'ol* in his poem יונה נשאתה על כנפי נשרים. See also Y. Levin, "Ha-sevel ba-mashber ha-riqonqistah be-shirato shel Yehudah Halevi" (Suffering in the crisis of the Reconquista in the poetry of Judah Halevi), *Oẓar Yehudei Sefarad* 7 (1964): 55.

3. On the phenomenon of conversion and apostasy in Halevi's generation and his personal involvement in the struggle against it, see D. Kaufmann, "R. Yehudah Halevi," *Sinai* 9 (1941/1942): 22, nn. 138–139; S. D. Goitein, "Ha-pareshah ha-aḥaronah be-ḥayyei R. Yehudah Halevi" (The last chapter in the life of R. Judah Halevi), *Tarbiẓ* 24 (1955): 35–48; H. Schirman, *Toledot ha-shirah ve-ha-drama ha-ʿivrit* (History of Hebrew poetry and drama), Vol. 1 (Jerusalem, 1979), pp. 292 and 336; E. Ashtor, *The Jews of Moslem*

As we shall see, in his earlier thought Halevi did not stress the full significance of the uniqueness of the Jewish experience. In that period he focused on practice—observance of the Torah commandments. In his later thought, by contrast, he dealt with other elements, such as intrinsic potential, origin, language, and country. Nevertheless, even at this stage in the evolution of his thought we see an increasing willingness to draw conclusions from this uniqueness, conclusions that are incompatible with the Philosopher's outlook.

Just as it is marked by the historical experience of his contemporaries, the evolution of Halevi's thought is also marked by his personal religious experience of "true dreams." Both his poetry and the *Kuzari* offer various indications of the centrality of these events in his life.[4] In his early thought, represented by Part III of the *Kuzari*, the Rabbi unhesitatingly proposes that the King learn from his personal experience—from "true dreams" (3,53). Such dreams can be summoned, because they are merely the result of proper observance of the commandments (ibid.). Halevi's confidence that one can have "true dreams" on order and that the pious individual can "discover secrets" through "reliable dreams" (3,11 [149/143]) is hard to understand unless we assume that it reflects his personal experience.[5] According to Halevi, a Divine call to man, on all its levels, emphasizes the

---

Spain, vol. 3, trans. A. Klein and J. M. Klein (Philadelphia, 1984), pp. 190–192; Salo W. Baron, "Yehuda Halevi, an Answer to an Historic Challenge," *Jewish Social Studies* 3 (1941): 252 and 259; M. Perlmann, "Ibn Hazur on Equivalence of Truth," *JQR* 40 (1950).

4. On the place and significance of Halevi's religious experiences in dreams, as reflected in his poetry, see Komem, "Poetry and Prophecy."

5. The King's dream is not explained against the background of any prior situation; see further Chapter 7, note 16. Note that "reliable dreams" appear here as part of a series that includes prophecy and the Urim and Tummim. Clearly he believes that such dreams are the only one of these means available to his contemporaries. Compare 1,4 and 2,60. See also Chapter 16, note 36. Saadia Gaon, too, was of the opinion that "there is also apt to be mingled with these dreams a glimmer of heavenly light in the form of a hint or a parable" (*The Book of Beliefs and Opinions*, trans. Samuel Rosenblatt [New Haven, Conn., 1948], Introductory Treatise, Chapter 5, p. 21). See also Leviticus Rabba 1,13, ed. Margoliouth; Genesis Rabba 52,5; E. E. Urbach, "Darshot Ḥazal ʿal neviʾei ʾummot ha-ʿolam ve-ʿal

fundamental importance of the human way of life—not only because of the didactic content of the call, but also because of the very fact of its occurrence, which embodies the Divine response to human action. This opinion contradicts that of the Philosopher, who believes that, just as the idea of a dream that pretends to be a Divine call to an individual and a new focus of the Divine will in the transient is absurd, it is similarly absurd to insist on the importance of a particular way of life.

Halevi only gradually came to realize the full significance for his doctrine of his religious experiences. Only in his later thought was he fully aware that these experiences are incompatible with the tenets of philosophy. In his earlier thought, the occurrence of reliable dreams (like other and more intense manifestations of Divine revelation) was explained in the context of a view of the deity that is chiefly Aristotelian, that is, on the basis of the eternal and unchanging ontological regularity that is the essence of divinity. This comes, of course, at the price of blurring the revolutionary, one-time, and unique nature of Divine revelations in the world. Only in his later thought did Halevi insist on this character of Divine revelations and evince a corresponding willingness to modify his theological beliefs. In his earlier thought, Divine revelation is only one of the two points of departure for his system, alongside philosophy; this bipolar origin is the source of the innate contradictions that riddle his earlier thought. In his later thought, by contrast, Divine revelation is the main point of departure. As we shall see, this determines both the image of God and the nature of His relationship to entities outside Himself, as well as the image of man and the nature of his link with the deity. This order is also reflected in the sequence of our discussion: When we focused on Aristotelian philosophy,

---

pareshat Bilʿam" (Talmudic homilies on Gentile prophets and the Balaam pericope), *Tarbiẓ* 25 (1957). On the meaning of dreams in the *Kuzari*, see L. Strauss, *Persecution and the Art of Writing* (Glencoe, Ill., 1952), pp. 105ff.; Schweid, *Taʿam ve-haqqashah*, p. 55.

the metaphysical issues came first; whereas when we consider Halevi's own thought, the issue of Divine contact with man takes precedence.

In addition to the biographical experiences that led Halevi to expand the fundamental themes of his thought, there were also internal developments within that thought. Over the years these produced an ever-widening gap between his later thought and Aristotelian philosophy. One expression of this change is his adoption of a critical attitude toward philosophy; another is his disposition to accord greater prominence to the primacy of empirical data over theoretical conclusions—a principle accepted by Aristotelian philosophy as well. In his earlier thought his only criticism of philosophy stems from his recognition of the boundaries of philosophical knowledge and his endeavor to expand them on the basis of the historical experience of the Jewish people and his own personal religious experiences. In his later thought, however, his criticism expands to include an exposé of the dogmatic nature of certain axioms of philosophy. This exposé maintains the relative superiority of Aristotelian philosophy over other world-views based on the human intellect that contemplates a world subject to natural law, but it also opens the way for the possibility of knowledge of a higher order.[6]

The superiority of empirical data is an important principle in Halevi's thought. The Rabbi notes, without reservation, that Aristotle too would have altered his opinion had he been granted an immediate or even mediated prophetic experience.[7] In Halevi's later thought this superiority becomes the principle of the a priori relativity of any world-view that originates in intellect (a relativity interpreted as contingent but not random). According to Halevi, Socrates (unlike Aristotle) acknowledged this fact: " 'Citizens, I do not contest your doctrine of God; I say only that I do not penetrate so far; I understand only the doctrine of

---

6. This ambiguity is reflected in the evaluation of the Philosopher's words as "convincing" (1,2 [10/38]).

7. 1,65; 4,30; 5,15.

man'" (4,13 [242/218]).[8] Based on the experience of revelation, Halevi was prepared to exchange even the fundamental axioms of philosophy for other assumptions. In his earlier thought, however, this relativism was only partial. This explains how, in the earlier thought, philosophy could in principle be open to supplements that take new empirical data into account (3,11; 3,17). As we shall see, the theme of the oldest stratum of the *Kuzari*, which expresses Halevi's earlier thought, is the polemic against Karaism rather than against Aristotelian philosophy. The latter dispute became central only in Halevi's more mature thought, when his differences with it became more profound, and is conspicuous in the portions of the book written later.

In light of the distinction between Halevi's earlier and later we can understand the two different titles of the book. The first title—*Al-Kitāb al-Khazarī* (The book of the Khazars [or of the king of the Khazars])—refers to the sections written first, which express his earlier thought. This name is given to the book on account of its main character—the king of the Khazars, who plays the role of a dispassionate judge before whom the Rabbi argues his case against Karaism. But this title, found in an autograph letter of Halevi's, refers explicitly to a work he sent to a Karaite scholar (or physician).[9] The later title—*Kitāb al-radd wa-ʾl Dalīl fī ʾl-dīn al-dhalīl* (The book of refutation and

---

8. See also 5,14. Because Halevi was aware of the problems inherent in this acknowledgment of the fundamental relativity of philosophy, he emphasizes that Socrates was a lover of truth. For the same reason, he refrains from indicting Aristotle. There seems to be room to make the skeptical attitude that accompanies metaphysical philosophizing depend on awareness of relativism. See 1,13; 4,16; 4,27; 5,14.

9. See S. D. Goitein, "Otografim mi-yado shel R. Yehudah Halevi" (Autograph manuscripts of R. Judah Halevi), *Tarbiẓ* 25 (1956): 393–412; D. Z. Baneth, "La-otografim shel Yehudah Halevi u-le-hithavvut sefer ha-kuzari" (On Judah Halevi's autographs and the development of the *Kuzari*), *Tarbiẓ* 26 (1957): 297–303. It is also plausible that the title *Al-Radd ʿalā al-Khawārij* (The book of answers to the sectarians), which appears in a twelfth-century list of books found in the Cairo geniza, refers to the same work. See Nehemiah Aloni, "Li-shemot shenei sefarim me-ha-sifrut ha-yehudit-ʿaravit" (On the names of two volumes from Judeo-Arabic literature)" *Qiryat Sefer* 38 (1963): 114.

proof on the despised faith)[10]—was given to the book as we have it before us, a large portion of which expresses Halevi's later thought; with slight variants, it appears in all extant manuscripts.[11] The book received this title because of the inclination of his later thought to defend Judaism—the despised faith—against Aristotelian philosophy, Islam, and Christianity. Needless to say, such a name is out of place for a work directed against Karaism. The despised status of rabbinic Judaism would be irrelevant in that dispute, because the historical destiny of Karaism was scarcely different from that of Rabbinism. The despised status of Judaism surfaces time and again in passages rooted in his later thought, but is mentioned only infrequently in passages that reflect his earlier thought. This distinction can also help us understand Halevi's partial reservations concerning the Rabbi's world-view, stated in the very first paragraph of the book: "I found among the arguments of the Rabbi many which appealed to me and were in harmony with my own opinions" (1,1 [4/35]). Halevi's more mature opinions compelled him to distance himself somewhat from the views of the Rabbi, who represents all stages in the evolution of Halevi's thought, including his earlier period.[12]

10. This Arabic title of the book, and its translation, are based on the scholarly edition of D. Z. Baneth (Jerusalem, 1977). See also Nehemiah Aloni, "Ha-Kuzari: Sefer ha-milḥamah ba-ʿarabiyyeh le-shiḥrur ha-yehudi" (The *Kuzari*: An anti-*arabiyyeh* polemic), *Eshel Beʾer-Sheva* 2 (1981): 119–143.
11. See the articles by Aloni cited in the last two notes.
12. As supporting evidence we should perhaps add Halevi's deprecatory words about the *Kuzari* in his letter; see Goitein, "Otografim." From our perspective, we can understand the "silliness" as just that, an expression of the author's reservations about the dominant trends of thought expressed in the book and the Rabbi's views in general. The reference is to the work intended for the Karaite scholar, which expressed his earlier thought. See Baneth, "La-otografim"; A. L. Motzkin, "Al ha-kuzari li-Yehudah Halevi ke-dialog aplatoni" (Judah Halevi's *Kuzari* as a Platonic dialogue), *Iyyun* 28 (1978): 213–215. Toward the end of the book, however, the character of the Rabbi comes to be identified with Halevi. He overtly draws on Halevi's autobiographical experiences (5,25) and prepares to emigrate to Eretz Israel. For another explanation of Halevi's reservations about the Rabbi's position, see Strauss, *Persecution and the Art of Writing*, p. 101, n. 17.

In our attempted reconstruction of the reasons for Halevi's gradual movement away from the traditions of Aristotelian thought we have noted three topics that philosophy could not deal with adequately: (1) the uniqueness of the Jewish people; (2) the importance of an individual's way of life; and (3) the significance of the religious experience—revelation in all its forms. These topics, which are the foci of the confrontation between Halevi's thought and philosophy, played an important role in the evolution of his thought from the earlier to the later period. They are central to Halevi's thought because of both their relations among themselves and their links with other fundamental issues. In the chapters that follow we shall deal extensively with these links.

2. The Uniqueness of Part III of the *Kuzari*

Various reasons have been offered to buttress the assumption that Part III of the *Kuzari* in fact represents the first edition of the book. Because this hypothesis fits in well with the main argument of the present chapter, let us start by surveying these reasons. S. D. Goitein discovered the Halevi autograph manuscripts and proposed that the *Kuzari* as we have it today goes back to a much shorter work that included an answer to various questions posed by a Karaite scholar.[13] It is this shorter work, the "first edition" of the *Kuzari*, about which Halevi made scornful remarks in his letter from a later period.[14] In a response, D. Z. Baneth agreed with Goitein that the *Kuzari* was written in two editions; he even endeavored to describe the first edition:

---

13. Goitein, "Otografim"; idem, "The Biography of Rabbi J. Ha-Levi," *Proceedings of the American Academy for Jewish Research* 28 (1959): 41–56.

14. Perhaps we should understand the scorn for the book only as an expression of the conventional manner in which authors referred to their works. If so, we can learn nothing about the way in which the book was written from this letter. See S. D. Goitein, "Judaeo-Arabic Letters from Spain," *Orientalia Hispanica* 1 (1974): 338, n. 2.

It seems plausible, then, that the first version of the *Kuzari* was relatively short and was meant primarily to answer the questions of the anonymous Karaite scholar. The framework of the dialogue between the king of Khazars and a rabbinic scholars was perhaps chosen to demonstrate that the Karaite rejection of the Oral Law undermines precisely those foundations that prove the Divine source of Judaism and raise it above the other religions, whose origin is human.[15]

Accordingly (and for other reasons as well), Baneth was inclined to view Part III of the *Kuzari*, which contains most of the anti-Karaite polemics, as a unit that could have been included as is in the first version of the book.[16] Relying on Pines,[17] however, he expanded the scope of the first version to include all of Parts I through IV. He did this even though it entails the assumption that Part I was revised before being incorporated into the second version of the *Kuzari*. As we shall see, a comparison of the other parts with Part III indicates that Baneth was mistaken. The hypothesis that Part III belongs to the first version of the book has received additional support from E. Schweid.[18] According to Schweid, the literary structure of Part III attests to its original unity, while its thematic and literary relations with the other parts attest to its independence of them. Like Goitein and Baneth, Schweid emphasized that the anti-Karaite polemic constitutes the core of the first version. However, he disagreed with them and held that the first version of the book comprised Part III only.

The scholarly works we have just mentioned focus chiefly on the composition of the *Kuzari* and the circumstances of its publication. Here, however, we are interested in the changes in Halevi's thought, in its themes as well as in its methodology. By comparimg the arguments in the various parts of the book, we shall attempt to demonstrate the following contentions: (1) Part III and certain groups of sections in the other parts reflect a

---

15. Baneth, "La-otografim," p. 299.
16. Ibid., n. 7.
17. Pines, "Shī'ite Terms," pp. 216–217.
18. Schweid, *Taʿam ve-haqqashah*, pp. 45–46.

particular doctrine. (2) This doctrine is in many ways close to the views of the Philosopher as he himself expounds them in Part I. This proximity of doctrine, as we have seen, attests to the relative earliness of this stratum. The first claim, that Part III expresses a specific doctrine, is compatible with its literary characteristics as unified and independent of the other parts. The second argument sits well with the idea that Part III belongs to the first version of the book. Of course, our assumption that there were two editions of the *Kuzari* says nothing about changes in Halevi's world-view, nor does the distinction between earlier and later thought imply anything about the manner in which the book was written. Even should the opinion that there were two version be refuted someday, the conclusions of the present work would remain valid. Hence, too, nothing in our demarcation of the boundaries of the first version is definitive proof that a particular section expresses Halevi's earlier thought. Nevertheless, the assumptions that Part III survives more or less intact from the first edition and that Part III in its entirety reflects Halevi's earlier thought are compatible and reinforce each other.[19]

An investigation of the nature of Halevi's earlier thought, including a clarification of how Part III fits into it, requires two things: (1) discovering Halevi's earlier opinions on central topics; (2) juxtaposing these views with Halevi's later views on parallel issues and with the views of the Philosopher.

---

19. It seems plausible that Halevi's thought evolved over many years. Hence the interest of Goitein's hypothesis that the first version of the *Kuzari* had already been written in 1125, whereas the second version was completed only around 1139. See Goitein, "Otografim," pp. 401–403, and the supplement on p. 412. Baneth, "La-otografim," p. 300, expresses a different opinion. It should be noted that the various references in the *Kuzari* indicating a date of 1140 or 1139 (the "about four hundred years ago" at the beginning of the book is a round number) actually come in the first part, in §1 and §47, which evidently reflect Halevi's later thought.

7

THE THEOLOGY OF THE EARLY THOUGHT

Halevi's thought (both earlier and later), like the Aristotelian philosophy of the *Kuzari*, is marked by the reciprocal relations between his epistemology—the conditions for knowing God— and his metaphysics—the meaning of divinity. This interrelationship is reflected in the relative importance of intellect among the attributes of the deity and the meaning with which all of them are endowed in this context.

There are no explicit discussions about the essence of God in Part III.[1] We can infer Halevi's opinions, though, from his

---

1. The absence of theological discussions in Part III provides additional support for the assumption that the first version of the *Kuzari* included the discussion of God's names and attributes (2,1–7). This topic was at the center of the controversy between Rabbanites and Karaites, with the latter accusing the former of endowing God with corporeal attributes. See: Y. Rosenthal, "Ha-maʿavaq neged ha-qaraʾut: Seqirat sifrut anti-qaraʾit" (The struggle against Karaism: A survey of anti-Karaite literature), *Meḥqerei Yerushalayim* 1 (1967): 224–238; the bibliography in Shimon Rawidowicz, *Iyyunim be-maḥshevet yisrael* (Studies in Jewish thought), vol. 1 (Jerusalem, 1969), p. 178, n. 11; Y. Baer, *A History of the Jews in Christian Spain*, vol. 1 (Philadelphia, 1961), p. 390, n. 45. It is plausible that the discussion on removing corporeality from descriptions of God appeared in the first version, which was mainly an anti-Karaite polemic.

remarks in this part on other topics, chiefly the various aspects of the relationship between human beings and God—its significance and the conditions in which it is constituted—as well as his explicit statements in the section on the names and attributes of God (2,1–7), which expresses Halevi's early thought. Note that there is also literary evidence that this passage is autonomous and was inserted at the beginning of Part II. It is not connected with what precedes or follows it and breaks the logical chain of thought, which begins in Part I and continues in Part II, about the intrinsic superiority of the Jewish experience and all its elements: the Torah, the Jewish people, the Land of Israel, and the Hebrew language.

In the first seven sections of Part II, Halevi focuses exclusively on a reinterpretation of the various Scriptural attributes

---

In light of the above, the story at the beginning of Part II must have been the introduction to the first version. Perhaps a Karaite scholar also participated in the debate in that version. On the other hand, the story at the beginning of Part I introduces an exposition of Halevi's later thought. It seems plausible that in the first version Halevi found the traditional description, wherein the act of conversion precedes the dialogue, to be more appropriate for his purposes. In that context the dialogue would concentrate on the question of reliable exegesis of the Scriptures—another topic at the center of the Rabbanite-Karaite controversy. In the second version, however, Halevi deviated from the traditional story and made the conversion the outcome of the dialogue. This order, starting with a dialogue about the status of Judaism as a revealed religion that believes in its own significance for all mankind, is more appropriate for the theme of the later version. Proof that the original version of the story at the beginning of Part II is independent of everything that precedes it can also be found in the contradictions between the plot lines at the start of Parts I and II. These contradictions survived the revisions of the original story aimed at permitting its merger with the story at the beginning of Part I. Whereas in Part I the King, with the Rabbi's help, uncovers the intent of the angel in his dream (1,98–99 [53]), the story at the beginning of Part II makes no reference to this success, and the King attains the "God-pleasing deed" only "in the mountains of Warsan" (2,1 [66/82]). Whereas in Part I it is the angel who speaks in the dream, at the beginning of Part II there is no angel. Whereas throughout Part I the Rabbi is already serving as the King's teacher and master, the implication at the beginning of Part II is that only at this stage did the Rabbi acquire this role. See also Yaakov Levinger, *Bein shigrah le-ḥiddush* (Routine and innovation), (Jerusalem, 1973), p. 143ff.; Yochanan Silman, "Ha-pan ha-sifruti shel sefer ha-kuzari" (The literary aspect of the *Kuzari*), *Daʿat* 31–32 (1994).

and descriptions of God that will reconcile them with God's unalloyed spirituality—a spirituality for whose truth the human mind is warrant (2,1). At this stage in the evolution of Halevi's thought there is still no fundamental distinction between the Tetragrammaton—God who appears at the horizon of prophetic knowledge—and *Elohim*—the universal philosophical God known through the intellect alone. Also absent is the complementary distinction between God as He is in Himself and God as He appears at the limit of prophetic and sensory knowledge.[2] The latter distinction allows Halevi, in his later thought, to maintain a radically transcendental view of God while at the same time accepting as given the material characterizations of God as expressed in His description and attributes. On the other hand, in the earlier thought, presented in these sections, Halevi held to the Aristotelian view that God in His essence, as He is for Himself, is intellect: "We also call [God] 'wise of heart' (Job 9:4), because He is the essence of intelligence and intelligence itself" (2,2 [72/86]).[3] This definition is perfectly compatible with

---

2. This is the case despite the special status accorded to God as Tetragrammaton in the earlier thought, where its exclusive denotation is God as Prime Cause. Accordingly, "the attributes connected with the Tetragrammaton describe creations of God, produced without any natural intermediaries" (2,2 [71/85]). Perhaps we should understand in this light his gloss on Exodus 6:3: The patriarchs, because of their greatness, did not require sensible prophetic experiences in order to know God (ibid.). In his later thought he believed otherwise. Compare 4,3; 4,17; 4,27.

3. This opinion is the Fourth Principle in 5,20 [325]; the Prime Cause is the intellect itself. These principles should not be viewed as expressing Halevi's thought when he wrote Part V. The reference (in this same principle) to the necessary conclusion as to the divine significance of the formal and intellectual aspect of the one and all-encompassing reality—a conclusion he vigorously rejects in 5,21—is another indication of the profound opposition between the later thought and the Mutakallimun. Note that it is when God is identified with the intellect (5,20) that the philosophical designation of God as Prime Cause appears; this designation alludes to the internal link between the existence of God and that of the world, which is a necessary consequence, as well as to the ontological role of God as First in the total context of existence. Nevertheless (as on other issues), Halevi recognized the educational and polemic value of his earlier views even when he himself no longer held them. Similarly, despite his reservations about the views of the Mutakallimun in 5,17, he takes the time to expound their opinions (5,18) out of consideration for the King's spiritual needs.

his idea that the human intellect has the capacity to know the essence of God (even if only partially) and to resemble the Divine intellect. As we shall see in Chapter 8, the human intellect's ability to commune with and resemble the Divine intellect underlies the doctrine of the immortality of the soul in the earlier thought.

In light of the preceding we can understand Halevi's reservations about the philosophers' description of God—reservations expressed in this part only in the argument that that description is incomplete. According to Halevi, the philosophers' characterization of God is negative—"all that the philosophers have preached regarding His sublimity and holiness" (3,17 [162/155])—and requires a positive complement, namely, God as "King and Lawgiver." Thus, despite his disagreement with the Philosopher's concept of the essence of God, in Part II Halevi does not arrive at an unambiguous confrontation between "the God of Abraham and the God of Aristotle" (4,16 [247])—between God who speaks with man and God as Prime Cause (1,4 [11]). In his opinion as stated here, the relationship between the deity who is presented in experience (whether individual or historical) and the philosophers' God, who is known through speculation, resembles the relationship between complementary aspects—aspects that, in principle, can be included in the meaning of the very same prayer (3,17 [162]). Accordingly, Halevi acknowledges that even those who venerate God only as a result of their own rational efforts merit reward (3,21).[4]

We can learn about Halevi's attitude toward the philosophers' God, in Part III of the *Kuzari*, from the description of the first of the Ten Commandments. Halevi (3,11 [150/144]) lists the beginning of the First Commandment, "I am the Lord your God," with the "laws of the mind" (*al-sharī'a al-nafsānīya*)—that is, the commandments that could be deduced

---

4. Similarly, Halevi did not reject the argument that "he takes care of you because you have shown him honor" (3,21 [168/160]). In the other parts of the *Kuzari*, though, Halevi held that philosophers merit reward only for their good works (1,111; 5,14; compare 4,19).

by human reason even in the absence of revelation.⁵ Just as the Rabbi demurs at the Philosopher's description of God in §17, so here too, in §11, he adds the corollary "that God observes not only the actions and words of man but also his secret thoughts, and requites good and evil" (ibid.). It is clear that this "corollary" (*ziyāda*) expands rather than contracts: It is not meant to call into question the independent positive value of the truth, which is explicitly asserted in the first words of the First Commandment. Not only can the intellect attain adequate knowledge of the existence of God, it can convert it into a concrete religious obligation. The "corollary" merely supplements the philosophers' God with the attributes required by God's involvement in human existence.⁶

Halevi's approach to the First Commandment underlies the question he put to his friend Abraham Ibn Ezra: "Why did He say, 'I am the Lord your God Who took you out of the land of Egypt' rather than 'Who created the heaven and earth and created you'?" (Ibn Ezra, long commentary on Ex. 20:1). Like Halevi in Part III of the *Kuzari*, in his reply Ibn Ezra reiterates that he accepts the questioner's postulate that one can learn about God by contemplating the world, through reason alone. He vigorously asserts that the truth expressed in the words "I am the Lord your God" can be attained by the intellect alone, divorced from historical experience. Note, incidentally, the agreement between the views of Ibn Ezra and of Halevi, as the latter are expressed in Part III of the *Kuzari* and in his earlier thought in general. But this interpretation, with its inherent world-view, was sharply and unequivocally rejected by the later Halevi, as we shall see in Chapter 15.

---

5. See Moscato on 3,11, *incipit* והתורות הנפשיות. Compare also 2,48. In all editions of Ibn Tibbon except for Hirschfeld's, the reading is "the ethical laws, which are the philosophical laws." But the added clause is not found in the Arabic original and is probably an exegetical interpolation (perhaps by Ibn Tibbon himself).

6. In his later thought Halevi acknowledged that the intellect can know God as *elohim*; but at the same time he denies that such knowledge can have any religious significance. God as *elohim* is merely the object of scientific curiosity (4,13 [241]).

1. God's Will and the "Divine Order"[7]

If the Divine essence is located in the intellect, there can be no alteration in the sphere of the Divine reality (2,2 [68]); this invariance is a necessary expression of the identity between the intellect that perceives and the perceived object. According to the philosophical tradition, which Halevi accepted,[8] the invariance of Divine truths is linked to their status as totally intelligible and as eternally fixed by the force of logical necessity. It follows that we cannot attribute to God a will that varies in time as a function of its occasional confrontations with ephemeral entities. Halevi was thus compelled to identify the Divine Will with the Divine Order: "call it will (*'irāda*), or order (*'amra*), or what you will" (2,6 [74/87]).[9] As the context makes plain, this

---

7. [The Hebrew *ha-ʿinyan ha-'elohi*, which Ibn Tibbon used to render the Arabic *al-'amr al-'ilāhi*, is an ambiguous and multivocal term. Heinemann's rendering is "the Divine Power." Hirschfeld almost always renders it "the divine influence" (in 2,24 [94/101] he has "Divine Providence"; in 1,95 [46/65] and 3,5 [44/139] "Divine Spirit"; and in 5,21 [329/291] "Divine command"). The author believes that this leans too far in the direction of "the Divine emanation" and suggested "the Divine Order," used by Pines in the first section of his important article, "Shīʿite Terms." This has been used throughout, replacing "divine influence" in quoted passages based on Hirschfeld's English. On this key term, see further Chapter 15, §4, "The Divine Order as a Mediating Factor"—LJS.]

8. As we shall see, we can infer Halevi's opinion on this issue from the way in which human beings draw nearer to God and from the ontological significance of this rapprochement.

9. Baneth ("Halevi and al-Ghazali," p. 309, n. 3) insisted that here Halevi is identifying *will* with the logos. This can also be deduced from 2,4; compare Pines, "Shīʿite Terms," p. 178. Compare further: "the Law is the outcome of His will (*'irāda*).... His wisdom (*al-ḥikma*) did not require Him to create angels on earth" (3,17 [159/152]); "after this the divine will and His wisdom ordained ... " (5,2 [281/249]). Halevi presents this as the view of the philosophers, opposed to his own opinion (in his later thought) that God's will does "what, how, and when He desires" (ibid.). Halevi attributed the opinion that the Divine Will and wisdom are identical to the author of *Sefer Yetzirah* (4,25) as well as to the Mutakallimun, and notes that this is also the opinion of the philosophers (5,18, Axiom 9). Here too we must see the exposition of the Kalam as reflecting Halevi's recognition, in his later period, of its educational and polemic importance. In 4,3, however, Halevi vacillates as to whether to endow God with a "will" in the literal sense or only metaphorically.

Divine will is an ontological factor that is the source of the cosmic order that rules the unchanging stratum of existence, such as the fixed courses of the heavenly bodies.[10] Similarly, this will "adapted the air to giving the sound of the Ten Commandments and formed the writing engraved in the tablets" (ibid.). According to Halevi, these acts, like miraculous deeds in general, are really manifestations of the eternal fixity of the primordial Divine will: "their origin was fixed by the primordial will in the days of creation on certain conditions" (3,73 [214/196]).[11]

In the earlier thought we can distinguish the special sense given to the common and ambiguous expression "the Divine Order." It also has a particular ontological sense, as one link in the chain of Divine emanations and as the immediate source of the rational order in the totality of non-Divine existence.[12] Halevi agreed with *Sefer Yetzirah* on three points: (1) the doctrine of emanation expresses the relationship between God and non-Divine reality;[13] (2) the rational nature of this reality, as subject to a uniform and fixed order; (3) the place of the Divine Order in the chain of emanations. Evidence of this agreement is Halevi's reliance on *Sefer Yetzirah* in his discussion of the Divine Order in Part III (3,17), where his reservations about that work, which

---

10. Compare the parallel critical discussion in his later thought—Part V, §§2–7.

11. Compare 5,18 [314]. H. A. Wolfson ("Judah Hallevi on Causality and Miracles," *Meyer Waxman Jubilee Volume* [Chicago and Tel Aviv, 1966], pp. 137–153) expressed a different opinion on this question. Nevertheless, in 2,2, miracles such as the Ten Plagues, the splitting of the Red Sea, the mannah, and the pillar of cloud are described as "intentional new creations"—the way Halevi characterized miracles in his later thought.

12. See D. H. Neumark, *Toledot ha-filosofiya be-Yisrael* (History of philosophy in Israel) vol. 2 (Jerusalem, 1971), pp. 288ff.

13. As we shall see in Chapter 15, in his later thought Halevi rejected the theories of emanation propounded by both Aristotelianism and *Sefer Yetzirah*. He held then that Abraham, the author of *Sefer Yetzirah,* abandoned the theory of emanations only after he had personally experienced the manifestation of the Divine will as a concrete and unique determination, which is not an expression of any predetermined law (4,27). Abraham Ibn Ezra was another partisan of the doctrine of emanation. Neumark (*Toledot*, p. 288) compared Halevi's and Ibn Ezra's positions. The matter appears otherwise in light of the distinction between Halevi's earlier and later thought. Compare Ibn Ezra on Ps. 119:3.

crop up in the parts of the *Kuzari* that express his later thought, are absent.[14]

From the perspective of his thought as a whole, though, the image of the Deity in his earlier thought requires the assumption about the Divine emanation as a process that constitutes the bridge between God and all other existence. The Divine Order cannot itself be subdivided into levels or internal aspects; its various actual embodiments are an inevitable consequence of the differences in those that receive its influence.[15] The order emanated from the Divine Order is actualized in the eternal cosmic order of superlunar existence and is expressed in the perpetual tendency to expand this order to sublunar existence. According to *Sefer Yetzirah*, the Divine Order is "*one*, whereas the difference among its actual embodiments is based on the difference of matter" (4,25 [261/233]). Halevi agrees and believes that the Divine Order is linked to "the community fit to receive it, as a smooth mirror receives the light" (3,17 [159/152]). That is, the extent to which the emanations of the Divine Order are absorbed depends only on the fitness of the object to receive it.[16] This emanation, expressed in the Revelation at Sinai, aims to establish the kingdom of God on earth, on the model of His kingdom in heaven: "The Torah is the outcome of His will to reveal His dominion on earth, as in heaven" (ibid.).[17] The

---

14. E.g., 4,27 and, implicitly 4,17; see also 5,14.
15. See Neumark, *Toledot*, pp. 288ff.
16. Or, as we read further on, "whether some few, or a whole community, are sufficiently pure" (ibid.). The pious individual makes sure that nothing will disturb "the purity of his soul during prayer" (3,11 [154/148]), in accordance with the Philosopher's demand to "strive after purity of soul. In sum, seek purity of heart" (1,1 [10/38]). In parallel, the "building of the Tabernacle" necessarily leads to the descent of the Shekhinah (3,23). According to the later thought, however, "we find that true visions are granted to persons who do not devote themselves to study or the purification of their souls" (1,4 [12/40]). As we shall see when we turn to the later thought, a Divine address to human beings does not necessarily depend on human initiative; this can also be inferred from the King's dream at the beginning of the book; see Chapter 22, note 6.
17. From this and the following citation, Efros (*Doctrines*, p. 189) inferred that Halevi considered the Divine Order to be the giver of the Torah. Although this inference does not necessarily follow from Halevi's text, Efros's

Israelites' acceptance of the yoke of the Torah—their cleaving to the Divine order, like that of the heavenly bodies—caused an additional emanation, which produced the physical ordering of the people in the order of the spheres: "The Divine Order, however, found next to the stars and spheres none who accepted his commands and who adhered to the course He had dictated, with the exception of a few.... The Divine Order rested upon them out of love, 'in order to be a God unto them.' In the desert he arranged them in the manner of the spheres, ... as is stated in *Sefer Yetzirah*" (ibid.).

The eternal fixity of the regularity of emanations, which stems from the Divine Order, is actualized in the innate universality of its various embodiments in sublunar existence. In and of itself it has no defined orientation. Thus it is regulated only by the initiative of the variable entities to which it applies. From this broad perspective, in Halevi's early thought the Divine Order resembles the Active Intellect of the Aristotelian philosopher.[18]

---

conclusion is extremely plausible from the perspective of the system as a whole. Ibn Ezra, too, seems to have favored this opinion at times; see his commentary on Deut. 4:35. See also Joseph Bonfils's supercommentary on Ibn Ezra, *Zafenat Paneah*, on Ex. 24:5. In other places, though, Ibn Ezra expressed a different view; for example, both his short and long commentaries on Ex. 20:20 and the short commentary on Ex. 33:21. Efros inferred from the attribution of the giving of the Torah to the Divine Order that the Divine Order is not a link in the chain of emanations. He did not take into account the distinction between the early and later thought, however. As for understanding the text, see Wolfson, "Hallevi and Maimonides on Prophecy," *Jewish Quarterly Review* 33 (1942–1943): 81–82, additional notes to §2. This passage is understood in a totally different sense by Meyer Waxman, *Ketavim nivharim* (Selected writings), (New York, 1943), vol. 1, pp. 99–100; he was followed by Even-Shmuel in his Hebrew translation.

18. The Philosopher identifies the Divine "light" with the Active Intellect: "to the perfect person there adheres a light of Divine nature, called Active Intellect" (1,1 [7/37]); Halevi, too, tends to identify them. See: 1,103; 2,50; 3,17; 3,20. In his system these concepts play a similar role. They bridge between unity and multiplicity and between unchanging and changing reality. Also worthy of note is the identification of the Divine Order with the Divine will, on the one hand, and of the Divine will with Divine wisdom (in the earlier thought), on the other. This identity can perhaps be inferred also from the doctrine of the immortality of the soul in the earlier thought (to be discussed later). In his later thought, Halevi

They disagree chiefly about the borders of its influence: In Halevi's thought, the Divine Order is responsible for the hierarchy of both the superlunar and sublunar worlds; for the Philosopher, the Active Intellect is responsible only for the order of the sublunar realm. As we shall see in later chapters, appropriate human activity can lead man (the individual or the collective, in life or after death) to union with the Divine Order. Accordingly, the disagreement between the later Halevi and the Philosopher focuses only on the concrete nature of this human activity. Like the Philosopher, the earlier Halevi holds that the Divine Order's providence and intervention in the course of human events is part of its nature: "The Divine Order resembles the rain which waters an area, if the inhabitants deserve it, although perhaps some of them do not deserve it: but they profit from the consideration of the majority; on the other hand, rain is withheld from an area whose inhabitants do not deserve it, although some of them might perhaps deserve it, but they suffer with the majority. This is how God governs the world" (3,19 [163/156]).[19] According to the axioms of the philosophical tra-

---

attributed the idea that the Divine Order is identical with the Active Intellect to the philosophers (5,4). On the one hand, "the Divine Order grudges nothing"; on the other hand, "there is no niggardliness with God, who allows every one his due. Philosophers call the giver of this degree Active Intellect" (5,10 [258–259]). See Wolfson, "Hallevi and Maimonides on Prophecy," pp. 81–82. We could also infer this from the King's remark to the Philosopher that, according to the latter's opinion, the Active Intellect is identical with the Divine Order: "This proves that between the Divine Order and the soul there are secret relations that are not identical with those you mentioned, O Philosopher" (1,4 [12/40]). Note that Moses Ibn Ezra, who strongly influenced the young Halevi, championed the idea that the Active Intellect is an emanation. The two differ, however, in the details of this idea. According to Abraham Ibn Ezra, the Active Intellect is the Creator. See *Zafenat Paneaḥ* on Gen. 1:26 and Ex. 24:10 and 33:12. In his first period, Halevi too may have held that the Divine Order is the creator. For example, "The pious man derives from his veneration of the Divine Order, near to him, what the servant derives from his master who created him" (3,11 [152/146]). But this passage can be understood in another way and requires study.

19. In 3,43 [188/174], Halevi associates the existence of injustice in the world with the "all-embracing wisdom" of the Creator; by this he must be referring to general providence only. Compare 3,11. In 3,19 he speaks

dition found in the *Kuzari*, individuality and corporeality cannot be sundered. Ontologically, the very existence of the individual qua individual is based on participation in the material dimension of existence. This material aspect, which is interwoven into the existence of individuals, is responsible both for their transitory nature and their unfitness to be fully known by any intellect, including the Divine intellect.[20]

2. The Theory of Creation

With regard to the source of the world, too, Halevi's earlier thought is close to Aristotelian philosophy, for reasons associated with his theology. Although we cannot extract the details of his opinions on this question, he does not seem to have been a partisan of ex nihilo creation.[21] It is no happenstance that in Part III (3,17) this is not enumerated among the basic tenets of Judaism.[22] In Part III he relies on *Sefer Yetzirah* with no qualifications (ibid.);[23] but in Part IV, which expresses his later thought, he says that the author of *Sefer Yetzirah* believed in

---

of providence in this world only, whereas in the world to come there is also individual providence. The distinction between this world and the world to come seems to be bound up with the fact that the principle of individuation in this world is base matter. We may, however, question whether the Rabbi truly believed, like Avicenna, in the immortality of the individual intellect.

20. This also seems to have been the opinion of Abraham Ibn Ezra (short commentary on Ex. 33:12, long commentary on Ex. 33:21).

21. This is also the opinion of Abraham Ibn Ezra; see his commentary on Gen. 1:1.

22. According to Halevi, the basic tenets of Judaism are included in the benediction of redemption recited after the morning Shema. Had Halevi really wanted to include belief in ex nihilo creation as one of these basic tenets, he could have found a proof text in the phrasing of this benediction—"You are first and You are last." Note that he does not include this dogma among the other meanings of the prayer; even in the benediction for the Creator of the heavenly lights, he stresses their innate wisdom, not the act of creation.

23. Only in Part III did Halevi unhesitatingly rely on *Sefer Yetzirah*; in Part IV (4,27) and Part V (5,14) he was careful to express his reservations about that work. See also 4,17, where he expressed misgivings about that work without mentioning it by name.

primordial matter (4,25). Evidently the later Halevi's willingness to treat the problem of ex nihilo creation (1,67) and his reading of *Sefer Yetzirah*'s view of the primordial status of matter (even though the text does not require such an interpretation) stem from his earlier vacillation, which he overcame in his later thought, without denying the problems caused by this dogma. According to his later thought, these problems caused the author of *Sefer Yetzirah*, the patriarch Abraham, to deny ex nihilo creation and individual providence—but only until he attained to his vision (4,27); after that he recognized "the Divine will and creation" (4,26 [269/239]) and "that no detail of his life escaped God, that He rewarded him instantly for his piety and guided him along the best path" (4,17 [247/223]).[24] This seems to be a retroactive explanation and apologia for the mistaken beliefs he had formerly held, before his own "dream" experience.

To sum up, in his earlier thought Halevi tended to the position of Aristotelian philosophy on this issue, which stands at the heart of the problem dealt with in the *Kuzari*. The Divine essence is located in intellect; accordingly the Divine Will, too, is reduced to the intellect and is identified with the Divine Order. This idea has many far-reaching consequences for the significance of the goal of man's rapprochement with God and the ways to accomplish this. It also determines the fundamental value of human action in general, as well as the rationale for the validity of the commandments of the Torah. We shall address these issues in the chapters that follow.

---

24. In parallel, the later Halevi held that Adam recognized God as Creator and the existence of individual Providence only after Eve had been created from his rib (4,3). Similarly, the Jewish people accepted the belief that the world is "created" only after "everyone who viewed those apparitions became convinced that the matter proceeded directly from God. It is to be compared to the first act of creation" (1,91 [45/63]).

8

ANTHROPOLOGY IN THE EARLIER THOUGHT

Judah Halevi's views on the immortality of the soul constitute a striking expression of his conception of the nature of man and of the ontological common denominator of God and man. It is no accident that the Rabbi deals with this issue at greater length in Part III than elsewhere in the book, for there it is a more crucial issue, anchored in the definition of man's supreme goal as union with God. Whereas in the other parts of the *Kuzari* the Rabbi's attention to this question derives chiefly from the dread of nothingness—of which there are various manifestations in both the *Kuzari* and Halevi's poetry—in Part III there is also the special interest raised by the ontological significance of the bond between man and God.

Like the Philosopher, Halevi asserted that the proof of "the survival of the soul after the destruction of the body" is the fact that it is spiritual, "of . . . incorporeal nature like . . . the angels" (3,43 [188/174f.]). He continues: "Pay no attention to the idea that the activity of the soul is halted during sleep or illness, which submerges the mental powers, that it is subject to the vicissitudes of the body, and similar disquieting ideas."[1] This

---

1. From the relevance that the Rabbi ascribes to the items he enumerates we may infer that in this section he is referring specifically to the immortality of the rational soul. Compare what the Rabbi says:

contradicts the explicit rejection, in Part V, of the philosophers' opinion and the contention that the doctrine of the immortality of the soul cannot be based on the assumption that, ontologically, the soul is "a spiritual substance that cannot be encompassed by space and is not subject to growth and decay" (5,14 [305/271])—an assumption whose truth he doubts. Among the reasons for doubting the assumption that the soul is a "spiritual substance," Halevi enumerated the problems he had described, in Part III, as no more than "disquieting ideas" (3,43). In Part V, though, Halevi, as is his wont in his later thought, made no ontological stipulations about either the soul or God as He is in Himself. Accordingly, the Rabbi argues that the immortality of the soul is possible only as an expression of Divine omnipotence (5,14).

But in Part III Halevi (echoing the Philosopher) attempted to explain the immortality of the soul as the end of an ongoing process entirely anchored in the authentic nature of human existence—a process in which the rational soul, while emerging from the potential to the actual, constitutes itself as a timeless entity. Accordingly, the immortality of the soul in no wise contradicts the nature of the soul, as Halevi believed in his later thought; rather, it is a necessary manifestation of its ontological essence as a "spiritual substance": "When arrived at this goal, do not be concerned that you must die. Your death is only the decay of your body, whereas the soul, having reached this step, cannot descend from it or be removed" (3,53 [198/183]). Just as the stages in the process of coming closer to God express the independent nature of this activity, the zenith of this process, the union, depends exclusively on the nature of the communing

---

"Altogether, [the body] is so arranged and prepared as to become fit to receive the guidance of the rational soul, which is an independent substance, and nearly approaches the angelic" (2,26 [103]). This is also the opinion of Abraham Ibn Ezra; see his comments on the biblical verse quoted here by Halevi (Dan. 2:11). See also the Rabbi's remarks at 5,10. Compare the Rabbi's observation at 1,89 and Ibn Ezra on Gen. 1:26, *incipit* נעשה אדם (as well as the fragmentary Genesis commentary—the "First Recension"—there); on Ex. 3:15; the preface to his commentary on Ecclesiastes; and on Dan. 10:21. Baneth ("Halevi and al-Ghazali," p. 316, n. 8) surmised that this topic marks a development in Halevi's thought during the period of the book's composition.

poles; there is no need to assume any further intervention by an omnipotent Deity. The process, which concludes with the immortality of the soul, depends on appropriate knowledge. This is what Abraham Ibn Ezra, in his commentary on Ps. 49:21, wrote in Halevi's name: "Rabbi Judah Halevi . . . said, 'Man with honor will not sleep'—meaning, there is something pertaining to man that does not sleep, and the sense is that it will not lie down and die—namely, the honor of the soul. Similarly, a man who has not learned will not understand this, like the beasts."[2]

Like the Philosopher, Halevi believed that the direct significance of death is restricted to the body (4,19; 5,12); its chief meaning for the soul is its liberation from "this unclean vessel"—"the sufferings of the body" (3,20 [166/159]). Hence in Part III Halevi tended to agree with the Philosopher's view that the fact of death has no meaning for the rational soul's union with the Divine Order. Human beings who rise to the level of prophecy, that is, those whose souls are "in contact with the Divine Order" (ibid.), attain during their lifetimes the closest possible proximity to God—a closeness unsurpassed even in the World to Come.[3]

Locating the human essence in the intellect has direct consequences with regard to man's supreme goal and the ways to attain it. As we shall see, the dualistic view of man, expressed in the polarization of man into essence and "vessel"—into intellect and whatever is not intellect—underlies Halevi's conception of the autarky of individuals who have actualized their essence and achieved independence of historical circumstances. Man's supreme goal is to establish an appropriate bond between himself and the intellects. Here the Rabbi agrees, in principle, with

---

2. Note that here too Ibn Ezra was citing the view that Halevi held in his earlier period.

3. See also 3,53. On this issue we must distinguish between the Aristotelian philosopher whose thought is sketched out in Part I and the philosopher mentioned in 5,14. Avicenna and Ibn Bajja differ on this point. Sometimes Ibn Bajja stresses that the union takes place during life; in other passages he holds that it takes place after death. See A. Altmann, "Ibn Bajja on Man's Ultimate Felicity," *H. A. Wolfson Jubilee*, vól. 1 (Jerusalem, 1965), pp. 47–87.

the Philosopher. This is how we should understand what the Rabbi says about attaining the "society of angels" (3,1 [139/135]) or cleaving to the "Divine light" (ibid. [139/136]), in the particular sense that the analogous terms have in the Philosopher's doctrine (1,1; 1,87)—a sense that the Rabbi explains in Part V: "At the same time there is an allusion to the seventh day in the words: 'He rested,' 'He blessed,' 'He sanctified,' because it marked the completion of the works of nature, which had a time limit, and placed man on a par with angels, which, being spirits, are above natural impulses and not bound by time in their works. Intellect can, as we see, picture heaven and earth in one moment. This is the world of celestial life and bliss, where the soul finds ease at the moment it attains it" (5,10 [288/256]).[4] Note that the significance of this union of the soul is discussed twice in §10 of Part V: The first time, where it is a doctrine attributed to the philosophers, the poles of the union are the Active Intellect, which is "an angel below God," and "man's intellect" ([292/259]). For the human intellect, this union is "his paradise and lasting life" (ibid.) The second time, it is discussed as a doctrine that the Rabbi, expounding Psalm 104, ascribes to the Psalmist. According to this, the poles of the union are the angels, which are intellects, and human souls [288/256]. This union is exemplified by man's situation as he enters the Sabbath day, the "world of rest," which is "like the World to Come." There seem to be no fundamental differences between these two approaches to union. In both, the union occurs in consequence of the common ontological essence of the communing poles and redeems the soul from its transience and the ills to which it is prey in this world. From this vantage point, we can understand the particular emphasis placed in Part III on the importance of knowing the truth. Because this knowledge, in and of itself, is shared by the human intellect and the upper intellects, it permits their

---

4. Compare 3,5. In the later thought, however, just as the Rabbi casts doubt on the spiritual nature of the soul, he also questions the spiritual nature of the angels. See 4,3 and Moscato ad loc.; 5,21. The exegetical passage in 5,10, relating to Psalm 104, cannot be reconciled with the latter thought. But it is a parenthetical and freestanding passage, as is clear from the text itself.

ontological union: "Among the prayers of petition the first place is that of the prayer for intelligence and enlightenment to serve the Lord; for in this way man approaches God" (3,19 [165/157]). It is not by chance that it is in Part III that the Rabbi enumerates the Principles of Faith, the "articles of faith which resume Jewish belief" (3,17 [160/154]), stressing that "whoever pronounces all this context with pure intention is a true Israelite and may hope to obtain that contact with the Divine Order, which is exclusively connected with the Israelite among all nations" (ibid.). That is, union with the Divine Order depends on an appropriate attitude toward the basic articles of faith. Similarly, in Part III Halevi lists sins of thought among those for which one should entreat forgiveness (3,19). Accordingly he prefers the Karaites to the Sadducees and Boethusians, who denied the tenets of faith and were heretics. This is not the case with the Karaites, who, whatever their deficiencies, "interpret the roots with their intellect" (3,65 [204/188]).[5] But in his later thought, where Halevi emphasized the importance of meticulous observance of the letter of the commandments, he brands the Karaites, too, as "heretics" (1,1).

This definition of man's goal—shared by the Rabbi of Part III and the Philosopher—explains the correspondence between the degree of philosophers like Socrates and the degree of the prophets or disciples of prophets (3,1). Both aim at the same goal: actualizing the inherent potential of the human soul, which is the intellect.

In Halevi's earlier thought, the rapprochement with God, in its various aspects, is associated with locating the meaning of the Deity in the web of necessary ontological relationships. This

---

5. Although in 3,49 Halevi points out the danger that Karaism may lead to heresy, he does not base this on nonobservance of the commandments, but on the potential danger to the unity of the Jewish people. See also D. Z. Baneth, "La-otografim shel Yehudah Halevi u-le-hithavvut shel sefer ha-kuzari" (Judah Halevi's autographs and the development of the *Kuzari*), *Tarbiẓ* 26 (1957): n. 7. Hence we can understand the importance of the intention to observe the commandments, even if the intention is not actualized. See 3,36 [169].

legitimizes speculative thinking as a method through which one can know God. In the discussion of the ontological common denominator of God and man, however, man's rapprochement with God in the realm of knowledge has ontological significance, in that it expresses the basic ontological bond between Divine existence and the formal aspect of non-Divine existence. In addition to the epistemological rapprochement with God, there is also a rapprochement in the realm of human action, on the ontological plane. The goal of action is to unite with the Divine Order. Similarly, the inherent redemptive significance of man's link to God—the possibility of being redeemed from human transience—is bound up with a process that has defined stages and takes place on the ontological plane shared by the human intellect and God. The core of the later development in Halevi's thought is the replacement of the ontological assumptions that permit an interrelationship between God and man with empirical facts that embody and presentify it.

9

THE HISTORICAL DIMENSION IN THE EARLIER THOUGHT

Halevi's earlier thought about history is strongly influenced by its location of the essence and goal of the individual human being on the intellectual plane. Initially he still agreed with the Aristotelian philosopher about the link between the individual and the collective. Like the Philosopher, he believed that individuals who had attained their supreme goal, such as Enoch and the prophet Elijah, should divorce themselves from human society and turn exclusively to the "society of angels" (3,1), because their participation in that realm can satisfy even their need for social life.[1] Like the Philosopher, Halevi in his earlier thought identified the angels with the divine intellects.[2] In this spirit, the Rabbi argues that individuals' prayers are accepted even if they

---

1. This is also the view of Abraham Ibn Ezra (commentary on Ps. 21:2; see also his commentary on Ps. 73:24 and *Yesod Mora* 7). Ibn Ezra, too, believed that Enoch "accustomed" his soul "to be in the company of the angels during his lifetime" (First Recension on Gen. 4:22; see also Ps. 49:16 and Deut. 32:39). For his opinion that the disciples of the prophets must lead a life of seclusion, see the end of the long commentary on Ex. 3:15.
2. Hence there is a fundamental difference between his earlier and later thought concerning the elite's attitude toward death. Compare 1,107–108, which expresses his later thought, with 3,1, which reflects the earlier thought.

do not participate in communal prayer, because their status before the Lord is on a par with that of the community at prayer (3,17).[3] These individuals are not subject to historical circumstances; they have the capacity to change them and permit their contemporaries to attain the prophetic degree even when the other conditions for this are lacking. During their lives they attain the degree of "worthy abode" for the Shekhinah and have the status of the Holy Temple: "their very existence helped their contemporaries gain the degree of prophecy" (3,65 [202/186]).[4]

Despite Halevi's agreement in principle with the Philosopher, he was unwilling to accord this position any actual significance for his contemporaries. Unlike the Philosopher, he believed that no one in his generation could attain the level of the elite and actualize the human goal in full—whether in the form of the perfect philosopher, like Socrates, or of the prophet or disciple of the prophets (3,1 [140/136]). In his opinion, in his era an individual who eschews human society "can count only on pain of soul and body" (ibid.). Furthermore, in his day and age one who prays must participate in public prayer (3,17; 3,19). This clear distinction between various historical periods acknowledges the existence of historical process and recognizes the importance of the nature of the human collective shaped by this process. The individual's spiritual evolution and the limits of that

---

3. The Rabbi emphasizes that "God commanded the building of the Tabernacle, and the whole people obeyed... and the necessary result was that the Shekhinah dwelled among them" (3,23 [170/162]).

4. Compare: "He who occupies such a degree has a right to be styled 'a man of God'" (4,3 [224/205]). Nachmanides refers to this view of Halevi's in his commentary on Deut. 11:22 (Lisbon edition); see also his commentary on Lev. 18:4. The idea is developed by Moses Hayyim Luzzatto in the *Paths of the Just*, Chapter 26, where it is explicitly linked to the idea that cleaving to God is also expressed in material deeds. This latter idea appears in the *Kuzari* in connection with the characterization of the pious man (3,11); see Chapter 16, note 9. For later avatars of this idea that the cleaving to God is manifested also in the "service of God in physical means," see Gershom Scholem, *The Messianic Idea in Judaism* (New York, 1971), pp. 203–227. On the other hand, in Part I of the *Kuzari*, §103 [57/74], conversing with a prophet does lead to "spiritualization," but the cleaving is only to "meekness and purity."

evolution depend on the unique guise assumed by the human collective at a particular point in history—and the Philosopher, too, is subject to this dependence. Needless to say, this view, which represents the first stage in a reevaluation of historical reality, is quite incompatible with the Philosopher's view of the autonomy and autarky of the intellect, which Halevi continued to accept. Nor is it compatible with his view, mentioned previously, that certain individuals, who are "abodes for the Shekhinah," have the capacity to replace the Holy Temple and enable their contemporaries to attain prophecy. But it is compatible with Halevi's view (here he differs with the Philosopher) that one must follow a fixed and defined way of life in order to draw closer to God—a way of life that of course depends, in part, on historical circumstances.

The figure of the pious man and his beliefs, in Part III, reflect the anti-Aristotelian trends in Halevi's ideas about history even in his earlier thought. The individual's dependence on the collective is conspicuous in his definition of piety as the highest spiritual level that can be attained and practiced in the present. The pious are involved in the life of society: in the life of their people, their society, and their families.[5] This involvement may originate in their spiritual requirements and natural inclinations, such as the need for family life, economic comfort, and helping the poor (3,1); or it may be imposed upon them by external circumstances, such as keeping company with children, women, or evil persons (3,5). Finally, this involvement may be rooted in the commands of the Torah itself: The injunction to circumcise a child must be fulfilled in a large congregation (3,8).

Not only do pious individuals require the community for prayer; prayer itself opens them up to the needs and problems

---

5. By contrast, R. Baḥya Ibn Paquda (*Duties of the Heart*, trans. M. Hyamson [Jerusalem, 1962], §9) characterized the pious man as one who leads an ascetic life. See also Joseph Dan, *Sifrut ha-musar ve-ha-darush* (Ethical and homiletic literature), (Jerusalem 1975), pp. 52–57; Eliezer Schweid, "Derekh ha-teshuvah" (The path of repentance), *Daʿat* 1 (Winter 1978); A. Lazaroff, "Bahaya's Asceticism Against Its Rabbinic and Islamic Background," *Journal of Jewish Studies* 21 (1970).

of the collective. Pious individuals pray, first and foremost, for the benefit of the collective, and for themselves only as part of the collective (3,17; 3,19). They see their relationship "to the commonwealth as the relation of the single limb to the body: should the arm, in a case where bleeding is required, refuse its blood, the whole body, the arm included, would perish; it is, therefore, the duty of the individual to bear hardships, or even death, for the sake of the commonwealth" (3,19 [164/157]). The pious individual's involvement in the life of the collective is not only an a posteriori dependence, but also an expression of his recognition of the absolute value of the existence and well-being of the collective, as opposed to the merely relative value of the existence of the individual—including the pious man himself.[6] Halevi accused the Karaites, unlike the pious man, of a sectarian factionalism liable to destroy the unity of the Jewish people. In his view, it is in the nature of heresy to lead to "the corruption of the nation and its abandonment of the pale of 'one law and one regulation'" (3,49 [191/177]).[7]

Not only are pious individuals involved in the life of the Jewish people in the present; they also see themselves as linked to its past and future. In their prayers they imagine the main events of the past (3,5); they find the meaning of and justification for the present lot of the people in the future (3,11). Even though pious individuals are far from philosophical equanimity about the concrete situation of the Jewish people in exile, they

---

6. We must distinguish between two degrees of the pious: First are the pious individuals (of the past and future) who are included with the prophets in the degree of the "purest essence (*al-'awaliyya*)" (2,44 [105/111]). This level is described as close to prophecy. Pious individuals of this degree enjoy some form of Divine inspiration (1,115; 2,14; 3,19). The second level of the pious individual is represented by the worshipper of the Lord (in Halevi's present) who is meticulous in the observance of the Torah commandments (Arabic *al-khayyir*). Halevi is referring to pious individuals of this second degree in the first sections of Part III. In §19, however, he is referring to the degree of the pious individual in the Messianic Age, that is, to the pious individual of the first degree (the Arabic is correspondingly *w'al-awaliyya*). Efros (*Doctrines*, p. 193) failed to distinguish between these two levels of piety.

do not attempt to change this situation through action. Despite being in exile, they know spiritual tranquility and live "a happy life" (3,12 [156/150]). Trusting in the promised future of their people, they "find no difficulty in picturing our restitution, though only one of us may have remained" (3,11 [156/150]).[8]

The pious individual's attitude toward historical reality stems from a twofold recognition of the fateful significance of the direction of the historical continuum: (1) Historical periods are qualitatively different, and this difference cannot be ignored; and (2) the successive epochs are linked as stages in a single process. This view of the historical continuum parallels the pious individual's characteristic awareness of time. The pious individual's life is marked by perpetual readiness—by his awareness of particular place in the temporal continuum. The importance of the latter stems from a qualitative perception of time.[9] The various moments of time are distinguished from one another by their own intrinsic qualities. The pious man prepares and directs his way of life in accordance with these distinctions. The time for prayer "constitutes the maturity and essence of time.... And just as these three times of daily prayer are the 'fruit' of his day and night, so is the Sabbath the 'fruit' of the week, because it is appointed to establish the connection with the Divine Order" (3,5 [144/139]).

7. Compare 3,10 and 3,39.
8. See also 2,32.
9. There is a parallel between the qualitative grasp of time and the qualitative grasp of place; see 1,79; 2,18–20; 4,7–9. In the Philosopher's doctrine, however, the temporal continuum has no significance. For the intellect, "the deduction of the conclusion is not dependent on time, since reason itself is above time" (5,12 [299/265]).

10

THE JEWISH PEOPLE, THEIR COMMANDMENTS, AND THEIR UNIQUENESS IN THE EARLIER THOUGHT

1. The Validity of the Torah Commandments

The essential distinction between knowing God in the context of ontological relationships and speculative thought as opposed to knowing Him as present in human experience has various implications for Halevi's thought. In his later thought (1,11–43) he held that the world-view of the adherents of the other revealed religions, namely, that God can be effectively known through reason alone, restricts the significance of revelation and limits its role to strengthening the bond between man and God instead of making a substantial change in man's theoretical knowledge of the deity. Revelation merely elucidates and expands the intellectual knowledge of God. In consequence, the meaning of God and the obligation to worship Him cannot be tied to the experience of revelation. This view, which Halevi attributed to Christianity and Islam in his later thought, was also that of his earlier thought.

In principle, the heuristic and theoretical elements of revelation can be separated from its other components. The fact that God revealed Himself to persons of a particular origin and spoke in a particular language at a particular place is secondary to the content of the revelation. From this follows the universality of Christianity and Islam—a universality stressed in the speeches of the Christian and Muslim scholars as well as by the Rabbi. Responding to the Rabbi's first speech, the King summarizes the position of the representative of those religions and contends that the Rabbi "should ... have said that you believe in the Creator of the world, its Governor and Guide, who created and keeps you, and such attributes which serve as evidence *for every believer,* and for the sake of which he pursues justice in order to resemble the Creator in His wisdom and justice" (1,12 [17/45]). Here, as in many other passages, the King is expressing Halevi's earlier view and stressing that the obligation to act is anchored in ontological relationships. The purpose of action is to resemble the Creator. This resemblance, when realized, has an objective value for every human being. The Rabbi acknowledges as much: "If the Torah were binding on us only because God created us, the white and the black man would be equally bound, since He created them all" (1,27 [21/47]). Thus, according to Halevi's earlier thought, the pious man yearns for the times of prayer, when "he becomes like the spiritual beings and is removed from the animal ones" (3,5 [144/139]). Similarly, on the Day of Atonement, the pious man is brought "near the angels" (ibid. [146/141]). So too, "man prays to be brought near to his Master" (3,19 [165/157]) through intelligence and enlightenment. It seems, then, that in Part III the Rabbi agrees, in principle, with the view that human deeds "are but means and instruments to attain spiritual rank" (3,65 [207/190]).[1]

---

1. There is no reason to assume that, for Halevi, Elisha ben Abuya's opinions depended on his singular experience; namely, that he had "ascended above human intelligence" (3,65 [207/190]). Only his error—thinking that he had attained this level, when he had really only gazed upon it—can be attributed to the influence of this experience. Compare Ibn Ezra on Deut. 32:39 and *Zafenat Paneah* ad loc. We should also compare this view of the intellects with the description of prophetic revelation in the later thought (4,5). See also Chapter 21, §3 "The Later Thought and the Dialogue Between God and Man."

Now we can understand why, in Part III, the Rabbi has no doubts about the relevance of revelation for those who did not experience it, nor second thoughts about the possibility of extracting the meaning of the revelation from its concrete sensory appearance. These problems arise, as we have seen, from the idea that the experience of revelation is an integrated whole, a position that Halevi did not yet advocate when he wrote Part III.

Just as the meaning of God's essence and the way to know Him are rooted in ontological relations, so too the process whereby human beings draw nearer to and increasingly resemble their God occurs on the same plane. This process of remaking oneself depends upon intentional human action—scrupulous observance of the Torah commandments, whose validity is grounded in this role. True, such meticulous observance depends, in general, on prior knowledge, and human beings can acquire this knowledge only through Divine Revelation (3,23; 3,49; 3,53). Still, this didactic need for Divine Revelation does not undermine the independent ontological status of observance of the Torah commandments as a self-motivated means to resemble God. Accordingly, in Part III the Rabbi asserts that the validity of the commandments is based on the objective relations between matter and form: "Religious ceremonies are, like the work of nature, entirely determined by God and beyond human power" (3,53 [196/181]). Following this line of thought, we should see observance of the commandments as a necessary and sufficient condition for advancing the process whereby human beings come to resemble their God.[2] This conception of the commandments allows Halevi to give a reason for observing

---

2. See also 3,7; 3,23; 3,49. Nevertheless, in 3,5 and 3,11 we find that the pious individual considers the commandments to be imperatives. Evidently we must not identify Halevi's early thought with the world-view of the pious man. Even though in Part III Divine providence is characterized as exclusively collective, the pious man believes in individual providence. In the passage on the creation of the world, the pious man subscribes to the Kalam notion that God is perpetually renewing the acts of creation (3,11); in the later thought, however, this view is ascribed to the "masses" (5,20). Furthermore (as we shall see on other central topics), certain of the pious man's opinions herald Halevi's later thought, where he returned to some traditional views.

them that avoids reliance on the will of God Who makes demands of human beings (concrete individuals)—a will whose existence Halevi denied in his earlier thought. The Torah commandments are not imperatives expressing the will of the Lord, but merely guidelines; God is not viewed as a deity who commands, but as a source of knowledge. In the overall context of Halevi's thought, the Rabbi's views concerning the essence of God, the ontological nature of the rapprochement to God, and the exclusively didactic and epistemological significance of revelation for the commandments are interwoven.

This interweaving, typical of Halevi's earlier thought, also surfaces in Part I, §§68–79, where it is accompanied by formal and literary indications that set these sections off from the rest of Part I, which reflects only Halevi's later thought. Section 68 begins: "The King: Thus far I find these arguments quite satisfactory. Should we continue our conversation, I will trouble you to adduce more decisive proofs. Now take up the thread of your earlier exposition" [32/54]. Section 80 begins, "Let us now return to our subject" [37/57], and continues §§1–67.

In addition to the formal and literary indications, there are important differences of content between the two groups of sections. These are particularly conspicuous if we compare the interrelated themes common to both groups, which include the reciprocal relations between God and human beings and the proofs that such a relationship exists. In §§1–67 this relationship is presented as unique, as a dialogue between God and human beings; the proofs offered for its existence do not depend on prior ontological assumptions. By contrast, in §§68–79 the two-way relationship is described as an intrinsic part of the fabric of ontological relations between form and matter. Similarly, the discussion of the relationship between human beings and God in §§77–79 is anchored in the same Aristotelian principles on which the relationship between God and non-Divine existence in general, discussed in the previous sections (68–77), is based.

According to §§68–79, communion with the deity emerges in the world through the general laws that determine how and to what extent matter "accepts" form. The Rabbi sums up the discussion as follows: "Do not deem it improbable for exalted traces of the Divine to be rendered visible in the lower world, when [low] matter is prepared to receive them. Herein lies the root of belief and unbelief" (1,77 [35/56]). Thus the principle that explains the communion between God and non-Divine existence is associated with the constitution of an appropriate material system: When matter is ready to accept form, form necessarily applies to it. The Rabbi hints, in the last sentence, that this general principle also has direct implications for any human initiative aimed at constituting an appropriate relationship with God. This arouses the King's astonishment: "How can the root of belief be also the root of unbelief?" (1,78 [35/56]). In response, the Rabbi explains the significance of this principle: "Belief" and "unbelief" have a single root in the sense that both derive from the same assumption; namely, that human initiative can shape matter in such a way that the Divine form will apply to it. The difference—what distinguishes "belief" from "unbelief"—stems from the fact that those who "believe" adopt the correct means for shaping matter so that the Divine form will apply to it: They observe the Torah commandments in all their details and particulars. "Unbelievers," by contrast, do not adopt the means that can shape matter and prepare it to accept the Divine form.

The reliable source of knowledge of the means—the commandments—is Divine revelation. Believers require Divine revelation to learn the appropriate means for shaping matter; whereas unbelievers endeavor to acquire these means in other ways. Of course, some unbelievers just happen to succeed (ibid.).[3] This follows from the axioms inherent in this line of thought. If the validity of the commandments is not anchored in revelation, but in their intrinsic benefit as means that function on their own, then adopting the appropriate means in and of itself guarantees the consequences. Accordingly, revelation serves only as a source of information about the proper way to observe the command-

---

3. Similarly, Halevi believed that human beings have the capacity to create certain animals as the result "of experiments," without knowing "their calculation and agency" (3,23 [171/163]; see also 3,53).

ments. Halevi notes, however, that it is not wise to rely on chance for acquiring knowledge of the appropriate means (ibid.). One should instead rely on God as the source of knowledge, as one relies on the directives of the "physician" who himself "prepared the medicines and explained the proper manner in which they were to be administered" (3,79 [37/57]).

2. Israel as the Chosen People

As we have seen already, if the validity of the commandments does not derive from the intentional Divine appeal embodied in revelation, there is no place for the assertion, typical of the later thought, that the Jewish people are unique because they alone are enjoined to observe the commandments and they alone can observe them with the special merit of acting out of obedience. In the earlier thought, in fact, the Jewish people's superiority to other nations is located exclusively on the plane of their practical way of life. According to Halevi in Part III, the Jewish people's excellence is manifested in their special care to observe the commandments to the letter. This meticulousness cannot be achieved by the nations: "It is just so with other imitations: no people succeeded in equalling us" (3,9 [148/142]). This failure of the nations is not due to a hierarchy of human degrees that are distinguished "in their essences" (1,39 [22/48]).[4] In Part III, it is explained by the nations' contempt for tradition rooted in revelation, which is the exclusive source for comprehensive and complete knowledge of the Torah commandments: "Speculation and reasoning about the Law do not lead to what pleases God. . . . We have, however, said that one cannot approach God except by His commands. For he knows their comprehensiveness, division, times, and places, and consequences . . . " (3,23 [169/162]).[5]

---

4. Note that even when Halevi, in his later thought, divided humanity into rational beings and prophets, he still held that rational beings, by virtue of their nature, can work improvements in earthly activity (1,35).

5. See also 3,21; 3,37; 3,53; 4,9; 4,11; 4,13; 5,20, Fourth Principle. Note that in 3,7 the Rabbi alludes to the parable of the physician's surgery (1,79), found in that portion of Part I (§§68–79) which, as we have seen,

It is no accident that the idea that no action whatsoever, including conversion, can totally abrogate the distinction between Jew and non-Jew is not found in Part III of the *Kuzari*. This notion is compatible only with Halevi's later view that the commandments are imperatives incumbent only on those enjoined to observe them. The later thought resolves the problems associated with the need to explain and justify the exclusive reference of the Divine imperatives to the Jews and to ensure the perpetuation of this exclusivity in the future. It is precisely in the light of the link between the validity of the commandments and the unanticipated determination of the Divine Will, as expressed in His imperatives-commandments, that the vital need for this guarantee can be understood. This guarantee is crucial also for the dispute between Judaism and the other monotheistic religions, which assert that the commandments are no longer in force. By contrast, in Part III, where the commandments are presented as guidelines anchored in a set of eternal objective relations, there is no need to ensure the eternal validity of the commandments, just as there is no need to explain and justify the superiority of the Jewish people over other nations, because it is already explained by their way of life.

In light of the distinction between Part III and the rest of the *Kuzari*, it is interesting to compare the discussion of the superiority of the Jewish people in 3,17 with the parallel discussion in 1,95. In Part I, Halevi tied this superiority exclusively to a heredity transmitted from Adam—the human being whose firstness includes his "unconditional" perfection—and to the uniqueness of the Jewish people. In Part III, by contrast, this excellence is presented as a particular application of the general principle that determines the conditions in which the "divine

---

expresses his earlier thought. Accordingly, the assumption that the commandments are like "medicines" that work by virtue of eternal law leads to the conclusion that even an ignorant man can provide benefit through chance. This can explain the emergence of new religions. Compare 3,23 and 3,53. Note also that in 3,23 [171/162] the Rabbi alludes in his words, "I gave you the example of the creation of the plant and animal," to 1,77. See Moscato on 3,23, *incipit* שעורם ומשקלם.

light" or Divine Order rests on human beings (and matter in general). Accordingly, in Part I this superiority (even if only potential superiority) has nothing to do with the concrete destiny of human beings or the lifestyle they actually follow; it depends exclusively on the individual's or the collective's affiliation with the chain that carries the appropriate heredity. In Part III, however, it is possible (at least in principle) to join the elite congregation, because "whenever some few, or a whole community, are sufficiently pure, the Divine light rests on them and guides them in an incomprehensible and miraculous manner that is quite outside the ordinary course of the natural world. This is called 'Love and joy.' The Divine Order, however, found next to the stars and spheres none who accepted his commands and who adhered to the course He had dictated, with the exception of a few between Adam and Jacob, who then became a people" (3,17 [159/153]). This piety itself is merely an expression of readiness to accept the comprehensive and eternal Divine Order: "in order to establish His dominion on earth; as it is in heaven" (ibid./152).[6] According to Halevi in Part III, success—whether of the individual or a people—in attaining "purity of the soul" does not depend on a special Divine initiative, but only on "favorable or unfavorable influences" (ibid./153).

---

6. Here Halevi explicitly bases his view on *Sefer Yetzirah*. We should note that in 4,27 [269/239] Halevi expresses reservations about the world-view of *Sefer Yetzirah* (see also 5,14). There he suggested that the book states the views of the patriarch Abraham after "divine power and unity dawned upon him" but before "the revelation accorded to him." In that period Abraham was still inclined to follow astrology and "other doubtful studies of nature" (ibid.). *Sefer Yetzirah* reflects this inclination and emphasizes the need for "the letters H W J or an angel or a sphere or other things" (4,26 [269/239]). Note that according to Halevi the world-view of the author of *Sefer Yetzirah* is close to that of the Philosopher; hence the Rabbi describes *Sefer Yetzirah* as one of the "relics of the natural science" (4,24 [253/228]). Compare 1,63; see also 4,27; 5,14. However, after "the Lord of the universe revealed Himself to him, called him His friend and made a covenant with him" (4,27 [270/240]), Abraham recognized the willful God Who addressed him. Recognition of God Who takes an interest in a unique individual comes precisely in the personal experience of a "vision." Hence Part III, in which Halevi unreservedly relies upon *Sefer Yetzirah*, must be earlier than the sections where he expresses reservations about the views of its author.

In 3,17 the Rabbi—like the Philosopher—does not recognize the existence (in the sublunar sphere) of a level of being superior to man, the "rational being." He does not distinguish, as he does in Part I, the first man, who was "son of God" (1,95 [47/65]), and those "who were like him" from others who by comparison are merely a "husk" (ibid.). Accordingly, neither does he distinguish between the intrinsic potential of the degree above that of rational beings and the intrinsic potential of rational beings. In this spirit the Rabbi proceeds to enumerate, in §17, the main tenets of Judaism; he notes: "Whoever pronounces all this context with pure attention is a true [Arabic *haqiqa*] Israelite, and may hope to obtain that contact with the Divine Order which is exclusively connected with the Israelite among all nations" (ibid. [160/154]).[7]

To sum up, in Halevi's earlier thought the election of Israel and the obligatory nature of the commandments is anchored in theology and anthropology. The earlier thought understands the Divine Will in a way that makes it impossible to see the Torah commandments as imperatives and reduces them to mere guidelines. Hence it cannot view the Jewish people as unique because they alone observe the commandments as a matter of obedience.

---

7. We should understand the end of this sentence in the manner of *Oẓar Neḥmad* (ad loc.), *incipit* מבלעדי שאר אומות עכו"ם, and not in the manner of Moscato, who has a clearly harmonizing bent here. That is, in this sentence the Rabbi is arguing that "a true Israelite" (perhaps "an Israelite in his essence" would be a better translation; see Efros, *Terms,* pp. 19, 51–52) is one who accepts certain tenets of faith on the basis of clear knowledge. The Rabbi goes on to make it plain that it is by virtue of this faith that he is a complete Israelite and the "Divine Order" that rests only on the Jews rests on him. This may also be how we should understand the Rabbi's words: "the truly righteous, who are the most select, namely, Israel" (3,73 [213/196]). However, in 3,73 the main trend is to reconcile with common sense, to the extent possible, various legendary traditions that a critical approach dismisses as implausible. Hence this view should not be seen as representing Halevi's own position. In any case, nowhere in the *Kuzari* does Halevi state that righteousness is the exclusive province of the Jews, excluding sincere converts.

Sometimes Halevi enumerated five levels in sublunar existence; like the Philosopher, he believed that the level of "rational beings" is the highest among these. He reached the number five by dividing the animals into two groups, marine and terrestrial, "those with fully developed senses and wonderful instincts" (4,3 [230/209]). Compare 5,10.

The absence of any Divine volitional intention toward human existence, which by its very essence is constantly changing, rules out seeing the election of the Jewish people as the result of a voluntary Divine act that determined once and for all the status of the Jewish people—the collective personality of the Jewish people throughout the generations—as the chosen people.

In the earlier thought the election of Israel is necessarily based on the order that emerges from human existence itself—an order that depends on observance of the commandments. This explanation of the election of the Jewish people depends on the importance ascribed to human action. But another aspect of Halevi's earlier anthropology, namely, the location of the human essence in the intellect, is totally incompatible with the crucial importance accorded to human action, even though it is compatible both with the belief that the highest human level finds expression in the actualization of intellectual potential and with the refusal to base the election of the Jews on some peculiar spiritual capacity (separate from intellect) inherent in their collective personality. This internal tension is one of the factors that led to new departures in Halevi's thought.

11

ERETZ ISRAEL AS THE CHOSEN LAND

One manifestation of Halevi's earlier thought about history is his opinion about the significance of Eretz Israel, the Land of Israel, for the Jewish people, with its practical corollaries. Many have noted the development in Halevi's tie to Eretz Israel: from a post factum acceptance of life in exile in the present to a call for emigration to Eretz Israel (*aliya*) and personally putting this doctrine into practice. Most of their proofs are drawn from his poetry.[1] We can provide added support for this thesis from a

---

1. Y. Baer, "Ha-maẓẓav ha-politi shel yehudei sefarad be-doro shel R. Yehudah Halevi" (The political situation of the Jews of Spain in the generation of R. Judah Halevi), *Ziyyon* 19 (1936): 22–23; idem, *A History of the Jews in Christian Spain*, vol. 1 (Philadelphia, 1961), pp. 68–76; H. Schirmann, *Toledot ha-shirah ve-ha-dramah ha-ʿivrit* (History of Hebrew poetry and drama), vol. 1 (Jerusalem, 1979), p. 293; A. Komem, "Bein shirah li-nevuah" (Poetry and prophecy), *Molad* 25 (1969): pp. 676–697; Salo W. Baron, "Yehuda Halevi, an Answer to an Historic Challenge," *Jewish Social Studies* 3 (1941): 255. Shraga Abramson ("Mikhtav R. Yehudah Halevi ʿal ʿaliyato le-ereẓ Yisrael" [A letter by R. Judah Halevi on his aliya to Eretz Israel], *Qiryat Sefer* 29 (1953–1954): 133–144) and Heinemann ("Philosopher-Poet," pp. 200–219) noted the parallel in his poetry between praise of Eretz Israel and deprecation of Greek wisdom. This parallel can be understood when we view the evolution of his attitude toward Eretz Israel in the context of his thought as a whole,

comparison of Halevi's earlier and later thought.[2] It may seem strange that in Part III, which is chiefly an anti-Karaite tract, Halevi refrained from explicitly dealing with one of the central themes of the Rabbanite-Karaite dispute—the bond between the Jewish people and Eretz Israel in the present—a topic that is addressed in the other parts. However, from his remarks on theodicy (3,11) we can understand that this silence is a consequence of his acceptance, in principle, of life in the Exile in the present. Hence we must see his remarks about living in exile as an indirect response to the Karaite's criticism of the Rabbanites for failing to mourn the destruction of Zion as they should and for not advocating emigration to Eretz Israel.[3] The King, summarizing the Rabbi's earlier statements, reaches the unequivocal conclusion that "such a man will live a happy life even in exile and gather the fruit of his faith in this world and the next. *He, however, who bears the exile unwillingly, almost loses his rewards in both worlds*" (3,12 [156/150]).[4] Not only did Halevi agree with the King, he developed the idea and contended that the sense of joy (derived from the commandment to recite a blessing over

---

distinguishing between its earlier and later strata. As noted, only in the later thought do the contrasts between Halevi's own view and Greek-Aristotelian philosophy become particularly acute.

2. Note that the common denominator of his poetry and the *Kuzari*, with regard to the development of his thought on the topic in question, can serve as a starting point for a future chronological description of the development of Halevi's thought throughout the *Kuzari*.

3. *Sefer Hayishuv*, ed. S. Assaf and L. A. Mayer (Jerusalem, 1944), vol. 2, pp. liii, 43–44; S. Assaf, *Tequfat ha-Ge'onim ve-sifrutah* (The Gaonic period and its literature), (Jerusalem, 1955), pp. 80–81; H. H. Ben-Sasson, "Demutah shel ʿadat ha-shoshanim ha-qara'it bi-yerushalayim" (A portrait of the Kara'ite community "Adat Hashoshanim" in Jerusalem), *Shalem* 2 (1976): 1–18.

4. Compare also Halevi's poem ים סוף וסיני למדוני (Brody, 4:212). In this poem Halevi is willing to give up life in Eretz Israel and settle for God's "society" and love. This line contradicts his later thought, in which he stressed that full observance of the Torah commandments is possible only in Eretz Israel. This is not only because of the fundamental importance of the commandments relating to the land as a condition for active prophecy (2,12; 2,14), but also because even the commandments that do not relate to the land can be perfectly observed only there (5,23).

both good and ill) perpetuates and strengthens the joy itself (3,13–15).⁵

Of course acceptance of life in the Exile is at odds with Halevi's later view that this very acquiescence prolongs the exilic era (2,24), whereas rebelling against exile and emigrating to Eretz Israel bring the redemption closer (5,27).⁶ Similarly, in Part III prophecy is associated, first and foremost, with living in a period when the Temple exists and its rituals are conducted as prescribed, and not necessarily with living in Eretz Israel.⁷ The emphasis is on the importance of actual participation in the Temple ritual (3,53 [195]) or on life in close proximity to the Temple (3,21 [169]), not on life in Eretz Israel per se, even when the Temple is standing. In consequence, no particular value attaches to living in Eretz Israel in the present, when the Temple is in ruins.⁸ By contrast, in his later thought Halevi believed that prophecy depends on living in Eretz Israel. He

---

5. The assumption that contemplation has the power to determine the meaning of events sits well with Halevi's earlier anthropology of the sovereign autarky of the human intellect. In his later thought, however, he did an about-face: Contemplation itself depends on the conditions of the milieu (5,23). This dependence reflects the essential dependency of the soul (and of the intellect) on the body (2,10), which is typical of the later thought.

6. This idea is also expressed in his poetry. See B.-Z. Dinur (Dinaburg), *Be-ma'avaq ha-dorot* (The struggle of the generations), (Jerusalem, 1975), pp. 214–217.

7. See also 3,39; 3,65; 3,73. However, particularly favored individuals who have attained the status of serving as an "abode of the Shekhinah" can attain prophecy and bring their contemporaries to prophecy, even in the absence of the Temple ritual (3,65). This is why the pious man aspires to attain prophecy even in exile (3,23 [169]). See also Moscato (ad loc.), *incipit* כל שכן עם המצא השכינה. Hence we should probably understand the expression "while no open vision exists (1 Sam. 3:1)" (3,1) as denying the widespread existence of prophecy in the present age, but not as totally ruling out the *possibility* of prophecy. Similarly, as we have already seen, those who have established intercourse with the world of spiritual entities are exempt from observing the commandments.

8. This view was held by those of Halevi's acquaintances who opposed his decision to emigrate to Eretz Israel. See his poem דבריך במור עובר רקוחים (Brody, 2:164). See also 5,22. In this section, as noted, the King is expressing Halevi's earlier view.

stresses the importance of the material, geographic, and climatic properties of the Holy Land, which are independent of the historical situation. This endows life in Eretz Israel with unconditional importance even when the Temple is in ruins (2,8–24). Accordingly, Halevi believes that although most of the Jews remained outside Eretz Israel, prophecy was attained (in Eretz Israel) during the Second Temple period, albeit to a limited extent (2,24).[9] Similarly, the Rabbi's decision to emigrate to Eretz Israel is interwoven with an emphasis on the importance of the dust and stones of the Holy Land (5,27 [334]).[10]

In the light of what we have already said about Halevi's earlier anthropology, including historical reality, we can propose internal reasons for the development of his thought on this matter.[11] The notion of the absolute superiority of Eretz Israel, as the only land where prophecy can be attained, and the concomitant idea of the election of the Jewish people, based on the assumption that only Jews can be prophets—which are a keynote of his later thought—are not found in his earlier anthropology. There, as we have seen, he holds that man's highest cognitive faculty is the intellect, which is totally sovereign, and that prophets acquire knowledge of God through the power of their intellect. Hence, just as there is no place for differentiating among human beings on the basis of their origin, there is no place for momentous distinctions among people who live in different countries. In the earlier thought, then (as in the Philosopher's doctrine),

---

9. Making prophecy depend on living in Eretz Israel arouses the difficulty of explaining the careers of prophets who lived elsewhere (2,13), including Abraham and Moses. This difficulty does not trouble his earlier thought, because those who served as "abodes of the Shekhinah" are not subject to this condition. It seems plausible that §§8–24 of Part II continue the development of the fundamental ideas presented in Part I (95, 109). These sections also reflect his later thought, as we shall see.

10. Compare 1,95; 4,17. See also Yochanan Silman, "Arẓiyyutah shel Ereẓ Yisrael" (The earthliness of Eretz Israel), in Moshe Hallamish and Aviezer Ravitzky, ed., *Ereẓ Yisrael ba-hagut ha-yehudit bi-ymei ha-beinayyim* (The Land of Israel in medieval Jewish thought) (Jerusalem, 1991), pp. 79–89.

11. See also the historical reasons adduced in the studies already cited in note 1.

the basic equality of all human beings rests on the fundamental assumption about the primacy and sovereignty of the intellect—a sovereignty that has the power to liberate human beings from absolute dependence on environmental conditions, including those that influence their physical state.[12] Furthermore, as we have seen, the sovereignty of the intellect is interpreted as an autarky that calls into question the unconditional value of human action, including collective and historical action.

The value of emigration to Eretz Israel, like the value of any deed, depends on its real significance as a means for actualizing the human purpose: attaining adequate knowledge of God. It goes without saying that the conditions of traveling to Eretz Israel in the Middle Ages and the conditions of life there could hardly encourage thought and contemplation. The King, who attempts to dissuade the Rabbi from emigrating to Eretz Israel, raises the very same arguments that had led Halevi, in his earlier thought, to justify his acceptance of life in exile. First he argues that "with a pure mind and desire, one can approach God in any place. Why will you run into danger on land and water and among various peoples?" (5,22 [331/293]). Responding to the importance that the Rabbi accords to observing the commandments in Eretz Israel, the King calls their fundamental importance into question and sees them as no more than "obligations"—obligations that depend on particular circumstances: "I thought that you loved freedom, but now I see you finding new religious duties which you will be obliged to fulfil in Eretz

---

12. It seems plausible that there is an echo of Halevi's earlier thought in the King's remark that "I see, then, that you admit the dominion of hours, days and places, as the astrologers do" (4,8 [237/215]). All the same, the Philosopher, followed by Halevi in his earlier thought, acknowledges that environmental conditions can delay or accelerate the process whereby human beings come nearer to God, especially in the early stages of this process, when the mind has not yet emerged from potential to actual. As we have seen, this opinion about the importance of environmental conditions grounds the theory of the commandments in the earlier thought and opens the door for a possible justification of the superiority of Eretz Israel even in the earlier thought. But Halevi did not take this path there.

Israel, which are, however, in abeyance here" (5,24 [332/294]).[13]
This disagreement between the King and the Rabbi as to the importance of emigration to Eretz Israel is a striking reflection of Halevi's attempt to come to terms with himself—an expression of the inconsistency between his earlier thought, represented by the King, and his later thought, represented by the Rabbi.

---

13. Note that latent in the dispute between the King and the Rabbi is a fundamental disagreement about the importance of the human body and, consequently, about the importance of material conditions for man's religious development. In the later thought, as we shall see, the superiority of Eretz Israel—its air and sky (4,17), its dust and stones (5,27)—rests on an integral anthropology in which body and soul are a single entity; whereas, as we have seen, in both the earlier thought and the Philosopher's doctrine man is viewed as a divided being.

12

AN OVERVIEW OF HALEVI'S EARLIER THOUGHT

1. The Earlier Stratum of the *Kuzari*

The distinction between Halevi's earlier and later thought is associated with certain assumptions about the order in which the *Kuzari* was written. As we have seen, the following sections express his earlier thought: all of Part III, §§68–79 of Part I, and §§1–7 of Part II. These constitute the earlier stratum of the *Kuzari*.[1] In the light of the clear-cut distinction in the various stages in the development of Halevi's thought and, in its wake, of the division of the book into earlier and later strata, we must reiterate that both Halevi's thought and the book are marked by an internal unity. This unity is sustained by the dialectic relations between the successive stages in the evolution of Halevi's thought. It is only natural, then, that the later thought builds upon the earlier stage (answering its implicit difficulties) and that the two strands are sometimes interwoven.

Just as Part III, which expresses the earlier thought and belongs to the earlier stratum of the *Kuzari*, includes concepts

---

1. The interesting question as to whether this stratum was ever circulated as a first edition of the *Kuzari* does not concern us here.

that foreshadow the later thought, those sections of the book that represent the later stratum incorporate ideas characteristic of his earlier thought. Thus far we have noted various instances of this interpenetration. We explained the appearance of later ideas in the earlier thought by the nonbinding character of the attitude of the pious man (§§5–11), by the polemic bent of the Rabbi's words in §73, and as an expression of the internal tensions that eventually spawned the next stage in the evolution of Halevi's thought. We also pointed out the interpolation of earlier ideas into the later stratum of the *Kuzari*. There are various reasons for this phenomenon, as we have seen: sometimes it creates a dialectic conflict between the earlier thought, represented by the King, and the later thought, whose spokesperson is the Rabbi; sometimes it legitimates the earlier ideas as opinions that a believer may hold, even though Halevi maintains that they are fundamentally mistaken. As we shall see, this tolerance stems from the fundamental superiority that the later thought accords to correct action over adequate theoretical knowledge.

Nevertheless, these explanations cannot eliminate the tension that runs through Part II, starting with §8. In these sections, Halevi elucidated the localization of the "glory" or "Divine Order" in Eretz Israel on the basis of the general principle that the extent to which form "rests" on matter depends on the degree to which the matter is suited to accept the form. The localization of the "Divine Order" in Eretz Israel accordingly depends on the peculiar disposition of various earthly factors possible only in Eretz Israel. This disposition also affects the inhabitants of the country: "there are places . . . where the inhabitants are distinguished by their form and character—through the mingling of humors resulting in the perfection or imperfection of the soul" (2,10 [75/88]). In the earlier thought it makes sense to rely on this principle, which explains the localization of the Divine Order but does not entail any assumptions about the existence of a Divine Will that is continually modified and renewed. Halevi later reiterated this principle explicitly: "The Divine Order is above change or damage" (2,26 [95/102]).² But, as noted, these sections reflect his later thought.³ As we shall see, at this stage in the development of his thought Halevi believed in the existence of a mutable Divine Will. Perhaps we should understand this principle as a necessary condition that limits the localization of the Divine Emanation but not as a sufficient condition that can guarantee Divine revelation (even though Halevi believed that when the Divine Presence rested on the First Temple every human being who had the intrinsic capacity to attain prophecy actually did so).

Starting from §8 of Part II, the principle of the differential suitability of matter to form is no longer invoked to save the absolute transcendence of the deity or to guarantee immutability in the Divine realm; it is used only to explain the localization of the Divine Emanation in Eretz Israel. It limits Divine activity a priori but does not bind it necessarily. As we shall see, the

---

2. This section does not express Halevi's personal opinion because, as he himself stressed, his argument there has chiefly didactic value. It was written out of consideration for "he ... who descends from this highest grade to scrutinizing" (ibid., 99/106). Compare 2,14 and 2,24. On the other hand, in §16 [80/92], it is God alone who determines the hierarchical order of time (the "seasons are fixed by him"). When it comes to the superiority of the Hebrew language Halevi proposed two explanations, one rooted in the inherent nature of the language and the other anchored in an irreducible Divine activity: Divine speech (2,68).

3. There is abundant evidence that Part II, from §8 on, expresses the later thought. As we have seen, the central role assumed by Eretz Israel in these sections of Part II implies that they express the later thought and belong to the later stratum of the *Kuzari*. In addition to the emphasis on the importance of Eretz Israel, Halevi highlighted the human body and the environmental conditions that permit a healthy physical life (2,50; compare the end of 2,62). As we shall see, there is a close correlation between the importance of the human body and the superior status of human action (2,50). Note further that in these sections Halevi distinguished among five or six different levels of being, including the unique degree occupied by members of the Jewish people (2,44)—an idea characteristic of his later thought (2,14). Similarly, the characterization of the Divine Will as perpetually renewed (2,50) is compatible with his later thought. The stress on the importance of the role that the Jewish people plays for all humanity (2,51–55) and on the parallel role played by the elite vis-à-vis the human collective (2,56) are further indications that these sections reflect his later thought.

theory of levels of existence plays a similar role in explaining why the Divine Order descends only on the Jewish people. Assigning the Jewish people to the prophetic degree does not guarantee that all of them will actually be prophets; it merely explains why in practice no non-Jew attains prophecy. Note that in Part II Halevi pointed out the parallel between the election of the Jewish people and the election of Eretz Israel: "The glory of God is only a ray of Divine light, which has a salutary effect on His people and on His country" (2,8 [74/88]).[4] To this the King immediately responds: "I understand what you mean by 'His people,' but what you say about 'His country' is less intelligible" (2,9 [74/88]). Later in Part II, Halevi again stressed that the unique historical destiny of the Jewish people must be understood against the background of voluntary Divine intervention (2,50). Hence the very act of pondering the unique destiny of the Jewish people leads all humanity to acknowledge that "God is eternal, and that the world was created. They look upon the Israelites and all that befell them as proof of this" (2,54 [113/116]). Before the nations became aware of Jewish history, though, they believed that there is no individual providence in the world (ibid. [112/116]).

2. The Internal Tensions of the Earlier Thought as the Background for the Evolution of Halevi's Ideas

Halevi's earlier thought has three outstanding hallmarks: (1) It refers chiefly to the controversy with Karaism rather than to that with Aristotelian philosophy. (2) It is anchored in the optimistic assumption that there are no substantive and irresoluble contradictions between the world-views of Judaism and of Aristotelian philosophy. (3) This assumption is called into question by the inevitable internal tensions that come to the fore as his thought evolves.[5]

---

4. See also 2,16.

5. As we have already seen, Halevi's increasing reservations about the Philosopher's ideas also stem from causes external to his thought: his own

On the one hand Halevi, like the Philosopher, attempted to base the hierarchical systems he believed to be characteristic of non-Divine existence on a clear-cut order inherent in it. This idea is associated with the concept of the Aristotelian God. Because God's internal properties necessarily express His essence, they are immutable. His relationship with transient being must be as an eternal, unvarying, and homogeneous emanation. Hence the hierarchy that characterizes this being can be understood only on the basis of its own inherent primordial and irreducible distinctions. God in this sense relates to non-Divine existence like an ideal righteous judge, whose verdicts and decisions differ only as a function of the differences in the various cases, rather than as a function of distinctions derived from the Divine realm itself (2,2, 2,4).[6] On the other hand, sometimes Halevi was forced to ground the hierarchical gradations in properties derived from the realm of Divine substance—a strategy incompatible with the Aristotelian notion of divinity.

Thus, on the one hand, Halevi makes the hierarchical ranking on the plane of action depend on qualitative distinctions inherent in that plane. In this he remains faithful to the spirit of Aristotelian philosophy. Accordingly, the validity of the Torah commandments stems not from the will of God but from the intrinsic quality of the act of fulfilling the commandment. On the other hand, his desire to establish the exclusive status of the Torah commandments, including those with no explanation, as a code of laws endowed with absolute validity and not to be modified leads him to base full and authoritative knowledge of

---

personal experiences—"the dream"—and pressing historical circumstances. Here we shall focus only on the internal tensions.

6. In Halevi's later thought this opinion is attributed to *Sefer Yetzirah:* "This also demonstrates that the one order is the work of a one-Master, who is God. And although things are multifarious and different from one other, their difference is the result of the difference of their material, which is partly of higher and partly of lower order, and of impure or pure character. The giver of forms, designs, and order, however, has placed in them all a unique wisdom and a providence that is in complete harmony with this uniform order and is visible in the macro-cosm, in man, and in the arrangement of the spheres" (4,25 [258/231]).

them on a unique Divine revelation in the past. The postulates of the earlier thought, however, are incompatible with the phenomenon of revelation as well as with its prescriptive content—the commandments. The giving of the commandments (even if only as "guidelines") is incompatible with the Aristotelian God who is totally inward-directed. From the perspective of Aristotelian anthropology, which locates the human essence in the intellect, there is no way to understand the extreme importance of the act of performing the commandments, an act in which human beings participate with their bodies and souls.[7]

In this context, revelation is seen as a unique concatenation of circumstances that cannot be summoned at will, embodied in a bond between God and a particular human being or a particular nation, through a particular statement uttered in a particular language, at a particular time, etc. In and of itself this localization establishes the superior status of its object, as well as of the chain of those who transmit the tradition of the revelation—a chain that bridges between the one-time event and human beings who have not had immediate experience of that revelation.[8]

This view of revelation necessarily leads to a profound internal contradiction in Halevi's earlier view of history. Halevi could not escape this contradiction, even though he limited the independence of the elite (including philosophers) from concrete earthly circumstances to defined historical contexts. This contradiction stems directly from his recognition of the fateful significance of the historic continuum—the distinction between historical eras and between concrete historical affiliations.

---

7. This last contradiction is the initial motif and starting point for the dialogue in Part I, which reflects Halevi's later thought. The contradiction surfaces in the juxtaposition of the King's dream (as an event in which the angel appears to the King and enjoins him to take action) with the Philosopher's presentation.

8. The emphasis on reason's inability to discover the precise regulations associated with the rational commandments and the principles of the nonrational ones, along with the emphasis on the need for a reliable tradition to transmit the fact of revelation from generation to generation, constitutes the central axes in Halevi's criticism of Karaism (3,23]). Its awareness of the inadequacy of reason distinguishes Judaism from other religions (3,7; 3,21).

The earlier thought also fails to provide an adequate explanation for the other unique lineaments of Jewish existence. It is difficult to reconcile Israel's past, marked by the various events in which God was revealed as particularly interested in the Jewish people in general or in individual Jews, with the concept of God propounded in it. Similarly, the historical destiny of the Jewish people in the present—their downtrodden status among the other nations—poses a fundamental problem. It cannot be ascribed to their failure to observe the commandments as prescribed, because the Jews are more meticulous in this than are other peoples.[9] What is more, their hopes for the future are associated with nonnatural events, analogous to the miracle of the Exodus (3,11). Halevi was cornered into explaining the possibility of such miraculous events through the preordained harmony between the Torah and natural law: "Nature claims to pursue its regular course, whereas the Torah claims to alter this regular course. The solution is that ordinary natural phenomena are altered within natural limits, since they had been primarily fixed by the Divine will and clearly laid down from the six days of creation" (3,73 [214/196]).[10]

In the third part of this book we shall see that, just as the internal and external tensions (the latter stemming from his personal experiences and the historical record) brought Halevi to hop between two branches in his earlier thought, it also led to the further evolution of his thought. This development, born of a desire to resolve the tension, continued for many years, eventually producing the system reflected in the later stratum of the *Kuzari*.

9. Halevi himself emphasized the superiority of the Jewish people as manifested in their more meticulous observance of the commandments (3,8; 3,9). In the later thought, though, where the commandments are considered to be imperatives, the inferiority of the nations has nothing to do with their failure to observe them, because they have not been enjoined to do so.

10. It is no accident that only in Part III did Halevi grapple with the Tempter, who seduces even the pious man and makes him despair, saying: "Can these bones live? (Ezek. 37:3)" (3,11 [156/150]).

PART III

HALEVI'S LATER THOUGHT

13

INTRODUCTION: UNIQUE FEATURES

Halevi's later thought was shaped by the controversy with Aristotelian philosophy, interwoven with self-criticism of his earlier thought, in which he was not yet aware of the intensity of the disharmony between Aristotelian philosophy and the revealed religions, including Judaism. In this later stage in the development of his thought Halevi had overcome the internal contradictions characteristic of his earlier thought. As we saw in the second part of this book, these contradictions are rooted in the attempt to sustain the postulates of Aristotelian philosophy while holding fast to the immediate and unique significance of fundamental elements of revelatory experiences. Only in his later thought was Halevi willing to abandon some of the Aristotelian postulates in order to extricate himself from these inconsistencies.

From the literary perspective, these contradictions are manifested throughout the dialogue that occupies the sections of the *Kuzari* that reflect his later thought; namely, Part I, except for §§68–79, Part II, except for §§1–7, and all of Parts IV and V. In these sections the Rabbi expounds Halevi's later position, while the King is sometimes the mouthpiece for philosophy and sometimes for the earlier Halevi.

The backdrop for this two-front struggle against Aristotelian philosophy and Halevi's earlier thought is his reevaluation of the ontological, epistemological, and psychological importance of sensory experience. As we shall see in the chapters that follow, experience is not simply a methodological point of departure for the later thought; it also determines its theoretical conclusions. On the one hand, experience reveals that human beings have the capacity to participate in revelation. On the other hand, it demonstrates the meaning of God as a deity who makes Himself available to human experience.

In the later thought, the debate among the revealed religions and Aristotelian philosophy focuses on three fundamental issues: (1) the meaning of divinity; (2) the nature of man, both as individual and as collective; and (3) the nature of the reciprocal relations between God and human beings. The significance of human action is particularly important for this last issue. Halevi was aware that there are necessary correlations among these issues. These correlations are already implicit in the King's *congé* to the Philosopher—his summary of the Philosopher's presentation and his outline of an alternative worldview (1,4). In the summary, the King makes plain that the Philosopher's view—that the relations between God and non-Divine existence are focused in their ontological common denominator—is bound up with the meaning his doctrine assigns to God, such that God, in His relationship to all other existence, is viewed as the "Prime Cause," which by its very nature as exclusively a "cause" does not "speak with mortals" (ibid. [11/39]). Postulating such an ontological common denominator entails defining man's essence as intellect. Man as intellect, even if only potential, can, at least in principle, unite with the Deity—the actual perfect intellect. To this notion the King opposes the possibility of dialogue between God and man: a Divine address to human beings and their response, in their full being—physical, psychological, and spiritual—to this address. On the psychological plane, this response is manifested in love and fear of the Lord; on the plane of action, it is manifested in observance of the commandments. The King understands that the dialogue depend on a different conception of man and of God—one in which sensory experience of God (even in a dream state) is possible: "Yet we find that true visions are granted to persons who do not devote themselves to study or the purification of their souls. *This proves that there are secret relations between the Divine Order and the soul, relations that are not identical with those you mentioned,* O Philosopher" (ibid. [12/40]).[1] We shall consider the nature of these correlations in the chapters that deal with these issues.

The later thought accords a prominent role to the problem posed by the actual present situation of the Jewish people. This effort involves more than contemporary historical circumstances, such as the Crusades and the Reconquista. It also stems from internal developments typical of Halevi's later thought, spurred by two considerations. (1) As we saw in the introduction to Part II of this book, the historical inferiority of Judaism, vis-à-vis Christianity and Islam, is a central issue in the dispute that pits Judaism against Aristotelian philosophy, Christianity, and Islam. (2) In the later thought, man's physical condition, including concrete historical situations, cannot be separated from his spiritual state: The concrete fate of human beings parallels the extent to which they please God. This parallel is sustained by Divine providence as well as by the monistic nature of man himself, which does not allow human beings to cast aside their earthly needs and focus exclusively on fulfilling their spiritual and religious aspirations. In proportion as the real conditions are worse and the physical needs are more pressing, so is it more difficult for human beings to ascend spiritually.

---

1. See Chapter 4, note 24. It is in this light that we should evidently understand Halevi's yearning in his poetry to attain Divine visions in his dreams. See Komem, "Poetry and Prophecy," p. 683.

14

HUMAN EXPERIENCE AND THE DIVINE PRESENCE

A reevaluation of the meaning of human experience is the unifying thread that runs through all the issues dealt with in Halevi's later thought and weaves them into a single philosophical system. Moreover, it is in the mirror of sensory experience that God's relationship to human beings acquires its particular meaning. All this takes place in the context of the overt confrontation with both the Philosopher's doctrine, in which this relationship is produced by the human intellect's contemplation of the cosmic order, and the ambiguous and hesitant position characteristic of Halevi's earlier thought.

As we shall see in the chapters to follow, the empirical nature of this bond between God and human beings is the cornerstone of the later thought. In this chapter we shall first consider the internal logic of sensory experience and then turn to the nature of the bond between God and human beings. The implications of this relationship for the rest of Halevi's system will be mentioned briefly, in the interests of completeness, with appropriate references to the relevant sections elsewhere in this book.

1. The Meaning of Sensory Experience

The double confrontation with Aristotelian philosophy and Halevi's earlier thought is waged against the background of his reevaluation of the epistemological, ontological, and psychological importance of human sensory experience, both waking and dreaming. In this chapter we shall focus on the epistemological and ontological aspects of sensory experience, deferring its psychological significance to later chapters.

The first twenty-five sections of the *Kuzari* hinge on the disagreement between the Philosopher and Halevi as to the status of sensory experience. This dispute is already implicit in the juxtaposition of the King's dream with the Philosopher's denial that the dream can have any theological significance and in the King's rebuttal. The King's response to the presentation of the Christian cleric contains the first explicit mention of the principle that experience is superior to the reasoned conclusions of speculative thinking (1,5 [14/42]).[1] Then, in his response to the Muslim scholar, the King enumerates the methodological requirements for verifying an experience as an event of objective theological significance (1,8). His recognition of the need to satisfy these methodological demands leads the King to invite the Rabbi to his palace. The Rabbi's presentation is strongly marked by the distinction between empirical and theoretical knowledge of God. The Rabbi attempts to explain this to the King through the parable of the king of India: Whereas the first part of this parable (1,19–20) deals with knowing God through speculation, its second part (1,21–25) deals with knowing Him through experience.

As stated, sensory experience is the starting point, with regard both to its place in the didactic sequence and to content. Didactically, Halevi emphasized both the irreducible primacy of

---

1. Note that the dispute with the Philosopher does not revolve around the validity of this principled superiority but around the adequacy of the traditional interpretation of the prophetic experiences related in the Holy Scriptures; that is, the application of the principle. Accordingly, Halevi argues that the Philosopher would change his mind were he to be persuaded of the reliability of this interpretation of experience.

sensory experience and its unqualified reliability. A sensory experience, when properly verified, has the capacity to attest to its own fundamental possibility, even when this seems quite unreasonable from the theoretical perspective.[2] In the light of verified sensory experience, human beings can even recognize the truth about God; namely, that "the Creator of this world and the next, of the heavens and lights, holds intercourse with this contemptible subject, I mean man, speaking to him, and fulfilling his wishes and desires" (ibid.). Seeing is believing: It has the intrinsic ability to liberate human beings from the need to bring further proof (1,15).[3] One who experiences divine revelation (direct or mediated) "despises all these rational proofs by means of which men endeavor to attain to knowledge of God's dominion and unity. Then he becomes a servant who loves his master and is ready to perish for the sake of his love" (4,15 [246/222]). The natural philosophers, too, acknowledge the existence of "strange phenomena," "which they would not believe if they only heard of them without seeing them; but when they see them, they discuss them and ascribe them to the influence of stars or spirits, because they cannot disprove ocular evidence" (1,5 [14/42]).[4] This approach allows Halevi to

2. Still, we must not think that Halevi had fallen into a naive realism. He believed that sensation can produce knowledge only of the external aspect of the presented object, not of its inner essence; see further in the next chapter.
3. Zifroni's Hebrew here has "proof" (the Arabic is al-ʿiyān). See Mosconi ad loc. Compare also 1,24 and 25). At 1,67 [31/54], "to contradict that which is manifest or proved," Zifroni has "proof" instead of "manifest" (in Hebrew this is a merely a matter of the vocalization of the consonants: $r^{\circ}ayah$ 'proof' vs. $r^{\circ}iyyah$ 'vision'). See also S. Horovitz, "Zur Textkritik des Kusari," in Hirschfeld, Sefer Hakuzari (1970), p. 18 n. 2 [first published in Monatsschrift für Geschichte und Wissenschaft des Judentums 41 (1897)]. Compare also S. A. Poznansky, "Liqqutim min Sefer Megalleh Setarim le-Rabbenu Nissim be-rav Yaʿakov mi-Kairouan" (Passages from the book Megalleh Setarim by R. Nissim b. R. Jacob from Kairouan), Ha-ẓofeh le-ḥokhmat yisrael, vol. 5 (Budapest, 1921; reprinted Jerusalem, 1972), p. 177. See also D. Kaufmann, Geschichte der Attributenlehre in der jüdischen Religions-Philosophie des Mittelalters von Saadja bis Maimuni (Gotha, 1877).
4. Compare 2,54; 4,3; 5,21. On the special importance of visual experience in Halevi's later thought, see Chapter 16.

intentionally ignore the Philosopher's trenchant theoretical arguments against the assumption that God displays interest in individuals and their deeds (1,1). The absence of a rebuttal can only be an acknowledgment that the Philosopher's point is justified theoretically. Nevertheless, Halevi rejected it because of prophetic experience, which is a manifestation of the interest that God actually displays in individuals.[5]

We must not be led astray to see the role of experience in the later thought as a token of antirationalism. Even the later Halevi remained a rationalist in many senses. True, he recognized the limits of human reason, the irreducibility of the sensory datum, the importance of cumulative sensory experience, and the superiority of action over introspection in determining human destiny. On the other hand, he continued to vigorously defend the position that nothing "in the Torah contradicts that which is manifest or proved" (1,67 [31/54]).[6] He recognized the power of unassisted human reason to discover the truth in various scientific disciplines (5,14). As we shall see, reason can even discover the truth about God, albeit only at the low level represented by knowing Him as *Elohim*. What is more, sensory data themselves require rational interpretation, to distinguish essence from accidents. Even the prophet needs this (4,3). Again, Halevi's basic inclination to demonstrate the truth of Judaism through arguments aimed at reason places him firmly within the rationalist camp. What

---

5. Similarly, the patriarch Abraham, after having had an experience—a dream-vision—abandoned the theoretical conclusions he had expressed in *Sefer Yetzirah* "and only strove to gain God's favor, having ascertained what this was and how and where it could be obtained" (4,27 [269/239]), without calling their *theoretical* validity into question. See also 4,17. Adam, too, escaped his theoretical doubts about the Deity—doubts he could not overcome through rational speculation alone: "Adam . . . would never have known God if He had not addressed, rewarded, and punished him, and created Eve from one of his ribs" (4,3 [219/200]). As we shall see in Chapter 16, the importance of sensory experience is also related to the weight assigned to the external aspect of existence—the aspect that is revealed to sensory experience. See also Poznansky, "Liqqutim," pp. 179–182.

6. Similarly; "Heaven forbid that we should assume what is impossible or what reason rejects as being impossible" (1,89 [43/62]).

distinguishes Halevi's later thought is that its point of departure is empirical sense data, rather than the theoretical postulates of Aristotelian philosophy.

The reevaluation of the role of experience entails further conflicts with Christianity and Islam, for two reasons: First, an emphasis on experience involves a fundamental uncertainty about the nature of religious truths that may be revealed in the future. Second, in some sense an emphasis on experience entails a preferential status for later periods over earlier ones, because the later era has a greater stock of experiences on which to draw. This openness and superiority of the future pave the way for Christianity and Islam to argue that they are superior to Judaism, because their seminal religious experiences postdate those of Judaism. As we have mentioned, though, in Halevi's later thought the dispute with Christianity and Islam has other motivations, associated with the historical circumstances of the period in which this thought crystallized. Hence we can understand that the King's summons to the representatives of Christianity and Islam, after he dismisses the Philosopher, do not simply reflect the need to deal with problems raised by pressing historical circumstances or the course of human history (which is significant in Halevi's philosophy); they are also rooted in the open nature of Halevi's later thought.

2. The Religious Experience as an Indissoluble Entity

The underived primacy of experience entails seeing it as an atomic entity that cannot be broken down into smaller factors. A major tenet of Halevi's later system is that thought cannot separate the God made manifest from the concrete situation of the epiphany and its particular components: "He, however, who knows how to distinguish one people from another, one person from another, one time from another, one place from another, and certain circumstances from others, will *perceive* that heavenly dictated events mostly came to pass in a particular land—the Holy Land—and among a particular people—the Israelites—and in that time and under circumstances which were accompanied by laws and customs" (5,20 [320/283]). As we shall see in the chapters that follow, this principle has many ramifications. Revelation, according to the Rabbi (who here stands isolated against the representatives of the other religions) is not simply an extraordinary opportunity to draw nearer to God on the ontological plane or a propitious moment when one can peer behind the veil and know what is on the other side of it—a glimpse that is altogether secondary to the content of the knowledge itself. The Rabbi holds that just as revelation itself is the only proof of the possibility of revelation, the fact of His revelation is the only possible characterization of the God who makes Himself manifest. God as revealed in prophetic experience cannot be abstracted; hence He has no generic name, but only a personal name, like "Reuben and Simeon" (4,1). He explains the divine name *ehyeh* (Exod. 3:14) in this fashion:

> It can be derived from the Tetragrammaton, or from the root *hayah*. It is meant to prevent the human mind from pondering over an incomprehensible but real entity. When Moses asked: "And they shall say to me, What is His name?" the answer was: "Why should they ask concerning things they are unable to grasp? . . . Say to them 'I am' [*ehyeh*], which means: 'I am that I am,' the existing one, existing for you whenever you seek Me. Let them search for no stronger proof than My presence among them, and name Me accordingly" (4,3 [202]).

The meaning of God that is relevant for the Jewish people is His very presence. These two aspects of God made manifest—the demonstration of His existence by revelation and His definition as God made manifest—are necessarily interdependent: By the same token that revelation grounds itself by its very presence, it is a unity that cannot be divided—"name Me accordingly." What is more, as we shall see in subsequent chapters, God's presentness in sensory revelation is expressed in the sensory nature of its visible and audible images. For Halevi's later thought, these images cannot be separated from God's meaning for human beings.

Prophetic experience as an integral whole encompasses those who actually participated in it—the Jewish people—as well as the land where it took place—Eretz Israel—and the language in which God addresses human beings—Hebrew. The experience requires all three factors: Only members of the Jewish people can witness the experience, which can take place only in the Land of Israel and only in God's language—Hebrew.[7] What is more, participating in a prophetic experience, even passively, directly influences all the factors included in this experience. The very fact that God is present in an experience determines its natural and supernatural properties—both internal and external—and hence its value as a means whereby human beings can attain their goal. Divine revelation is a cross-section of concrete circumstances in different spheres of existence. The factors that participate in revelation occupy the summit of the hierarchy in each sphere of existence. The place of all other factors in the hierarchy is a function of their relative "distance" from this pinnacle.

As we shall see, the prophetic encounter has a major influence on the external aspect of those who participate in it. Thanks to this influence, prophetic experience has a meaning that goes beyond those who attained it immediately—the prophets—to acquire a universal and historical significance. By virtue of this influence, the participants themselves become foci of immediate sensory experience. Consequently they can convey the fact of

---

7. Baneth ("Halevi and al-Ghazali," pp. 322–323) contends that Halevi held that Israel had a special religious preparation—a doctrine that "somewhat resembles the racialist theories of our own day.... It was forced on Halevi by the facts in the Holy Scriptures, according to which no true knowledge of God, prophecy and miracles, or reward and punishment are to be found for a people in this world, except for Israel." In light of our discussion, we should expand this argument to the other components of the Jewish experience as well. However, as we shall see later, when we consider the specific meaning of *race* in Halevi's thought, it is important to stress that, so far as his system is concerned, Halevi's starting point is not the authority of Scripture—an authority that stems from its sanctity—but the independent epistemological status of the data of sensory experience (5,6 [283]). Even the sanctity and authority of the Holy Scriptures are grounded on these data. Halevi did derive his information about these data from Scripture as an authoritative source, but because he accepted the documentary reliability of the age-old tradition collected in it—a tradition that satisfies precise methodological requirements (1,44–59).

revelation to those who did not have immediate experience thereof. In the wondrous and supernatural events that happen to prophets, "God made manifest to the people that He is in connection with them" (1,43 [48]). Human beings who are present when a prophet prophesies undergo an alteration in their very being: "He who converses with a prophet experiences spiritualization during the time he listens to his oration. He differs from his own kind in the purity of his soul, in a yearning for the higher degrees and attachment to the qualities of meekness and purity" (1,103 [57/74]).[8] Similarly, the nations, thanks to the physical presence of the Jewish people among them, witnessed supernatural events through which they discovered "that the world had a King who watched and guarded it, who knew both great and small, rewarded the good and the wicked, and directed the hearts" (2,54 [112/116]).[9]

The centrality of experience in Halevi's later thought is reflected also in the accent on one-time events that cannot be understood according to the laws of nature, events that are in part creation ex nihilo and in part creation ex rebus. These events, which are given in sensory experience, find expression in the narrative strand of the book, in the biographies of individuals, nations, and humanity as a whole. They appear also as central motifs in the meaning that man attributes to God. Unlike the Philosopher (who purifies God of all variability and intentional association with mutable existence and liberates individuals who have actualized their intellects from all obligatory associations with transient concrete existence), the mature Halevi,

---

8. So, too, "waiting upon the king" depends on "costly raiment"—"the visible light" that appeared on the face of Moses (1,109 [60/76f.]). Similarly, "prophets and pious Sages are spoken of in similar terms, because they, too, are original instruments of the Divine will which employs them without meeting with unwillingness and performs miracles through them" (4,3 [224/204]).

9. In this function, the Jewish people resemble the sun, which "next to God ... is the cause of being.... Its light produced sight and colors" (2,53 [111/115]); see also 2,50. See Chapter 17, note 30. See also R. Nissim b. Reuben Gerondi, *Derashot* (Homilies), ed. Leon A. Feldman (Jerusalem, 1973), the Eighth Homily.

going beyond the hesitant and ambiguous position of his earlier thought, emphasized the importance of such one-time events that cannot be generalized and grounded on any eternal system of laws. Experience of these events plays a vital role in acquiring adequate knowledge of God. Thanks to these experiences, human beings learn of the existence of God who transcends Himself, through the interest that He displays in the particularity of existence outside himself. From these events human beings learn the significance of the Divine Will as a spontaneous will that continuously redefines itself, selecting a segment of existence on which to focus its influence. Experience also has the power to set boundaries and steer the evolution of the individual, of the human collective, and of all humanity.

In the later thought, this voluntary focus of the Divine Influence on selected segments is not restricted to the human realm. It also involves other spheres of existence and constitutes hierarchies in them as well. These hierarchies derive from a divine initiative and express a new determination of God's will, even when the initiative encounters the "inflexibility" of the existence on which it focuses. As we shall see, these hierarchies occupy different planes—national, linguistic, territorial, and others. In the chapters that follow we shall consider the nature of the relations among these hierarchies and the internal relations within each of them.

15

GOD AND THE WORLD

Theology stands at the center of Halevi's later thought, despite the paucity of explicit references to it.[1] His theology is based on the factual events in which God made Himself manifest to human beings. Knowledge of God depends, both methodologically and thematically, on these sensible events. Hence the image of God cannot be divorced from the manner in which He appears in private or collective human experiences—experiences discussed in the previous chapter. Because, as we shall see in Chapters 16, 17, and 22, Halevi's anthropology rests on these very same experiences, there are correlations between the image of God and the image of man. Similarly, his theology underlies his doctrine of the Torah commandments and election of the Jewish people, to be discussed in Chapter 18.

1. God as Manifest versus God as Intelligible

Theology is one focus of the controversy between Halevi and Aristotelian philosophy and a linchpin of Halevi's own hesita-

---

1. Perhaps we should attribute this reticence to Halevi's preference for the action and sentiment with which human beings respond to God's address over intellectual knowledge of God. He holds that the ancestral tradition is reason enough for worshipping the Lord: one must "obey the authority of [one's] father and...ancestors in their belief in the God of

tions in his earlier thought. Consequently, the *Kuzari* begins by juxtaposing the personal deity, who relates to the Khazarian king and reveals His will to him, to the impersonal and totally introverted Aristotelian deity whose characteristics are fixed for all eternity. The Philosopher begins with an unequivocal rejection of the concept of God that lies at the heart of the revealed religions; he points out the contradiction between God's perfection, on the one hand, and the postulates that His will emerges from the potential to the actual and that His knowledge is perfected by learning about mutable existence, on the other. The King, dismissing the Philosopher, stresses the antithesis between the philosophers' God as "Prime Cause" and a God who speaks to ephemeral individual human beings. In consequence, the King calls in the Christian and Muslim scholars with the aim of learning about the revealed religions, which maintain that God speaks with human beings and assert that they know about the "secret relations" between the "Divine Order and the soul" (1,4 [12/40]). At the very beginning of the dialogue between the King and the Rabbi, Halevi has the King expound the fundamental problem: "Should you not have said, Jew, that you believe in the Creator of the world, its Governor and Guide, who created and keeps you, and such attributes which serve as evidence for every believer, and for the sake of which he pursues justice in order to resemble the Creator in His wisdom and justice?" (1,12 [17/44]). The Rabbi replies by pointing out the intentional parallel between the beginning of his reply and the beginning of God's address to His people: "God commenced His speech to the assembled people of Israel: 'I am the God whom you worship, who has led you out of the land of Egypt'; He did not say, 'I am the Creator of the world and your Creator.' In the same style I spoke to you, Prince of the Khazars, when you asked me about my creed" (1,25 [20/46]). Halevi's accentuation of this parallel indicates the centrality to his system of the distinction between the philosophers' God, known syllogistically and in the

---

Abraham, Isaac, and Jacob, whose solicitude was with them"; there is no need for "a complete knowledge of God" (5,21 [330/292]).

context of ontological relations, and God who makes Himself present in immediate historical experience. In his later thought, Halevi held that the substantial difference between Judaism and the other religions lies precisely in this distinction (1,109).[2] This is why this concept crops up again in the remarks that constitute an "introduction" for non-Jews to the tenets of the Jewish faith.

In Judaism, then, God is defined "in such terms as are quite clear to the eye" (1,24 [20/46]). As we saw in the previous chapter, this "seeing" requires no further verification: it is "the very proof [and] evidence" (1,15 [18/45]).[3] The Rabbi stresses that the Torah is binding because of a direct Divine address spoken to man in his uniqueness (1,27).[4] Halevi himself noted

---

2. It is no accident that the representatives of the other religions open their descriptions of God not with a reference to revelation but ontologically, as the Philosopher does. Note that here the Rabbi describes the appropriate relationship between human beings and God, on the practical plane—"to serve him" (1,21 [19/46]), and not to become like Him. See also Y. Heinemann ("Helekh ha-raʿyonot shel hathalat sefer ha-Kuzari" [The current of ideas at the start of the *Kuzari*] in Zemora, *R. Yehudah Halevi*, pp. 246–247), who left a large gap to plug. The truth is that Halevi, at this stage in the development of his thought, believed that the theoretical concept of God cannot be known without personal experience of the Divine Presence, because the intrinsic meaning of the objects of experience can never be fully conceived (4,5, 4,6).

3. Similarly, "to those endowed with prophetic vision it appears too bright and resplendent to require any other proof" (5,21 [328/291]). This emphasis on the role that vision and the eye play in knowledge of God stems from Halevi's position on the epistemological and psychological status of visual experience (discussed in the next chapter). The reliability of sight is independent of whether the "inner eye," on which prophetic vision depends, is an additional sense or an internal sensation derived from the imagination (4,3). This question arises only in the context of the problem of the ontological status of the objects of vision—the forms. See also Meyer Waxman, *Ketavim nivharim* (Selected writings), vol. 1 (New York, 1943), p. 125.

4. This is why the Rabbi makes a special effort in Part I (in §§80–96, which are associated, both doctrinally and literarily, with §§1–67) to stress that the Exodus was "directly from God" (1,91 [45/63]). In the same vein, the Rabbi draws an analogy between the initial Creation (1,89; 1,91) and the "great scenes," including the Exodus. This view is at odds with that of Abraham Ibn Ezra in his short commentary on Exodus 13:21— "even though the verse states 'Who took you out of the land of Egypt,' he did so by means of an angel." Obviously Ibn Ezra intends to reject

the serious problems this causes for his system by calling into question God's spiritual nature (1,88) and unity (4,3), the relevance of Judaism for the non-Jew (1,25; 1,27), and perhaps also the relevance of the ancestral tradition for the generations to come.[5]

In light of what we have said it is clear that the later Halevi, having abandoned his earlier position (3,11), did not believe that the second half of the First Commandment—"Who brought you out of the land of Egypt"—is merely an addendum to the first half; on the contrary, it is the crux of the matter (1,25). Its purpose is to disqualify rational thinking as a suitable method for acquiring adequate knowledge of God: theoretically, as an appropriate content of faith; psychologically, as an appropriate emotional relationship; and practically, as constitutive for the validity of the Divine Law. In Part III, Halevi incorporated the Hebrew verse into his Arabic text without translation, whereas in Part I he translated or rather paraphrased it as "I the Lord Whom you shall serve am the

---

any unmediated relationship between God and physical reality. In Part III of the *Kuzari*, too, Halevi held that the Exodus "was a deliberate act of God, and not... achieved by mediation of... angels... or other beings, but by God's commandment alone" (3,73 [212/194]). Still, as we shall see, sometimes Halevi did attribute the Exodus to "the Divine Order."

5. Because it does not fit in with the overt course of the discussion, the unsupported equation of tradition with personal experience (1,25) indicates that Halevi entertained doubts on this issue. Instead of clarifying the problems that his opinion about unmediated experience poses for the value of tradition and interpersonal communication in general, he contents himself with a laconic and dogmatic aside. Although here (and at the end of 5,14) Halevi unreservedly compared tradition with visual experience, when he enumerated the criteria for authentic sensory experience he demanded immediate sensory experience— "who saw it distinctly and did not learn it from reports and traditions" (1,8 [16/43]). What is more, Halevi states that the Gentiles' worship of the Lord has no significance because it is the result of "hearsay and tradition" only (4,3 [220/201]). Similarly, knowledge of God as "My God and Holy One" depends on immediate personal experience of the presence of God (ibid. [222/203]). The distinction between immediate and mediated knowledge of God is crucial for Halevi, in light of the decisive influence that immediate experience has on human beings, as we shall see in the next chapter. See also the end of Chapter 19.

One Who took you out of the land of Egypt." In this rendering, the phrase "I am the Lord your God" is not understood as a sentence with subject and predicate; instead, "the Lord your God" is in apposition to the subject "I," and the predicate is supplied by the second half, "Who took you out of the Land of Egypt." That is, in the context where it is possible to worship Him, God is the one who brought the Jews out of the land of Egypt.[6]

2. God—Phenomenon versus Essence

If adequate knowledge of God is the result of human experience, there is a fundamental distinction between God's meaning for human beings and His essence for himself. In this section we shall consider this distinction in its epistemological sense; its ontological senses will be discussed later.

Alongside his contention that it is fundamentally impossible for human beings to know God's essence—"it would be a defect in Him if we could grasp [His nature]" (5,21 [329/291])—Halevi denied that the Aristotelian concept of God has any religious significance. The Aristotelian God is only an object of man's intellectual curiosity (4,13), although the later thought admits a sense in which God can be known through rational speculation (2,54; 3,15; 4,1). If God is known by the intellect, however, His meaning for human beings does not go beyond the intellectual plane and has no import for action or emotions, as we shall see in the next chapter. Halevi's position that man cannot know God in His essence—as He is in Himself and for Himself—rests on the assumption that by its very nature sensory knowledge can include only the attributes perceived by the senses (4,3), as well as on metaphysical arguments about God's absolute transcendence. For these reasons, the later Halevi also denied that God in His essence is actual intellect—an identifi-

---

6. This can also be deduced from a comparison of the First Commandment with Moses' address to Pharaoh (ibid.). Compare also Heinemann, "Helekh ha-ra'yonot," p. 247. See also Even-Shmuel's note on 1,25 (p. 249).

cation that he did accept in his earlier thought. In his later view, *only* God is essentially incorporeal; everything that is not God *is* corporeal. This fundamental dichotomy rules out knowledge of His essence: "There is surely an incorporeal being which guides all corporeal substances, but which our mind is inadequate to examine. We therefore dwell on His works, but refrain from describing His nature" (5,21 [329/291]).[7] Accordingly, Halevi understood the verse "let us make man in our image and likeness" (Gen. 1:26) as meaning that human beings were created in the likeness of God's angels and servants, not in the image of God Himself (4,3).[8] Halevi's recognition that God's essence is unknowable leads to a fundamental change in the meaning he attaches to man's rapprochement with God: Instead of uniting with God on the ontological plane, in the later thought human beings approach God on the plane of action, by complying with His injunctions—His commandments.

Paradoxically, this distinction between God's meaning for human beings and God in Himself allows Halevi to satisfy the internal exigencies of his thought and provide a literal explanation of biblical anthropomorphisms. God, as perceived through sensory revelation, is necessarily perceived in sensory and physical images; the prophets "without doubt saw the divine world with the inner eye; they beheld a sight which harmonized with their natural imagination. They endowed whatever they wrote down with attributes as if they had seen them in corporeal form. These attributes are *true* as far as regards what is sought by inspiration, imagination, and feeling; they are *untrue* as regards the reality that is sought by the intellect" (4,3 [228/208]). That is, although these images do not relate to God in Himself; they are not merely allegorical.[9] At the same time, these anthropomor-

---

7. See also 4,3. This is also Saadia Gaon's opinion; see his commentary on Dan. 7:9, in Y. Kapah, trans., *The Book of Daniel and Scroll of Antiochus, with the Translation and Commentary by R. Saadia Gaon* [Hebrew] (Jerusalem, 1981).

8. This is also the opinion of Abraham Ibn Ezra. See his commentary on Gen. 1:26 and the short commentary on Ex. 23:20.

9. In this respect there is a great proximity between Halevi and the Kabbala.

phisms are also associated with how the later thought views man (see the next chapter).

If the idea of God as phenomenon depends on cumulative human experience, it is dynamic. Just as the history of the Jewish people is played out under the sign of divine revelations, so too the idea of God as phenomenon is marked by the annals of Israel. This is how we should understand the Rabbi's opening words: "I believe in the God of Abraham, Isaac, and Israel, who led the Israelites out of Egypt with signs and miracles; who fed them in the desert and gave them the (Holy) Land, after having made them cross the sea and the Jordan in a miraculous way" (1,11 [17/44]). All these events, as well as the individuals who participated in them, are constitutive and indispensable elements of the concept of God.[10] Accordingly, when the Rabbi asks, "how would you describe him, then, if asked?" (1,23 [19/46]), the King replies, "in terms that are quite clear to my eye" (1,24 [20/46]).[11] Similarly, the unique status of the Jewish people, as the nation of the Torah, is anchored in their knowledge of the God Who brought them out of Egypt; for if acceptance of the obligation to observe the Torah involved knowledge of God as Creator of the World, "the white and the black man would be equally bound, since He created them all" (1,27 [21/47]).[12] Just as the encounter between divine existence and human existence constitutes the human essence in its fullest sense—raising individuals from their original level to the degree of prophets and raising the Jewish people to the degree of a nation of prophecy—so too it gives God His authentic religious meaning: "Sometimes the

---

10. See also 2,50.
11. Similarly, the "Divine attributes" originate in prophetic experiences—in forms. See also Moscato on 4,1, *incipit* בכלל נקרא אלקים כי היה.
12. Even though the Rabbi recognizes the status of the righteous convert who "joins us," this status applies to converts as individuals. He is not willing to go further and recognize that an entire community could acquire a special status by accepting the Torah. The conversion of any nation involves its assimilation into the Jewish people (1,27). See also Even-Shmuel's note on this section, p. 249.

name 'Lord' was applied to the connecting link between God and Israel.... For there exists no connection between God and any other nation, as He pours out His light only on the select people. They are accepted by Him, and He by them. He is called 'the God of Israel,' while they are 'the people of the Lord,' and 'the people of the God of Abraham' " (4,3 [220/ 201]).[13] For Halevi, the purpose of the creation of the universe is fulfilled in this disclosure of God's meaning for human beings. In fact, as Halevi noted, God is not referred to as *Adonai Elohim* in Genesis until after He first appears to Adam (4,15).[14]

Another reflection of the fact that this idea of God as phenomenon depends on repeated human experiences is that it cannot be exhausted conceptually. Halevi stressed that YHWH is a proper noun, like Reuben and Simeon, unlike *elohim*, which is only a generic or common noun (4,1; 4,15).[15] This phenomenal meaning is not an exhaustive definition of God-made-manifest. It can merely hint at such a definition, and the hint is meaningful only for someone who has had the experience of revelation (4,2; 4,3). In consequence, not only is any adequate knowledge of God as phenomenon derived from human experience, past and present; this salient meaning—God as pure presence—is progressively confirmed by the kaleidoscopic permutations of human experience and must always be reacquired. This is how Halevi explained the name with which God first identified Himself to the Jews, *ehyeh*: "Say to them 'I am' [*ehyeh*], which means: 'I am that I am,' the existing one, existing for you whenever you

---

13. See also 2,50–56, and Ibn Ezra on Deut. 26:17.

14. Ibn Ezra, too, vacillated as to why the name *YHWH elohim* first appears only after God has manifested Himself to Adam (First Recension on Genesis 1:2). His answer is based on a distinction among the divine names that is quite different from that drawn by Halevi.

15. The dichotomy between generic name and individual name is bound up with the dichotomy between the intelligible God Who is known as a concept through rational speculation and God Who is known through the senses as a sensory datum. This dichotomy is also compatible with that between a view of God that, at least in principle, can admit both polytheism and monotheism (4,1) and the view of God that can lead only to monotheism. Logically, a generic name is indifferent in its denotation (4,3), whereas a proper name is fundamentally unique (ibid.).

seek Me. Let them search for no stronger proof than My presence among them, and name Me accordingly" (4,3 [221/202]). Thus God as God-made-manifest includes an allusion to God Who has not yet been revealed but will be there when sought.[16]

3. Transcendence versus Immanence

The infinite distance that the later thought places between the transcendent deity and all other entities theoretically rules out any possibility of relations between them. Nevertheless, the paradoxical existence of such relations is undeniable: They are attested to by experience, to which the later thought gives unassailable status. A striking literary expression of Halevi's awareness of the paradox posed by the existence of these relations can be found in a liturgical poem (an *ōfon*) for the Festival of the Rejoicing of the Law (Simḥat Torah):

> Lord, where shall I find Thee?
> High and hidden is Thy place!
> And where shall I not find Thee?
> The world is full of Thy glory!

> Found in the innermost being,
> He set up the ends of the earth:
> The refuge of the near,
> The trust for those far off.
> Thou dwellest amid the Cherubim.
> Thou abidest in the clouds,
> Yet art raised above their praise.
> The [celestial] sphere cannot contain Thee;
> How then the chambers of a temple?

> And though Thou be uplifted over them
> Upon a throne high and exalted,

---

16. Compare: "Not everyone who wishes is permitted to say, 'My God and Holy One!' except in a metaphorical and traditional way. In reality only a prophet or a pious person with whom the Divine Order is connected may say so. For this reason they said to the prophet: 'Pray to the Lord, thy God' (1 Kings 13:6)" (4,3 [222/203]).

> Yet art Thou near to them,
> Nearer than their own spirit and their flesh.
> Their own mouth testifieth for them,
> That you alone art their creator.
> Who shall not fear Thee,
> Since the yoke of Thy kingdom is their yoke?
> Or who shall not call to Thee
> Since Thou givest them their food?
>
> I have sought Thy nearness;
> With all my heart have I called Thee;
> And going out to meet Thee
> I found Thee coming toward me.
> Even as in the wonder of Thy might
> In the sanctuary I have beheld Thee.
> Who shall say he hath not seen Thee?—
> Lo, the heavens and their hosts
> Declare the fear of Thee
> Though their voice be not heard.
>
> Doth then, in very truth,
> God dwell with man?
> What can he think—every one that thinketh,
> Whose foundation is in the dust?
> Since Thou art holy, dwelling
> Amid their praises and their glory,
> Angels proclaim Thy wonder,
> Standing in the everlasting height;
> Over their heads is Thy throne,
> And Thou upholdest them all![17]

God's interest in the world and in human beings, like their desire to draw nearer to God—to find Him—seems paradoxical in light of God's transcendence. From this vantage point the question, "Lord, where shall I find Thee?" with its immediate

---

17. Trans. Nina Salaman (*Selected Poems of Jehuda Halevi* [Philadelphia, 1924]), but silently adopting, for exegetical purposes, some of the changes proposed by Isaak Heinemann in his commentary to the poem, appended to his edition of the *Kuzari*.

answer, "High and hidden is Thy place," is a hopeless aspiration that cannot be realized. God, who is high and lofty, is also hidden and unknowable. Because He is transcendent He cannot be found, not even in the Temple: "The [celestial] sphere cannot bear Thee; how then the chambers of a temple?"[18] For the same reason, it is impossible to understand God's interest in the world or in human beings: "Doth then, in very truth, / God dwell with man? / What can he think—every one that thinketh, / Whose foundation is in the dust?"[19] Nevertheless, man's yearning to commune with God cannot be eliminated, since it is rooted in immediate experience of the Divine immanence that permeates non-Divine existence—the universe and man: "And where shall I not find Thee? / The world is full of Thy glory!"[20] God, who is nearer to human beings than their own flesh and spirit—God who is "found in the innermost being"—imposes His perpetual presence on human beings: "Who shall not fear Thee, / Since the yoke of Thy kingdom is their yoke? / Or who shall not call to Thee / Since Thou givest them their food?" This human desire to draw closer to God derives from the radical tension between the infinite distance separating and the infinitesimal proximity bringing together man and God.

18. In the Temple, human beings have clear vision of God (2,14; 4,9).

19. This is of course a rhetorical question (compare 1,8). As is made clear by the position of this liturgical poem in the morning service and the reference to "angels" in its last stanza, the question applies to all non-Divine existence: Halevi was referring to the contradiction between Divine transcendence and the existence of any link between God and non-Divine entities. It should be emphasized that this problem is more acute in Halevi's later thought than in the Philosopher's doctrine. The strict transcendence of the later thought rules out the solution offered by the Aristotelian philosopher; namely, the theory of emanations (5,14).

20. As we shall see later, Divine "glory" is one of the designations of the Divine immanence in the world. Note, though, that there is no other allusion in this poem to a distinction between God as made manifest to human beings and God as He is in Himself. Evidently one of the main roots of the paradox of the relation between the immanent and transcendent God is precisely the lack of any distinction between them. The distinction in the later thought between the immanent and transcendent God is itself an expression of the vital need to explain and overcome the psychological difficulty of accepting this fundamental paradox.

In theory there is no solution to the paradox that stems from the relationship between Divine transcendence and Divine immanence: They are mutually exclusive. Either God is "high and hidden" or, antithetically, "the world is full of [His] glory." Against the background of the Divine transcendence, the Divine immanence that is given in experience is "a wonder." As the poem concludes: "Angels proclaim Thy wonder, / Standing in the everlasting height; / Over their heads is Thy throne, / And Thou upholdest them all!"[21]

According to the poet, human beings can draw nearer to God only on the plane of action, not of thought. Thus, despite the theoretical difficulties, the poet "goes out" to find God: "I have sought Thy nearness; / With all my heart have I called Thee; / And going out to meet Thee / I found Thee coming toward me."[22] Nevertheless, this tension between the transcendent and the immanent—an essential feature of Halevi's later thought—is dispelled by the various explanations Halevi offered for the reciprocal relations between God, on the one side, and man and the universe, on the other. These explanations seek to demonstrate that the distance between the transcendent Divine sphere and all other existence is bridgeable—that the spiritual, one, and unvarying God can indeed have relations with mutable and multifold material existence.

---

21. This last stanza parallels the first one. The wonder proclaimed by the angels who stand in the highest sphere of the universe is the relationship between the Divine immanence—"Over their heads is Thy throne"—and the Divine transcendence—"And Thou upholdest them all."

22. This "going out" seems to refer to observance of the commandments. Compare the poem שובי נפשי למנוחיכי (Brody 3:35). But Heinemann, "Philosopher-Poet," p. 185, interpreted this "going out" in another fashion. Similarly, Abraham, after he conceived the Divine Order by "tasting, not by speculating, . . . observed that no detail of his life escaped God, that He rewarded him instantly for his piety and guided him along the best path, so that he moved forwards or backwards only according to God's will. How should he not despise his former speculation? The Sages (BT Shabbat 156a) explain the verse: 'He brought [Abraham] forth' (Gen. 15:5) as meaning 'give up thy astrology!' That is to say: He commanded him to leave off his speculative researches into the stars and other matters and to devote himself to the service of Him whom he had tasted" (4,17 [247/223]). See also 4,27.

Halevi's conjectures all require the assumption of the existence of mediators and of the validity of an all-encompassing causal law to which both God and non-Divine existence are subject. This forced him back to Aristotelian postulates that, were it not for this explanation, would have no place in his later thought and whose inclusion engenders serious internal inconsistencies.

The ambiguous meaning of the mediating agents stems from their role as intermediaries between transcendent and spiritual Divine existence and corporeal non-Divine existence, including the sublunar realm and its characteristic materiality.[23] On the one hand, their proximity to God requires some semblance between them and God, if not indeed their identity with some aspect of divinity itself; this proximity is expressed in their ontological status as wholly spiritual. On the other hand, their association with non-Divine reality entails a common denominator between them and that reality, which is sometimes expressed by according them a material essence. Of course these two aspects are quite incompatible; what is more, each harbors many fundamental internal contradictions.

The spiritual nature of the mediating agents is incompatible with God's unity and oneness, as Halevi himself contended when rejecting the philosophical doctrine of emanations: "We take ... no heed of the words of philosophers who divide the divine world into various degrees. As soon as we are free from our bodies there is for us only one divine degree. It is God alone who controls everything corporeal" (5,21 [329/291]). Their hierarchization of the Divine leads the philosophers to "adopt

---

23. Recall that the Philosopher holds that God's association with sublunar existence involves only the form impressed upon it; in principle this was also Halevi's opinion in his earlier thought. In his later thought, Halevi emphasized the relations between God and matter, including man, this "contemptible piece of clay" (1,8). Of course the later opinion exacerbates the paradox. With regard to the relations between God and human beings, it is reflected in the problem of positing that God can speak to human beings or that they can respond to His wishes (ibid.). With regard to God's relations with the universe as a whole, the paradox finds expression in the difficulty in believing in ex nihilo creation, as we shall see.

many gods" (ibid.). But if the mediators are corporeal, they cannot be mediators, since they would themselves require mediation to come into relation with spiritual Divine existence. In addition, the existence of such mediators, like God's subordination to causality, necessarily weakens the sense of Divine transcendence, God's unlimited freedom and omnipotence.[24] Nevertheless, as we shall see in Chapter 19, these explanations and their underlying assumptions do not so much express Halevi's own views as they reflect the didactic and polemic interests that take precedence over pure theory in his later thought.

4. The Divine Order as a Mediating Factor

The expressions that refer to the mediating agents can be divided into two groups. The first explains the path from transcendent Divine existence to non-Divine existence; that is, the possibility that the transcendent God can become immanent. The second explains the path from human existence to Divine existence. The former group includes the Divine Order, Divine Presence or Shekhinah, Divine Light, Glory of God, Holy Spirit, kingdom of God, and the angels. The second group includes man of God, son of God, exceptional individuals, chosen people, and prophet. Particularly conspicuous in the first group is the Divine Order,[25] a term that recurs frequently in central passages

---

24. To some extent God's need for mediation indicates His subordination to laws that limit His activity. Thus, in contrast to the philosophers' God, in whom Divine existence is divided into degrees, Halevi offered the image of the sovereign God, "who controls everything corporeal" (5,21 [329/292]). The most conspicuous expression of God's unlimited sovereignty is ex nihilo creation, an act in which God's omnipotence is embodied in a single moment and God creates everything at once, without a process whose stages depend on one another. By contrast, in 4,25 God is described as the guide of the spirituals; see note 41.

25. As we shall see later, however, this expression, like others of the first group, frequently appears in other senses as well and plays other roles in Halevi's system. One of these is to explain the path from non-Divine reality to God. In that sense the expression belongs to the second group.

of the *Kuzari* and has consequently received particular attention in the scholarly literature. Many studies have endeavored to uncover the primary meaning of the expression, on the theory that this would open the way to understanding its many other meanings as secondary and derived. But scholars hold widely divergent views about the degree of substantiation of the Divine Order as an independent ontological entity and about the nature of the relations that prevail between it and other ontological factors. Here we shall start from the multiplicity of meanings itself, which is rooted in the internal tension characteristic of Halevi's later thought.

In his later thought (but not the earlier thought) Halevi rejected the Aristotelian version of the theory of emanations—a theory based on dividing Divine existence into a chain of ontological agents. According to the later Halevi, this theory dissolves the inner unity of God into a multiplicity of separate Divine agents (5,21). The Aristotelian theory of emanations rests on the postulate that God belongs to the formal and rational facet of existence, an assumption that Halevi rejects in his later thought. Hence the theory cannot be reconciled with the later concept of Divine transcendence, which has no place for the Divine Order in the sense of a necessary and eternal link in the chain of emanations that begins in the Divine essence.[26] Even in the later thought, though, the Divine Order sometimes plays the role of a mediating agent—one meant to explain, to the extent possible, the possibility of mutual relations between transcendent Divine existence and non-Divine existence. Consequently, when he wants to explain how the Divine Order relies on concrete existence, even in his later thought Halevi must have recourse to some version of the theory of emanations. In this sense, the Divine Order is a created ontological agent, identified with God as He appears in human experience.

---

26. Similarly, in his later thought Halevi rejected the idea that appropriate preparation can in and of itself guarantee reception of the Divine immanence. He also explicitly demurs at the Philosopher's concept of the Active Intellect (1,87 [41]; 5,14 [308], 21 [330]). See also Wolfson, "Hallevi on Design," p. 112; Davidson, "The Active Intellect," p. 374.

But we frequently encounter the "Divine Order" in the sense of an aspect of Divinity itself[27] or in the sense of a concrete embodiment of the Divine immanence in the world. What these last two senses have in common is that the Divine Order does not serve as a mediating agent between transcendent Divine existence and non-Divine existence. It is plausible that Halevi's vacillation among the various senses of the term reflects the radical tension between the heuristic and didactic inclination and the philosophical inclination. For the latter, the confrontation between the testimony of experience concerning Divine immanence and the theoretical truth of Divine transcendence entails the paradox, which cannot be explained rationally, that there is a relationship between the transcendent God and non-Divine reality.[28]

As a mediating agent, the Divine Order is the foundation of the concrete manifestations of the Divine immanence in the world, but is not identical with it. Thus, when Moses presents the people's hypothetical question about His essence to God, God replies:

> "Why should they ask concerning things they are unable to grasp? . . . Say to them 'I am' [*ehyeh*], which means: 'I am that

---

27. Efros, *Doctrines*, pp. 189ff. At the other extreme stands Waxman, *Ketavim nivḥarim*, pp. 95ff. In light of our discussion, both of them went too far, each in his own direction. See also Wolfson, "Hallevi and Maimonides on Prophecy," *Jewish Quarterly Review* 33 (1942–1943): 81; Davidson, "The Active Intellect," p. 391.

28. Compare Baneth, "Halevi and al-Ghazali," p. 318, n. 4. From the literary perspective, Halevi, when discussing the possibility of Divine speech, expressed both his personal stand and his response to the objective difficulties that others have in accepting this stand. At the beginning of the discussion he emphasized, in no uncertain terms, that "tangible speech" is "of Divine origin," in the case of "the words of God spoken face to face" (1,87). After the King has accused him of corporealizing God (1,88), however, he retreats to the noncommittal: "the air which touched the prophet's ear assumed the form of sounds" (1,89 [44/63]). In 1,91 Halevi himself expressed cautious reservations about this suggestion and returned to his original position: "the matter proceeded directly from God" (ibid. [45/63]). Similarly, Halevi viewed the Ten Plagues as unmediated Divine acts, whereas the King scrupulously ascribes them to the Divine Order (1,83–84).

I am,' the existing one, existing for you whenever you seek Me." . . . This is followed by a similar phrase, namely, "The God of your fathers, the God of Abraham, the God of Isaac, and the God of Jacob," persons known to have been favored by the Divine Order perpetually (4,3 [221/202]).

We learn that the Divine Order is not identical with the Divine essence, which is unknowable, nor with the particular manifestations of God's immanence in the world. The Divine Order *is* identical with the God Whom human beings find when they seek Him. All the manifestations of God in the world are His manifestations, but He is not exhausted by them. In this vein Halevi distinguished between God as "holy," an epithet that applies to God as transcendent—"God is too high, too exalted, too holy, and too pure for any impurity of the people in whose midst His light dwells to touch Him"—and "the Holy One of Israel," which refers to the Divine Order as it communes with man: "to rule and guide them, not merely to be in external contact with them" (ibid.).

Accordingly Halevi refered to the Divine Order as *elohim* (*'ilaha*): "The Divine Order, one might say, is attendant on the man who appears worthy of the favor, waiting to be attached to him and to be his God, as in the case of the *prophets and the pious man*" (2,14 [79/92]). Again, "The Divine Order grudges nothing" (5,10 [291/258]), which is restated at the end of the same section as "there is no niggardliness with God."[29] It

---

29. Again; there was no "direct union with the Divine Order (*'amr 'ilāhī*) . . . until Jacob begat the Twelve Tribes, who were all under this Divine Order (*l'il-'amr al-'ilāhī*). Thus the Divine element (*al-'ilāhīyya*) reached a multitude of persons" (1,47 [24/49]). This identification of the Divine Order with God also appears in the earlier thought (3,11; 3,17). There, as in the later thought, the Divine Order plays the role of a mediating agent that has direct influence on the concrete world. As we have seen, however, there are fundamental differences between the earlier and later thought with regard to the nature of the relations between the Divine Order—God—and transcendent Divinity. Compare Efros, *Doctrines*, pp. 188ff.; Wolfson, "Hallevi and Maimonides on Prophecy," *Jewish Quarterly Review* 32 (1941–1942): 353–370, and the note to §2 on p. 381; Waxman, *Ketavim nivḥarim*, p. 95; Davidson, "The Active Intellect," pp. 391ff. See also Pines, "Shī'ite Terms," p. 172.

follows that the Divine Order is identical with God (*'ilaha*). Because of God's unique relationship with the Patriarchs, with the Jewish people, and with Eretz Israel, Halevi also refered to the Divine Order as "the God of Abraham," the "God of Israel," and "the God of the Land." Note that these designations are generally associated with the possibility of sensible knowledge of God.[30] We can infer, then, that such epithets have nothing to do with God in His transcendent essence, but only with God as He appears in human experience.[31] Abraham, after "conceiving the Divine Order by tasting, not by speculating," became steadfast in the worship of the Divine Order: He "devoted himself to the service of Him who he had tasted, as it is written: 'Taste and see that the Lord is good' (Ps. 34:9). *The Lord [Adonai]* is therefore rightly called 'God of Israel,' because this seeing is not found among others [i.e., the Gentiles], and 'God of the land,' because the peculiarity of its air, soil, and climate aids this vision" (4,17 [247/223]). In other words, it is the Divine Order that, although not identical with God in His essence, watches over Abraham; what is more, the Divine Order guides Abraham to follow the just path: "He . . . observed that no detail of his life escaped God, Who rewarded him instantly for his piety and guided him along the best path, *so that he moved forwards or backwards only according to God's will*" (ibid.).

It is in this vein that we should understand the Rabbi: "In this way I answered your question. In the same strain Moses spoke to Pharaoh, when he told him, 'The God of the Hebrews

---

30. For example, "Thus we also speak of the 'devouring fire on the top of the mount' (Ex. 24:17), which the common people saw, as well as of the spiritual form which was visible only to the higher classes: 'under His feet as it were a paved work of a sapphire stone' (ibid. v. 10). He is further styled: *Living God*" (4,3 [224/204]). [Thus in the Arabic; both Ibn Tibbon and Even-Shmuel "emend" in accordance with the biblical verse and have "they called this 'the God of Israel.'"] Again, referring to the same biblical passage: "[Moses] . . . invited the Seventy Elders, and they saw it, as it is written: 'They saw the God of Israel' (Ex. 24:10)" (4,11 [240/217]). See other passages to be cited later.

31. The term *elohim* itself has many meanings. This is not the place to elucidate them, except to the extent that they shed light on the meaning of *Divine Order*.

sent me to you'—namely, the God of Abraham, Isaac, and Jacob. For the story of their life was well known to the nations, who also knew that the Divine Order was in contact with the Patriarchs, caring for them and performing miracles for them" (1,25 [20/46]).[32] That is, the Divine Order is known to the nations as "the God of Abraham, Isaac, and Jacob" because it guided the Patriarchs and worked miracles for them. Similarly,

> Behold how the Divine Order attached itself to Abraham, and afterwards to his whole "picked progeny" and to the Holy Land. This Order followed him everywhere, and guarded his posterity, preventing the detachment of any of them. . . . He is, therefore, called "God of Abraham" and ["God of Isaac"],[33] "Dwelling between the Cherubim," "Dwelling in Zion," "Abiding in Jerusalem"—these places being compared to heaven, as it is said: "Dwelling in heaven." His light shines in these places as in heaven, although through the medium of a people fit to receive this light, and on whom He sheds it. This shedding is called "God's love" (2,50 [110/114).

"God of Abraham" does not allude only to God's special relationship with Abraham—a relationship that made the Patriarch's special vision possible; it also refers to the Jewish people's role as a mediating agent, thanks to which God—the Divine Order—acquires His universal significance. The Divine Order "sheds its light on them" and they in turn retransmit the light to all of humanity. From this perspective they are superior to the sun, which "next to God . . . is the cause of being" (2,53 [111/115]).[34]

32. Compare: "This is followed by a similar phrase, namely, 'The God of your fathers, the God of Abraham, the God of Isaac, and the God Jacob,' persons known to have been favored by the Divine Order perpetually" (4,3 [221/202]).

33. Ibn Tibbon's Hebrew reads "God of Isaac" instead of "God of the Land," found in the Arabic MSS; compare 4,17.

34. Compare: "In reality only a prophet or a pious person with whom the Divine Order is connected may say so. For this reason they said to the prophet: 'Pray to the Lord, thy God' (1 Kings 13:6). The relation of this nation to others was to have been like that of a king to ordinary people, as it is written: 'Holy shall ye be, for holy am I the Lord, your God' (Lev. 29:2)" (4,3 [222/203]). We can infer from the context that the king

From all these passages we learn that in the later thought *Divine Order* sometimes means an ontological agent that is identical with God—reciprocal relations exist between Him and man—but is not to be identified with transcendent Divinity itself, Which cannot be known by created beings, whereas the Divine Order can be seen and must therefore have a corporeal nature.[35] This corporeal nature of the Divine Order is already evident from the general ontological dichotomy between the transcendent spirituality of God and the corporeality of all other existence.[36] Hence we should identify the "Divine Order" with

---

is "the Lord your God" and is the Divine Order. The communion between prophets or pious individuals and the Divine Order must be expressed in holiness, which is expressed in veneration and—like the Divine Order itself—in a desire to influence those who have not yet attained this level. Accordingly there is no reason to emend the text to read "angels" instead of "king," as Even-Shmuel did. See what follows: "Even after these two comparisons, imagination can give Him no other form than that of the noblest human being, who arranges order and harmony for the rest of mankind, in the same systematic way as God has done for the universe" (ibid. [231/209f.]). Compare: "It was He who initiated our delivery from Egypt in order that we become His chosen people and He our King, as He said: 'I am the Lord your God, who brought you out of the land of Egypt, to be your God' (cf. Lev. 22:33, Num. 15:41)" (2,50 [111/115]). In this last passage the Divine Order is said to be responsible for the Exodus from Egypt. See also 1,84.

35. This vision must be understood literally, as a sensory relationship to an entity that occupies space, even when Halevi attributed it to the "inner eye." See, for example, 1,87; 4,5; 4,11. We can also learn that vision must be understood literally from Halevi's conception of the "Glory of God," and especially from the distinction between the glory that can be known by human beings and the glory that cannot—a dis-tinction we shall consider later. See also Waxman, *Ketavim nivḥarim*, p. 125 n. 148.

36. We should perhaps also understand the presence of the Divine Order in defined places such as the Temple, Jerusalem, and Eretz Israel as an expression of its corporeality. We must not infer from 2,26 that the Divine Order does not occupy space, because on a number of other issues this section does not reflect Halevi's later thought—e.g., the essence of the influence of the Divine Order, which "does not refuse [its guidance] nor hesitate to shed light, wisdom, and inspiration [over a being prepared to receive its guidance]" (ibid. [95/102]), and the affinity between the rational soul and the angelic substance (ibid.), here stated to derive from the common spiritual nature of the rational soul and the angels. Halevi himself implied in this section (2,26) that its importance is polemical and didactic:

the "Divine world" (*al-ʿālam al-ʾilāhī*). The prophets saw "the divine world[37] with the inner eye; they beheld a sight which harmonized with their natural imagination. They endowed whatever they wrote down with attributes as if they had seen them in corporeal form. These attributes are *true* as far as regards what is sought by inspiration, imagination, and feeling; they are *untrue* as regards the reality that is sought by reason, as we have seen in the parable of the king" (4,3 [228/208]). Here Halevi is referring to the parable of the king (ibid.), in which the relationship between the Divine world and the transcendent essence of God is compared to the relationship between a king's body and his mind and will. The king's body puts on and takes off forms—"previously he was a body that was subject to the royal will alone" (ibid. [226/206]). It is through these forms that the king appears to his subjects: "in the shape of a king or judge, seated on his throne, issuing commands and prohibitions, appointing and deposing officials" (ibid. [229/208]). The king's body is not identical with his essence; nevertheless, the body is an ontological entity that exists and persists by its own right.

5. "The Glory of God," Angels, the Shekhinah, and "the Light of God"

In light of these descriptions of the Divine Order, it should be included, in this sense, in the list of the agents that (according

---

"I do not . . . assert that the intention of that service was exactly as here expounded; indeed it is more obscure and loftier. It is commanded by God; and he who accepts it with all his heart, without scrutiny or scruple, is superior to the man who scrutinizes and investigates. He, however, who descends from the highest grade to scrutinizing does well to seek a wise reason for these commandments, instead of casting misconstructions and doubts upon them, leading to corruption" (ibid. [99/106]). Compare Davidson, "The Active Intellect," p. 386.

37. The 1880 Warsaw edition of Ibn Tibbon's Hebrew version reads "Divine Order" instead of "Divine world." This was evidently the reading before Moscato (ad loc.). In 5,21, "the Divine world" should be understood as synonymous with "the Divine Order," except that there, evidently, the "Divine Order" is identical with transcendent Divinity itself.

to a tradition that appears to go back to Saadia Gaon) mediate between the essence of Divine existence and non-Divine existence, and especially human existence.[38] This list includes "the Glory of God," "the Divine presence" (*shekhinah*), "the angels of God," and "the light of God"; sometimes "kingdom" (Hebrew *malkhut*) is substituted for "angels" (Hebrew *mal'akhut*) (4,3).[39] All these concepts refer to an entity that, by virtue of its corporeal nature, can appear at the horizon of sensory experience and thereby serve as a mediating agent between God in His spiritual essence and sensory knowledge, which deals with corporeal objects only. The mediating function of this entity is expressed in the inherent ambivalence of its essence: Although it is corporeal, its corporeality is not of the sort that pertains to sublunar existence; it is a "fine substance"—a substance whose essence positions it between the corporeality of sublunar existence and the perfect spirituality of the transcendent God. The fine substance is embodied in the concrete incarnations of this entity:

> "Glory of God" is that fine substance which follows the will of God, assuming any form God wishes to show to the prophet. This is one view.... This includes the glory which the prophet's eye could bear; there are things in its wake that even our eye can behold, like the "cloud" and "the devouring fire," because we are accustomed to see them. The higher degrees of these are so fine that even prophets cannot perceive

---

38. Gershom Scholem, *Pirqei yesod be-havanat ha-qabbalah u-semaleha* (Basic chapters for understanding kabbalah and its symbols), (Jerusalem, 1976), pp. 271–272; Joseph Dan, *Torat ha-sod shel ḥasidut ashkenaz* (The arcane lore of the German pietists), (Jerusalem, 1968), pp. 105ff. The tradition actually goes back to the Karaite scholar Benjamin Nahaondi. See Efros, *Doctrines*, p. 196.

39. On the influence on the Kabbalah of the identification of "kingdom" with "glory" and "presence," see Gershom Scholem, *Reshit ha-qabbalah ve-sefer ha-Bahir* (The beginnings of kabbalah and the Bahir) (Jerusalem, 1962), pp. 83–84. On the identification of the angels of God with the kingdom of God, see Efros, *Doctrines*, p. 197; Baneth, "Halevi and al-Ghazali," p. 323, n. 5. For another view on this subject, see Wolfson, "Hallevi and Maimonides on Prophecy," p. 49, n. 89.

them.... Such is the explanation of the "Glory of God," "the Angels of the Lord," and the "Shekhinah of the Lord," as they are called in the Bible (4,3 [233/211]).[40]

The angels, too, have a corporeal nature, whether they are created for a fixed period or are eternal and arise from "fine elementary corpuscles" (4,3 [232/211]); that is, from the "Glory of God."[41] Accordingly, angels, too, are seen by the prophets.[42] Similarly, the Divine Presence has a corporeal

---

40. This passage should be understood in light of Saadia's distinction between the upper and lower glories. See Dan, *Torat ha-sod shel ḥasidut ashkenaz*, pp. 110ff. Saadia's influence is particularly strong in this section. Compare *The Book of Beliefs and Opinions*, trans. Samuel Rosenblatt (New Haven, Conn., 1948), Treatise II, end of Chapter 12, p. 130: "I say, then, invoking the aid of God in the effort to reveal and clarify all this...." See also Saadia's commentary on Ex. 33:23: "I shall remove My cloud so that you may see the end of My glory, but you shall not see its beginning."

41. There is no difference between these two views of angels with regard to the essence of the Glory of God, but only to its concrete embodiments. In the former view, its embodiments are forms created for a fixed period, whereas the latter view holds that they include only "imperishable things" (4,3 [233/211]). See Moscato ad loc. The difference seems to rest on different conceptions of the relationship between the Glory and its concrete embodiments. In the former view, God creates the forms from the Glory, like the creation of the lower world from primordial matter. As we shall see, the later Halevi did not totally reject this doctrine of creation. In the second view, which reflects his earlier thought, the embodiment of The glory is a necessary stage in the process of emanation: The Glory is not a created entity, but an emanated and eternal one, which can emanate in immediate fashion only eternal entities. In 2,4 [72/87]—a section that, as already noted, expresses the earlier thought—the Glory of God arose "from the ethereal and spiritual substance which is called 'holy spirit'." According to *Sefer Yetzirah*, though, the angels and souls are spiritual and were created from the "spirit of God," which it identifies with the "Holy Spirit." In the same vein, the Divine Order is also the director of the "spiritual entities" (4,25 [263]). Wolfson ("Hallevi and Maimonides on Prophecy," pp. 55ff.) argues that Halevi never explicitly declared that the Glory of God, the kingdom of God, and the Shekhinah are eternal entities; but this seems problematic in view of the second opinion, in which the Glory is the source from which the eternal angels emanate. As stated, the second view expresses only Halevi's earlier and not his later thought.

42. 1,109; 3,11; 4,5.

nature,[43] is found in defined places,[44] is created,[45] and can be seen.[46]

Divine Light, too, sometimes refers to a mediating ontological factor, in a sense close to these terms. Abraham's reception of the Divine Light, like his communion with the Divine Order, is reflected in the expression "the God of Abraham" (2,50).[47] The Divine Light, like the Shekhinah

---

43. Moscato on 2,7, incipit שכינה.

44. 1,109; 2,20; 2,23; 3,19; 3,23. We must not understand these statements other than in their literal sense.

45. See Scholem, *Pirqei yesod*, p. 272.

46. 2,14; 3,11; 3,19; 5,23. Sometimes the Shekhinah appears alongside angels and as distinct from them: "the Indian messengers are the Shekhinah and the angels" (1,109 [60/77]); "as if the Divine Presence were with him continually, and the angels virtually accompanied him" (3,11 [152/146]). Sometimes *Shekhinah* and the *Glory of God* refer to a particular angel of a degree higher than the other angels; in this sense it can be seen, even if only partially. Sometimes the terms refer to the common and amorphous ground of all the heavenly forms, including the angels. On the relationship between the Shekhinah and the Divine Order, see Davidson, "The Active Intellect," pp. 288ff. Davidson seems to have overemphasized the importance of the distinction between the visible Shekhinah and the unseen Shekhinah. We should identify the unseen Shekhinah with the potential Shekhinah, and the visible Shekhinah with the actual Shekhinah—as may perhaps be inferred from the last passage referred to in this note.

47. See also 4,3. Compare 2,8 with 3,17. As noted, this last section expresses Halevi's earlier thought. Here too the Divine Light is synonymous with the Divine Order and is referred to as "love." This Divine Light—the Divine Order—which is the source of any deviation from the laws of nature, is focused in the Patriarchs and their descendants, the Jewish people. At 3,17, however, God's "will" or "pleasure" is identified with the Divine "wisdom," whose manifestations are subject to eternal and unchanging law: "His wisdom did not demand of Him to create angels on earth, but mortals of flesh and blood, in whom natural gifts and certain characteristics prevail according to favorable or unfavorable influences, as this is explained in *Sefer Yetzirah*. Whenever some few, or a whole community, are sufficiently pure, the divine light rests on them and guides them in an incomprehensible and miraculous manner that is quite outside the ordinary course of the natural world" (3,17 [159/153]). That is, the descent of the Divine Light—Divine Order—is an expression of the law inherent in the Divine emanation, a law that governs the Divine influence only in the sublunar world. In 2,50, however, the emanation of the light of God is also governed by the spontaneous determination of the sovereign Divine Will: "it originally came from Him, but not from us" (ibid. [110/115])—a will distinctly reflected in ex nihilo creation (ibid.).

and the Divine Order, is located at a defined place (4,9, 4,11) and can be seen.[48] The term is also used as a synonym for "glory" (2,8).[49]

Hence we must not infer a multiplicity of mediating agents from the multiplicity of terms that refer to the mediation between the transcendent God and non-Divine existence. This proliferation of concepts is not due to the inner logic of the system, but to the Jewish and philosophical traditions that antedated Halevi, which he interpreted according to their various contexts and as alluding to the mediating agent. Nevertheless, we must not totally exclude the possibility that Halevi some-

---

48. 2,14; 4,7; 4,9; 4,11; 4,20. The Divine Light, like the Shekhinah, the angels, and the Kingdom of Heaven, is an object of the pious man's vision (3,1; 3,11; 3,19; 3,20). It is plausible that the earlier Halevi understood this vision as merely a consequence of the imaginative faculty; in fact he suggests this possibility: "It is possible that this [inner] eye [which sees things as they really are, without any alteration] is the power of imagination as long as it is under the control of the intellect" (4,3 [228/207]). This is also the opinion of the Aristotelian philosopher (1,87). Note that sometimes Halevi's earlier thought identifies the Divine Light with all the angels taken together: On the one hand, one who attains the degree of Enoch or Elijah is in the company of angels, who are "his associates" (3,1 [139/135]); on the other hand, "he ... who ... would like to retire into ascetic solitude ... has no intercourse with the divine light and cannot associate himself with it as the prophets" (ibid. [140–141/136]).

49. On the relationship between the Holy Spirit and the Divine Light, see Wolfson, "Hallevi and Maimonides on Prophecy," p. 51; Waxman, *Ketavim nivḥarim*, p. 133. Sometimes the Divine Light is synonymous with the Shekhinah: in the Land of Israel "there were the altars of the Patriarchs, who were answered by fire from heaven and the Divine light. The binding of Isaac took place on a desolate mountain, Mt. Moriah. In the days of David, when it was inhabited, the secret was revealed that it was the place specially fit and suitable for the Shekhinah; Araunah the Jebusite tilled it at that time. Thus it is said: 'And Abraham called the name of the place the Lord sees—about which will one day be said, In the mount the Lord shall be seen' (Gen. 22:14)" (2,14 [77/91]). That is, the "secret"—the special virtue of Mount Moriah as a place where human beings are answered by the Upper Fire and the Divine Light—was known only to the Patriarchs and not revealed to other human beings until the time of David. Halevi identified the Upper Fire and the Divine Light with the Shekhinah and with the Tetragrammaton.

times distinguished among these concepts as different aspects of the single mediating agent, taking their contexts into account.[50]

6. Mediation and Emanation

All the same, the interposition of a mediating agent between transcendent Divinity and non-Divine existence is not enough to explain the Divine immanence. In the later thought, as we have seen, the relationship between the transcendent God and the mediating agent is based on God's free will and omnipotence, which render this relationship inexplicable.[51] On the other hand, when Halevi explains the relationship between the mediating agent and non-Divine existence, his explanation resembles that advanced by the Aristotelian philosopher for the relationship between God and non-Divine existence. Like the philosopher's God, the mediating agent works in a fixed framework, which is embodied in a process of emanation (2,50)—a process in which some fitness in non-Divine existence ensures the reception of an appropriate Divine emanation through the mediating agent.

Thus the unequal distribution of the influence of the mediating agent among non-Divine entities goes back to the differential fitness of various segments of non-Divine existence to receive the Divine emanation: "Divine Providence gives man only as much as he is prepared to receive; if his receptive capac-

---

50. See Wolfson, "Hallevi and Maimonides on Prophecy," pp. 49ff.
51. In principle, another reason why this relationship cannot be explained is that it stems from the totally free determination of God's will; as such it is not governed by any prior state of affairs and therefore cannot be deduced through any rational argument. Accordingly, the Greek philosophers rejected everything "that was not revealed to [speculation] as the result of its activity" (4,3 [232/ES163/210]). Similarly, the natural philosophers, after experiencing "strange phenomena," endeavor to find out their causes (1,5). That is, in the *Kuzari* the explanation depends on "causes," and this is Halevi's opinion as well. Hence any veritable beginning cannot be explained. Similarly, there is a subjective difficulty in believing in events that are supposed to manifest Divine creation, whether this is a limited creation—miracles—or a comprehensive one—the creation of the universe.

ity be small, he obtains little, and much if it be great" (2,24 [94/101]). In this regard, the agent that promotes communion with the Divine Order is rooted in an alteration of circumstances in non-Divine existence:

> The Divine Order, one might say, is attendant on the man who appears worthy of the favor, waiting to be attached to him and to be his God, as in the case of the prophets and the pious man; thus Reason is attendant on those whose natural gifts are perfect and whose soul and character are so harmonious that it can find its perfect dwelling among them—that is, philosophers. Likewise, the Soul is attendant on a being whose natural powers are perfected to such a degree that a higher power is able to dwell within it—that is, animals. So too Nature (organic power) is attendant on a harmonious mingling of qualities in order to dwell therein and to form the plant (2,14 [79/92]).

In other words, the principle that determines whether the Divine Order inheres in human beings is the same principle that determines the particular status of each individual at every level of existence to which it belongs. Hence it seems that a single ontological agent is the exclusive source of the emanation of order and law to non-Divine existence in its various levels. This is in accordance with the principle of fitness, which explains the concrete nature assumed by this emanation in any particular segment of existence.[52] From this perspective, then, the mediating agent plays the role of the Aristotelian God and resembles the mediating agent in Halevi's earlier thought.

There is a fundamental difference between the role of the mediating agent in the thought of Saadia Gaon and R. Nissim Gaon and its place in Halevi's later thought. For the first two, the theory of Divine glory serves chiefly to explain the Divine immanence, as this is manifested in the visual and aural motifs

---

52. Compare 4,15. This was Halevi's opinion in his earlier thought—2,26; 4,25. See also Waxman, *Ketavim nivḥarim*, pp. 78ff.; Y. Heinemann, "Temunat ha-historiyyah shel R. Yehudah Halevi" (R. Judah Halevi's picture of history), *Ziyyon* 9 (1944): 155ff.; Davidson, "The Active Intellect," pp. 374ff.

present in prophetic experience.[53] By contrast, Halevi's theory of mediation explains the plenitude of the Divine immanence reflected in non-Divine existence in its entirety.

Nevertheless, there is a great difference between Halevi's later view, which he raises only as part of his didactic efforts, and his earlier view, which he shares with the Aristotelian philosopher. Halevi in his later thought believes that the mediating agent is itself a created entity; in this context, the necessary laws to which it is subject are a conspicuous manifestation of God's free will.[54] What is more, as we shall see in Chapter 18, in the later thought the Divine imperative, which is an exemplary expression of God's free will, constitutes a direct two-way relationship between God and human beings. The degree to which human beings respond to the Divine imperative determines also the nature of the bond between them and the mediating agent: "man can only attain to Divine Order through Divine ordinance" (1,98 [53/70]). Similarly, the "connection" of the Jewish people with the Divine Order is "through the laws He has placed as a link between us and Him" (2,34 [101/108]).[55] Hence even when Halevi had to assume the existence of a mediating agent, he endeavored to preserve the sovereignty of the Divine Will over non-Divine existence and even vis-à-vis the mediating agent.

Still, nothing in all this can totally rule out some contraction of the Divine sovereignty—a contraction rooted, despite its autonomous source, in God's need for mediation and His subjection to the principle of the fitness of matter. It follows that the theory of mediation, invoked to explain God's immanence,

---

53. See Dan, *Torat ha-sod shel ḥasidut ashkenaz*, p. 107; S. A. Poznanski, "Liqqutim min Sefer Megalleh Setarim le-Rabbenu Nissim be-rav Yaʿakov mi-Kairouan" (Passages from the book *Megalleh Setarim* by R. Nissim b. R. Jacob from Kairouan)," *Ha-ẓofeh le-ḥokhmat yisrael* 5 (Budapest, 1921; reprinted Jerusalem, 1972), p. 177; Shraga Abramson, *R. Nissim Gaon, Libelli Quinque* [Hebrew], Chapter 4, p. 345; D. Kaufmann, *Geschichte der Attributenlehre in der jüdischen Religions-Philosophie des Mittelalters von Saadja bis Maimuni* (Gotha, 1877), p. 167, n. 121.

54. This contradicts Ibn Ezra's position that the "Divine Glory" is created. See Dan, *Torat ha-sod shel ḥasidut ashkenaz*, p. 117.

55. Similarly, "These are ... the ordinations especially given to Israel as a corollary to the rational laws. Through this they received the advantage of the Divine Order" (2,48 [106/112]).

is quite incompatible with Halevi's primary interest, in his later thought, in a Divine presence that expresses a spontaneous Divine Will, which does "what, how, and when He desires" (5,2 [281/249])—a presence that, as we have seen, is a basic empirical datum.[56] In the later thought, then, the inability of the mediating agent to explain the immanence of transcendent Divine existence derives not only from very meaning of transcendence, but also from the significance of Divine immanence as an immediate datum of human experience. Because Halevi vigorously insisted upon the dichotomy between transcendent Divine existence and non-Divine existence—a dichotomy that rests on epistemological and metaphysical considerations as well as on postulates drawn from Jewish tradition—the assertion of Divine immanence in the world inevitably becomes paradoxical. Even though the assertion cannot be explained on the theoretical plane, it must be accepted, because of the various manifestations of the Divine immanence in human experience. If in the later thought it is explained by means of a mediating agent, the argument is not rooted in Halevi's system as a whole, but in the level of propaganda and polemics—levels whose significance for his system will be discussed in Chapter 19. Further demonstrations of the present contention will be advanced in subsequent chapters, where we shall be discussing the various manifestations of the relationship between human beings and God, marked by the assumption that there is an unmediated Divine presence in the world.

7. The Embodiments of the Divine Immanence as Mediating Agents

Halevi's reservations about the doctrine of mediation as a means to explain God's immanence in the world come through in the alternate meanings he proposes for its key terms. In Halevi's

---

56. See Heinemann, "Temunat ha-historiyyah," pp. 175ff.; Baneth, "Halevi and al-Ghazali," pp. 318–319; Julius Guttmann, *Philosophies of Judaism*, trans. David W. Silverman (Garden City, N.Y., 1966), pp. 146–151; Waxman, *Ketavim nivḥarim*, pp. 79ff.; Davidson, "The Active Intellect," p. 380.

later thought, the concepts we discussed in previous sections as referring to the mediating agent are frequently associated with concrete embodiments of God's immanence in the world; that is, with events or entities (including human beings) that are the object of human experience and display signs of the Divine immanence. Sometimes these signs of immanence are inherent in the specific form of the event or entity; elsewhere they are the result of unmediated causal links with God, "divine effects" (5,20 [316/280]) that "have no other causes except God's will" (ibid.). As we shall see, these embodiments of the Divine immanence exempt defined areas of non-Divine existence from the laws of nature or the laws of history; they can even spur human beings to love and fear God. What is more, they themselves become objects that are the only medium through which human beings can address, pray to, and worship God. These mediating agents, which constitute the path from the human sphere to the Divine realm, differ from the agents meant to mediate between Divine and non-Divine existence. Halevi was uncomfortable with the theoretical implications of the latter group of agents, but assigned a central place in his system to the former group. These embodiments constitute hierarchical systems on the different levels where man is found—hierarchies that are the only way man (individual and collective) can draw near to God. Similarly, "ADONAI, spelt *alef, daleth, nun, yod,* points to something that stands at such an immeasurable altitude that a real designation is impossible. Indication is possible in one direction only. We can point to things created by Him, and which form His immediate tools" (4,3 [223/203]). That is, there is an intrinsic self-contradiction in the idea that human beings communicate directly with God, because it implies a limitation of Divine being, which by its very nature cannot be limited. It follows that this Divine name does not refer to God as He is in His essence, but only to "a divine being (*shai 'ilāhī*)" (ibid. [224/205]), a concrete entity that embodies God's immanence in the world and that human beings can address: "In speaking of a divine being we use the appellation Adonai—*alef, daleth, nun, yod*—as if we wished to say: 'O Lord, You are my ruler'" (ibid.).[57] The Divine immanence can be embodied in some object as a result of human craft, whereby spiritual forms are copied and impressed upon physical objects. Thus "the form of the Tabernacle was shown to Moses on the mountain; that is, God caused the tabernacle, the tent, the table, the candelabrum, the ark, and the surrounding court, with its pillars, coverings, and all appurtenances, to appear to him in their real shape, in the form in which He commanded to have them executed" (1,99 [55/72]). Following this line of thought, in the affair of the Golden Calf the Israelites' "sin consisted [only] in the manufacture of an image, which was forbidden to them, and in attributing Divine power to a thing made and chosen by themselves without God's command" (1,97 [51/68]).[58]

The embodiments of the Divine immanence in human beings, whether as individuals or groups, have extreme importance. When a human being communes with the Divine Order, an essential change takes place in his nature and he acquires "the most perfect soul and ... the loftiest intellect that it is

---

57. Compare 1,97. In this entire section *Divine Order* denotes an attribute or form deriving from God and inherent in various objects. It also refers to the object in which the attribute or form inheres. The latter sense is appropriate in the passage quoted. The pillar of cloud is included in the list of things that appeared through the prophets and that may be designated by the names *Glory of God, angel of God,* and *Shekhinah* (2,7). Compare 4,3.

58. Halevi and Abraham Ibn Ezra held the same opinion about the incident of the Golden Calf; see Ibn Ezra's long commentary on Ex. 31:18. This seems to be how we should interpret 1,98 [53/70]: "man can only attain to Divine 'order' through Divine 'ordinance,' viz., through actions ordained by God." In other words, man can attain the Divine Order only through the Divine object, which is "something visible" (1,97 [50/68]), and on condition that these are "actions ordained by God." Taken in this light, the rest of the section alludes to mediation such as the worship of the calf—which was "done by the advice of the astrologers and magicians among them" (1,97 [52/69]); but the words "through Divine 'ordinance' " are not in the Arabic. Compare Even-Shmuel's Hebrew translation here; Wolfson, "Hallevi and Maimonides on Prophecy," n. 75. See also the comparison between Ahab's party and Jeroboam's party (4,13). See also M. Breuer, ed., *Sefer Niẓẓaḥon Yashan (Nizzahon Vetus)* (Ramat-Gan, 1978), p. 60.

possible for a human being to possess, and, surpassing intellect, the Divine power (*al-qūwa al-ʾilāhīyya*), that is, an eminence enabling him to enter into communication with God and spiritual beings and to comprehend the great truths without instruction, after slight reflection.... Thus the Divine Order descended among them from the earlier to the later generations" (1,95 [46/64]).[59] Here participation in the Divine immanence means communion with the Divine Order—receiving the "Divine power." Through this power human beings can comprehend great truths without "instruction" (*taʿlīm*); that is, without the discursive process required to discover the truth through reason alone.[60] Similarly, one who attains the degree of prophetic vision, "ascends, so to speak, from his kind and joins the angels, 'another spirit' (Num. 14:24) entering in him.... All these are symbols of the Holy Spirit, which enwraps the prophet in the hour of prophecy.... All previous doubts of man concerning *elohim* vanish then" (4,15 [246/222]).[61] Prophets or pious sages merit the epithet *divine* because they "are original instruments of the divine will, which employs them without meeting with unwillingness and performs miracles through them.... He who occupies such a degree has a right to be styled 'a man of God,' a description comprising human and divine qualities, and as if one would say: a godly man" (4,3 [224/204]).[62] Thus, as we

---

59. See also 5,21. Sometimes Halevi identified the Divine Order, in this sense, with the "Divine glory" (1,27).

60. Similarly, Adam and "those of his descendants who are like him"—"sons of God" who attained the "divine power"—communed with "God and spiritual beings" and knew "the great truths without instruction" (1,95 [46/64]). According to Abraham Ibn Ezra, Halevi glossed the verse, "the sons of God saw the daughters of men" (Gen. 6:2) as follows: " 'the sons of God' refers to the sons of Seth, who was a righteous man; 'the daughters of man' refers to the daughters of Cain" (First Recension ad loc.). See also 2,14.

61. See also 1,42; 5,20. Compare 3,53.

62. See also 1,103. According to this, Divine speech itself stems directly from a "Divine cause": "The speech of a prophet at the time when he is enwrapped by the Holy Spirit is in every part directed by the Divine Order, the prophet himself being powerless to alter one word" (5,20 [321/284]). Perhaps its wondrous influence on its hearers, too, is bound up with its ontological status as a "divine effect" (ibid. [316/280]).

have seen, the prophet's outward appearance changes,[63] and the course of his life is not determined exclusively by natural law. Analogously, the destiny of the Jewish people, the nation of prophets, unlike the destiny of the other nations, is not determined by the laws of history.

We see that the later thought, marked by the fundamental tension between empirical elements and theoretical and metaphysical elements, has no explanation for the Divine immanence. Even though he is aware that his system cannot accommodate such an explanation, Halevi, to satisfy didactic needs, was compelled to advance the theory of mediation to explain the Divine immanence. At the same time he endeavored to safeguard, to the extent possible, the role of Divine sovereignty and the spontaneity of the Divine Will in his system. Thus, when he rejected the Philosopher's doctrine of emanation, which he supported in his earlier thought, he gave the mediating agent the status of a created entity. Unlike God in His essence, this mediating agent operates according to defined laws and its action is expressed in emanation.

Alongside this theory of mediation, which is intended to explain the immanence of the transcendent God, Halevi, for reasons crucial to his doctrine as a whole, developed a second theory of mediation that could explain and ground a human attachment to God. In this second theory of mediation the mediating agents are the concrete embodiments of the Divine immanence in the world.

Later, in our discussion of creation, we shall find that the subjective problem associated with accepting the idea of ex nihilo creation—the idea of an absolute beginning—forced Halevi to limit the demands he made on the believer and to accept alternative beliefs about the origin of the world. Even these alternative beliefs, however, must posit the sovereignty of God and the spontaneity of His will.

63. So too, when the "Light of the Shekhinah" leaves human beings, "their intelligence wanes, their bodies deteriorate, and their beauty fades" (2,62 [118/121]). That is, the manifestations of beauty in the world are themselves expressions of Divine immanence. See p. 250.

8. Divine Spontaneity and Creation

The contrast between the God of Abraham—the visible God—and the God of Aristotle—the intelligible God—is not limited to the epistemological plane; it has fundamental importance on the ontological plane as well. Unlike the autarkic Aristotelian God, the God who is manifested in human experience goes beyond Himself. This emergence is expressed in intentional involvement in existence external to Himself, focusing on the human realm. The three expressions of this emergence are: (1) God's active role in prophetic experiences; (2) the manifestation of His will—His commandments; and (3) His intervention in historical processes and the miracles that He works.[64] Knowledge of this aspect of God who goes beyond Himself—expressed as knowledge of Him as the Tetragrammaton—is the loftiest knowledge that human beings can have. God as the Tetragrammaton is known through His unmediated actions, as they find expression in the prophetic experience peculiar to members of the Jewish people (4,3). Through His immediate acts manifested in the prophetic experience unique to the Jewish people, God reveals to mankind as much of the truth as they require to be able to respond to God's appeals to them. For example, the name *ehyeh*, with which God introduced Himself to the Israelites (Ex. 3:14), is intended "to prevent the human mind from pondering over an incomprehensible but real entity" (4,3 [221/202]). A cognate term is the *Glory of God*, which, according to one opinion, "is that fine substance which follows the will of God, assuming any form God wishes to show to the prophet" (ibid. [233/211]). Accordingly, "those endowed with prophetic vision" know God as "an incorporeal being that guides all corporeal substances." At the same time, they are aware of the limitations of human cognition: "We therefore dwell on His works, but

---

64. By contrast, in the earlier thought, the "attributes" of the Tetragrammaton have a cosmic context: "The attributes connected with the Tetragrammaton describe creations of God, produced without any natural intermediaries, as, e.g., Creator, Producer, Maker, 'who *alone* doeth great wonders' (Ps. 136:4), i.e., by His bare intention and will, to the exclusion of any assisting cause" (2,2 [71/85]).

refrain from describing His nature. For it would be a defect in Him if we could grasp it" (5,21 [329/291]).⁶⁵

The teleological and intentional nature of God's emergence beyond Himself and its focus in concrete human reality are the foundation of Halevi's later thought and at the center of his dispute with Aristotelianism. This dispute, as we have seen, revolves around two main axes. The first crux is the purpose of this Divine emergence. Positing such a purpose requires distinguishing potential Divine Will, which has not yet actualized its goal but aspires to do so, from actual Divine Will, which has already actualized its goal. The second crux involves the direction of this Divine emergence. The Divine emergence, because aimed at human existence in its uniqueness, contingency, and mutability, must be seen as selective and as varying in direction and in intensity. This selectivity and variability stem from God's own internal decisions, which change from time to time, that is, from spontaneous determinations of the sovereign Divine Will. Similarly, the Divine emergence forces us to ascribe a potential dimension to Divine existence—the potentiality of will and the potentiality of knowledge—a potential whose actualization depends on the constitution of a bond that can mediate between God and material entities. Such a bond entails the possibility of divine speech that is physical and addressed to human ears (1,89) and of "forms" that are directed at human eyes (4,3).

As we have seen, the Aristotelian philosopher rejects, as a matter of principle, both the teleological intentionality of this Divine connection and its particular focus in human beings. Halevi, however, views them as the keystones of Judaism and of the revealed religions in general. This basic opposition finds literary expression in the confrontation at the beginning of the *Kuzari* between the dream, with its intrinsic message, and the Philosopher's doctrine. The dream, as an individual experience, is a manifestation of a voluntary Divine initiative—an initiative that Halevi intentionally avoided explaining in any way. The dream expresses, in its own occurrence and content, a

---

65. See also 4,17; 4,27.

spontaneous determination of the Divine Will, focused on a particular individual, the king of the Khazars. But the Philosopher begins by denying that dreams have any theoretical value; whatever value human action has, it is "not in order to receive favor from [the Prime Cause] or to divert its wrath" (1,1 [9/38]).

The spontaneous ability of the Divine Will to alter itself has various empirical manifestations—extraordinary events, which are in part ex nihilo creation and in part ex rebus creation. These manifestations are an integral part of direct prophetic experience—a Divine call—or of indirect prophetic experience—wonders and portents (5,21).[66] The later Halevi believed that these manifestations are the only way that human beings can become aware of the existence of a Divine Will that can modify itself. The knowledge that "God has intercourse with man" depends on the occurrence of "a miracle that changes the nature of things, so that man may recognize that God alone, who created them from nought, is able to do so" (1,8 [16/43]).[67] The possibility of God's evincing an interest in concrete human existence, with its mutability and uniqueness, depends on the existence of such a Divine Will. Similarly, Abraham set aside his speculations "and only strove to gain favor of God, having ascertained what this was and how and where it could be obtained" (4,27 [269/239]), only after he had had a vision that led him to "believe in the Divine will and creation" (4,26 [269/239]).[68] Similarly, the Jewish people's awareness of a "beginning" that originates with God depends on their presence at the

---

66. See also Wolfson, "Hallevi on Design," p. 159.

67. In this section (1,8) the King presents an argument with three parts: (1) "God has intercourse with man"; (2) "a miracle which changes the nature of things"; and (3) a creator who "created them from nought." It is clear from this section that the problem of Divine revelation and response to an individual is merely one facet of the difficulty of positing "intercourse" between God and a "contemptible piece of clay" (cf. "creatures made of low and contemptible material"—1,68 [33/54]).

68. The Philosopher, by contrast, denies the possibility of any alteration of the Divine Will; of creation, whether ex nihilo or ex rebus; and of an intentional association between God and human beings.

Revelation at Sinai—an event accompanied by events that recapitulate Creation: "The result was that everyone who viewed those scenes became convinced that the matter proceeded directly from God. It is to be compared to the first act of creation. Thus the belief in the law connected with those scenes was as firmly established in the mind as the belief in the creation of the world, and that He created it" (1,91 [45/63]).[69] Now we can understand that it is no accident that the later Halevi tended to associate experiences that represent a new creation with recognition of a changeable Divine Will and God's interest in human beings—an interest manifested, as we shall see, in His commands and imperatives.[70]

In the previous chapter we demonstrated that God's awareness of man entails the existence of a personal providence, because of the personal nature of such intentional awareness. Accordingly, the later Halevi holds that God knows individuals in their moments and their smallest actions. For example, Abraham, after "conceiving the Divine Order by tasting, not by speculating, observed that no detail of his life escaped God and that He rewarded him instantly for his piety" (4,17 [247/223]). The Israelites maintained this belief in individual providence even when they were awash in idolatry (4,23). This awareness of individual providence derives from the experience of extraordinary events that embody creation in little (2,54).[71] It is only thanks to such experiences of ex nihilo creation that human beings realize that it was God who spoke to them as individuals (1,8).[72] As we have seen, these events are the foundation of the

---

69. Compare 1,81. The suddenness is an essential element of Creation (ibid.). All things, including all species of animals, were created in the same instant (1,91; 4,26; 5,14). Seeing is the most appropriate method of intuiting suddenness, as we shall learn in the next chapter.

70. See also 1,67; 1,83; 2,54; 5,21; and see further the Appendix.

71. Compare 5,6. The Philosopher, who does not believe in Creation, also rejects the possibility of individual providence (4,13). The Mutakallimun, however, derive individual providence from the creation of the world (5,18, Axiom 7).

72. Similarly, Adam became cognizant of individual providence only after the creation of Eve—a creation that changed the nature of things (4,3).

coalescence, continued existence, and actualization of the historical and universal vocation of the Jewish people (2,54).

Now we can understand Halevi's doctrine of Creation as well. Although, as noted, he vigorously maintained the fundamental importance of knowledge of events that embody creation in little, he also belittled the value of knowing the truth about the creation of the world as a whole—even though he unambiguously asserted that the world was created from nothing, that the world "came into existence by the will of God at the time He desired" (5,14 [305/270]).[73] Halevi's view of Creation is not central to his later thought. He held that Judaism is unique precisely in that this doctrine is not the foundation of God's interest in human beings or the ground of man's association with this interest (1,11; 1,12).[74] Nor does it underlie the special interest that God manifests in a particular human collective—that is, the election of Israel (1,27). The greater import that Halevi attributes to events that embody creation in little, vis-à-vis the creation of the world as a whole, stems from the empiricist trends mentioned previously. These events are possible objects of human experience; but the creation of the world is not the object of any experience whatsoever. Its veracity and meaning are derived only from abstract syllogisms. It is no accident that the main discussion of the creation of the world (1,60–67) is merely an aside, part of the reply to the King's polemic question whose real thrust is to question the reliability of the entire chain of tradition.

---

73. We can infer from 1,67 (as well as 1,8 and 1,89) that Halevi's willingness to recognize the legitimacy of belief in creation from primordial matter is granted under compulsion.

74. The Christian and Muslim scholars begin their presentations by declaring their belief in the creation of the world, whereas the Rabbi initially ignores this issue. Halevi returns to this in §25 (ibid. [20/46]): "In the same way God commenced His speech to the assembled people of Israel: 'I am the God whom you worship, who has led you out of the land of Egypt'; He did not say, 'I am the Creator of the world and your Creator.'" The analogy between the Rabbi's introductory remarks to the King and God's first words to the Israelites is intended to underscore the importance that Halevi attributes to this position.

Halevi rejects, though without enthusiasm, the Aristotelian position that the world is eternal.[75] He is, however, cognizant of the difficulties that lurk for the believer; hence he accepts the legitimacy of the opinion that the world was created from "an eternal substance and the existence of many worlds prior to this one" (1,67 [31/54]), on condition that its advocates believe that "*this* world was created at a certain epoch, and that Adam and Noah were the first human beings" (ibid.).[76] Halevi was even tolerant of the exegetical identification of the concepts *tohu wabohu, water,* and *darkness* with the primordial matter from which the world was created, provided that the act of Creation itself be understood as an expression of a spontaneous and intentional determination of the Divine Will: "Some people believe that the 'water' spoken of in the biblical account of the creation is an appellation for this matter, and that 'the spirit of the Lord hovering over the surface of the water' only expresses the divine will which penetrates all atoms of matter, with which

---

75. It should be emphasized that the Rabbi's rebuttal of the Aristotelian view that the universe is eternal is intentionally vague. In the central passage dealing with this opinion (1,67) he refrains from an explicit condemnation of those who advocate it; their error can be inferred only indirectly: this opinion is not included in the list of the views that do not impugn the belief of their advocates. Evidently we should also distinguish between those whose faith is imperfect and those who are excluded from the congregation of the faithful. If so, those who maintain the eternity of the universe do not thereby excommunicate themselves from the congregation of the faithful. See H. A. Wolfson, "The Platonic, Aristotelian and Stoic Theories of Creation in Halevi and Maimonides," *Essays in Honor of J. H. Hertz* (London, 1942), p. 438.

76. From the Rabbi's emphasis that "*this* world was created" (1,67 [31/54]) we can infer that the doctrine of the multiplicity of worlds preceding this world refers to an infinite multiplicity thereof. With regard to the assumption of some eternal entity alongside God, there is no difference between this doctrine and the theory of the eternity of primordial matter, attributed to Plato. Neither doctrine must assume that a spiritual God is the cause of the existence of matter. See Wolfson, "The Platonic, Aristotelian and Stoic Theories of Creation." Wolfson is inclined to explain the theory of multiple worlds as relating to a finite multiplicity. Theories of an infinitude of consecutive worlds are mentioned by Abraham bar Hiyya in the name of the "the divine philosophers." See Abraham bar Hiyya Savasorda, *Megillat ha-megalleh,* ed. S. A. Poznanski and J. Guttmann (Berlin, 1924), p. 10; Scholem, *Reshit ha-qabbalah,* p. 179.

He does what, how, and when he desires, as the potter with the shapeless clay. The absence of form and order is called darkness and *tohu wabohu*" (5,2 [280/249]). Similarly, Halevi attributed to the Patriarch Abraham, whom he held to be the author of *Sefer Yetzirah*, the view that the world was created from *tohu*—"the primary matter, not qualified" (4,25 [264/235]),[77] even though the vagueness of the text in *Sefer Yetzirah* admits another interpretation, compatible with the doctrine of ex nihilo creation.[78]

In addition, the King's response to the Rabbi (4,26 [269/329]) reflects Halevi's belief that the author of *Sefer Yetzirah* maintained that the world was created from primordial matter: "Why should the letters H W J or an angel or a sphere or other things be required if we believe in the Divine will and creation, and if we believe that God created the immense variety of things and species in one moment, as is related in the Book of Genesis?" Here the King is criticizing the position of *Sefer Yetzirah* on the creation of the world, while noting the link between the meaning of the Divine Will and the manner in which the world came into existence. In the next section (4,27), the Rabbi agrees with the King and goes on to make both the meaning of the Divine Will and the manner in which the world came into existence depend on the nature of the association between God and human beings. Abraham, before the Lord spoke to him,

---

77. See D. Kaufman, "R. Yehudah ha-levi ve-shitato ʿolam qadmon" (R. Judah Halevi and his doctrine of a primordial world), *Meḥqarim be-sifrut ʿivrit shel yemei ha-beinayyim* (Studies in medieval Hebrew literature), (Jerusalem, 1962), pp. 208–211; D. H. Neumark, *Toledot ha-filosofiyah be-yisrael* (History of philosophy in Israel) (Jerusalem, 1971), vol. 2, pp. 304–306; Waxman, *Ketavim nivḥarim*, pp. 75ff. Waxman (ibid., n. 35) distinguishes between "first matter" and "primordial matter." There is no support for this distinction in the text itself; we may assume that had it been accepted by Halevi he would have explicitly noted this.

78. Thus Saadia Gaon interpreted *Sefer Yetzirah* as follows: "and its interpretation is: He created things ex nihilo, and what is from what is not, and quarried great pillars from impalpable air" (*Sefer Yeẓirah, with the Commentary of R. Saadia Gaon*, trans. Y. Kapah [Jerusalem, 1972] [Hebrew], 4,5, p. 121). See also Scholem, *Reshit ha-qabbalah*, pp. 45–47.

wrote what he wrote in *Sefer Yetzirah;* but after that vision "he gave up all his speculations and only strove to gain God's favor, having ascertained what this was" (ibid.). From the previous section we can infer that Abraham's new knowledge of God's will also involved a change in his view of Creation. Of course, the very ascription to Abraham of the view that the world was created from primordial matter endows it with some measure of legitimacy, despite Halevi's own reservations about it.[79]

Now we can understand how rejection of the Aristotelian theory of an eternal universe and qualified acceptance of the view of creation from primordial matter are compatible with the later Halevi's focus on the nature of the bond between God and the world, and in particular with man, rather than on learning the abstract truth about how the world came into being. Halevi was less concerned with God as Creator of the universe than with God who "controls everything corporeal" (5,21 [329/292]), who "watches and guards it, who knows both great and small, rewards the good and the wicked" (2,54 [112/116]). God's unlimited sovereignty is perfectly compatible with the view that the world was created from primordial matter, since that theory, too, entails the assumption that this world, in its concrete particularity, is the consequence of a new determination of the Divine Will, which governs "all atoms of matter, with which He does what, how, and when He desires" (5,2 [281/249]).[80] According to Halevi, God's sovereignty in the world can be deduced from extraordinary events that are ex rebus creation—the conversion of "one thing into another"—and not necessarily from ex nihilo creation—"new creations": "[The Torah] tells of miracles and transformations of the normal cause of things, either through new creations or by changing one thing into

---

79. Note further that Halevi did not enumerate ex nihilo acts of creation among the "divine effects" (5,20). He merely distinguished Divine acts that are in accordance with natural law from those that violate natural law. See also H. A. Wolfson, "Judah Hallevi on Causality and Miracles," *Meyer Waxman Jubilee Volume* (Chicago and Tel Aviv, 1966), pp. 137–153.

80. Here the word *how*, which does not appear in Zifroni's Hebrew text, reflects the emendation proposed by Baneth, "Halevi and al-Ghazali," p. 319, n. 3. See also 1,67; 1,83; 1,89; 5,4.

another, to testify to the power of the Creator, who accomplishes whatever He wills, and whenever He wills it" (1,67 [31/193]).[81] Thus Adam recognized God as the creator of the world after "He had ... addressed, rewarded, and punished him, and created Eve from one of his ribs. By this he was convinced that He was the Creator of the world" (4,3 [219/200]).[82] Because this degree of sovereignty, which guarantees God's unlimited dominion over man's fate, suffices for Halevi's system, he is willing to consider the objective theoretical problems posed by the concept of ex nihilo creation—but only on condition that one believe that God created the world, even if from primordial matter.

We should not overlook the fact that Halevi's willingness to recognize a priori a believer's right to maintain an erroneous theory of creation derived also from his basic view of pure theoretical knowledge in general. As we saw in the previous chapter, in his later thought Halevi was disposed to make light of the intrinsic value of this realm. The status of human beings before God is determined by their actions, not by their beliefs.

---

81. Again, "We see substances changed, the course of nature altered, and new things produced without craft" (5,21 [329/291]). It seems likely that "new things produced" refers to ex nihilo creation, because "substances altered" clearly refers to ex rebus creation.

82. Nevertheless, Halevi tended to assume that those who have experienced events that embody ex rebus creation are inclined to acknowledge the ex nihilo creation of the world. By the same token, as a consequence of the nations' pondering the destiny of the Jewish people and "all that befell them" (2,54 [113/116]), "today the whole civilized world acknowledges that God is eternal and that the world was created" (ibid.). It seems likely that "was created" refers to ex nihilo creation of the universe—hence the juxtaposition of the eternity of God with the created status of the world. It also seems that Adam deduced that God created the world ex nihilo from his experience of extraordinary events of ex rebus creation (4,3). Similarly, Abraham, after his vision, recognized God as Creator of the world (4,26–27), where the context suggests that the reference is to ex nihilo creation. Only the God who created the universe ex nihilo can work a wonder that "changes the nature of things" (1,8 [16/43]). This seems to contradict what Halevi says in 1,67; namely, that sometimes a "believer in the Torah" holds the theory of ex rebus creation and that miracles alone cannot teach that the world is created. Only the prophetic tradition can vouch for the creation of the world.

Halevi's interest in the theoretical plane focused on its influence on other provinces of human existence.

But even if belief in creation from primordial matter can be tolerated, because it is compatible with God's sovereignty over the world and the possibility of intercourse between God and human beings, the Aristotelian view that the world is eternal must be rejected. Halevi's opposition stemmed chiefly from the theological assumptions about the essence of Divinity that underlie this view, because, as we have seen, they cannot be reconciled either with God's sovereignty over the concrete world—a mutable multiplicity—or with the possibility of intercourse between God and human beings. From the outset (1,4) the King associates belief in the creation of the world in six days with belief in a God who holds intercourse with human beings. He believes that the Philosopher's postulate of the eternity of the world, like his denial of the possibility of Divine intercourse with an individual, is rooted in his view of God as Prime Cause—a view that rules out new Divine initiatives, whether toward human beings or the world. The possibility of God's speaking to individuals—through prophecy, true dreams, or miracles—requires a different concept of God.[83]

Another reason for Halevi's rejection of the idea that the world is eternal is that it contradicts the Torah—and this contradiction calls into question both the reliability of the received tradition and the reliability of prophetic revelation in general.[84] Against the philosophers who deny the existence of Adam as an expression of their view that the world is eternal—"philosophers . . . teach the eternity of matter and that man never arose otherwise than from semen and blood" (5,14 [304/270])—Halevi argued that "according to the Torah, it was God who created the world, together with animals and plants. There is no

---

83. God as Prime Cause implies an impersonal deity for whom speech, in the normal sense of this term, is quite irrelevant. As we have seen, it also includes the idea of God as autarkic, a being totally withdrawn into its own internal necessity—a necessity that leaves no place for any true innovation, whether with regard to human beings or with regard to the world as a whole.

84. One of the tasks of prophecy is to teach about the past (1,43).

need to presuppose intermediaries or combinations [of elements]" (ibid.).[85]

From everything we have said it follows that the discussion of the creation of the world, in the later thought, is largely apologetic and polemic. It deals chiefly with the Aristotelian view that the world is eternal, because its theological postulates contradict those of Judaism. From this perspective, the issue of creation is subsumed under theology.

In summary, the theology of the later thought is marked by empiricist trends. These find expression both on the epistemological plane—a preference for knowledge of God through sensory experience—and on the theological plane—the characterization of God as a pole of human experience. As we shall see in the next chapter, these trends are also expressed on the psychological plane. The importance of sensory experience in the knowledge of God is manifested in the anthropomorphisms associated with Him as well as in the distinction between God who appears in experience—God as involved in intercourse with man—and God as He is in Himself. This distinction, rooted in the common view of the nature of sensory perception, makes it possible to preserve the transcendent concept of God as He is in Himself, and with even greater stringency than in Aristotelian philosophy.

In the chapters that follow we shall see that just as the theology is marked by God's role in His intercourse with human begins, so the anthropology is marked by man's place in that same intercourse.

85. See also 1,67; 4,3; 4,26.

16

THE LATER ANTHROPOLOGY

Halevi's anthropology is associated with the general empiricist trends of his later thought and the special significance it accords to revelation. This empiricism mandates the importance of the senses and of the external aspect of human experience, which alone can be perceived by the senses. His view of revelation leads to many parallels between his anthropology and his theology. These parallels are manifested in a recognition of the importance of the concrete individual, with his or her integrity, mutability, and historical affiliations. The anthropology has fundamental implications both for Halevi's historiosophy, as we shall see in the next chapter, and for the significance of the commandments of the Torah; indirectly it also affects his doctrine of the election of the Jewish people, as we shall see in Chapter 18.

1. Man as Individuum

The salient empiricism of Halevi's later thought is accompanied by a concept of man as *individuum*, in the two senses of this term: (1) in the older sense, as a whole that cannot be divided into parts; and (2) in the more modern sense of the term, as an entity possessing certain traits that cannot be absorbed or nullified. In polar antithesis to the Philosopher's concept of man, Halevi believed (1) that the essence of man is not located exclusively in the mind, but includes body and soul, imagination and reason, emotions and senses; and (2) that man, in his essence, is not an individual in the first (and older) sense, but only in the second sense, ontologically autonomous and with a fate determined by its own selfhood.

The concept of man as an integral whole entails his uniqueness. Similarly, the inclusion of the corporeal and material dimension in the totality of human existence leads ipso facto to man's uniqueness. This accords with the Aristotelian principle (which Halevi does not question) that it is matter that constitutes individuality.

In Halevi's system, this concept of man parallels the nature of the reciprocal relations between God and man. These relations are anchored not only in the ontological realm, but also, and chiefly, in the ongoing dialogue between God and man. Man's position as one pole of the intercourse between himself and God utterly annihilates his anonymity and gives him both his uniqueness and his internal unity. As we shall see, just as this notion of man follows from the Divine call to man, it also follows from the appropriate way in which human beings should respond to this call. As early as the dream at the beginning of the book, the angel addresses a particular human being—the king of the Khazars.[1] There is a similar emphasis on the personal nature of the call in the thought experiment where the King is asked to imagine that he has received a message from the king of India (1,21). The messengers of that monarch are not street evangelists, but are dispatched to a specific individual—the king of the Khazars; they bring him a personal letter from the king of India, medicines to cure him, and poisons for his

---

1. This call is not through the intellect but through the imagination—in a dream. The King himself notes that true dreams or visions are granted "to persons who do not devote themselves to study or the purification of their souls" (1,4 [12/40]). See E. Schweid, "Ha-mivneh ha-sifruti shel ha-ma'amar ha-rishon min ha-Kuzari" (The literary structure of Part One of the *Kuzari*), *Tarbiẓ* 30 (1961): 257–272; idem, *Ta'am ve-haqqashah*, pp. 55–56.

enemies. They do not offer him spiritual guidance only; they also tend to his body.² In answer to the Rabbi's question, "would this make you beholden to him?" (1,21 [19/46]), the King, aware of the personal dimension of the message from the king of India, responds: "Certainly. For this would remove my former doubt that the Indians have a king. I should also acknowledge that a proof of his power and dominion has reached me" (1,22 [19/46]). Another manifestation of the personal plane is that God's words obligate only those to whom God calls. The King concludes from this that the Torah was given only to the Israelites (1,26).

2. Action, Intention, and Abstract Thought

The integrated conception of man and the emphasis on the importance of the external aspect of human experience also underlie the superiority of action over an as-yet unrealized intention to act and over abstract knowledge of truth. This is because action alone allows human beings to function with their full physical and spiritual being: the limbs, senses, reason, emotions, and imagination. In a period when prophecy is unattainable, the pious individual, the ideal servant of the Lord, "concedes to the senses their fair share according as he requires them, using hands, feet, and tongue for necessary or useful actions, likewise hearing, seeing, and the general perception which unites them, as well as imagination, instinctive judgment, thought, and memory; finally will-power, which commands all these, but is in its turn subservient to the decision of the intellect. He does not allow any of the limbs or faculties to perform their various tasks without restriction, nor does he allow them to encroach on each another" (3,5 [142/137]). His will power "stimulates all his organs

---

2. Similarly, God's attachment to the Jewish people is manifested in a concern for their political and economic needs: "For if the divine presence is among you, you will perceive [it] by the fertility of your country, by the regularity with which your rainfalls appear in their due seasons, by your victories over your enemies in spite of your inferior numbers" (1,109 [59/75]). See further Y. Baer, "Eretz Yisrael ve-galut be-ʿeinei ha-dorot shel yemei ha-beinayyim" (Eretz Israel and the Diaspora in the eyes of the medieval generations), *Ziyyon* 6 (1934): 149–171.

to work with alertness, pleasure, and joy. They stand without fatigue when occasion demands; they bow down when he bids them to bow; they sit at the proper moment. The eyes look as a servant looks at his master; the hands do not play nor join together; the feet stand straight; all limbs are frightened and anxious to obey their master" (ibid. [144/139]).[3] Halevi and the Philosopher disagree, as we have noted, about the value of action; there are also fundamental differences between Halevi's earlier and later thought. As we shall see in the chapters that follow, the implications of this disagreement extend to both individual activity and collective-historical activity.

The value of action is the starting point of the *Kuzari* as both a literary work and as a philosophical system. In the very first section the King is confronted in his dream by the angel's uncompromising demand for particular deeds, and, at the same time, by the angel's great moderation regarding his theoretical predispositions as a priest serving in a pagan temple.[4] When the

3. In this regard, devotion expresses the perfect response of the servant of the Lord to serve his God with his entire being, as we shall see in Chapter 18.

4. In his poetry Halevi held that, in the final analysis, many pagans actually intend the worship of the one God. For example, in his poem ישעך יכירו עם בך יזכירו (Brody, 3:13): "those who were intended to be among his servants / in their hearts declare the unity of the one God, / and if with their mouths they deny it, inside them they bear witness to it." See 1,98 and 4,15. See also Heinemann, "Philosopher-poet," p. 202 n. 8. But we must not associate the angel's lenience with this opinion, because we cannot take Halevi to mean that he agrees with their intention. We can learn this also from the general context—the juxtaposition of the King's dream and the Philosopher's remarks later in §1. Furthermore, in the *Kuzari* Halevi straddled the fence on this issue; he also championed the contrary view, namely, that idolators do not have worship of the one God in mind, either because they have not acknowledged Him or because "they admitted the existence of God, but maintained that to serve Him was of no use" (4,1 [217/194]); see also 1,79. See further Chapter 4, note 46. See also S. Pines, "Al ha-munaḥ ruḥaniyyut u-meqorotav ve-ʿal mishnato shel Yehudah Ha-levi" (On the term 'spirituality' and its sources and the doctrine of Judah Halevi), *Tarbiẓ* 57 (1988): 529.

Now we can understand why there is no presentation of basic tenets of faith in the sections that reflect the later thought. By contrast, in Part III, which expresses Halevi's earlier thought, there is a list of "the articles of creed which complete the Jewish belief" (3,17 [160/154]). There is also an enumeration of the principles of the Mutakallimun (5,18 [310]).

King's unassisted endeavors to find an appropriate answer to the angel's demand fail to bear fruit, he turns to the Philosopher, from whom he learns that contemplation and intention are superior to action. But this position is the polar antithesis of what the angel had said in the dream. Hence the King is confronted by the fundamental problem of the value of action. It is the need to deal with this problem that compels him to call in representatives of the revealed religions.[5]

We can also learn about the inferiority of unrealized intention, in the later thought, from Halevi's explanation of the Binding of Isaac: This trial was set in order "to render [Abraham's] theoretical obedience practical, and to let it be the cause of his prosperity. [God] says subsequently: "Because thou hast done this thing ... I will bless thee (Gen. 22:10)" (5,20 [319/282]).[6] Similarly, Aaron was a participant in the sin of the Golden Calf because, like the Philosopher, he erroneously believed that people are judged by their intentions; he "sinned in causing what was only a sin of intention to become a sin in deed" (1,97 [52/69]).[7] Accordingly, Halevi asserted that even when human beings confess to nonobservance of a commandment, and even when observing it is impossible, their confession is only "somewhat useful" (5,27 [333/295]). This position spawns the activist trends of the later thought. As we shall see, this activism finds expression, inter alia, in his views about aliya to Eretz Israel.

In his later thought Halevi (unlike the Philosopher and unlike his own earlier view) believed that abstract truth itself acquires epistemological and existential significance only after it is embodied in human action: "The observance of the Sabbath is itself an acknowledgment of His omnipotence, an acknowledgment, however, through the medium of deeds; for he who observes the Sabbath because the work of creation was finished

---

5. Similarly, the fundamental difference between the revealed religions is located on the plane of action. See 1,2; 3,9; 4,13.

6. This idea also appears in 2,56.

7. This explanation may allude to the lackadaisical attitude toward observance of the commandments that was common in Halevi's time among the Jewish courtiers in Spain—a lenience that involved accepting the philosophical emphasis on intention and deprecation of action.

on it acknowledges, no doubt, the creation itself; and he who acknowledges the creation acknowledges the Creator and Originator; he, however, who does not believe in it, tends to the belief in the eternity of the world, and his conviction concerning the Creator is not undisturbed" (2,50 [109/114]). This dependence on action of the epistemological and existential significance of abstract truth is easily comprehended in light of the integrated conception of man—a conception that leaves no faculty, including the rational, totally independent. Thus, disputing the Philosopher's opinion, Halevi admonished:

> Do not believe someone who considers himself wise and thinks that he is so far advanced that he can grasp all metaphysical problems with the abstract intellect alone, without the support of anything that can be conceived or seen—such as words, writing, or any visible or imaginary forms. You cannot even collect the burden of your prayer in thought alone, without reciting it. Neither can you reckon up to a hundred without speaking, still less if this hundred be composed of different numbers. Were it not for the sensible perception that encompasses the organization of the intellect by means of similar sayings, that organization could not be maintained (4,5 [235/213]).[8]

An integrated notion of man is also latent in the content of the Divine call to man—the Torah commandments. Human beings are bidden to serve God in their full concrete being—their reason, emotions, feelings, and bodies. In this sense the integration of the personality is manifested in the mutual interdependence of its various elements.[9] Hence meticulous observance of the commandments of the Torah does not impair any

---

8. Halevi does not seem to have taken this view to its ultimate conclusion.

9. According to Halevi in his earlier thought, the pious individual "examines his sensations, and devotes part of them to God. Tradition teaches that the smallest measure of praise that it is man's duty to offer to God consists in a hundred blessings daily. First among these are the ordinary ones; then he supplements them in the course of the day by the blessings that accompany the savoring of odors, eatables, and things heard and seen. Whatever he does beyond those is a gain, and brings him nearer to God" (3,11 [153/147]). This is in utter contrast to the way of life of the ascetic

faculty of soul or body. The Torah "imposes no asceticism on us. It rather desires that we keep the balance and grant every mental and physical faculty its due, as much as it can bear, without overburdening one faculty at the expense of another" (2,50 [108/113]).[10] Observance of the commandments as a result of thought and intention leads to a joy that is expressed in song and dance, which are themselves "worship and a bond of union [with] the Divine Order" (ibid. [109/113]).[11] Hence the

---

(3,1). Compare Ibn Ezra on Eccles. 7:16. Again, "if the pious individual remembers [his dependence on God] with every movement he first acknowledges the Creator's part in them" (3,11 [152/146]). Furthermore, the pious individual serves God even in the difficulties associated with observing the commandments: Whenever he has done a good action it is "as if he had paid, as it were, a tribute to his Lord in enduring hardships in order to obey Him" (ibid. [151/145]). See also Heinemann, *Taʿamei miẓvot be-sifrut Yisrael* (The rationale for the commandments in Jewish literature), (Jerusalem, 1966), p. 152, n. 57. In these sections Halevi described the pious individual but did not identify with him. As we have seen in other matters, here too the pious individual sometimes expresses, in his personality and opinion, views that Halevi would adopt in his later thought. See H. H. Ben-Sasson, "Yiḥud ʿam yisrael le-daʿat benei ha-meʾah ha-shteim ʿesreh" (The uniqueness of the Jewish people according to the people of the twelfth century), *Peraqim* 2 (1969–1974), p. 157. Compare Saadia Gaon, *The Book of Beliefs and Opinions*, trans. Samuel Rosenblatt (New Haven, 1948), Treatise X, Chapter 1.

10. Compare 3,5.

11. It is no accident that the King responds to this position in the next section: "This sentence seems to go too far, and is overbold in expressing that the Creator is glorified through mortal man" (2,51 [111/115]). Starting in the next section (§52), and continuing through §62, the Rabbi endeavors to provide a rationale for God's glorification through "flesh and blood." Similarly, the Jews' circumcision is a warrant of their "connection with that Divine Order" (2,34 [101/108]). Compare 3,7. See also Ben-Sasson, "Yiḥud ʿam yisrael," p. 157; S. Pines, "Note sur la doctrine de la prophétie et la réhabilitation de la matière dans le Kuzari," *Mélanges de philosophie et de littérature juives* 1–2 (1956–1957): 253–260; and N. Simḥoni, "R. Yehudah Halevi be-tor meshorer leʾummi (R. Judah Halevi as a national poet), *Ha-ʿivri he-ḥadash* (The new Hebrew), (Warsaw, 1912), pp. 56–78. Compare 3,5. There, despite the emphasis on the importance of worshipping the Lord with the body, it becomes clear toward the end of the section that the goal is to liberate the soul from its animal and physical nature. This dichotomous view of the human condition is typical, as we have noted, of Halevi's earlier thought.

duty of song is placed on "the aristocracy of the people, that is, the Levites, who made practical use of [songs] in the holy house and in the holy season. For their maintenance they relied on the tithes, since music was their only occupation" (2,64 [120/123]).

We see, then, that the later Halevi gave primacy to life in this world, where man is in "the bonds of this life in spite of the hardship of this world" (1,106 [58/74]), rather than to continued existence after death, when human beings are released from their bodies, senses, and earthly needs (1,109).[12] This is despite his agreement that one who witnesses great historical events "no doubt longs for the perpetual separation of his soul from his material senses, in order to enjoy that light. It is such a person who would desire death" (1,108 [58/74]). Prophets are duty-bound to squelch this ineluctable desire, rooted in their legitimate aspiration to remain at their higher spiritual degree, because its realization would prevent them from fulfilling their mission in this world. From this perspective, the prophets' vocation outweighs their individual status (ibid.).[13] Hence whenever there is any suspicion that a human being may ignore his body and

---

12. In this section Halevi again stressed the difference between Judaism and other religions with regard to the vocation of the human servant of God. In Judaism, the vocation is observance of the commandments, and the reward is paid in this world. In the other religions, however, human beings are supposed to resemble the Deity, and this is realized only in the world to come: "All the promises of the other religions have the same basis, namely, the anticipation of being near God and His hosts" (ibid. [ES41/76]; see Even-Shmuel's note ad loc.). Compare also 3,1, where a fundamental distinction is drawn between the "servant of God" in the present and the elect of bygone generations. Still, the former, too, loves the world and length of days. In his earlier thought, Halevi explained that this is "because it affords him opportunities of deserving the World to Come" (ibid.). See M. Buber, *Bein ʿam le-ʾarẓo* (Jerusalem, 1985), pp. 71–72.

13. Accordingly, just as the parable in 1,109 relates to the last part of the section—"these companions are the Children of Israel"—it also relates to its first part (and to the previous section, 108): Taking leave of the king and returning to the wilderness represent Moses' descent from Mount Sinai, but they also symbolize the prophets' return to their senses after having been sundered from them during the period when they enjoyed "that light" (1,103 [57/74], 1,108 [58/75]; compare 4,15). To the "longing" for "the perpetual separation of his soul from his material senses ... [and desire for] death" (1,108 [58/74]) the Rabbi opposes the ideal of "remaining

physical needs and earthly vocation, it is the angels' duty to put him right: "Whoever of you comes to me, and ascends to heaven, is as those who, themselves, dwell among the angels—and the angels call them, 'son of man,' in order to distinguish them from the angels who stand in their midst" (1,109 [58/75]).[14]

---

in the ... Holy Land" (1,109 [59/75]). This section, which refers back to §105, is also a direct continuation of the previous section (but see the different view of Moscato ad loc.). The integrated view of existence that is expounded by the Rabbi from §103 through the end of Part I is countered by the King's multifaceted criticism; we should understand §109 as an answer to one of these criticisms (1,108). Unlike the Philosopher, the Rabbi stresses the ontological proximity of this world and the next, of body and soul, of action and contemplation, of the prophetic species and the angelic. There are two manifestations of this closeness: (1) the fundamental possibility of two-way commerce between heaven and earth—whose participants are both angels and prophets (in their bodies) (1,109; see also Moscato ad loc.); and (2) the unmediated presence, in this world, of the soul and the reward (though the latter is chiefly in the world to come) (§§103–105). This presence is an indication of the immortality of the soul and of the existence of the reward in the world to come (1,103, 1,109); it is strong enough to instill in human beings a sense of confidence in their continued existence in the world to come. See note 39. This confidence is the starting point for the King's criticisms. He rejects the Rabbi's factual assertion (ibid.), basing himself on his own personal experience (1,106). The Rabbi counters that only those who saw the great events of history are witnesses of this presence (1,107). The King accepts this answer but directs the Rabbi's attention to the internal contradiction in his existential conclusions, which follow from his doctrine of the immortality of the soul and reward in the world to come. The King argues—and the Rabbi agrees—that confidence in a reward in the world to come should lead to a "longing for death" (§§106–108). But this longing is incompatible with the need for a concrete prophetic presence in this world, a need felt even by those who were not present at the great historical events (§103). In other words, the King asserts that the Rabbi reaches the paradoxical conclusion that the more fit a man may be for the life of the world to come, and therefore seeks death, the more do other human beings need him. Section 109 is the Rabbi's attempt to deal with this fundamental paradox.

In §§110–115 the discussion focuses on an additional problem, associated with Halevi's view of the relationship between human action and reward in this world. This relationship is not compatible with the concrete historical fate of the Jewish people in exile.

14. Hirschfeld, followed by Zifroni, deleted the end of this passage ("and the angels call them, 'son of man,' in order to distinguish them from the angels who stand in their midst"). But this emendation seems unjustified. The sentence is a concise expression of one of the important conclusions of

One of the clearest manifestations of Halevi's new anthropology in his later thought is his view of personal immortality. He holds that the survival of the soul after death is not the result of an ontological process, as the Philosopher believes, and as Halevi himself believed in his earlier thought. Personal immortality is explained by God's omnipotence—it is evidence of his capacity for ex nihilo creation (5,14); but Halevi was careful to avoid any ontological assertion as to the nature of the soul. As part of the discussion of personal immortality, Halevi, evidently under the influence of Galen, hypothesized that the soul is neither an "intellectual body" nor spiritual, but corporeal (ibid); this seems to be his true opinion.[15] In light of our discussion, it is clear that he does not offer this theory by chance; rather, it is of a piece with his later thought. It is rooted in the primary status accorded to the reciprocal relations between God and man—relations that are sustained despite the polarity between God and man. The theory is also compatible with the disposition to decrease the ontological distance between the different components of man.

3. Individuals and Their Biographies

Halevi, unlike the Philosopher, believed that human beings are determined over time by the events that befall them. People are not molded exclusively by the emergence from potential to actual.

---

this section: the focus of human life in this world, the importance of the body and material conditions in general, and the emphasis on the status of the human being as an individual—all of which are interrelated. See also Even-Shmuel's note ad loc. Compare: "His wisdom did not demand of Him to create angels on earth, but mortals of flesh and blood, in whom natural gifts and certain characteristics prevail according to favorable or unfavorable influences" (3,17 [159/153]). There the "demand" is only an expression of the eternal order imprinted on existence by the Divine emanation.

15. This can also be deduced from his notion of the angels. As we have seen, in his later thought he holds that the angels are corporeal beings and that man was created in the image of the angels (4,3). Only God is totally spiritual (5,21). Abraham Ibn Ezra, in his commentary on Gen. 1:26, also states that man was created in the image of the angels, but maintained a different view as to the nature of the angels.

Circumstances, lifestyle, and historical affiliations play an active role in defining who and what a person is. The biography of a human being is not merely a passive backdrop to the process of his actualization; however, his unique essence is shaped by his experiences. This position is compatible with Halevi's view of the nature of man. Man's multifaceted nature spurs him on to greater involvement in many spheres of existence. This involvement, expressed by an interest in external reality and hence by the importance attributed to action, is also expressed in the relationship between human beings and their biographies. In this section we shall consider how dramatic one-time events shape a life. In the next section we shall turn our attention to the significance of the unique long-term affiliations of human beings and to the laws that control the shaping of individuals or human collectives.

The plot of the *Kuzari* is not just a literary scaffolding with no particular relevance to the theoretical content of the book. Rather, it spins out, concomitant with the systematic exposition of the philosophy, the web of circumstances in which human beings find themselves when they prepare to adopt particular theoretical ideas. The literary form chosen—the dialogue—reflects the correlation between the philosophical system and the order of human cognition.

At the very start of the book Halevi linked an incident in the King's life—the inexplicable recurrent dream—with the monarch's willingness to search for religious truth outside the context of his ancestral tradition by appealing to philosophy and then with his hesitation to accept philosophy as absolute truth.[16] Latent in this emphasis on biographical circumstances as the reason for turning to philosophy, as well as for the King's doubts about it, is a conception of man antithetical to that held by the Philosopher. For Halevi, one cannot separate a human being's intellectual achievement from the incidents of his or her life. The King's destiny depends in part on his encounter with the Philosopher. Only in the light of philosophy does he come to

---

16. See Schweid, *Taʿam ve-haqqashah*, pp. 55–56.

understand that the problem facing him is not merely to discover the essence of acts that are pleasing to God; first he must clarify whether there exists a God who is conscious of individual human beings and their deeds. It is the need for such an inquiry that renders the Muslim scholar's presentation (1,8–9) unsatisfactory.[17] Ultimately, the King would never attain the goal of his quest if he did not meet the Rabbi.

Like the King, the other characters in the book grow by virtue of their unique experiences. Even though Adam was "perfection itself" (1,95 [46/64]), he did not recognize the oneness of God nor God's interest in individuals until after "He had ... addressed, rewarded, and punished him, and created Eve from one of his ribs" (4,3 [219/200]). Similarly, Abraham did not arrive at a correct notion of God on his own powers and did not understand the importance of human action until after "conceiving the Divine Order by tasting, not by speculating" (4,17 [247/223]).[18]

As we have already seen (Chapters 14 and 15), in Halevi's later thought Divine Revelation acquires a distinctly ontological significance, because of the strong accent on the voluntary and dramatic aspect of the God-made-manifest. Divine Revelation as mediated by the prophet has a significance that is not merely epistemological and goes beyond its literal content. When human beings find themselves in circumstances that are evidence of their proximity to God, their status undergoes a major ontological change. The altered status is something new in all respects and cannot be grounded on their latent potential.

---

17. See Schweid, "Ha-mivneh ha-sifruti."

18. See also 4,27. Here Ibn Tibbon's translation seems more exact, especially because Halevi brings Ps. 34:9 as his prooftext. Halevi wished to present the spiritual resonance of sensory experience, which he called "taste," as a power that dissipates man's interest in theoretical knowledge of God and focuses his interest on worship of God—an interest that reaches its zenith in a willingness to give up one's life (4,16). On the emotional plane this is expressed by the fear and love of God. See also Efros, *Doctrines*, pp. 191–192.

4. Man's Dependence and Limitations

We have been considering the image of man from two vantage points: the relationship between human beings and their biographies, and the essence of human beings as individuals. Now we shall focus on man's limitations. These limitations are expressed in the subordination of individuals to an internal law that predetermines their possible course of development, as well as to the conditions of their environment. When we discussed the relationship between human beings and their biographies we encountered their dependence on one-time events, but did not deal with the internal logic in the order of their occurrence or with the laws that explain how these events influence them.

A comparison of the various accounts in the *Kuzari* reveals that, at a certain stage in the development of humanity—both individuals and collectives—Aristotelian philosophy was the norm. Adam, Abraham, the Jewish people as a whole, and all mankind accepted the philosophical method—the syllogism—as the only method for acquiring knowledge of God and used it to draw philosophical conclusions. They were liberated from the method and its conclusions after they experienced Divine Revelation, whether direct or mediated.[19] According to Halevi, it is no chance that Aristotelian philosophy appears at the horizon of human awareness; rather, it is the necessary outcome of any rational activity that is faithful to its essential method—the syllogism. Hence Halevi agreed that the Aristotelian philosopher represents the intellectual acme of mankind (2,14). Were there no revelation, philosophy would justly be accepted as the only

---

19. Similarly, in the life of pious individuals, perception of "the degree of the intellect" precedes that of "the divine degree" (3,5 [143/138]). See also 2,48 [106/111] on the relationship between "the rational laws" and "the Divine law." The latter is rooted in the theory of levels of existence. According to both the Rabbi and the Philosopher, existence is distributed into levels: the vegetative, the motive, and the rational. To these the Rabbi adds the level of the prophet. The relationship among the levels is such that each includes all of the perfections of those below it. See 1,31; 2,48; 3,23; 3,53; 4,3; 4,15. Compare further 1,95 and 2,26.

expression of truth. What is more, their encounter with philosophy provides human beings with the appropriate tools for discerning true Divine Revelation and attaining a proper understanding thereof. Hence man's spiritual development must start by passing through the philosophical stage; only then is he ready for the stage of Divine Revelation. It is in light of this idea that we should see Halevi's inclusion of the Philosopher in the frame story of the Khazar king's conversion to Judaism.

Halevi's conception of the integrated nature of human existence and the importance of one-time events for an individual's destiny led him to highlight the importance of an individual's affiliation with unique spheres of existence: spiritual and physical milieu, origin, and historical period. These can set an upper bound on the abilities of individuals, cause them to be content with their spiritual achievements, or spur them on to additional exertion. The spiritual destinies and world-views of the major characters in the *Kuzari*—the King, the Philosopher, the Christian and Muslim scholars, and the Rabbi—are determined by their particular set of affiliations. The King (after he abandons his pagan creed) and the Philosopher do not belong to any of the revealed religions; hence they are able to investigate the axioms shared by all the historical revealed religions. But the King, unlike the Philosopher, relates seriously to these assumptions, because of the particular circumstances of his life (his dream). The spiritual destiny of the representatives of the revealed religions is determined by their ties to their traditions: the Christian, who grew up on the knees of his faith, believes in things that "logic tends to rejects" (1,5 [14/42]); whereas the Muslim, whose mother tongue is Arabic, is so impressed by the Koran that he holds it to be the word of God (ibid.).[20]

An individual's national affiliation, which includes both genetic and cultural aspects, is also important. In Halevi's philosophy, the election of the Jewish people is associated with an emphasis on the importance of a person's national affiliation in

---

20. Similarly, the prophets saw "sight[s] that were in harmony with their natures and habits" (4,3 [228/208]).

determining his or her destiny. In the earlier thought, the election of the Jewish people is anchored in the cultural aspect of national affiliation, as expressed in the appropriate manner of life; whereas in the later thought the emphasis is on the genetic aspect.

Halevi also attributed great importance to an individual's physical environment. Consequently, when he described the superiority of Eretz Israel over all other countries, he highlighted the physical conditions that make it special: The land "possesses a special power in its air, soil and climate, which . . . assists in improving the species" (4,17 [247/224]).[21] Jacob "ascribed the vision which he saw, not to the purity of his soul, nor to his belief, nor to his integrity, but to the place" (2,14 [78/91]). The Rabbi's valedictory speech is typical of this attitude: "Jerusalem can only be rebuilt when Israel yearns for it to such an extent that we sympathize even with its stones and dust" (5,27 [334/295]).[22]

An individual's dependence on environmental conditions entails far-reaching distinctions between different periods of history. When the Temple existed, a Jew in Eretz Israel could attain the level of prophecy; but this is not possible in other eras (2,14). Accordingly, Halevi held that the Greek philosophers could not have attained religious truth—the truth of revelation—because, as a matter of historical record, they had no opportunity for direct sensory experience of the prophets among the Israelites: "Had the Greek philosophers seen [the prophets] when they prophesied and performed miracles, they would have acknowledged them, and sought by speculative means to discover how to achieve such things" (4,3 [232/210]). This emphasis on

21. Compare 1,95; 1,109; 2,10; 2,20. See also Baer, "Eretz Yisrael ve-galut."

22. This notion of the importance of material conditions for the spiritual development of human beings is compatible with Halevi's integrated conception of man. Similarly, Egypt has both a climatic (2,50) and spiritual (2,22) superiority over all other countries (except for Eretz Israel). The Hebrew language has a material and phonetic superiority over other languages (2,80) and this superiority entails excellence in other respects as well (1,100–101; 2,66; 2,68; 5,20). See also Chapter 19, note 12.

the importance of human history, like the emphasis on the importance of an individual's biography, reflects an empiricist disposition associated with an accent on the cumulative nature of the acquisition of knowledge as an ongoing process in time.

The accent on the importance, for the shaping of their personality, of the general context in which individuals find themselves leads Halevi to limit man's accountability and to maximize causal explanations. Thus, as we have already seen, Halevi cites the reasons that led those opposed to the worldview of Judaism to adopt their particular outlooks and does not reproach them; he states explicitly that no blame should be attached to the Aristotelian philosopher.[23] On the other hand, Halevi explained mankind's descent from the original level of Adam to that of "husks" by an analogy to the growth of trees. It seems plausible that he believed that the laws that govern the development of humanity resemble those that govern organic development in general.[24] This general disposition to limit human accountability is probably the reason that the *Kuzari* contains no specific discussion of the source of sin. This disposition may also explain Halevi's vacillations with regard to the problem of human freedom.[25]

5. Sensation, Reason, and Emotion

The empiricism of Halevi's later thought stems from a reevaluation of the importance of sensory experience. This reevaluation underlies the quarrel between Halevi's later thought and Aristotelian philosophy. According to Halevi, human beings can

---

23. See 1,64; 4,13; 4,16; 5,14.

24. Compare 1,47; 1,95; 4,15. A similar botanical explanation is invoked to explain the return of the human race to the level of Adam (4,23). On the biological conception of humanity and the Jewish people, see also Y. Heinemann, "Rabbi Yehudah Ha-levi: Ha-ish ve-hogeh ha-deʿot" (R. Judah Halevi: The man and the thinker), in Zemora, *R. Yehudah Halevi*, pp. 131–165.

25. S. Pines, *Toledot ha-filosofiyah ha-yehudit* (History of Jewish philosophy), ed. Y. Igra (Jerusalem, 1965), pp. 72 and 91. For another opinion, see Baneth, "Halevi and al-Ghazali."

recognize the possibility of God's calling to man, and its actual occurrence, only through sensory experience.[26] Furthermore, God derives His particular significance as the God of Israel from the unique sensory experiences of the Jewish people.

This meaning of God has epistemological, normative, and psychological aspects. As noted, it is only by dint of this experience that human beings become aware of the existence of God who is conscious of them as individuals. This Divine consciousness of the individual or of a particular nation constitutes God's significance for human beings and obligates them to respond to Him in deeds.

Hence the roles played by sensation in constituting the relations between God and man are bound up with an appropriate evaluation of the relative importance of the faculties of knowledge: reason and the senses. This evaluation reveals two causes for the superiority of the physical senses—particularly sight—over reason: first, the immediate link between the senses and external reality; and second, their capacity to take in, in a single moment, the manifold objects of sensation, in their concrete complexity (4,5; 4,6). The advantage of the senses over reason is not only that the latter requires the former as its primary and indeed exclusive source for knowledge of God. Even reason cannot free itself from their specific quality: the physical nature of sense data as they are perceived.

This disagreement with the philosophers underscores the further superiority of vision.[27] Prophetic sight reaches farther than logical analogy: a prophet's sight "reaches up to the heavenly host direct; he sees the dwellers in heaven and the spiritual beings that are near God and others in human form" (4,3 [230/209]). As we saw in the previous chapter, Halevi frequently

---

26. 1,8; 1,49; 1,87; 1,91; 4,11.
27. Ibn Ezra disagreed with Halevi and gave pride of place to hearing. See Uriel Simon, *Four Approaches to the Book of Psalms*, trans. Lenn J. Schramm (Albany, N.Y., 1991), p. 161. In his long commentary on Exod. 3:6 and 20:1, and in the short commentary on 19:17, however, Ibn Ezra agreed with Halevi. See also D. Kaufmann, *Die Sinne* (Budapest, 1984), p. 56, n. 53.

referred to vision, the visible, and the eye when he described knowledge of God or of the Divine Order. This preference stems from the particular capacity of sight to encompass and process in a single moment a manifold of data, in all their details. This is not the case with reason and hearing, which at each instant can focus on only a single topic and acquire only partial and incomplete knowledge: "Thinking is like narrating, but one cannot recount two things at the same time. Even were this possible, no one who hears them can absorb them simultaneously. The details of a country and of its inhabitants that can be seen in one hour would not find room in a large volume" (4,6 [236/214]).[28] As we saw in Chapter 11, it is of the essence of Divine Revelation that it cannot be broken down into elements and can be known only as a unified whole. However, this primacy of sight is not restricted to the epistemological plane; it extends to the psychological dimension as well. Only through vision can the emotions of love, fear, or hatred emerge.[29] Halevi goes on to assert that "in one moment love or hatred of a country could enter my heart. If all this were read to me from a book it would not impress me so greatly" (ibid.).[30] Hence the preference for the compact moment of vision over the continuum of rational action is not just a matter of degree. It is the intrinsic quality of vision that underlies the fundamental difference between the later Halevi and the Philosopher as to the significance of the bond between human beings and their God: "Such are the visions that the prophet sees in one second. Thus fear and love come to him naturally and remain in his heart for

---

28. Sight's ability to encompass a manifold of data in a single moment is of the highest importance because of the characteristic suddenness of prophetic experience. This suddenness stems from the status of this experience as a new creation.

29. Unlike his later opinion, in his early thought Halevi believed that fear and love could develop from observance of the commandments (3,11).

30. Here Halevi offered another reason for the inferiority of thought: It would "confuse my mind, being mixed up with errors, fancies, and previous impressions. And nothing would be completely clear." This rationale, too, is rooted in the discursive nature of thought, which leaves time and space for "confusion."

the whole of his life. He even yearns and longs to behold the vision again and again. Such a repetition was considered a great event for Solomon, in the words: 'The Lord who has appeared to him twice' (1 Kings 11:9). Will a philosopher ever achieve the same result?" (4,5 [236/214]).[31] These emotions, which arise in the heart of one who sees, can lead to a willingness to sacrifice one's life: "Then [a man] becomes a servant who loves his master and is ready to perish for the sake of his love, finding the greatest sweetness in his connection with Him, the greatest sorrow in separation from Him" (4,15 [246/222]). Accordingly, Abraham was even willing to sacrifice his son Isaac, after "conceiving the Divine Order by tasting, not by speculating" (4,17 [247/223]). Similarly, a desire for death is ignited in those "who witnessed those grand and divine scenes" (1,107 [58/74]).[32]

Note that the factor that mediates between vision, on the one hand, and hatred, fear and love, on the other, is not theoretical speculation but spontaneous emotion. Love grows from the immediate impression of a beautiful visage; hatred and fear stem from an immediate impression of a repulsive and loathsome appearance. Halevi grounded these opinions in sensory experience itself: "We see that the human soul shows fear whenever it meets with anything terrible, but not at the mere report of such a thing. It is likewise attracted by a beautiful form which strikes the eye, but not so much by one that is only spoken of" (4,5 [235/213]).[33] Thus, to a prophet, "in one sudden flash [there] stands revealed this grand and majestic figure, which was created for him, with its splendor, its characteristics, the instrument which typify power, etc. the uplifted hand, the unsheathed sword, fire, wind, thunder and lightning which obey his behest" (ibid.).[34]

---

31. This section contains a vivid description of multiple simultaneous experiences.

32. Compare 3,65. A similar idea can be found in al-Ghazali.

33. The impressions stimulated by the sensible appearance of a city can directly stimulate hatred or love (4,6). Such an impression resembles the prophetic experience, discussed in the previous section (4,5).

34. On the relationship in Halevi's poetry between love of women and love of the Creator, see Yaakov Levinger, "Ahavah ke-vittui

In the later thought, prophetic experience of the Divine Presence or of the presence of the Divine Order is manifested by apprehension of images in space—whether in real space or only in the spatial imagination of the prophet (4,3), whether waking or in dream.[35] The pious individual, who has not actually attained this vision, nevertheless endeavors to apply the faculty of imagination "to produce, with the assistance of memory, the most splendid pictures possible, in order to approach the Divine Order which it seeks, e.g., the scene of Sinai, Abraham and Isaac on Moriah, the Tabernacle of Moses, the Temple service, the presence of (God's) glory in the Temple, and the like. The pious man then orders his memory to retain all these, and not to forget them" (3,5 [143/138)]).[36]

In Halevi's doctrine, the preference for contact with God through vision is paralleled by legitimation of the sensible anthropomorphic images of God or of the Divine Order, interpreted literally: "Do not reject everything that has been said concerning such verses as 'The similitude of the Lord shall he behold' (Num. 12:8) and 'they saw the Lord of Israel,' nor *ma'aseh merkabah and Sheur Komah,* because in the opinion of some interpreters the reverence of God is implanted in the human mind, as it is written: 'That His fear may be before

---

la-ḥavayyah ha-datit ʾeẓel RYHL." (Love as an expression of the religious experience in R. Judah Halevi), *Mishnato he-hagutit shel R. Yehudah Halevi* (The philosophical doctrine of R. Judah Halevi), (Jerusalem, 1978), pp. 217–229. See Chapter 15, note 63, and Chapter 18, note 15.

35. For the importance of vision for the prophet and the pious individual, see 1,87; 1,91; 1,100; 2,48; 3,19; 4,3–8; 5,23. See also Chaptor 6, note 5. On the importance of dream experiences, see Chapter 17, note 6.

36. The description of the manner in which the pious individual meditates may well reflect Halevi's personal experiences. Compare his poem אלוקי, משכנותיך ידידות (Brody 2:160). He seems to be referring to these experiences in his poetry as well. See Komem, "Poetry and Prophecy"; see also Chapter 4, note 24, and Chapter 13, note 1. Of course, the way of piety is of special importance in a period when actual prophecy is impossible. The figure of the pious individual retains its relevance even in the later thought, albeit for different reasons than in the earlier thought. Compare Chapter 9; Chapter 22, note 4.

your faces'" (4,3 [234/212]).[37] This favorable attitude has implications on the practical level as well. Moses ascended Mount Sinai in order to bring down to the Israelites "something visible from God on which they could depend, as they followed the pillars of cloud and fire when they departed from Egypt" (1,97 [50/67]). Again, "The first leader, Moses, caused the people to stand before Mount Sinai, that they might see the light which he himself had seen, so far as they should be able to see it in the same way. He, then, invited the Seventy Elders, and they saw it, as it is written: 'They saw the God of Israel' (Exod. 24:10)" (4,11 [240/217]). When it comes to the meaning and role of the personification manifested in anthropomorphic images, the later Halevi was poles apart from the Aristotelian philosopher. According to the latter, such personification is an unexceptionable necessity—a didactic means that the prophet-philosopher is compelled to adopt when addressing those who lack the capacity to conceive of God without personification. By contrast, the later Halevi believed that although such personification can play a didactic role, it in fact expresses an irreducible Divine activity. To the extent that human beings become more refined and attain immediate sensory experience of these images, their bond with God intensifies. The sin of the Golden Calf lay only in "the manufacture of an image, which was forbidden to them, and in attributing Divine power to a thing made and chosen by themselves without the order of God" (1,97 [51/68]). According to Halevi, not only is there is no transgression in worshipping the Lord through "an object," such worship is actually rooted in the revelation at Sinai. In other words, the Israelites sinned not despite their having received the Torah, but because of it: "The people waited for (Moses') return, clad in the same apparel in which they had witnessed the drama on Sinai, without removing their jewels or chang-

---

37. The association of these images with God entails an emphasis on the limits of sensory perception and on the fundamental distinction between God as phenomenon and God in His essence (see Chapter 15).

ing their clothes, remaining just as he left them, expecting every moment to see him return" (ibid. [50/68]).[38]

Sight is privileged in interpersonal relationships, too. Halevi ascribed extreme importance to an immediate face-to-face encounter with the prophets and to observing the prophets as they prophesy. The act of prophesying entails visible actions. From this perspective, the prophet's appearance to the people resembles God's appearance to the prophet. The "spiritual light that dwelt in the soul of Moses" resembles "the visible light [that] appeared on his countenance" (1,109 [60/77]). The prophet is one who "walks into the fire without hurt, or abstains from food for some time without starving, on whose face a light shines which the eye cannot bear," and so forth (1,41 [23/48]). It is through the external "characteristics of the undoubted prophets," which can be sensed, that "God made manifest to the people that He is in connection with them, that there is a Lord who guides them as He wishes, according to their obedience or disobedience" (1,43 [23/48]). Indeed, "had the Greek philosophers seen [the prophets] when they prophesied and performed miracles, they would have acknowledged them" (4,3 [232/210]).[39] Thus, as we shall see in the next chapter, the external dimension of existence, that is, concrete

---

38. Compare the King's reaction to the account of the revelation at Sinai, which, according to the King, entails belief in the corporeality of God (1,88). In the Rabbi's reply he carefully distinguishes between phenomenon and the underlying essence (1,89). Similarly, in the future the Shekhinah will be manifested to the eye (5,23). See what Halevi wrote about the sin of Jeroboam (4,14).

39. It is in this light that we should understand the significance of the polemic remarks directed against the belief in the immortality of the soul held by adherents of other religions. The inevitable expression of the fact that this belief has no anchor in sensory experience, because "during this life nothing points to [it]" (1,105 [58/74]), is that they do not relate to it with full seriousness: "I have never seen anyone who believed in these promises desire their speedy fulfillment" (1,106 [58/74]). By contrast, drawing closer to a prophet and listening to his words, as he prophesies, is "a manifest proof... and a clear and convincing sign of reward hereafter" (1,103 [57/74]; see also 1,109). This explains the advantage of living in Jerusalem when the Temple existed (see 2, 14; 3,21), as well as the great importance of seeing Eretz Israel (2,20).

historical destiny, is crucial for Jewish people's fulfillment of their universal mission (2,54 [112]).

But Halevi also gave great weight to hearing. Music can work revolutionary changes in human nature (2,65). The great moment of the immediate personal bond between two human beings depends both on seeing the other's face and in hearing his or her voice. The possibility of perfect communication between human beings, which would transmit "the idea of the speaker into the soul of the hearer" (2,72 [125/126]), depends on both the dynamics and rhythm of the spoken sounds and the facial expressions and gestures that reflect the speaker's emotional state: "Verbal communication finds various aids, either in pausing or continuing to speak, according to the requirements of the sentence, by raising or lowering the voice, in expressing astonishment, question, narrative, desire, fear or submission by means of gestures, without which speech by itself would remain inadequate. Occasionally the speaker even has recourse to movements of eyes, eyebrows, or the whole head and hands, in order to express anger, pleasure, humility or haughtiness to the degree desired" (ibid.). Accordingly, Halevi again underscored the physical quality of Divine speech, which takes the form of voices that reach the prophet's ear (1,89).[40] In this explicit confrontation with the Philosopher (1,87), Halevi was fully aware of the fundamental difficulties of his position.[41]

The significance accorded to the esthetic dimension in the later thought can be understood in the context of Halevi's integrated conception of man.[42] For Halevi, human beauty and ugliness are a function of a person's nearness to God. Beauty and ugliness diffuse through the human soul, body, clothing,

---

40. Hence the goal of human beings, even after they have been separated from their organic senses—in the World to Come—is to behold the angelic light and hear the Divine speech (1,103). Halevi also stressed the importance of the sound of the prophet's voice (ibid.)

41. 1,4; 1,8; 1,9; 1,49; 1,87–89.

42. See also H. H. Ben-Sasson, "Ha-ḥevrah be-haguto shel RYHL" (Society in the thought of R. Judah Halevi), *Mishnato he-hagutit shel R. Yehudah Halevi*, p. 96.

and domicile.[43] From this perspective we can compare the Divine Presence in Israel to the vital spirit in the human body (2,62 [118/121]). Just as the "weak nerves" of women and children are manifested in physical symptoms, such as "black and green marks" when they go out at night, so too, as the Divine Presence is more remote from human beings, "their intelligence wanes, their bodies deteriorate, and their beauty fades" (ibid.).[44] On the aural plane, Halevi noted the beauty of the sounds of the Hebrew language—the holy tongue—in the past (2,80). In the present, however, it has been impoverished, in parallel with the declining fortunes of the Jewish people (2,26). By the same token, in the past music occupied an important place in the life of the Jews: "Music was the pride of the nation, which distributed its songs in such a way that they fell to the lot of the aristocracy of the people, that is, the Levites, who made practical use of them in the holy house and in the holy season" (2,64 [120/123]). Now, however, their music has deteriorated, just as the nation has fallen from its glory (2,65). This appreciation of the esthetic dimension as an expression of the bond between God and man, in body and soul, is rooted in a recognition of the Divine source of beauty and is perfectly compatible with a recognition of the decisive influence of the senses and with the view that body and soul are inseparable—an individual's spiritual condition is reflected in his or her physical condition, and vice versa.[45]

6. Conclusion

The difference between the Philosopher's conception of man and that held by Halevi in his later thought is implicit in their

---

43. As we shall see, the reevaluation of the human body in the later thought is paralleled by a reevaluation of man's material environment. This explains the importance that Halevi attributed to clothing and housing. As stated, the appearance of the material environment (such as the appearance of a city) can stimulate a person to love or hate. On the importance of clean clothing, see 3,10.

44. Compare 2,58.

45. For a comparison of Halevi's views on music with those of Moses Ibn Ezra and Abraham Ibn Ezra, see Simon, *Four Approaches to the Book of Psalms*, pp. 175–176.

diametrically opposed positions on the nature of the internal relations among the various strata of human existence. The Philosopher's anthropology is marked by an ontological polarization of human existence, whereas Halevi's features an internal ontological unity. The bipolarity of human existence in the Philosopher's system is reflected in the location of man's essence in his intellect. This has a number of implications: (1) the location of man's essence in his participation in the domain of intellect; (2) a preference for intellectual and contemplative activity over concrete action; and (3) an emphasis on the sovereignty of man's essence over the other strata of his existence, personal history, and his unique affiliations. By contrast, in Halevi's later thought the unity of human existence is expressed by locating man's essence in his concrete integrity. This has the following implications: (1) an emphasis on the importance of man's uniqueness and unity; (2) an emphasis on the importance of human action—an activity in which man participates with his full stature; and (3) an emphasis on man's dependence on the concrete circumstances of his life and his unique affiliations. In Aristotelian philosophy, then, the emphasis on the superindividual and eternal dimension of man entails his internalization and noninvolvement in events that take place outside the intellect and, consequently, the accent on the sovereignty of man qua rational being. By contrast, Halevi's emphasis on the individual and episodic dimension of man entails a demand for action and a corresponding accent on man's dependence on his environment and circumstances.

Note that the opposition between the two views of man stems from the fundamental difference in the nature of the universal bipolarity: For the Philosopher, it is a dichotomy of form and matter; for Halevi, of Creator and created. Form-and-matter dualism cuts through every manifestation of existence. By contrast, the division into Creator and created highlights what the two dimensions have in common, and this unifies all aspects of created existence. Near the end of the *Kuzari* Halevi referred explicitly to this contrast: "If we have reached this degree, we say that there is surely an incorporeal being that guides all corporeal substances, but which our mind is inadequate to examine. We therefore dwell on His works, but refrain from describing His nature. For it would be a defect in Him if we could grasp it. We take, however, no heed of the words of philosophers who divide the divine world into various degrees. As soon as we are free from our bodies there is for us only one divine degree. It is God alone who controls everything corporeal" (5,21 [329/214]). Under the sign of God's unlimited sovereignty over non-Divine existence—that is, of the Divine will that is realized on all levels of the world—the most salient fact is the fundamental uniformity of non-Divine existence.[46]

In summary, the view of man as an individuum, in both senses of this term—as indivisible and as irreducible—stems from the empiricist leanings of Halevi's later thought. On the ontological level, these result in a perception of man's essence in his full concrete stature. On the epistemological level, they are manifested in an emphasis on the importance of sensory perception.

Similarly, the two-way relations between God and man are dialectic: God's personal call to the individual, in his concrete individuality, is answered by man, first and foremost, through an activity that expresses the full man—observance of the commandments.

46. Compare also 4,5. See further Chapter 21, §3, "The Later Thought and the Dialogue Between God and Man."

17

HISTORY IN THE LATER THOUGHT

Like the other aspects we have been examining, the theory of history implicit in Halevi's later thought is marked by the attempt to resolve the fundamental contradictions in his earlier thought and to interpret the unique historical experiences of the Jewish people.

As noted, the key to Halevi's later thought is the idea that individual destiny is determined by environmental conditions, including those of the human environment, which are strongly rooted in historical affiliation. This idea derives from his new, non-Aristotelian concepts of God and man. We have also seen that God's voluntary and autonomous attention to particular events leads to a hierarchization within each of the various levels of existence. At each level, factors that participate actively and directly in those events occupy the pinnacle of the hierarchy. Agents and events are a unified whole; their interactions underlie their preferential status. Just as the status of an agent depends on the event, so the occurrence of an event depends on the agent. The election of Israel among the nations, of Eretz Israel among the lands, and of Hebrew among the languages depends on revelation; conversely, revelation depends on the coincidence of these factors in a single environment. The coincidence itself depends on concrete historical circumstances, which are always changing.

This idea that an individual human being or a nation is conditioned by environmental conditions also derives from Halevi's new conception of man as a unified entity. Because this binds human beings to their environment, it exposes them to environmental influences. Accordingly, the later thought emphasizes the epistemological and psychological importance of experience and the primacy of action over intention and contemplation. This stress on experience and action leads to a reevaluation of historical reality and its various aspects.

Man's dependence on the environment and the importance of experience and action rule out the distinction, found in Halevi's earlier thought, between the ideal human goal, allotted to the favored few of earlier generations, and the real human goal that can be attained in the present.[1] In consequence, he rejects out of hand the Aristotelian notion that the human goal is ahistorical in nature.[2]

1. Historical Eras, Human Collectives, and Religious Experiences

The epistemological importance of experience gives new meaning to the differences among historical periods and among particular human groups. The experience of an event in which God's interest in mankind is revealed can be the grounds for hierarchies of historical ages and of nations. The new sense given to the differences among periods is associated with the nature of this experience, whose content is unique and fragmentary, and which cannot be invoked at will. Knowledge that such an experience took place depends, therefore, on individuals' links to a human collective that has a reliable tradition, which can bridge the generations and accumulate into an integral whole

---

1. See Chapter 9.
2. See Chapter 4, §2, "The Goal as the Actualization of Human Potential"; Chapter 5, §8, "Asceticism as the Philosopher's Way of Life."

the lessons derived from the proliferation of individual and fragmentary experiences. David commanded Solomon "to obey the authority of his father and his ancestors in their belief in the God of Abraham, Isaac, and Jacob, whose solicitude was with them, and who fulfilled His promises [to them]" (5,21 [330/292]). But those persons, such as the Greek philosophers, who have no opportunity to relate to the appropriate traditions are doomed, whether they will or not, to an inferior religious perception: "We cannot blame philosophers for missing the mark, since they only arrived at this knowledge by way of speculation" (4,13 [241/218]). By contrast, the King's enlightenment comes from what he learns from the Rabbi.[3]

The dependence of the individual's destiny on the human collective has far-reaching consequences for Halevi's theory of history. This dependence underscores the importance of the directionality of human history, which is, on the one hand, a progressive and evolutionary process. Because of the accumulated experience of the generations, later periods have an advantage, in principle, over earlier ones. With the appearance of the Jewish people on the stage of history, with their extraordinary experience of the presence of a personal God Who takes an interest in human beings, a fundamental change took place in human history, a change that cannot be negated or ignored: "All who came after them could not detach themselves from their principles, so that today the whole civilized world acknowledges that God is eternal, and that the world was created. They look upon the Israelites and all that befell them as a proof of this" (2,54 [115/116]).[4] On the other hand, the later generations are inferior to their predecessors. One source of their inferiority

---

3. This explains the need for investigating the reliability of a tradition. See 1,44–59. The discussion of the same issue in 3,64–67 is part of the anti-Karaite polemic.

4. The representatives of the revealed religions are in fundamental agreement concerning the theological significance of the elements of Judaism found in Christianity and Islam. The representatives of Christianity and Islam see these elements as necessary but partial and insufficient indications of their religious truth, whereas Halevi sees them as manifestations of the process whereby Judaism will become the religion of all mankind. See Schweid, *Ta'am ve-haqqashah*, p. 65.

is the superiority of immediate experience over experience mediated by the chain of tradition; another source is that catastrophic historical events can engender a temporary retreat in the course of human evolution. Such catastrophes may result from this very dependence of the individual or collective on environmental circumstances. This explains the superiority of past generations, when Israel lived in its land and the Temple was standing in Jerusalem. At one and the same time, then, the idea of human dependence underlies both the concept of historical progress and that of a temporary relapse in the historical process.

Note, however, that because historical reality can be affected by divine intervention, its processes cannot be described exclusively from the evolutionary vantage point. Divine intervention cuts through the bounds of natural law; its results, ontologically speaking, are new creations. For example, the Israelites' entry onto the stage of history as the people of the Torah was associated with a divine act of creation: "A religion of divine origin arises suddenly. It is bidden to arise, and it is there, like the creation of the world" (1,81 [38/58]). The tablets of the law were a new creation (1,97); so was the splitting of the Red Sea (1,89; 2,2). Viewed from this angle, the historical process incorporates turning points where its continuity is ruptured by sudden jumps—revolutionary changes that cannot be understood solely on the basis of previous stages in the process. In Halevi's thought, the serial continuity of the processes that shape mankind are associated with the continuous hierarchy of human degrees, in which, according to the Aristotelian philosopher, "every individual on earth has its completing causes" (1,1 [7/36]). This is also the opinion of Halevi in his earlier thought. By the same token, any discontinuity in these processes must be linked to a discontinuity in the human hierarchy—a discontinuity manifested, in Halevi's later thought, by the election of Israel.

The reevaluation of the human collective and of the differences among the various groups that compose it is associated with an exclusive reliance on religious experience. This reliance depends on finding a way to reinforce the objective and obligatory significance of such an experience. The need for reinforcement has two sources: the unremitting suspicion of the religious experience engendered by its uniquely "dreamlike" nature, as a one-time and personal event; and the difficulty of accepting the existence of the God who is supposed to be made present in this experience or who at least provokes its occurrence. Halevi endeavored to allay this suspicion in two ways: (1) Such one-time experiences can be compared with others of their ilk. This comparison can indicate the obligatory and objective validity of the experiences, despite their undeniable affinity with the individual domain. This type of comparison was employed by the prophets (4,3; 4,11). (2) Certain religious experiences do take place in the public domain—before the masses—and leave their imprint on history.

The individual's dependence on the collective, then, is not simply a matter of a limitation of the possibilities open to individuals and a delineation of the paths for actualizing them or of individuals' interest in supplementing their partial and incomplete experiences. It is also manifested in a rupturing of the bounds of the individual domain itself. By granting primacy to the human collective, the later Halevi distanced himself as far as possible from the aristocratic views he had formerly shared. An intimate experience, such the King's dream, located entirely in the private domain, finds its objective and obligatory significance only when opened to the public domain. Only in light of historical experiences can it be verified as a real occurrence that is neither fantasy nor magic spell. As the King tells the Rabbi:

> The human mind does not incline to believe that God has intercourse with man, except by a miracle that changes the nature of things, so that man may recognize that God alone is able to do so, who created him from nought. Such a miracle must also have taken place in the presence of great multitudes, who saw it distinctly, and were not told about it by someone who saw it in a dream or learn about it from reports and traditions. Even then they must examine the matter carefully and repeatedly, so that no suspicion of imagination or magic

can enter their minds. Then it is possible for the mind to grasp this extraordinary matter, namely, that the Creator of this world and the next, of the heavens and lights, holds intercourse with this contemptible subject, I mean man, speaking to him, and fulfilling his wishes and desires. (1,8 [16/43])[5]

In the same vein, the Muslim scholar directs the King's attention to the Jewish tradition, which attests to religious experiences that satisfy the methodological demands the latter has put forward: The experiences recounted by that tradition took place in the public domain, in history (1,9).

The literary correlative of the breaching of the bounds of the private domain is the casting of the King as the central character in the book. The King represents the individual, who is characterized by the degree of sovereignty he possesses. This sovereignty is a warrant of maximum personal autonomy as expressed in maximum involvement in public life. More than other human being, the King, by virtue of his royal status, is someone in whom the private and public domains are mutually open and sustaining. The King's private experience (his dream) and his proximity, as ruler, to major historical events (wars of religion) are interwoven in his response to the Philosopher (1,2). Although he does not reject the Philosopher's presentation on theoretical grounds, he explains his discomfort with the Philosopher's concluding remarks and his decision to continue the quest for religious truth in the specific context of his biography, which include both personal and historical experiences. Both kinds of experience are marked by man's need to cope with the divine demands on individual and collective. A comparison of the situation at the beginning of the book with the parable of the king of India (1,21–24) is instructive, because the latter is meant to exemplify the most important

---

5. The passage "and were not told it by someone who saw it in a dream," found in the Arabic MSS, is not found in Ibn Tibbon's Hebrew and Hirschfeld's and Heinemann's English. Here the King seems to be alluding to his own dream as well. He acknowledges that his dream cannot prove the existence of a God who has intercourse with flesh and blood. It seems plausible that there is also an allusion to Muhammad's dream.

innovation introduced by the Rabbi. In both parable and plot, experience has a personal character. In the plot, this personal character finds expression in the fact that the King is addressed when he is unquestionably in the private domain—dreaming; in the parable, the personal character of the call is expressed both in the addressee of the mission and the miraculous powers of the drugs and potions, which are precisely adapted to the King's medical condition. Yet there is a difference between the two. Whereas, in the plot, the experience is acted out entirely within the private domain,[6] in the parable of the king of India the public and private domains are interconnected: the unquestioned source of the drugs, the credibility of the letter, and the improvement in the king's health are manifest to all. In addition, the arrival of the messengers affects the collective destiny as well, through the drugs and potions they bring with them: The king's enemies are destroyed without open and bloody warfare. This juxtaposition of private experience and collective experience endows personal experience with its objective meaning—both theoretical and practical: The arrival of the messengers and their gifts "would remove [the king's] former doubt that the Indians have a king. I should also acknowledge that his dominion and his word had touched me" (1,22 [19/46]).[7]

6. From the King's political experiences—specifically, from wars of religion—he learns not only that dreams are relatively frequent in human history, but also about the power of fantasy and imagination, especially when different dreams contradict one another: "it is impossible to agree with both" (1,2 [11/39]). Nevertheless, suspicions about the objective significance of experiences that are located entirely in the individual domain do not undermine their power to exert practical influence on the individual who experienced them—again as can be learned from wars of religion and from the effect of the King's own dream on himself. The inner power of these experiences is determined by their content and their direct impingement on the senses. See Chapter 13, note 1; and note 30 in the present chapter.
7. The parable of the king of India certainly alludes to the exodus from Egypt; compare 1,83–84. After the King is persuaded that the historical experience parallel to the hypothetical experience in the parable of the king of India did in fact take place, he understands the objective meaning of his own dream (1,98).

2. The Vocation and Destiny of the Jewish People

In the later thought, the link between individual and collective depends on more than just the individual's own spiritual interests. It also depends on a reevaluation of the situation of the human collective. This has important implications for the significance of the historical destiny of the Jewish people and its status among the nations. God evinces greater interest in the fate of a human collective than in that of an individual. In Chapter 14 we saw that a religious experience, because it is public but nevertheless peculiar to a particular human collective, endows the collective that has witnessed it with a uniqueness and relative superiority. Hence (in contrast to the position taken in the earlier thought) individuals—even one who has attained the highest degree, such as Moses—must subordinate their individual interests to fulfilling their role in advancing the destiny of the human collective. Accordingly, "if there were no Israelites there would be no Torah. They did not derive their high position from Moses, but Moses received his for their sake. The divine love dwelt among the descendants of Abraham, Isaac, and Jacob. The choice of Moses, however, was made in order that the good fortune might come to them through his instrumentality. We are not called the people of Moses, but the people of God" (2,56 [113/117]). Similarly, the "rabbi," Moses, who had been allowed to come "before the king," was compelled to take leave of him and return to the "companions"—the Israelites in the wilderness—and teach them the "shortest and straightest route." What is more, "honor and rank" were granted to him by the king, "who knew that he was one of these friends, and who had also known their fathers, former comrades of his" (1,109 [59/76]).[8]

Running parallel to the preceding in Halevi's later thought is a universalist perspective that gives the general human vocation absolute priority over the self-interest of any particular

---

8. Thus, as we saw in the previous chapter, the prophet has a duty to remain and live in this world, so that he can fulfill the prophetic mission entrusted to him (1,109); see Appendix.

human collective, including the Jewish people. From this vantage point, the election of the Jewish people—the nation of prophets (potential or actual)—is based on the pan-human historical role that this election is supposed to fill. Of particular interest here is the analogy that the Rabbi draws between the sun and the Jewish people (2,50–56): If the creation of the sun reflects "glory on its creator" because of "its great power" (2,53 [111/115]), how much the more so is God glorified by the Jewish people, because of their decisive influence on all humanity (2,54).[9] From these passages we learn that, although the special relationship between God and the Jewish people—the people of prophets—emerged thanks to the presence of "the proper matter for it" (2,50 [115]), the presence of this matter is only a necessary but not a sufficient condition. The Jewish people acquire their special ontological status from the role they play vis-à-vis the other nations (2,50; 2,54). As we shall see in the next chapter, this mission was assigned to the Jewish people by God, in an autonomous determination of His will. The protracted exile of the Jewish people, even though it prevents their own ascension, is meant to refine the nations (4,23). The Jews are compared to a seed that falls on the earth and loses its peculiar excellence, vegetative matter that declines to the status of the inanimate and "undergoes an external transformation into earth, water, and dirt" (ibid. [251/226]).[10] This comparison

---

9. Just as the sun is the "cause of being," on both the physical level—"by its means night and day and the seasons of the year are determined; minerals, metals, plants, and animals were developed through its instrumentality"—and on the epistemological level—"its light produced sight and colors" (2,53 [111/ 115]), so the Jewish people are the cause, both on the physical level—"to be worthy of seeing miracles that changed the course of nature" (2,54 [112/116])—and on the epistemological level—"to understand that the world had a king who watched and guarded it" (ibid.).

10. We must not infer that the change is only apparent (which is how Moscato [ad loc.] understood the passage and how Heinemann, but not Hirschfeld, translated it). The Arabic *al-ẓāhir* means "uncovered"—that is, the change is visible to all. Compare: "We are not like dead, but rather like a person sick unto death, who has been given up by the physicians . . . which means that, on account of his visible (*al-ẓāhir*) deformity and repulsive visage . . . " (2,34 [102/108]). Or again, "So it is concerning the religion of Moses: all later religions are transformed into it, though *externally*

of the Jews in exile to a seed that falls on the ground attests to the importance the Rabbi ascribes to immediate contact between the Jewish people and the nations, which can take place in full only when the Jews are in exile. This contact is a precondition for the Jews' fulfilling their historical role.[11]

But the subordination of the private interests of the favored individual, the prophet, to the general interest of the favored nation, the Jewish people, as well as the subordination

---

they may reject it. They merely serve to introduce and pave the way for the expected Messiah: he is the fruit" (4,23 [252/227]). Compare 2,54; 3,1. Compare also the discussion on the degree of Terach (1,95). In 4,23 the Rabbi is sparring against Christian beliefs. The universal and Messianic role of the Jewish people is associated with suffering, but this suffering is the lot of the entire nation and not only of the Messiah. Christianity, however, which believes that the Messiah has already come, can, in truth, merely "introduce and pave the way for the expected Messiah" (4,23 [252/227]). See also Y. Baer, "Eretz Yisrael ve-galut be-ʿeinei ha-dorot shel yemei ha-beinayyim" (Eretz Israel and the Diaspora in the eyes of the medieval generations), *Ziyyon* 6 (1934): 162.

With regard to the protracted exile of the Jewish people, however, the Rabbi sometimes associates it with the absence of "yearning to such an extent that they embrace her stones and dust" (5,27 [334/295]; 2,24). See also B.-Z. Dinaburg (Dinur), "Aliyato shel R. Yehudah Halevi le-ʾereẓ Yisrael ve-ha-tesisah ha-meshiḥit be-yamav" (Judah Halevi's immigration to Eretz Israel and the messianic fervor of his age), *Minḥah le-David (Sefer ha-yovel le-R. David Yellin)* (David Yellin jubilee volume), (Jerusalem, 1935), pp. 157–182. In 1,115 [63/79], however, the Rabbi explains the length of the exile by the absence of an appropriate spiritual attitude toward exile: "If the majority of us ... would learn humility towards God and His law from our low station, Providence would not have forced us to bear it for such a long period." See also 4,22–23. See also H. H. Ben-Sasson, "Yiḥud ʿam yisrael le-daʿat benei ha-meʾah ha-shteim ʿesreh" (The uniqueness of the Jewish people according to the people of the twelfth century), *Peraqim* 2 (1969–1974): 145–218. But this rationale is insufficient to explain the continued exile in the present. The Rabbi considers the Jews' suffering in exile to be punishment for their coming to resemble the Gentiles (2,44).

11. Sometimes, however, Halevi argued that the influence of the Jewish people on the nations depends chiefly on their living in Eretz Israel in the past (5,20; compare 2,54; 4,5). This internal contradiction stems from the tension between Halevi's interest in preserving the fullness of the prophetic experience as given, as explained in Chapter 14, and his interest in explaining the long sojourn of the Jewish people in exile and in making its universal vocation compatible with its downtrodden status in the present.

of the self-interest of the Jewish people to the interest of all of humanity, does not exhaust the relations among them. The Divine vocations imposed on the prophet and on the Jewish people are to motivate the Jewish people and all mankind to realize their true, divine goals—that is, to raise them to their own level: The prophet's task is to raise the Jewish people to the degree of prophecy; that of the Jewish people is to elevate the nations and convert them to Judaism.[12] The respective goals of the Jews and the Gentiles are achieving prophetic status and conversion to Judaism. Looked at from one side, the rationale of Jewish suffering is to fulfill the Jews' pan-human role; from the other side, the rationale of humanity is to accept Judaism: "Now we are oppressed, whereas the whole world enjoys rest and prosperity. The trials that meet us serve to purify our piety, to cleanse us and to remove all taint from us. If we are good, the Divine Order is in this world. You know that the elements gradually evolved metals, plants, animals, man, and finally the pure essence of man. The whole evolution took place for the sake of this essence, in order that the Divine Order should inhabit it. That essence, however, came into existence for the sake of the highest essence, namely, the prophets and pious" (2,44 [104/110]).[13] "The servant of the Lord"—the Jewish people—suffers on account of his sins (2,35), which derive from the influence of their Gentile milieu on the Jews in exile (2,54). But life in a Gentile environment is itself a precondition for the Jews' affecting all of humanity; their influence on the Gentiles

---

12. Halevi held that in the Messianic era the nations will all be absorbed into the Jewish people (2,23). This opinion is not compatible with his doctrine of degrees of existence.

13. In our reading there is no contradiction between this section and 2,56. See Moscato, *incipit* ולולא בני ישראל (2,56). Nor is there any contradiction between this section and 4,23. Our view is reinforced by Halevi's explicit reference in 4,23 to his gloss (2,34) on the verse, "Indeed, My servant will prosper" (Isa. 52:13). Its direct continuation is §54. We can infer from this reference that even in 4,23, when he proposes his doctrine of the universal mission of Judaism, he continues to maintain the doctrine (expounded from 2,29 to 2,54) that the status of the Jewish people is the goal.

requires their physical presence in exile (2,44; 4,23). From this perspective, the suffering of the servant of God is indeed associated with the elevation of the Gentiles. This sense of the reciprocal influence of the Jews and the Gentiles is adequately represented by the metaphor of the seed (4,23); only after the seed "undergoes an external transformation to earth, water, and dung" does it have the capacity to "transform earth and water into its own substance, carrying it from one degree to another, until it refines the elements and makes them like itself" (ibid.).[14] In parallel, the Rabbi—who, as we have noted, also stands for the entire Jewish people—remains in exile and is forced to abridge his service of the Lord, since "many of the Israelite laws lose their force for one who does not live in Eretz Israel" (5,23 [331/293]). Only after the Rabbi concludes his mission and the Khazar people—who represent all of humanity—have been converted to Judaism can he emigrate to Eretz Israel.

3. The Jewish People: Loftiness and Subjection

In the later thought, the discussion of the historical destiny of the Jewish people in the present is of major importance, as evidenced by one of the two titles of the book: "The Book of Refutation and Proof on the Despised Faith."[15] In the later thought, this subjection and humiliation take on a sense that transcends the historical dimension, because they undermine any assumption of the exalted status of the Jewish people in the present as God's chosen people. This argument is used by Christianity and Islam in their long dispute with Judaism: the actual status of the Jewish people among the nations—their

---

14. Compare 4,10 and 4,11. There too Halevi focused on the two-way relations between the Jewish people and the Gentiles, among whom they live in exile. On the one hand, the Jews influence the "later religions" (4,10 [238/215]); on the other hand, "we, through our sins, incline daily more and more towards them" (4,11 [239/216]). We need hardly mention that this idea resembles the kabbalistic notion of "descent for the sake of ascent."

15. As we already noted (p. 114), this seems to be the title given the book in the spirit of Halevi's later thought.

degradation—is evidence of their inferior status before God (1,112–113). Accordingly, when the King resolves to summon the representatives of the monotheistic religions, he sees no reason to include a spokesperson for Judaism, because "I am satisfied that they are of low station, few in number, and generally despised" (1,4 [12/40]). It is no accident that the theme of abasement appears in the *Kuzari* only in the context of the invitations to the representatives of the revealed religions. This summons reflects the King's willingness to consider the axiom (which the Philosopher rejects out of hand) that from time to time God displays special interest in an individual human being or a particular group of people. This assumption, shared by all the revealed religions, makes the Jews' current abasement problematic. At a later stage in the discussion, after the Rabbi has asserted that God rewards human beings for their good deeds and concluded that the status of a human being after death parallels his or her closeness to God during life (1,111), the King responds, with a note of sarcasm: "Apply this also in the other direction, and judge their degree in the next world according to their station in this world" (1,112 [62/78]). But the Christian, the first representative of the revealed religions, has already expressed this line of thought and argued that the lot of the Jewish people in the present manifests a spiritual inferiority derived from sin— their attitude toward Jesus—despite the Christian's recognition that the Jews were exalted over all other peoples in the past— before that sin. The Muslim, who does not explicitly refer to the Jews in the present, relies on Koranic stories that refer to the unique experiences of the Jews in the distant past. In all human history, only these public experiences can attest to the existence of a deity who speaks with human beings and fulfills their requests (1,9). Thus, despite the Muslim's failure to refer to the situation of the Jewish people in the present, he too must acknowledge that his doctrine is based on traditions associated with them; in this fashion he indirectly acknowledges their lofty status, even if only in the past, in the pre-Islamic epoch. What is more, the Muslim scholar must rely, willy-nilly, on an actual representative of the Jewish religion living in the present—the

Rabbi—to buttress the foundations of Islam.[16] This dependence constitutes an acknowledgment of sorts of the absolute superiority of the Jews, as the exclusive bearers of the evidence that there is a "divine law on earth" (1,10 [17/44]), over all other peoples.[17]

The abject state of the Jewish people in the present, with its political, social, economic, and spiritual facets, acquires its full tragic sense in the later thought, against a dual background: (1) the belief that God takes an interest in particular human beings, and especially the Jewish people; and (2) the integrated concept of man (discussed in Chapter 16) and the concept of experience as a single unit that cannot be atomized (Chapter 14). In the context of this view of man, the annals of a people, like the biography of an individual (and including, in both cases, the degree of their closeness to God), depend on a system of causal circumstances—human, physical, and territorial. This entails the great importance that Halevi, in his later thought, attributed to living in Eretz Israel, with the influence of its physical aspects, as a condition for attaining prophecy (4,17). The Rabbi's valedictory stresses the importance of the stones and soil of Eretz Israel (5,27).[18] The ideal conditions for the spiritual development of human beings exist only in Eretz Israel, the land of prophecy (1,95): "Heart and soul are perfectly pure and immaculate only in the place that is believed to be specially selected by God" (5,23 [293]).[19] This is why Eretz Israel is the land that human beings have desired and fought over in all generations. Already Cain and Abel came to blows over it,

16. See Schweid, *Ta'am ve-haqqashah*, p. 66.
17. This is also Halevi's opinion; see 2,54; 4,10; 5,20. Note that Halevi prefers Islam to Christianity, as can be inferred from a comparison of the King's responses to their spokesmen. This preference is compatible with his general philosophy of history, which posits human progress as history proceeds. The main stages of this progress are reflected in the order of the audiences with the King.
18. It is in this light that we should understand the parable of the vineyard (2,11–15). See Baer, "Eretz Yisrael ve-galut." This also underlies the importance of Eretz Israel's geographical location in the center of the temperate zone (1,95 [47]).
19. Compare 2,10; 4,8–9.

because "they desired to know which of them would be Adam's successor and heir to his essence and intrinsic perfection; to inherit the land and to stand in communion with the Divine Order, while the other would be merely the 'shell' " (2,14 [76/89]).[20] After them, Isaac and Ishmael fought over it, and then Jacob and Esau (ibid.). In subsequent periods, "all the nations make pilgrimages to it, long for it" (2,20 [89/98]).[21] The centrality of Eretz Israel explains the severity with which the later Halevi viewed the life of the Jewish people in exile. Living outside Eretz Israel prevents the Jewish people from attaining their intrinsic spiritual level; namely, prophecy.[22] However, living in exile has implications that go beyond the Jews' separation from Eretz Israel. The Jews are impoverished (4,21), dispersed (ibid.),[23] enslaved by the nations (4,23), declining in numbers (1,4), and hated by all (ibid.).[24]

This awareness of the gulf that separates the situation of the Jewish people in the present from the conditions necessary for actualization of their unique potential stands at the core of Halevi's later thought. He held that, despite this gulf, passage between the abject state and loftiness of the Jewish people is

20. Note that, according to this passage, the status of human beings as "essence" or "shell" is determined exclusively by their association with Eretz Israel. Similarly, "Jacob ascribed the vision which he saw, not to the purity of his soul, nor to his belief, nor to his integrity, but to the place" (ibid. [78/91]).
21. This is a clear echo of the Crusades. See also 2,23 and 4,11.
22. This leads to bitter criticism of acquiescence in living in the Diaspora (2,23–24; 5,23–27), criticism that, as we have noted, belongs to Halevi's later thought.
23. See also 2,30 and 2,32. As we have seen, Halevi's chief argument against the Karaites, in his earlier thought, is that they divide the nation (3,49).
24. Halevi tended to "understand" this enmity to the extent that it is the outcome of objective circumstances, namely, that the Jewish people in exile resemble "an unclean thing, which man only beholds with disgust, and rejects; 'despised and shunned by men,' 'a man of suffering,' 'familiar with disease' (Isa. 53:3)" (2,34 [102/108]). Compare 2,58 and 2,62. For manifestations in his poetry of the abject state of the Jewish people in exile, see the article by A. Mor, "Galut u-ge'ullah be-shirat RYHL." (Exile and redemption in the poetry of Judah Halevi), *Sinai* 10 (1947): 131–142; see also note 10.

possible, in both directions. The intrinsic excellence of the Jewish people, manifested at Sinai, led directly to their spiritual nadir—the sin of the Golden Calf. Similarly, the loftiness of the Jewish people, as the bearers of a universal vocation, is inseparable from their ignoble state—their dispersion among the nations. On the other hand, this wretched state itself will ultimately lead to the Jews' exaltation through the actualization of their Divine vocation—the refinement and elevation of all humanity. Furthermore, the Jews' survival in exile is additional evidence of the special bond between God and this people (2,32).[25] Similarly, the Jews' steadfast adherence to their faith, in the conditions of exile, attests to their excellence, because they "could escape this degradation by a word spoken lightly, become free men, and even surpass their oppressors. But they do not do so out of allegiance to their faith" (4,23 [251/226]). Nevertheless, Halevi believed that nothing in the dialectic between the Jews' degradation and excellence can bridge the gap between these two states. The passage from the actual state of the Jews in the present to their anticipated future condition is not a continuous and natural process, but the result of jumps that express God's intervention in the course of history. The Jewish people resemble a sick person whose physicians have given up on curing him; nevertheless, he "hopes for recovery through miracles or extraordinary events, as it is said: 'Can these bones live?' (Ezek. 37:3)" (2,34 [102/108]).

4. Historical Action and Redemption

In Chapter 16 we said that, for the later Halevi, human action takes precedence over any intellectual or mental disposition. This activist attitude has implications on the historical plane, too, given the importance of (1) historical destiny in the lens of

---

25. The Jews' excellence is also manifested in the strict punishments meted out exclusively to them. These punishments, which indicate that the destiny of the Jewish people is not determined by the laws of nature, also attest to a special Divine Providence for the Jewish people (1,109; 2,32; 2,58; 4,3 [220]). This evidence has an effect on the nations, too (2,54).

his anthropology; (2) the Jews' urgent need to change the face of historical circumstances; and (3) God's interest in the human condition in general, as this is embodied in mankind's historical destiny. Whereas the human condition in general and the Jews' special concern with historical destiny lead to activity aimed at steering the course of history, God's interest in history entails a human obligation to engage in such activity and is the warrant of its success. Halevi's activism rests also on an assumption about the intrinsic potential of human action as such, including action that is not a priori intended to change the face of history. As we saw in our discussion of Halevi's earlier thought, he believed in the importance of human action, both as a unifying factor that consolidates individuals into a group and as a dividing factor—different ways of life can disrupt human collectives. In the unique situation of the Jews, who are dispersed among the nations, human activity is of the utmost importance.[26]

The later Halevi underscored the importance of action intended to change historical circumstances and advocated action explicitly aimed at bringing closer the redemption of the Jewish people (5,27). In his opinion, it is incumbent on his contemporaries to emigrate to Eretz Israel, even if this involves some physical danger. Such danger "does not come under the category of 'You shall not tempt the Lord' (Deut. 6:16)" (5,23 [332/293]).[27] Accordingly, Halevi sometimes blamed the Jews themselves for their continued exile. As for the King's outspoken criticism that he sees no evidence of a readiness on the part of the Jews to leave their exile and emigrate to Eretz Israel (2,23), the Rabbi can only agree: "That is a justified reproach, O king of the Khazars" (2,24 [93/100]). He acknowledges that

---

26. Similarly, the construction of synagogues in the present is justified, because they are needed to maintain the unity of the Jewish people (1,97). On the historical role played by the observance of the Sabbath and festivals, see 3,10.

27. Locating the goal of human life on the historical plane leads, in the later thought, to a displacement of the center of gravity from the destiny of the individual to the destiny of the collective. According to Halevi, Judaism is unique in that it holds that the chief goal of human beings is to be found in collective life in this world (1,109).

the Jews make do with prayer—"Bow to His holy hill, bow to His footstool" (Ps. 99:9,5), "He who restoreth His glory to Zion"—and denigrates this as resembling "the chattering of the starling and the nightingale" (ibid. [94/101]). Halevi's activism links the beginning and end of the story: The *Kuzari* begins with a preference for individual action over intention, as the angel tells the King in his dream—"Your intention is indeed pleasing to the Creator, but your way of acting is not pleasing" (1,1 [3/35])—and concludes with an accent on the importance of action on the historical plane, as the Rabbi says: "Jerusalem can only be rebuilt when Israel yearns for it to such an extent that they embrace her stones and dust" (5,27 [334/295]).[28]

According to Halevi, the historical activism of the Jews is also found in Christianity and Islam, and for the same reasons. (This position is the antithesis of the Philosopher's view.) The activism of Christianity and Islam is embodied in the missionary expansionism that lies at the core of their belief and is highlighted in their representatives' stress on their universalism, as manifested in their call to all nations to subscribe to their faith.[29] This tenet resurfaces in the Rabbi's remarks about Christians and Muslims: "The leader of each of these parties maintained that he had found the divine light at its source, namely, in the Holy Land, and that there he ascended to heaven, and was commanded to lead all the inhabitants of the globe in the right path" (4,11 [239/216]). This is the angle from which Halevi observed the major international events of his age—the wars between the Christians and Muslims, who had divided the "inhabited world" between them. At the very start of the *Kuzari*, when the King juxtaposes the revealed religions with the doctrine of the philosophers, Halevi cited holy wars as symptomatic of the revealed religions—a manifestation of the centrifugal force

---

28. At the end of the story the Rabbi, who is to be identified here with Halevi himself, draws personal conclusions and sets out for Eretz Israel.

29. The Christian and Muslim note that their faiths' concern for all nations is an essential tenet thereof. The Christian presents this as a contrast with the Jewish attitude (1,4). Compare 1,100–103.

of human action on the plane of international relations. These wars, as actions that are deeply anchored in the plane of history, stem from historical circumstances in which human activity does not respond to the Divine Will; their aim is to correct this distortion. They are a striking manifestation of the willingness of individuals to bear the heaviest burden for the sake of action that has historical significance.

Judaism, too, participates in the struggle to mold the image of humanity, but it does this in its own hidden ways: "So it is concerning the religion of Moses: all later religions are transformed into it, though *externally* they may reject it. They merely serve to introduce and pave the way for the expected Messiah: he is the fruit; all will be his fruit, if they acknowledge him, and will become one tree. Then they will revere the root they formerly despised" (4,23 [252/230]). Perhaps we should see the plot of the *Kuzari*, which starts with the dream of a pagan king and ends with the conversion to Judaism of the entire Khazar people, as symbolic of the process through which all humanity passes on the road from paganism to Judaism, with all its characteristics, stages, and conditions.[30] The King's conversion symbolizes the process whereby all mankind will accept Judaism, while the order in which the spokesmen appear symbolizes the stages in the realization of this historical process.

5. Conclusion

As we noted in Chapter 16, Halevi's anthropology evolved through an increasing recognition of the intrinsic unity of human existence. In the evolution of his theology we can distinguish a transition from the Aristotelian notion of a God who has

---

30. In this process, religious visions and dreams play a leading role. Human beings may have these visions, whatever their ethnic origins. The role of the Jew (represented in the *Kuzari* by the Rabbi) is to expound the correct meaning of these dreams and provide them with objectively valid foundations, by juxtaposing them with the public experiences of the Jews, and with a specific exegesis, by juxtaposing them with the Torah commandments. See Chapter 13, note 1.

no interest in reality outside Himself to the concept of a God who transcends His own sphere and is aware of non-Divine existence, including mutable material existence. These two processes are interdependent.

In the first part of this book we saw that the Philosopher's anthropology rests on a concept of human existence that is split between its essence—intellect that is above time—and a nonessential stratum that is mutable and not intellect. The human goal is actualized in the emergence of this essence from potential to actual; that is, the disclosure of the substantive gap between intellect and whatever is not included in it. By liberating the intellect from its dependence on ephemeral existence, by self-contemplation, human beings come to resemble the Active Intellect and unite with it. This concept of man is also reflected in the Philosopher's attitude toward concrete human existence, whose path is determined in the course of history. For the Philosopher, the distinctions between different groups and different periods in mutable historical existence are not rooted in the rational stratum of human existence. This attitude has implications both for his evaluation of the individual's historical affiliations and for his evaluation of all aspects of human action.

In the second part of this book, where we discussed Halevi's earlier thought, we saw that, as a matter of principle, he still held to the Aristotelian notion of the essence of human existence and continued to believe that man's goal is located chiefly in the rational stratum of his personality. Accordingly, like the Philosopher, he believed that individual redemption is humanity's highest ideal. But he saw no possibility of actualizing this human ideal in the circumstances of life in the actual present. This realization that, in contemporary circumstances, the goal cannot be realized constitutes an acknowledgment of sorts of the weight of historical circumstances. The only ideal that can be actualized in the present is that of the pious life, which recognizes the importance of the religious act and of the individual's involvement in collective life. But this ideal of the pious life is not compatible with the fundamental axioms of Aristotelian anthropology.

Halevi's later thought, both theology and anthropology, is marked by a significant change of direction. In polar antithesis to the Aristotelian philosopher, Halevi now juxtaposed the God endowed with a will, Who is interested in the fate of mankind, with the integrated human condition, an existence that can respond fully to God's will. The integration of human existence is reflected both in the idea of the individual human being as a unique entity that cannot be atomized and in the concept of the human collective as a unique and irreducible entity that cannot be built up from any other entity—not even from the individuals who compose it. The integration of the human collective is grounded in the intrinsic relations between the concept of the individual and the concept of the collective and in the relations between God and the collective. The integrated view of human existence has three implications: (1) recognition of the importance of one's historical affiliation as a set of conditions that determine the individual's destiny; (2) recognition of the importance of the human historical continuum as a process in which the goal of humanity is actualized; and (3) emphasis on human action, including action intended to influence historical circumstances and implement the Divine vocation of all humanity.

18

THE JEWISH PEOPLE, THEIR COMMANDMENTS, AND THEIR UNIQUENESS IN THE LATER THOUGHT

In the preceding chapters we have seen that the contrast between Halevi's thought, both earlier and later, and the Philosopher's view of the status of the ethical hierarchy in the practical realm stems from a fundamental disagreement as to the nature of God's relation to ephemeral concrete multiplicity. According to Halevi, God's intentional and discriminating association with man produces a hierarchy of action, one level of which includes the commandments—actions that are pleasing to God in and of themselves. Because the Philosopher utterly rejects the possibility of such a relationship, he also denies the existence of this hierarchy of actions.

Halevi understood the bond between God and man in different and even contradictory senses. In his earlier thought, it is purely informational, and the commandments are merely guidelines; in his later thought, however, God's relationship with man extends to the normative dimension. The divine injunction grounds the validity of the Torah commandments, which have imperative force.

In both the later and earlier thought the significance of the election of the Jewish people depends on the significance of the commandments; and the significance of the commandments, whether taken as guidelines or as imperatives, depends on parallel theology and anthropology. The very act of commanding reveals God as having a will that is continually re-created—a will that is aware of the totality of concrete human existence. The integrated notion of man is latent in his status as commanded. Hence this chapter, which deals with Halevi's doctrine of the commandments, is the culmination of the preceding chapters on his theology and anthropology.

Nevertheless, Halevi's view of the election of Israel is also associated with his concept of history, which we discussed in Chapter 17. The meaning of Israel's election depends on the meaning of the commandments, because the objective and obligatory validity of the commandments, as imperatives, requires that they be linked with the concrete existential status in which human beings (individual or collective) know themselves to be commanded. One can deduce from the logical significance of this imperative that it applies only to the personality (individual or collective) to which it was addressed. On the other hand, the commandments as guidelines leave no place for such an association, because the rationale and validity of guideline-commandments does not depend on any specific way in which they apply to man.

1. The Foundation of the Validity of the Torah Commandments

In Halevi's earlier thought, the Torah commandments are guidelines for attaining an ontological rapprochement between man and God; their effectiveness, anchored in a given and independent order, depends on their meticulous observance. In this view of the commandments, God is understood to be a teacher, not a monarch. In the later thought, by contrast, the Torah commandments are considered to be divine imperatives—immediate manifestations of the Divine Will; at the same time, Halevi sticks to his belief in the direct impact of observance of the commandments per se—an impact based on a fixed order.[1] This influence has great importance for his system as a whole, because it gives meaning to observance of the commandments by one not commanded to do so—"any Gentile who joins us" (1,27 [21/47])—and he too will "share our good fortune" (ibid.).[2] Clearly this opens the way to universalizing Judaism and provides an answer to the King's query, "then your belief is confined to yourselves?" (ibid.). In the later thought, however, the direct ontological impact of the commandments no longer grounds their obligatory validity, as we can learn from the opening episode of the book. The angel in the King's dream demands that he perform deeds because they are pleasing to God (1,1).[3] Later the King, too, explicitly refers to commandments as imperatives: "You confirm the opinion I formed through meditation and through what I saw in my dream: that man can only attain the Divine Order through Divine ordinance, namely, through actions ordained by God" (1,98 [53/70]).[4] Similarly, the prophet sees God "with the mind's eye" in the image of "a king or judge, seated on his throne, issuing commands and

---

1. 1,99; 2,14; 2,60; 4,9.
2. Note that, according to Halevi, one who is not commanded but nevertheless acts receives a reward in the world to come as well; see 1,111.
3. As we have seen, the Philosopher rejects out of hand the possibility of a Divine Will that has any intention of actualization; consequently he also denies the possibility of actions that are intrinsically pleasing to God (1,1).
4. Similarly, in the first parable of the king of India—a parable that has many points of contact with the dream at the beginning of the book—the dominant view is of the commandments as imperatives: Accepting the yoke of the Torah and commandments is understood to mean accepting the yoke of obedience and service (1,21). This is also the view of the commandments underlying the second parable about the king of India (1,109); see also 2,46; 2,48; 5,20. The idea of the commandments as imperatives can be traced as far back as the description of the pious individual in Part III (3,5; 3,11). As we saw in the second part of this book, the views of the pious individual sometimes correspond to those of Halevi in his later thought.

prohibitions, appointing and deposing officials, and knows that this figure is appropriate to a powerful prince" (4,3 [229/208]). Accordingly, the Torah commandments express God's will to directly guide the Jewish people: "We do not find in the Torah: 'If you keep this law, I will bring you after death into beautiful gardens and great pleasures.' On the contrary, it is said: 'You shall be my chosen people, and I will be a God unto you, who will guide you' " (1,109 [58/75]).[5]

It should be noted, though, that Halevi's remarks about the objective goal of human obedience to Divine imperatives are ambiguous. Sometimes he implied that the point of obeying these imperatives is simply acceptance of the yoke of heaven: "The cause of obedience is the command to obey" (5,20 [323/286]).[6] On the other hand, sometimes the goal seems to be *communion* or *connection*. True, this communion is not between the essence of man and the Divine sphere; it is not a "union of dependence and external contact" (4,3 [ES156/203]), but rather a relationship of "ruling and guiding" (ibid.).[7] When human beings comply with a divine injunction, their will becomes an instrument of the Divine Will. Thus the prophets and sages and pious individuals "are original instruments of the divine will, which employs them without meeting with unwillingness and performs miracles through them. In illustration of this the Sages said: 'The words: Thou shalt fear the Lord thy God' also refer to scholars. He who occupies such a degree has a right to be styled 'a man of God,' a description comprising human and divine qualities" (4,3 [224/204f.]). By the same token, the Jewish people and the Divine Order are connected "through the covenant He has placed as a link between us and Him" (2,34

---

5. Nevertheless, as we have seen, God's direction reaches all of humanity through the medium of the Jewish people.

6. This can also be inferred from the parable of the king of India. The king of the Khazars does not see himself "beholden to him" (1,21 [19/46]) because of a strong desire to cleave to God, but because "proof of his power and dominion has reached me" (1,22 [19/46]).

7. Here Even-Shmuel's Hebrew seems to render the meaning better than Ibn Tibbon's. On the meaning of *communion* or *connection*, see Efros, *Doctrines*, pp. 191ff. See also Chapter 9.

[101/108]).[8] Sometimes, however, Halevi explained this "connection" as a result of the sanctification of the human will itself and not simply as a subordination of the former to the latter—to God's commandments. In consequence, the joy that stems from observance of the commandments itself becomes "worship and a bond of union between you and the Divine Order" (2,50 [109/113]); that is, the joyful response is an inseparable part of the act of fulfilling the commandment.[9] This identification is interpreted as true freedom: "His service is freedom, and humility before Him is true honor" (5,25 [332/294]).[10] Accordingly, the subjective rationale for observing the Torah commandments is, as we shall see, love of God who gave the commandment (ibid.).[11]

2. The Meaning and Rationale of Acceptance of the Commandments

In the previous section we focused on the grounds that validate the commandments; now we shall consider the subjective mean-

---

8. The covenant is an expression for "connection with the divine influence and happiness in the world to come" (2,14 [90]).

9. On the other hand, in the earlier thought (3,11), joy is an additional and independent commandment. The rationale of the commandment of joy is that it makes it possible to praise the Lord who gave the commandments (ibid.).

10. In these concluding sections of the *Kuzari*, which deal with the Rabbi's emigration to Eretz Israel, consciousness of this freedom is associated with an emphasis on the importance of actually worshipping the Lord, as against the King's view that observance of the commandments is merely "service." The King places the accent on intention, which faithfully reflects the extent to which the human will is subordinated to God's will. For the King, man achieves the full duty of his service merely by having the appropriate intention. The Rabbi, however, argues that a person who is aware of the full identification of the human will with the Divine Will cannot remain content with intentions alone and can be satisfied only through full actualization of the divine intention in the world. Compare his poem, עבדי זמן עבדי עבדים הם (Brody 2:300). However, as we have seen, the importance of deeds is associated also with Halevi's theology and anthropology.

11. As we shall see in the next section, for Halevi it is of the nature of love that it can be fully actualized only through arduous deeds—deeds that require some measure of self-sacrifice. In this light we can see love as the emotional and subjective side of freedom.

ing for human beings of observing the commandments. The idea that the Torah commandments are imperatives is associated with a view of the commandments as "divine service." Whereas the commandments are considered to be service in the parable of the king of India (1,21), this idea is absent from the parable of the fool (1,79), which expresses Halevi's earlier thought. In the latter parable, where the Torah commandments are considered to be guidelines, any means or intentions involved in the observance of the commandments are secondary to its outcome. The method or agents that induce human beings to accept the "medicines" have nothing to do with their effectiveness or ineffectiveness. Action is merely a means for drawing closer to God. In Halevi's later thought, by contrast, where the Torah commandments are considered to be imperatives, human action has its own intrinsic goal, whether this inheres in acceptance of the yoke of Heaven or in a qualitative change in will. The communion between the Divine Order and human beings—the covenant between man and God—is actualized in man's readiness to serve God. Moses "had received commissions and treaties, and in return he had to swear fealty to the king" (1,109 [60/76]): life in this world takes precedence over life in the world to come (ibid.). Accordingly, Halevi attributed the fundamental difference between philosophers and "believers" regarding the status of human action to their antithetical notions of the essence of the relationship between God and man. The philosopher locates this essence exclusively on the intellectual stratum, whereas "the believer seeks God for the sake of various benefits, apart from the benefit of knowing Him" (4,13 [241/217]).[12] The believer draws near to God on many levels, not just the intellectual. Observance of the commandments can lead human beings to view themselves as if they were God's "guest, invited to His festive board" (2,50 [109/113]).[13]

---

12. As we saw in Chapter 16, however, the difference is inherent also in their opposing views of the essence of man.

13. In his description of the ideal state of the soul in the World to Come—the "reward" for observance of the commandments—however, Halevi persisted in his earlier view (3,1) that "the only result to be expected from

Just as the remarks in Halevi's later thought about the objective goal of observing the commandments are open to several interpretations, so too there are multiple senses to what he says about the subjective rationale of accepting the yoke of the commandments. For Halevi, these are in fact complementary paths by which one can draw nearer to God: "Our law, as a whole, is divided between fear, love, and joy; by each of them one can approach God" (2,50 [108/113]).[14] Note that several directions of thought can be discerned in what Halevi said about love as a rationale for observing the commandments. On the one hand, observance of the commandments expresses the desire of human beings who love God to respond with all their might to the will of the beloved deity. This is the source of their joy at the opportunity given them by this deity through the commandments He imposed on them: "You shall delight in the law itself through love towards the Lawgiver and consciousness of how He has distinguished you; feel as if you had been His guest, invited to His festive board, and thank Him in mind and word" (2,50 [109/113]). The servant of the Lord is not content with thought; he aspires to deeds that "by their nature are difficult to perform, and are yet performed with the utmost zeal and love" (2,56 [114/117]).[15] The Rabbi asserts that the Jews suffer "scorn" and "slavery" in their exile on account of their

---

this is that the human soul becomes divine, being detached from material senses, joining the highest world, enjoying the vision of the divine light and hearing the divine speech" (1,103 [57/74]). This ideal underscores the tragic sense of the sacrifice offered by the prophet on the altar of his earthly mission.

14. Even though it seems that in this section, too, Halevi gave precedence to joy and love over fear, he did stress the didactic importance of fear of punishment as a deterrent to sin (2,58). The Philosopher, however, who does not expect any reward, "need not care what he does" (4,19 [249/25]). Similarly, the Rabbi's opening remarks (1,11) include only the doctrine of reward and punishment.

15. According to Halevi, not only does love have the power to induce human beings to self-sacrifice, by its very nature it cannot be fully actualized without sacrifice. The same applies to love between human beings. Halevi addressed his beloved in his poem, לקראת חלל חשקך (Brody 2:34). In another poem he addresses God: מאז מעון האהבה היית (Brody 4:232).

religion, but do not attempt "to escape this degradation by a word spoken lightly. . . . [This is] out of devotion to their faith: is not this sacrifice the way to obtain intercession and remission of many sins?" (4,23 [251/226]).[16] That is, the suffering associated with observing the Torah is a sacrifice that can atone for many sins. On the other hand, Halevi sees observance of the commandments as an expression of the lover's desire that his beloved God continue to love him and of his anxiety that failure to comply with His demands might destroy that love: "Then he becomes a servant who loves his master and is ready to perish for the sake of his love, finding the greatest sweetness in his connection with Him, the greatest sorrow in separation from Him" (4,15 [246/222]).

3. Observance of the Commandments and Self-Sacrifice

In Halevi's later thought, self-sacrifice derives from man's bond to God—a bond that is a precondition for the possibility of man's ability to conform with divine injunctions as well as for the creation of an appropriate emotional substrate.

On the historical plane, wars of religion are an expression of self-sacrifice in the service of the deity. These wars, the hallmark of believers in the religions based on revelation rather than of those who accept the philosophers' creed, have sundered the civilized nations who profess the revealed religions into two camps, which are fighting to the death. Unlike the contemplative activity that remains wholly in the individual domain, human action by its very nature affects the public domain; in certain historical circumstances it necessarily leads to jihad and crusade: "There must no doubt be

---

It seems that in the *Kuzari*, as well, the Rabbi emphasizes the relationship between things that are "difficult to perform, and are yet performed with the utmost zeal and love" (2,56 [114/117]; 4,15). See also Yehuda Ratzhabi, "Yesodot she'ullim be-fiyyutei Yehudah Halevi min ha-shirah ve-ha-filosofiya ha-ʿaravit" (Elements in the liturgical poems of Judah Halevi borrowed from Arabic poetry and philosophy), *Molad* 7 (1975–1976): 165–175.

16. See also 5,23.

a way of acting, pleasing in itself, and not through intentions. If this be not so, why then do Christian and Muslim, who divided the inhabited world between them, fight with one another, each of them serving his God with pure intention, living either as monks or hermits, fasting and praying? Nevertheless, they vie with each other to kill their fellows, believing that this is a most pious work and brings them nearer to God. They fight in the belief that paradise and eternal bliss will be their reward" (1,2 [11/39]). The Philosopher, who, unlike Halevi, denies the existence of "actions pleasing in themselves," has nothing good to say about holy wars (ibid., 3). There are even situations in which he holds it appropriate for individuals to adopt a new creed so as to escape mortal peril (2,49): In times of danger there is no need to sacrifice one's life for one's beliefs (4,16). The inevitable conclusion is that the Jews' fidelity to their traditions is irrational, because in the contemporary world this fidelity entails a willingness to live in abjection and humiliation.

On this front, in his later thought Halevi was contending with two different world views, which arrive at the same practical conclusion—namely, that there is no reason for the continued existence of the Jewish people and the Jews should therefore abandon their religion. One view is that of the revealed religions—Christianity and Islam—which postulate their absolute superiority to Judaism, given the inferior historical condition of the Jewish people. The second view is that of the Philosopher, who, although he rejects the absolute superiority of any particular historical religion over others, nevertheless believes that various religions may be endowed with relative superiority in given historical circumstances. Halevi grappled with both views; his struggle, as we have noted, constitutes one of the main axes of his later thought. Halevi attempted to justify and in a sense even to assert a positive value for the abject condition of the Jewish people—a degradation associated with devotion and self-sacrifice—and thereby to justify and assert the value of the Jews' survival. In rebuttal to the spokesmen of the revealed religions, Halevi argued that even they consider observance of religious commandments out of devotion and in conditions of abasement to be a supreme religious value; hence their doctrine, if consistent, cannot infer anything about the ostensible spiritual inferiority of the Jews from the latter's abject physical condition (1,113). In response to the Philosopher, Halevi pointed to the intrinsic value of human action in order to justify the meaning and value of self-sacrifice.

Nevertheless, in the later thought the demand for self-sacrifice is not intended merely to ensure observance of religious commandments or to disseminate the creed among infidels; the intention that underlies the self-sacrificing deed also has crucial weight. Even though Jews do sacrifice their lives to sanctify the name of God (1,115; 4,23), their intention is not appropriate. The King compares the Jews unfavorably with the Christians' and Muslims' endurance of humiliation and martyrdom: "Should I see the Jews acting in a like manner for God's sake, I would place them above the kings of David's house.... The light of God enters only into the souls of the humble" (4,22 [250/226). The Rabbi can only agree: "You are right to blame us: our degradation has not yielded any result" (4,23 [251/226]). So great is the importance ascribed to self-sacrifice for the right reason that the absence of the proper intention is the only reason the Jews remain condemned to exile. The proper intention should be expressed in an a priori willingness to serve God at any cost and with no reservations. The classic exemplar of this kind of self-sacrifice is Rabbi Akiva, martyred in the name of God: "During his torture he asked his pupils whether the time of reciting the Shema had arrived. They answered: 'Master, even now?' He replied: 'All my days I was afflicted by reason of the commandment: "Thou shalt love the Lord thy God with all thy heart and all thy soul (Deut. 6:5), that is, even if He takes away your soul"; now, the opportunity being given, shall I not fulfill it?' And he protracted the word *eḥad* till his soul fled" (3,65 [207/190]). Rabbi Akiva attained the degree at which self-sacrifice is no longer a means for reaching a goal external to itself and has become a goal in and of itself—indeed, the ultimate goal and focus of his life.[17] So too Abraham, after his prophetic experience, was willing even to sacrifice his son Isaac (4,17). This devotion, expressed in full identification of one's own will with God's will—in an unqualified waiver of the present and of continued existence in the future—was the expression par excellence of his love for God, a love that evolved from God's revelation to Abraham. The capacity of the human soul to accept martyrdom depends on love of God, as we saw in Chapter 16; this in turn depends on sensory and visual experience (4,15).

4. The Election of Israel: Genetic Origin versus Way of Life

In the later thought, as in the earlier, the significance of the election of Israel depends on the meaning of the Torah commandments. Because the later thought gives a different meaning to the Torah commandments than the earlier thought does, it also differs about the meaning of Israel's election. In the later thought, the commandments are Divine imperatives—expressions of the sovereign will of a deity who is aware of individual human beings and their lives. The obligation applies only to those (individual or collective) who were so commanded by God—the human beings to whom the "power and dominion" of God relate personally (1,22 [19/46]). Furthermore, as we have seen, a person's spiritual readiness to respond appropriately to the Divine injunction depends on his or her actual presence at the event where the Divine Will is revealed. Nevertheless, even those who were not commanded in an actual prophetic context draw nearer to God and acquire the status of proselytes when they accept the Torah and commandments. In addition, the vocation of the Jewish people is to bring the nations of the world to accept the Torah and commandments.[18]

---

17. Rabbi Akiva's attitude toward martyrdom cannot be justified in the context of Halevi's earlier thought.

18. Halevi himself seems to allude to the problematic status of the proselyte. At the end of the book he hints that the Rabbi's success as a

This concept of the commandments appears already in the Rabbi's first speech, where he bases the Torah commandments on Divine injunctions conveyed to the Jewish people by messengers (1,11). It follows that the Torah was given to the Israelites alone (1,26), as he states explicitly: "In the same style I spoke to you, O Prince of the Khazars, when you asked me about my creed. I mentioned to you what is convincing for me and for the whole of Israel, who knew these things, first through personal experience, and afterward through an uninterrupted tradition, which is equal to experience" (1,25 [20/46f.]). Not only is "personal experience" a prerequisite for knowledge; it is also the condition without which there is no obligation. As the Rabbi reiterates, it is the rationale for the obligatory force of the Torah commandments that determines the scope of their incumbency: "If the Torah were binding on us because God created us, the white and the black man would be equally bound, since He created them all. But the Torah [is binding on us] because He led us out of Egypt and remained attached to us. For we are the pick of mankind" (1,27 [21/47]).[19]

The Jews' unique status as the nation that received the Torah and commandments constitutes their superior link with God on two interdependent bases: (1) their unique status as the only people *obliged* to perform the Torah commandments; and (2) their unique opportunity to observe the command-

---

teacher was only partial, because he was unable to get the King to comprehend the abstract significance of observance of the commandments—a theme that stands at the center of the problems of the later thought. Even at the end of the book the King posits as self-evident that "through pure intention and strong desire we may approach to God in any place" (5,22 [331/293]). Despite the Rabbi's explicit statement about the fundamental importance of action (5,23), the King (5,26 [333/294]) repeats that "the mind is free before God"; to which the Rabbi replies: "Actions must be perfect to claim reward" (5,27 [333/295]). The next section, the last in the book, offers no evidence that the King has fully comprehended the Rabbi's meaning. On this issue the King's opinion seems to remain that of the earlier Halevi. See Yaakov Levinger, *Bein shigrah le-ḥiddush* (Routine and innovation), (Jerusalem, 1973), p. 149. See also p. 302.

19. On the doctrinal difficulties posed by this position, see Chapter 15, note 6.

ments as those who have been enjoined to do so and fulfill their duty. On the first basis, Israel's election does not depend on actual observance of the commandments; on the second, it does. These two points are crucial for explaining various aspects of the unique historical destiny of the Jewish people: They explain its ability to survive in conditions of abasement, give sense and reason to this humiliation, and thereby open the door to hope for a better lot in the future (2,32). The unique Divine leadership of the Jewish people is expressed, on the plane of human-Divine relations, by God's gift of the Torah and commandments. On the historical plane, its reflection is that the Jews are exempt from the dominion of "natural law," whatever lifestyle they lead. Nevertheless, the concrete destiny of the Jewish people does depend on their way of life (1,109). As for the nations, by contrast, the Rabbi argues that "even supposing some nations had followed Him and worshipped Him, being converted as the result of hearsay and tradition, where do we find His acceptance of them and His connection with them, His pleasure in their obedience, His anger at their disobedience? We see them left to nature and chance" (4,3 [220/201]).

Grounding the election of Israel on Divine initiative, rather than on human action, makes it imperative to explain and justify this Divine initiative. The later thought does so through the doctrine of hierarchical existence. Because the Divine initiative involves the Jewish people only, any explanation of it must relate to the biological plane. In addition, basing Israel's election of Israel on a Divine initiative, the result of God's free will, invites the argument advanced against Judaism by Christianity and Islam; namely, that God has replaced His religion and people.[20] The doctrine of levels of existence is a warrant for both the eternal validity of the Torah of Israel and the election

---

20. The Rabbi is seeking to rebut this when he says: "Sometimes the name LORD was applied to the connecting link between God and Israel.... For there exists no connection between God and any other nation, as He pours out His light only on the select people" (4,3 [220/201]); see also the Appendix, note 3.

of the Jewish people. The Rabbi invokes the genetic difference between the Jews and other nations to show that the Divine initiative itself is subject to eternal laws.

Thus the theory of levels of existence is not the cornerstone of the idea of the election of Israel, as many have thought. On the contrary, its role is to provide a theoretical explanation for an idea that, according to Halevi, rests on an independent empirical foundation—the fact that God has made demands only on the Jews and is present only among them. The hierarchical theory of existence appears in the *Kuzari* only after Halevi has provided a foundation for the election of Israel, as an attempt to provide an ontological explanation for God's presence among the Jews (1,26). It crops up again in his attempt to provide an ethical explanation of this, in reply to the King's question: "Would it not have been better or more commensurate with divine wisdom had all mankind been guided in the true path?" (1,102 [56/73]). To which the Rabbi responds: "Would it not have been best for all animals to have been reasonable beings?" (1,103 [56/73]).

In fact, the hierarchical theory of existence is not really compatible with fundamental tendencies in Halevi's later thought, even when he adds a fifth level—that of the prophets (1,39; 1,43)— to the four Aristotelian levels. The hierarchical theory of existence does not sit well with the tendency of the later thought to emphasizes the sovereignty of God as the ex nihilo Creator, because the theory, in all its variations, sets limits to God's power. It is incompatible with other trends in Halevi's later thought as well. It cannot explain the oneness of the human race. It does not permit transitions from level to level. Its postulates cannot support the possibility that some of Adam's descendants are at are the level of "husks" (1,95). Nor can it explain how, at the end of days, after generations of being split into different levels of existence, the human race will again be one (4,23).[21]

---

21. See J. Guttmann, *Dat u-madda* (Religion and science), trans S. Asch (Jerusalem, 1955), p. 81.

19

AN OVERVIEW OF HALEVI'S LATER THOUGHT

As compared with the earlier thought, Halevi's later thought is marked by a greater willingness to fully work out conclusions that stem from the unique Jewish experience. As we have seen in the previous chapters, this leads to the replacement of some Aristotelian axioms by new axioms compatible with this experience. In the present chapter we shall survey the later thought through the lens of the characteristic order inherent in many systems prevailing in many realms, that is, hierarchical order. As we shall see, the similarities among the various hierarchies are rooted in the doctrinal and empirical foundations of Halevi's later thought, embody its unity and uniqueness, and reveal its typical problems.

In Aristotelian philosophy, the constitution of an undifferentiated relationship between God and non-Divine reality depends on the Divine essence, but its actual embodiment in the hierarchical order of non-Divine reality depends only on the variety of non-Divine existence. In his earlier thought Halevi still tried to have it both ways. On the one hand, he adhered to the Aristotelian axioms and endeavored to base the hierarchical order on primary distinctions that are inherent in non-Divine existence as such. On the other hand, he was forced to retreat from the philosophical position on a number of major issues. The unique nature of the Jewish experience and his conception of the Torah commandments as actions that cannot be replaced by others required him to posit that the hierarchical order rests on Divine intervention (in some sense) as well. In the earlier thought, this fundamental deviation from Aristotelian philosophy did not modify the orientation of Halevi's theology and anthropology, as consistency would require. In the later thought, however, Halevi had no qualms about adopting the view that the hierarchical order originates in voluntary Divine intervention. He drew the appropriate conclusions about the nature of the hierarchical order, about God's meaning for human beings, and about the nature of man. But in his later thought, too, as we have noted, Halevi relied on the regularity and order implicit in non-Divine existence to explain the involvement of a transcendent deity in the affairs of the world.

1. The Source of the Hierarchical Order

Unlike the Aristotelian position that God's relationship to non-Divine existence emerges from the unchanging nature of God—whence its indefiniteness and eternal fixity—in Halevi's later thought this relationship expresses God's defined interest in non-Divine existence and is a manifestation of voluntary intentionality focused on a particular segment of non-Divine existence. This spontaneous focusing of the Divine Will finds expression in the arrangement of concrete multiplicity into hierarchical orders—whether these hierarchies depend exclusively on the Divine Will (as a necessary and sufficient condition) or depend also on the nature of the existence that is affected by God (as a necessary but not sufficient condition). This identification of God as the source of the hierarchical order is associated with the concept of the deity that characterizes this stage in the development of Halevi's thought—the acknowledgment of a spontaneous Divine Will.

The specific resolves of the Divine Will and the dispositions of the hierarchical orders that stem from it are not entailed by any prior state of affairs; rather than the outcome of a gradual process, they constitute a totally new beginning: "Why should the letters *heh vav yod* or an angel or a sphere or other things be required if we believe in the Divine will and creation, and if we believe that God created the immense variety of things and species in one moment" (4,26 [269/239]).[1] Hence the theme of the benediction "with eternal love Thou lovest us" is that "[the beginning] came from Him, not from us" (2,50 [110/115]). So too the intrinsic status of the Jewish people as a nation that has assumed the obligation of observing the Torah and commandments is a sudden innovation: "A divine law arises suddenly. It is bidden to arise, and it is there, similar to the creation of the world" (1,81 [38/58]).[2] The prophets' resemblance to the angelic degree, too, results from a sudden act—prophetic vision (4,9).[3] All this helps explain the proliferation of hierarchical orders in the later thought, in stark contrast to the fundamental unity of the hierarchical order in Aristotelian philosophy. In the later thought, the multiplicity in the world stems from the infinite states of the Divine Will. In Aristotelian philosophy, the unitary aspect of the world arises from the singleness and uniformity of God and from His ontological status as actual existence.

Despite the multiplicity of hierarchical orders, there are fixed relations among them, as we have seen. The topmost rung of hierarchical ladders in the sublunar sphere is occupied by various aspects of Jewish existence: The elect among the nations

---

1. See also 5,14. Similarly, heaven "is employed to carry out the divine will directly and without the assistance of intermediary factors" (4,3 [223/204]).

2. The Ten Plagues were intended to help the Israelites overcome the difficulty of believing in new Divine initiatives that "were ordained by God, who does what He wills and when He wills, and that they were not ordinary natural phenomena, nor were they wrought by constellations or by accident" (1,83 [39/59]). See also 5,20; 5,21.

3. Compare J. Schlanger, "La doctrine de la hiérarchie dans le livre du *Kuzari* de Jehuda Halevi (1085–1141)," *Colloque international sur le néoplatonisme, Royaumont, 9–13 juin 1969* (Paris, 1971), pp. 339–353.

is the Jewish people;[4] among historical periods, that future age when all humankind will be assimilated into the Jews (4,23); among languages, Hebrew; among countries, Eretz Israel; among sources of knowledge, prophecy; among ways of life, observance of the commandments that are unique to the Torah, which is the "divine law" (2,48 [106/111]); and among the festivals, the Jewish festivals (2,16). The location of the elements of Jewish existence at the pinnacle of the hierarchical scales of the sublunar realm expresses their immediate relationship with the Divine Presence in the world, a relationship distinguished by its own degree of intensity: "He who is capable of gauging these matters is the real prophet; the place where they are visible is the true place of worship. For it is a Divine place, and the law coming forth from it is the true religion" (4,9 [238/215]). The Jews are "the people of the Lord" (4,3 [220/201]).[5] The Divine Order rests on the multitude of Israel (1,95).[6] Eretz Israel is the "inheritance of God" (2,16 [80/92]) and "the land of prophecy" (1,95 [47/65])—"the country distinguished by the Divine Order" (ibid. [48/66]). Hebrew is the language created by God (4,25).[7] Observance of the Torah commandments is a condition for attaining the Divine Order (1,98).[8] The Jewish holidays

---

4. Ontologically, the Jewish people stand at the summit of the ladder of the levels of sublunar existence.

5. See also 2,16.

6. See also 2,48 and 4,3. The Divine Order can rest on individual Jews even in exile. The pious individual attains the Divine Order (3,11). Human beings can commune with the Divine Order by means of joyful service of the Lord (2,50). For our present purposes we need not consider the distinctions among between the various senses of *Divine Order*, which were discussed in Chapters 7 and 15.

7. See also 2,2. The Hebrew language was created directly by God and is the language in which the universe was created (ibid.). Hence it inheres in nature, whereas all other languages are based on convention. In principle, on this point the later Halevi still agreed with *Sefer Yetzirah* (5,20). For a comparison with the opinion of Abraham Ibn Ezra, see Uriel Simon, *Four Approaches to the Book of Psalms*, trans. Lenn J. Schramm (Albany, N.Y., 1991), p. 267, n. 53.

8. See also 2,34; 2,46; 2,48; 4,13. Conversely, attaining the Divine Order is a condition for a psychological readiness to observe the commandments (4,17).

are the festivals of the Lord, instituted by God Himself (2,16), and "the Divine Order is connected with" the Sabbath (1,86 [40/60]).[9]

The influence of the Divine presence on the elements of Jewish existence is not limited to determining the intensity of their relationship with God. The Divine presence can annul the previous nature of the elements and give them a new nature. For example, the history of the Jewish people is not subject to the laws that rule the history of the Gentile nations.[10] By the same token, the physical laws that determine rainfall and harvests do not apply to Eretz Israel (1,109). Note that this exemption is a direct result of the participation in an event that embodies the Divine presence in the world. The Divine presence radiates its essence on the environment and elevates the components of the latter to a higher degree. Hence an event that embodies the Divine presence in the world can be viewed as the tangent point of concrete circumstances in different spheres of existence. In every sphere, the factor that participates in the event stands at the pinnacle of the hierarchy; all other factors find their place in the hierarchy as a function of their relative "distance" from it.

Note, however, that even in his later thought Halevi was sometimes at pains to explain that God becomes present in one particular segment of existence rather than another because of

---

9. This suggests that in his later thought Halevi inclined to the idea that there can be qualitative distinctions within the temporal continuum itself: The holiness of the Sabbath applies to a defined unit of time, the seventh day, just as the holiness of Eretz Israel and the holiness of the Hebrew language apply to the entities themselves. Sometimes, however, the later Halevi attributed the quality of times and places to the influence of the spheres (4,7–9), as did Abraham Ibn Ezra (*Yesod Mora*, §9). In his earlier thought, by contrast, Halevi ascribed the special nature of the Sabbath and festivals to observance of the specific commandments that apply to them. Accordingly, the Sabbath "has been appointed to establish the connection with the Divine Order" (3,5 [247]), a function actualized by the particular rules of conduct for the Sabbath day that are incumbent on the Jews.

10. 1,109; 2,32; 2,33; 2,48; 2,54; 2,58; 4,3; 5,20. Similarly, the prophet is exempt from the laws of nature (1,41–43; 1,109; 2,62; 3,17). See also J. Guttmann, *Dat u-madda* (Religion and science), trans. S. Asch (Jerusalem, 1955), p. 71.

a primary, prevoluntary hierarchical order inherent in non-Divine existence. For example, the special relationship between God and members of the Jewish people is explained by their particular excellence, which is innate and has been passed down from generation to generation, going back to Adam.[11] Similarly, Eretz Israel has a particular virtue that allows it to be the land of prophecy: "This area was also privileged. Whenever a person was found in it who fulfilled all the necessary conditions, these sights became distinctly visible to him, 'visibly, and not in dark speeches'" (4,3 [231/210]). Again, "He is also called God of the land, because this possesses a special power in its air, soil, and climate" (4,17 [247/224]). Eretz Israel is also distinguished by its geographical location "in the center of the inhabited world" (2,20 [82/93]) and in the middle of the temperate zone (1,95).[12] The Hebrew language has a phonetic superiority and is distinguished by the beauty of its sounds (2,80). It outranks other languages on the semantic plane as well: Its words allude to the essence of things (4,25); the tra-

---

11. 1,41–43; 1,95; 4,3; 4,15.

12. Similarly, the Temple is in the "center" (3,17; 4,25). Compare Saadia Gaon, *The Book of Beliefs and Opinions*, trans. Samuel Rosenblatt (New Haven, Conn., 1948), beginning of Treatise IV, and Ibn Ezra's short commentary on Exodus 8:18. In his commentary on Exodus 23:20, though, Ibn Ezra denies that the mean has any special value. See A. Altmann, "Torat ha-ʾaqlimim le-RYHL." (Judah Halevi's theory of climates), *Melilah* (Manchester, 1944), pp. 1–17; Y. Heinemann, "RJHL: Ha-ʾish ve-hogeh ha-deʿot" (R. Judah Halevi: The man and the thinker), in Zemora, *R. Yehudah Halevi*, pp. 166–235; S. Rawidowicz, *ʿIyyunim be-maḥshevet Yisrael* (Studies in Jewish thought), vol. 1 (Jerusalem, 1969), p. 158. Evidently Halevi vacillated as to whether it is the physical data, or the events in which God was revealed, that establish the election of Eretz Israel. This indecision is reflected in conflicting views about the status of Egypt. On the one hand, he included Egypt among the lands where prophecy is possible (2,14; 4,3; compare also 2,22; see also his poem, למצרים עלי כל שיר תהילה [Brody, 2:180]). This view is compatible with the idea that election depends on Divine revelation. Elsewhere, though, he excluded Egypt from the lands that are fit for prophecy (2,14)—a view compatible with the idea that election depends on physical conditions. See Altmann, "Torat ha-ʾaqlimim," n. 2.

ditional cantillation signs facilitate the comprehension of clauses and sentences (2,72–73).[13]

In the mirror of Halevi's thought as a whole, the last-named hierarchical orders should be seen as expressing particular states of the sovereign Divine Will. These states were latent in the original act of Creation. The fact of direct creation by God guarantees the perfection of creation, "because no flaw could be found in a work of a wise and Almighty Creator, wrought from a substance chosen by Him, and fashioned according to His own design" (1,95 [46/64]). As we have seen, the intrinsic qualities of the Jewish people derive from Adam (ibid.).[14] Similarly, Hebrew is the language created by God; the perfection of Eretz Israel expresses the importance of the "mean," established by the act of Creation itself.[15] By the same token, the special quality of particular dates on the Jewish calendar is bound up with the Creation (2,20).[16] But this reliance on hierarchical orders anchored in the Creation engenders grave problems for Halevi's system as a whole.

2. The Relations Among the Hierarchies

In Halevi's later thought the various hierarchies influence one another, even though they do not derive from one another.

---

13. 2,66–81; 5,20. On the excellence of the Hebrew language, see Nehemiah Aloni, "Qedushat ha-safah ha-ʿivrit" (The sanctity of the Hebrew language), *Turei Yeshurun* (Sivan–Tammuz 5735 [1975]): 13–15.

14. The Jews still bear the full human potential with which Adam was endowed when he was created, whereas the nations carry only part of this potential. This deficiency of the nations is an expression of the degeneration that turns them into "husks" (1,95).

15. The virtues of Eretz Israel, as the country for which the Sabbath and festivals are determined, are bound up with Creation, and specifically with the creation of light and the sun: It was at the hour of sunset for Eretz Yisrael that "the first light was created, the sun being created later on" (2,20 [84/94]).

16. See Eliezer Schweid, *Moledet ve-ereẓ yeʿudah* (Tel Aviv, 1979), pp. 63–64 [English Version: *The Land of Israel: National Home or Land of Destiny*, trans. Deborah Greniman (Rutherford, N.J., 1985)].

Hence the fate of the components of Jewish existence parallels the extent to which they are actualized.[17] The observance of the Torah commandments by Jews in Eretz Israel is a precondition for attaining the level of prophecy, that is, for communion with the Divine Order: "The land also has its part in this and so have the religious acts connected with it, which I would compare to the cultivation of the vineyard. But no other place could share the influence of the Divine Order" (2,12 [75/88]).[18] Similarly, full observance of the Torah commandments is possible only in Eretz Israel: "Many of the Israelite laws lose their force for one who does not live in Eretz Israel" (5,23 [331/293]).[19] The determination of the times of the festivals and Sabbaths, and of the sabbatical years and jubilee years, depends exclusively on the Land of Israel (2,18–20).[20] Whether the Hebrew language flourishes depends on the situation of the Jewish people (2,68). In short, the condition of one element of the Jewish experience influences its other elements. Any weakening of the bond between the people and their land prevents them from attaining prophecy[21] and deprives the land of its particular virtue; at such times, the "visible" Divine Presence that rests on the Land of Israel is hidden (5,23). The Jews' regression from their lofty status leads to the decline of the Hebrew language as well: "It

---

17. Note that Halevi was aware of the parallels among the various hierarchical orders and frequently draws analogies between different hierarchies. The central axis of the discussion in 2,8–24 is the analogous locations of "God's people" and "God's land" in their corresponding hierarchies (see also 1,95). He also draws analogies between the Hebrew language and the Jewish people (2,68), between God as the Lord and the "favored few" and the Jewish people (4,3), and between special places and times (4,8–9).

18. See also 1,109; 2,14; 2,16; 4,3; 4,11; 4,17; 5,23. Sometimes, however, Halevi explained the human hierarchy, too, on the basis of its correlation with Eretz Israel, and not only on the possibility of actualizing a given potential. Thus "Eber represented the essence of Shem, the latter that of Noah. He inherited the temperate zone, the center and principal part of which is Canaan, the land of prophecy" (1,95 [47/65]).

19. See also 2,18 and 2,56.

20. See Schweid, *Moledet ve-ereẓ yeʿudah*, pp. 63–64.

21. 1,95; 2,12; 2,14; 4,11; 4,17; 5,23.

shared the fate of its bearers, degenerating and dwindling with them" (2,68 [122/124]).[22]

The reciprocal influence among the hierarchies and, in its wake, the parallel in the destinies of the elements of the Jewish existence are linked by the ontological relations among the hierarchies. But the hierarchies are also connected by their common goal, which depends on this reciprocal influence.

3. Hierarchies and Teleology

One of the major lineaments of Halevi's later thought, as a unified system, is inherent in the meaning of hierarchical order. Unlike Aristotelian philosophy, where the all-encompassing hierarchy (the succession of emanations) and an entity's place in that hierarchy derive from defined ontological orders, in Halevi's later thought they rest on the goals that they actualize or are supposed to actualize. In Aristotelian philosophy the hierarchy resembles a down-staircase; because it descends it can be exploited by those who wish to ascend. In Halevi's later thought, by contrast, the hierarchy resembles ladders that are dropped down, from time to time and on purpose, to help actualize the Divine purpose of elevating existence in this world to the level of the heavenly sphere. Thus the role and purpose of the Jewish people are to make God's "light" visible on earth, to a degree matching its appearance in heaven (2,50).[23] The prophet as an individual and the Jewish people as the nation of prophets have a duty to fulfill their universal vocation, even if this delays their

---

22. The Jewish people's fall from their lofty status is connected with their "inclinings" to the nations (2,54). Similarly, the corruption of Hebrew poetry stems from "imitation" of the conventional meters of Arabic poetry, which are foreign to the spirit of the Hebrew language (2,73).

23. This idea can be found already in Part III (17 [159/152]): "The Torah is the outcome of His will to reveal His sway on earth, as in heaven." As we have noted, this section, which describes the way of life and views of the pious individual, should not be read as expressing Halevi's own beliefs in his earlier thought. On this point, too, the later Halevi came around to the opinion of the pious individual.

own ascent. As we noted in the previous chapter, the purpose of the Torah commandments is to lead human beings to accept the yoke of the kingdom of the Lord. All the other elements of the Jewish experience also participate in constituting this kingdom: "He, however, who knows how to distinguish one people from another, one person from another, one time from another, one place from another, and certain circumstances from others, will perceive that heavenly dictated events mostly came to pass in the chosen and holy land, and among the privileged Israelite people, and in that time and under circumstances that were accompanied by laws and customs the observation of which was beneficial, while their neglect wrought harm" (5,20 [320/283]). Thus Eretz Israel was "appointed for the instruction of mankind and apportioned to the tribes of Israel from the time of the confusion of tongues" (2,16 [79/92]).[24]

That the hierarchies include a goal—a lodestone to help those in the lower levels ascend—stems from the theology of the later thought. This goal manifests God's interest in non-Divine existence and reflects the Divine aspect that faces outward—His "kingdom." God constitutes His kingdom by means of the "instruments"—the elite entities at the summits of the various hierarchies. These chosen entities embody this kingdom through their manifest presence—their destiny and deeds—and thereby magnify the kingdom of the Lord. In the heavenly, angelic sphere, this "kingdom" actually exists in perfection; in the terrestrial sphere, by contrast, it is progressively objectified by means of the elect (1,109), who serve as "original instruments of the divine will, which employs them without meeting with unwillingness and performs miracles through them" (4,3 [224/204]).[25] This resemblance between prophets and angels, grounded on their common vocation, is reflected in the proximity of their

---

24. Hence the Jewish people's right to Eretz Israel derives from their intrinsic essence as the nation whose members are fit to be in communion with the Divine Order (1,95; 2,14).

25. Hence Halevi attributed great importance to the visible external appearance of the elect; see Chapter 14; and Chapter 15, note 62.

degrees in the overall hierarchy.[26] The prophets actually attain the level of the angels or come very close to it.[27] Halevi explained that Adam was created in the image of the angels.[28] This closeness to the level of "the divine and celestial" is valid only for "the noblest human being, who arranges order and harmony for the rest of mankind, in the same systematic way as God has done for the universe" (4,3 [231/209]).[29]

---

26. The proximity between Jewish existence and the angelic degree is also reflected in the angels' particular affinity for the Hebrew language. The angels "employ it in preference to any other" language (4,25 [256/251]). The proximity between Eretz Israel and the heavenly spheres is expressed by the fact that Eretz Israel is "the next step to paradise" (2,14 [77/90]). Hence it fell to the lot of Seth, the "son of God" (ibid.). Abraham Ibn Ezra, citing Halevi as his source, wrote that "the sons of God" are the descendants of Seth (Ibn Ezra, First Recension on Gen. 6:2, *incipit* בני אלוקים). Seth, the "son of God," who perfectly embodied the angelic form, was allotted Eretz Israel, which thereafter passed down to those who resembled him in their virtues (1,95). Accordingly, the "gates of heaven" are located in Eretz Israel (2,14; 2,23).

27. Halevi vacillated about the relationship between the prophetic and angelic degrees. Sometimes he inclined to the opinion that the prophets are merely close to the level of the angels (1,103; 1,109; 2,26); elsewhere he held that their level is the same as that of the angels (1,42; 3,23; 4,15; 5,20, Fourth Principle). This vacillation seems to be associated with his similar uncertainty concerning the nature of the angels, which we discussed in Chapter 15. Because Halevi held that the angels are corporeal, he could maintain that human beings can attain their level. For Ibn Ezra, too, the nature of the relationship between the angelic and prophetic degrees depends on the nature of the prophets. But he held that the angels are spiritual, so their level is higher than that of human beings. See Ibn Ezra on Gen. 1:1, *incipit* ברא; on Ex. 23:20 (short commentary), *incipit* הנה אנכי; and on Ex. 25:40 (short commentary), *incipit* וראה.

28. This is also the opinion of Ibn Ezra on Gen. 1:26, as well as in the First Recension ad loc. In contrast to Halevi's later thought, however, Ibn Ezra located the common denominator between angel and man in the spiritual nature of the angel and the human soul; according to Ibn Ezra, it is the spirituality of the soul that guarantees its eternity. As noted, this was Halevi's opinion in his earlier thought; in the later thought, however, he denied the spiritual nature of both the angels and the soul.

29. This seems to be how we should understand the level of the "man of God," which is "a description comprising human and divine qualities" (4,3 [224/205]). Such a person is "divine" in the sense of angelic, because he is a primary instrument of the Divine Will (ibid.). Evidently this is also

4. Mission, Action, and Freedom

Basing the hierarchy on its teleology leads to conclusions that totally contradict the stance of Aristotelian philosophy and Halevi's earlier thought. It entails a recognition of the supreme importance of activity that actualizes the Divine purpose and a devaluation of the intention to realize the purpose. It also involves a fundamental preference for action over contemplation and, within the sphere of action itself, a preference for historical and collective action over action that mainly implicates the actor's own fate. As we saw in earlier chapters, these conclusions also follow from Halevi's later anthropology.

The supreme importance of the actualization of the goal sheds additional light on Halevi's ambivalent position, in his later thought, about the meaning of human freedom. Freedom in the sense of free choice (i.e., freedom *to*) is not a precondition for actualizing the goal; what is more, by its very nature such freedom undermines any possibility of planning aimed at the achievement of some particular outcome.[30]

In light of this, we can understand the significance of the fundamental disagreement on this issue between Saadia Gaon and the later Halevi. For Saadia, the ultimate goal of the Divine Creation lies in God's will to do good; because there is no greater good than rewarding an action that expresses obedience to a command[31]—an action possible only if the obeying creature is free—God created human beings with free will.[32] This freedom endows human beings with their status at the pinnacle of the hierarchy of creatures and makes

---

the level of the "sons of God" (1,95; 2,14). Note that in 5,20, Fourth Principle, Halevi argues that observance of the commandments is sufficient to elevate human beings to the level of the angels.

30. One might argue that God, with His foreknowledge of the future, can create the futures to be chosen as required. Opinions about this argument, which has been discussed by various thinkers in recent years, are divided.

31. Saadia Gaon, *The Book of Beliefs and Opinions*, III, beginning.

32. Ibid., IV,1.

it possible for them to rise above the level of the angels.[33] From this perspective, Saadia's thought is distinctly anthropocentric.[34] For Halevi, though, who saw the Divine goal as the ultimate ideal set by the Creator for His creatures, and not as the intrinsic rationale of the Deity,[35] the reward is only a by-product of correct action, not the objective. Accordingly, human freedom does not occupy a central place in his system, as it does in Saadia Gaon's philosophy. Adam was "the noblest creature on earth" (1,96 [49/67]), but his nobility had nothing to do with his practical choices. Nor does the prophet stand (at least not exclusively) at the summit of the hierarchy of all creatures.[36] From this perspective we can hardly describe Halevi's thought as anthropocentric.

In Halevi's later thought, then, the Divine injunction must be understood as a manifestation of the Divine Will, exclusively intended to lead human beings to action, and not, as for Saadia, to provide an opportunity for human beings to freely choose to respond to the Divine imperative. By the same token, Halevi explained the need for Divine injunctions, even though God knows in advance whether human beings will serve Him or defy Him, only on the grounds that the commandment itself is an

---

33. See Efros, *Doctrines*, pp. 130ff.

34. Saadia Gaon, *The Book of Beliefs and Opinions*, IV,1 and VII,1. This is from the perspective of the creator and not that of the creature. See also E. Schweid, "Torat ha-musar ha-datit shel R. Saʿadiah Gaon" (The religious ethics of R. Saadia Gaon), *Meḥqerei Yerushalayim be-maḥshevet Yisrael* 3 (1982): 15–32.

35. Halevi did not follow Saadia's path and offer an ethical rationale for God's interest in non-Divine existence, even though that would refute the Philosopher's argument that a God who evinces interest in others is necessarily a deficient God. Evidently Saadia and Halevi disagreed as to the validity of ethical norms. Saadia adhered to the Mutazilite, Halevi to the Aristotelian tradition. Even though Halevi recognized the validity of the "rational laws" (2,48 [106/111]; 3,7; 3,11), their rationale is chiefly utilitarian and human and their validity limited to human beings. See L. Strauss, *Persecution and the Art of Writing* (Glencoe, Ill., 1952) pp. 118ff.

36. This depends, as we have noted, on the relationship between the prophetic and angelic degrees.

"intermediate cause" (5,20) and not that the command opens the door to obedience out of choice.[37]

5. Tolerance in the Later Thought: Rationale and Manifestations

The preference for action over contemplation is reflected in Halevi's general policy in his final revision of the *Kuzari*, made, of course, from the perspective of his later thought. Here he favored pragmatic, didactic, and apologetic interests over purely theoretical ones—the discovery of absolute truth for its own sake.[38] According to Halevi's own testimony, the *Kuzari* was intended to refute the arguments put forward by "philosophers and followers of other religions and also against [Jewish] sectarians who attacked the rest of Israel" (1,1 [3/35]). His answers do not relate merely to the literal and theoretical sense of these attacks; they take into account the concrete situation of the critics: their objections, abilities, and circumstances. From the literary perspective, this approach is embodied in the dialogue that runs through the book.[39] In Halevi's opinion, although it is possible to persuade even a pagan to accept the commandments (the King's conversion is evidence of this), it is far more difficult and sometimes even impossible, relying exclusively on rational argumentation, to induce human beings to abandon the predispositions that underlie their world-view. Halevi deliberately has the Rabbi fail in his protracted attempts

---

37. Accordingly, the sole purpose of the Binding of Isaac was to make Abraham's piety emerge from potential to actual, not to implement this piety by means of a spontaneous act of free choice (5,20). This notion of the Divine imperative may explain how the Land of Israel was enjoined to observe the Sabbatical year just as the people of Israel were commanded to observe the Sabbath day (2,18). Halevi may have held that the Sabbatical year commandments apply to the Jewish people because of the Sabbath that is imposed on the land (ibid.).

38. See Baneth, "Halevi and al-Ghazali," p. 317; Yaakov Levinger, *Bein shigrah le-ḥiddush* (Routine and innovation), (Jerusalem, 1973), p. 138.

39. The *Kuzari* was written in dialogue form for other reasons as well, as we shall see later.

to persuade the King that action has primacy over intention.[40] Ultimately the Rabbi has no choice but to rest content with his partial success, take his leave of the King, and emigrate to Eretz Israel.

This provides an insight into Halevi's tolerance of opinions and beliefs he considers erroneous. As we have seen, this tolerance also rests on his conception of man's limitations and dependence on the theoretical plane, given the circumstances imposed upon him, as well as on the knowledge that world-views and religions evolve from and rest on earlier ones. His tolerance applies to Aristotelian philosophy as well as to Christianity and Islam. Hence the preference given to practical considerations does not derive merely from pressing historical circumstances; it is justified by the fundamental principles of his doctrine. Whereas the recognition that the world-views of human beings depend on their biographical circumstances exempts them, a posteriori, from responsibility and guilt and, in certain circumstances, foredooms any attempt to modify their outlooks, the preference for action over contemplation a priori subordinates thought and contemplation to practical interests. The acknowledgment that doctrines and religions contribute to the spiritual development of humanity endows them with a relative positive value.

It follows that one of Halevi's main criteria for the acceptability of a particular view is how he evaluated its practical and didactic influence. Recognizing the King's spiritual needs, he complied with his request and explains the main tenets of the Mutakallimun (5,16–18).[41] At the same time, he took into account the difficulty of persuading individuals of fundamental axioms and was willing to compromise with believers who could not accept ex nihilo creation, himself suggesting that they persist

---

40. See Chapter 18, note 18.
41. See Baneth, "Halevi and al-Ghazali," p. 317. In the same vein, the Rabbi reviews the doctrine of *Sefer Yetzirah* (4,28), even though he explicitly demurs at it (4,26). Compare 2,26; 5,1. And, as we shall see below, Halevi incorporated into the final version of the *Kuzari* elements of his earlier thought that he no longer accepted.

in the idea that the world was created from some primary matter.[42]

The pragmatic inclination of Halevi's later thought explains its inconsistency, which we discussed in Chapter 15. A concern for the psychological difficulty of accepting the fundamental possibility of ex nihilo creation that takes place without cause or reason—a difficulty that can be overcome only through personal prophetic experience—requires Halevi to try to explain certain matters that, in truth, can be told but not explained.[43] In these explanations he relied on Aristotelian postulates that no longer have a place in his later thought. For example, as we saw in Chapter 15, Halevi proposed explanations even for the Divine immanence in the world. By their very nature these explanations rely on a system of law that stands on its own and on agents that mediate between the utterly transcendent God and the world. As we saw, both such a system of law and the mediating agents are quite incompatible with the Divine sovereignty that expresses God's free will. They are also incompatible with God's absolute transcendence, which leaves no place for agents that, by virtue of their intrinsic ontological status, mediate between God and the world. Similarly, in rebutting the arguments advanced against Judaism by rival religions, namely, that from God's bond with the Jewish people in the past nothing can be inferred as to their election in the present—arguments for which there is no empirical refutation—Halevi had to rely on Aristotelian theories of levels of existence, accepting the distinc-

---

42. Similarly, Halevi had reservations about the idea that the world is re-created from time to time, inter alia because the proponents of this theory tend to be apathetic to miracles (5,20). Still, in 4,20 the King seems to maintain this view and the Rabbi makes no objection. By the same token, one must come to terms with the superstitions associated with synagogues, because they are vital for maintaining the unity of Israel (1,97).

43. According to Halevi, psychological need causes natural scientists to offer explanations even for events that clearly deviate from logic (1,5). These explanations are in fact schemes and sophistications (ibid.); that is, they have no theoretical justification. For another view, see Y. Heinemann, "Temunat ha-historiyyah shel R. Yehudah Halevi" (Judah Halevi's picture of history), *Ziyyon* 9 (1944): 147–177.

tion between form and matter and the principle that the acceptance of form depends on the readiness of the matter. On the basis of these theories Halevi justified God for having chosen one nation out of all nations in the past and for having chosen the Jews in particular and guaranteed their continued election in the present and future. This guarantee is of supreme importance, because in Halevi's thought there is no distinction between the significance of the Jews' unique historical destiny and their status as the chosen people. Explaining the election of the Jews on the basis of intrinsic characteristics that preceded their election is hardly exceptional, as we have seen. Halevi used a similar argument to explain the election in the context of other hierarchies as well.[44]

6. The Earlier Thought in the Light of the Later Thought

Now we can understand why Halevi incorporated his earlier thought into his book, despite the radical changes that had intervened in his world-view. It seems plausible that Halevi believed that his earlier thought was not unique to him, but was characteristic of human beings who, in a process of spiritual evolution, have risen above the rationalist philosophical level but have not yet attained the level of his later thought. He could find support for this idea not only in his own biography and the experience of others,[45] but also in the location of the earlier thought between philosophy and his later thought.[46] And, as we

---

44. See also Baneth, "Halevi and al-Ghazali," p. 318.

45. Halevi's early view on many key issues was the same as or close to that of many of his friends, including Abraham Ibn Ezra. All of them were influenced by the prevalent philosophical currents. This similarity reinforced the view we are ascribing to Halevi here. Accordingly, the fact that Halevi's earlier thought provides the starting point for many of the King's questions reflects the status of the latter as a person dissatisfied with Aristotelian philosophy who has yet to find anything better.

46. From this perspective there is a parallel between the earlier thought and *Sefer Yetzirah*: Both express ideas located somewhere between speculative philosophy and empiricism. The conclusions of *Sefer Yetzirah*

have seen, Halevi considered Aristotelian philosophy to be a necessary and well-defined stage in the spiritual development of human beings. The earlier thought was an appropriate response to the theoretical questions that are posed by people at the transition between the stages—a response appropriate to their level of perception and whose practical conclusion is observance of the commandments. Clearly the far-reaching compliance with the demands of rational thinking,[47] as well as the emphasis on the meticulous observance of the commandments, makes the earlier thought extremely significant in the context of the dispute between Rabbanites and Karaites. Here the front line of the debate is shortened and focused on what Halevi considered to be the main point: observing the commandments according to the tradition of the Sages. In Part III, Halevi acknowledged that the Karaites "turned their attention to the fundamental principles"; his main argument against them is that they "deduce the special laws... by means of arguments" (3,65 [204/188]). As we have seen, Part III was originally written as part of a debate with a Karaite, a dispute that focused on issues directly linked to observance of the commandments as prescribed by the Sages.

Halevi's belief that his earlier thought was not a chance episode and the practical conclusion he drew from this belief—meticulous observance of the commandments—underlie the superior status allotted to this thought in the *Kuzari* vis-à-vis other world-views that are also rejected on theoretical grounds.

---

are demonstrated with even greater force than are the conclusions of philosophy (5,14), but its own author scorned it after he had experienced Divine revelation (4,17). As we have seen, on a number of points the earlier thought is indeed close to *Sefer Yetzirah*. Also, like the earlier thought, whose theoretical invalidity does not abrogate its practical and didactic value, so too *Sefer Yetzirah*, despite its theoretical invalidity, maintains its place among the holy books and is an example of "the relics of natural science" that survived among the Jews (4,24 [253/228]).

47. It seems plausible that the main tenets of the Mutakallimun are included in the *Kuzari* (5,16) in deference to the Karaite world-view. As is well known, the views of the Mutakallimun were accepted by Karaite thinkers.

Whereas Halevi recognized the legitimacy of the other views only a posteriori and with great reservations,[48] when it came to his earlier thought Halevi went no further than expressing partial disagreement with the Rabbi's presentation (1,1), without specifying which points he opposed—those that reflect his earlier thought—and which he accepted—those that reflect his later thought. The blurring of the border between the earlier and later thought must be understood as the partial rehabilitation of the earlier thought, a rehabilitation based on his recognition of the vital importance of its didactic elements. As we have seen, in his later thought Halevi came to prefer these to purely theoretical interests.

48. He explicitly expressed reservations only about *Sefer Yetzirah* (4,17; 4,27) and the opinions of the Mutakallimun (5,16).

PART IV

THE UNITY OF THE *KUZARI*

20

INTRODUCTION: THE STRUCTURE OF THE BOOK AND ITS UNITY

In the first three sections of the present volume we focused on the distinctions between the contrasting threads in the Kuzari, each of which has a large degree of internal consistency. As we saw, they represent particular stages in the development of Halevi's thought. By the same token, the division of the book into parts and groups of sections is related to their affiliation with these stages and their connection to these threads. In this last section of our book we shall attempt to show that, despite all these distinctions, the *Kuzari* is many senses a unified whole. What is more, the confrontation between the philosophical systems it presents—the dialogue between the various stages in the evolution of Halevi's thought—is one pillar of this unity.

As we have seen, the stages are distinguished by their principal orientations. Whereas the earlier Halevi was interested chiefly in anti-Karaite polemics, Aristotelian philosophy is the debating partner of his later thought. The stages are also distinguished by their theoretical outlook: The earlier Halevi remained a faithful disciple of Aristotelian philosophy; later he deviated from it and consolidated his own independent system. But as we saw in the previous chapter, the consolidation of his own system led him to recognize the relative legitimacy of beliefs and opinions that he no longer accepted. This legitimacy derives from his preference for action over contemplation as well as from polemic and didactic considerations—central criteria of the later thought. Another manifestation of this tolerance is the inclusion of his earlier thought in the *Kuzari*, even though the book's final redaction was made from the perspective of his later thought. It follows that the inclusion in the *Kuzari* of contradictory trends of thought stems from fundamental doctrinal principles.

As part of our consideration of the relations between Aristotelian philosophy and Halevi's earlier and later thought we discussed several aspects of the dialectical unity of the book. This unity is not merely an a posteriori acknowledgment of the legitimacy of views and opinions in the light of contingent circumstances; it is also a recognition of their status as intrinsic to the philosophic doctrine itself. One reflection of this unity is that the earlier thought provides answers to questions that cannot be answered in the context of Aristotelian philosophy; subsequently, the later thought resolves the problems, both internal and external, that mark the earlier thought. From this perspective, the book is unified by the internal logic of its constituent systems, which consolidates them into a single philosophical doctrine based on jumping as needed from system to system, where comprehension of the difficulties besetting one system is a precondition for understanding the next. Hence an understanding of Halevi's earlier thought depends on understanding the problems of Aristotelian philosophy; and understanding the later thought depends on understanding the problems typical of both the earlier thought and Aristotelian philosophy. What is more, these theoretical relationships within his system have a concrete biographical and historical manifestation (which Halevi believed is demonstrated by actual human existence) in the different stages of the process whereby human beings aspire to actualize their supreme goal—drawing nearer to God. From this perspective, the unity of the book derives also from the status of the different systems of thought as essential stages in a single continuous process found in the history of individuals, peoples, and even all humanity.

In this section we shall consider another facet of the unity of the *Kuzari*. In Chapter 21 we will focus on the correlations between the theology and anthropology. As we shall see, Halevi was fully aware of the existence of these correlations in all stages of the development of his thought. In Chapter 22 we shall consider the literary manifestations of the unity of the book, which parallel the theoretical and material aspects thereof.

21

THEOLOGY AND ANTHROPOLOGY

There are correlations between the various characterizations of God and man and their mutual interaction in each of the three stages of the development of Halevi's thought, including the Philosopher's doctrine, which is the initial stage. In this chapter we shall investigate these correlations within each stage as well as the relations among the stages.[1] As noted previously, these correlations are the keystone uniting the various stages into a single structural and philosophical whole.

1. The Philosopher's System

The descriptions of Aristotelian philosophy in the *Kuzari* make the tripartite correlation among theology, anthropology, and the relationship between God and man explicit, starting from theology. This theology, in which the Divine essence precedes its concrete

---

1. These correlations are found in pagan creeds as well: Fireworshippers believe that the essence of the soul is fire (2,54). Similarly, belief in many gods is associated with a belief that the soul is compounded of many forces (4,1). See Moscato, *incipit* וטענו קבוץ הכחות וכו' שהנפש ל"כ.

manifestations, is paired with an anthropology in which the human essence precedes its concrete manifestations. The relationship between God and man is focused on the ontological plane.

The priority of the Divine essence over its concrete manifestations is manifested both when divinity withdraws into itself—when God contemplates Himself—and when it expands beyond itself—in the process of emanation. These two ontological states are totally dependent on the Divine essence; and this essence, which is actual existence, is in principle immutable.

To the extent that the relationship between God, as prime cause, and non-Divine existence depends on God alone, it is absolutely invariant. For the universe as a whole, this property of the Divine relationship appears in the eternal chain of emanations; for the sublunar realm, it is manifested in God's exclusive interest in its inherent rationality; that is, in the eternal laws of nature and the existence of species and genera. This focusing of the Divine relationship in the world has far-reaching conclusions, both for the Philosopher's anthropology and for his definition of the relationship between man and God and how it is constituted.

Anthropology and theology are necessarily intertwined, as Halevi was well aware. Summarizing the main points of the dispute between the Philosopher and the adherents of the revealed religions, the King stresses these links: "What could be more erroneous, in the opinion of the philosophers, than the belief that the world was created, and in six days, or that the Prime Cause spoke with mortals[?]" (1,4 [11/39]). According to the philosophers, the fundamental error of the adherents of the revealed religions is latent in their belief in Creation, in the sense of a creative act that begins at a particular moment and ends at a particular moment. For this compels them to posit, alongside the created world, a God whose existence is continually renewed—a deity whose will is continually determined and redetermined. They also believe that God speaks with individual human beings. According to the Philosopher, their error is twofold. God, as He really is, that is, as Prime Cause, cannot speak, nor is it possible for Him to have any relationship whatsoever with an individual human being.[2] Because God has no interest in individuals, according to the Philosopher, the relationship between the individual and God cannot be understood as compliance with the latter's desires: "not in order to receive favor from the Prime Cause or to divert its wrath" (1,1 [9/38]). The individual's link with God has only an ontological basis and is expressed by cleaving to the reality of God, that is, by "becoming like the Active Intellect" (ibid.).

The constitution of an ontological relationship with God depends on the fundamental ontological identity between the poles. This identity stems from the underlying ontological unity of the chain of emanations on all its levels, which are distinguished from one another only by the intensity of the Divine emanation (5,21). It also derives from a dualistic notion of man that locates the human essence in the intellect and denigrates the body and its faculties as a mere "vessel." Man, participating in the chain of emanations as intellect, can establish a relationship of ontological proximity to God (5,12). Another expression of the ontological resemblance between the Divine and human intellects is the priority of essence over actual manifestations in the human sphere as well. The nature of the human intellect as potential intellect endows it with the aspiration to actualize itself—to perceive or know. The intellect orients this actualization in the process of cognition, determines the appropriate means for this actualization by means of the syllogism, and demarcates its ontological boundary—its goal of union with the active intellect (ibid.). This ontological conversion of potential intellect into actual intellect also has the power to divest this intellect of its individual status, thereby liberating it from mutability.

---

2. Later in this section the Christian representative, as the first speaker for the revealed religions, expounds the main tenets of belief in Divine revelation to man. In place of God as Prime Cause he proposes God the Creator; in place of man who lacks an essential identity he proposes the particular individual and the defined, elect human collective. Similarly, the Philosopher stresses the fundamental difference between God as "cause of causes" and God as Creator (1,1). Compare 1,6 and 1,87. See Chapter 3, note 8.

When, however, it comes to individual human beings and their destiny—to the extent that this destiny is inherent in the human essence—their actualization depends on circumstances that do not depend on their essence. The biography of an individual, with all its elements—genetic, causal, and historical—determines the success of the process whereby his or her intellect emerges from potentiality into actuality and can accelerate this process or suspend it in midstream (4,19). But destiny, to the extent that it is shaped by factors that are not present as intellect in the human realm, is a deviation—stubborn factual reality, devoid of all sense and meaning. Authentic human existence, which embodies the true human vocation, derives from the unique human essence.

2. The Earlier Thought

In his earlier thought Halevi still accepted, in principle, the axioms of Aristotelian philosophy. Nevertheless, one can already discern his endeavor to explain and even to modify them in the light of opinions and beliefs derived from Jewish tradition and in light of his own personal experiences and of the historical experiences of the Jewish people in the past and present. This is the case for the current issue, too: Halevi still held to the Aristotelian view that only through intellect can one know God. In Part III he classified the first of the Ten Commandments, "I am the Lord your God," with the "rational laws," that is, the laws that, in principle, can be comprehended by reason (3,11), and evidently believed that one should indeed arrive at it through ratiocination. Accordingly, it is incumbent upon the worshipper, when reciting the benediction of the "Sanctification of the Name," to have in mind "all that the philosophers have preached regarding His sublimity and holiness" (3,17 [162/155]). The earlier Halevi also maintained the Aristotelian view that the essence of God is intellect: "We also style Him wise of heart, because He is the essence of intelligence and intelligence itself; but [intelligence] is not an attribute of His" (2,2 [72/86]). This fundamental assertion is perfectly compatible with his view that, epistemologically, the human intellect can know God's essence (even if only partially) and, ontologically, can resemble the Divine intellect.

Halevi, like the philosopher, believed that God's concrete manifestations depend exclusively on His essence: "The Divine Order is above change" (2,26 [95/102]). Accordingly, the earlier Halevi, like the Philosopher, continued to champion a theory of emanations that constitute an ontological bridge between divinity and mutable non-Divine reality; whence his identification of the Divine Will with a particular entity in the chain of emanations and his assertion that the states of this will are eternal (2,6). Halevi emphasized that the philosophers, too, accept this theory (ibid.). This theory of the Divine Will is poles apart from his later theory of the Divine Will as a spontaneous volition that refashions itself from time to time out of absolute freedom—a will that does "what, how, and when it desires" (5,2 [281/249]). Halevi proposed an explanation of miracles in this vein: "Ordinary natural phenomena are altered within natural limits, since they had been primarily fixed by the Divine will and clearly laid down from the six days of creation" (3,73 [214/196]). For similar reasons, he believed that the Divine Providence in the world is concentrated in fixed and enduring rules and not in mutable details (3,19).

Just as God's essence precedes God's concrete manifestations, in the human realm essence comes before destiny. Thus, as we saw in our discussion of the Philosopher's outlook, the earlier anthropology, too, rests on a dualistic concept of man: The body is only an "unclean vessel" (3,20 [166/159]), whereas man's essence is concentrated in his intellect. This theory of man is the basis on which the earlier thought grounds the various aspects of the constitution of the relationship between human beings and God. The constitution of this relationship is associated with four things: (1) It takes place through a slow, continuous, and gradual process that passes through defined stages. (2) This process stems from the characteristic potential of humanity as a whole. (3) This potential is located in the human essence—the intellect. (4) The process takes place on the ontological plane; that is, the constitution of the relationship is a process of drawing nearer to or establishing communion with God. In the context of this view, the observance of the Torah commandments receives a distinctly ontological interpretation. The commandments are guidelines—"drugs or medicines" whose internal properties render them a major factor advancing the ontological rapprochement between man and God. At each stage of the process, however—the degree of piety, for example, or the stage in which individual or collective reaches the prophetic degree—the level attained is a necessary outcome of the ontological process that preceded it: "Whenever some few, or a whole community, are sufficiently pure, the divine light rests on them and guides them in an incomprehensible and miraculous manner that is quite outside the ordinary course of the natural world" (3,17 [159/153]).[3] This process is the framework in which Halevi explained the immortality of the soul, it too considered to be a necessary outcome of ontological processes originating in human life. This process is possible because the soul is not physical, but is "as far removed from corporeality as the angels are" (3,43 [188/175]). The survival of the soul depends on the knowledge it possesses—another view shared with the philosophers.[4] Halevi argued, accordingly, that the benediction on knowledge deals with "intelligence and enlightenment to serve the Lord. For in this way man approaches God" (3,19 [165/157]). For the same reason, it is in Part III that Halevi expounded the main tenets of Judaism while underscoring their importance as the principles whose acceptance defines membership in the Jewish people: "Whoever pronounces

---

3. Similarly, "to the same category belong tales of visions of spirits, a matter that is not strange in such pious men. Some of the visions they saw were the consequence of their lofty thoughts and pure mind; others were really apparent, as was the case with those seen by the prophets" (3,73 [212/195]). Note the role played by purity, whether of the soul (3,5; 3,21) or of the intellect (3,73), in the ontological process. This resembles the position of the philosophers (1,87) rather than Halevi's later thought.

4. Note the great similarity not only in the conclusions but also in the argumentation about the immortality of the soul in Halevi's earlier thought (3,20) and in the philosophers' doctrine (5,12).

all this with pure intention is a true Israelite and may hope to obtain that contact with the Divine Order which is exclusively connected with the Israelite among all nations" (3,17 [160/154]).

The earlier thought is marked by inconsistency and by vacillation between incompatible positions. Many of the internal contradictions are associated with various aspects of the two-way relationship between God and man. The Jewish religious experience is incompatible with the narrow and unambiguous meaning given to this relationship by Aristotelian philosophy— an ontological relationship based on the ontological similitude of essences: the Divine intellect and the human intellect. Halevi's earlier thought attempts to build a bridge between this sense of the two-way relationship and its manifestations in religious experience; but this is impossible. The inability to bridge this gap explains the eventual sea change in Halevi's conception of God and, in parallel, of man.

On the one hand, Halevi held to the Philosopher's notion of the human essence. On the other hand, basing himself on the unique historical experience of the Jewish people and evidently on his own personal experience as well, he believed that God addresses human beings. At this stage in the development of his thought Halevi still attempted to maintain both views. In the benediction of the "Sanctification of the Name" the worshipper ought indeed to have in mind the philosophical notion of God, but only after he has thought, in the benediction of "Mighty Deeds," that "the course of the world is ruled by God eternally and not, as asserted by the natural philosophers, by the known elements. He realizes that He 'revives the dead' whenever He desires" (3,17 [161/154]). As we have seen, Halevi knew that the Philosopher's theology and anthropology locate man's relationship to God on the theoretical and intellectual plane. But he also reiterated the fundamental importance of the practical commandments and made their meticulous observance a precondition for drawing nearer to God. As a path for approaching God, intellectual contemplation was suited only to individuals who lived in the distant past (3,1). The idea that man's relationship to God is located exclusively on the intellectual plane is also incompatible with the religious experience of life, as this experience is characterized in Part III itself: The pious individual is distinguished by the fact that he serves God with his full stature, with his limbs and emotions. This definition of the worship of God makes no sense if the relationship to God is located on the intellectual plane. In his later thought Halevi attempted to resolve these problems.

3. The Later Thought and the Dialogue Between God and Man

Halevi's deepening recognition that if God's essence is active intellect there is no possibility of a voluntary Divine call to human beings or of God's speaking with an individual or a particular group of human beings wrought a revolution in his thought. Whereas for the Philosopher and the earlier Halevi metaphysical theology is the starting point for the God-man relationship, in his later thought the starting point is the empirical fact that such dialogue has taken place, as is attested by the experience of individuals and groups. True visions, as primary and irreducible data that are not the result of an ongoing ontological process of perception and purification of the soul, indicate that there is "a secret that is not identical" with the Philosopher's concept of the Divine influence and of "souls" (1,4 [12/40]).[5] The Rabbi's first speech and the King's response to it already contrast man's link to God, based on metaphysical reduction and focused on the ontological plane as an attempt "to resemble the Creator in His wisdom and justice" (1,12 [17/45]), with man's relationship to God that stems from the presence of a redeeming and commanding God—a relationship embodied in compliance with Divine injunctions. For Halevi, this distinction underlies the difference between "speculative

---

5. At the beginning of the *Kuzari* Halevi deliberately stressed that true dreams are not a consequence of spiritual purification. In this he was rejecting the idea maintained by the philosophers, and by himself in his earlier thought, that prophetic phenomena are the result of an ontological process with defined stages. See also 1,87; 2,14.

and political religion" and religion that is rooted in experience (1,13 [18/34]). In polar opposition to the Philosopher, he believes that the closer human beings draw to God, the more they are aware of the infinite distance between themselves and Him. God is manifest in prophetic revelation, where He appears as "a created figure" representing His absolute mastery: "Many angels stand humbly before Him" (4,5 [236/213]).[6]

Just as the dialogue between God and man leads to a new conception of the human individual, so too it gives rise to a new conception of the human collective and of humanity as a whole. At the same time it gives a new sense to the relations between individual and community and between a particular community and all mankind. This new conception of the human collective and of mankind, as entities that stand on their own and by their own power and are in several senses superior to the individual, is rooted in the nature of God's encounter with the individual and of the unmediated encounter between God and the human collective.[7]

---

[6]. Similarly, God is grasped as He who "controls everything corporeal," quite unlike the philosophers' God (5,21 [321/292]). Similarly, "All the promises of the other religions have one basis, namely, the anticipation of being near God and His hosts" (1,109 [ES41/76]). (Ibn Tibbon's translation of this passage is corrupt, and Hirschfeld's ambiguous; see Even-Shmuel's note, p. 255.) In this vein we can understand the beginning of 1,109, where the Rabbi says that the angels insist upon the intrinsic ontological status as human beings, with a task to perform in this world, of those mortals who have ascended alive to heaven. Compare the conflict between the desire to remain in the palace and the obligation to go out to the wilderness (ibid.). Halevi seems to be referring to this distinction between man's association with God on the basis of ontology and on the basis of obedience in his remarks about the epithet "Holy One of Israel" (4,3). See Even-Shmuel's translation and note there.

[7]. The encounter between God and the individual leads in and of itself to a dependence of the individual on the collective, for the following reasons: (1) This encounter, as an individual and personal experience, acquires its objective and compelling status through juxtaposition to prior collective experience. (2) The contingent and fragmentary nature of experience is necessarily bound up with dependence on the human collective, which transmits the tradition of past revelations down through the generations. (3) With regard to content, the motif of a historical mission is central to the Divine demands made of man in these encounters; see the Appendix.

The reliance on experience completely changes the meaning of God and, in parallel, of man. On the one hand Halevi had reservations about making any metaphysical affirmation about God and the human soul, as they are in themselves. On the other hand, he did give a new epistemological and existential sense to God and to man, based on the unique epistemological quality of sensory experience and its sweeping influence on human beings—on the individual in his or her concrete integrity and on the human collective in its full historical uniqueness. The theological and anthropological implications of the assumption that God addresses human beings are inherent in the nature of the address itself: (1) Ontologically, this call is an event that, like Creation, cannot be derived from previous conditions. (2) With regard to its direct consequences, the call works revolutionary changes in those who participate in the event; these changes, too, are analogous to Creation. (3) Epistemologically, the call is an event that is in principle available to sensory perception. (4) From the axiological perspective, the call institutes the human obligation to bow to Divine authority.

4. The Dialogue as a Starting Point for the Later Anthropology

First let us consider the aspects of the later anthropology that reflect the internal logic of the relationship between man and God. The Divine call, as an irreducible event, cannot be invited by human beings. Hence reliance on the experiences of the past acquires extreme importance. This reliance is conditioned by individuals' particular biographical circumstances: their historical affiliations, biographies, and way of life. Thus, in contrast to Aristotelian philosophy, where the human essence has primacy over its actual manifestations, in Halevi's later thought the intrinsic quality of individuals or human collectives is a consequence of their concrete biographies. The emergence of this quality is extremely important for participation in an event wherein God addresses human beings. The experience of such an event has ontological significance and is not limited to the cognitive and didactic planes. Hence we must not see the plot of the *Kuzari* as merely an unimportant literary frame for presenting its ideas. The plot spreads out before us, in parallel to the exposition of doctrine, the circumstances in which human beings who are ready to adopt particular theoretical concepts find themselves.

Still, the innovation in the later anthropology goes beyond a reevaluation of the relations between man's essence and actual life and presents a new idea of this essence. Whereas the Philosopher's notion of the human essence is marked by the latter's concentration in one stratum of the personality—the intellect—in Halevi's later thought man is grasped as a unique and unified entity composed of body and soul, intellect and imagination, emotions and senses. Unlike the conception of man held by the Philosopher and the earlier Halevi, here the human essence is to be located in the total being of the individual and in a human collective defined by its unique historical destiny. The Aristotelian dualism of man, which permits the constitution of a relationship between man and God on an ontological basis, has no weight in the later thought. There the relationship rests on God's interest in man, so there is no need to accept ontological postulates about the human essence. What is more, God who calls to human beings (individual or collective) in their entirety, through their senses and imagination, their emotions and body, and demands that they act, divests them of their anonymity and, by this very call, makes them unique and singular. Just as the Divine call for action endows the material world—the world in which the acts take place—with importance, so too it gives moment to particular human bodies and the limbs with which the deeds are performed. And just as God makes each individual unique through the demands He makes on him or her, so too He bestows a unique identity on a community through the historical destiny He imparts to it.

In the later thought, the emphasis on the significance of human action involves a concomitant devaluation of beliefs and opinions—this too in polar opposition to the Philosopher and to Halevi's earlier thought. Accordingly, Halevi displayed tolerance of opinions and beliefs that he rejected out of hand as totally invalid.

Another manifestation of his integrated anthropology has to do with the immortality of the soul. According to the later Halevi, this is not the culmination of a continuous ontological process, as the Philosopher believes and he himself had once thought. The immortality of the soul is to be understood against the background of God's omnipotence, as a manifestation of His capacity for ex nihilo creation (5,14). Halevi deliberately refrained from making any ontological assertions about the essence of the soul. He also avoided taking a position as to whether the soul is a spiritual "intellectual entity" rather than a physical entity (ibid.). In the light of our discussion, it is clear that the reference to the possibility that the soul may be physical is a typical feature of Halevi's later thought rather than a chance remark. It stems both from his inclination to ground the human relationship with God without recourse to a priori metaphysical postulates and from his general inclination to contract the ontological distance between the various components of the human personality.

5. The Dialogue as a Starting Point for the Later Theology

The changes in Halevi's later anthropology are paralleled by fundamental changes in his theology. Just as human beings cannot know their own essence, neither can they know God's essence. Halevi reached this conclusion for both metaphysical and epistemological reasons. By contrast, the idea of the Aristotelian God, which the later Halevi agreed can be attained through syllogistic reasoning (4,3; 4,15), has no authentic religious significance. The doctrinal need for a clear distinction between a God Whose meaning derives from ontology and Who is known through reason, and a God Who is known through experience, is concisely and definitively satisfied by the distinction between the Divine names: *Elohim* refers to the ontological sense (4,1), whereas the Tetragrammaton refers to God in the empirical context.

In Halevi's later thought, just as an individual's biography precedes the determination of his or her intrinsic quality, the concrete manifestations of God in the world precede His meaning for human beings. The meaning of God coalesces through repeated human experiences. The later Halevi, in diametrical opposition to the Philosopher's position, holds that God is not revealed in regular and continuous processes that express the emergence from potential to actual, but in extraordinary events wherein the normal bounds of natural law, with its various manifestations, are shattered. The experience of these events generates the image of God as intentionally transcending His boundary in the direction of existence outside Himself—an image utterly at variance with the God of Aristotelian philosophy. The outstanding expression of this notion of God is His characterization as Creator. In the later thought, this characterization does not follow from a priori metaphysical arguments, nor is its primary source belief in the verity of the Scriptures. Instead, it is rooted in the experience of God's call to human beings. The recognition of the factual authenticity of this call and the characterization of God as ex nihilo Creator are interdependent. The call, if genuine, is "a miracle that changes the nature of things" (1,8 [16/43]). As a "start" (1,87) that cannot be based on natural factors, this call resembles ex nihilo creation.

Just as the dialogue between God and man molds the identity of God while defining Him as a deity who goes beyond His pale, it also adds a voluntary dimension to His identity. Unlike the Philosopher's definition of the Divine Will, here the Divine Will is one that does "what, how, and when He desires" (5,2 [281/249]).[8] The voluntary dimension involves both God's interest in human beings, as embodied in the very fact of the Divine call, and the specific message in which it is expressed—the commandments. This dimension is perfectly compatible with the ephemeral nature of the occurrence. What is more, the later Halevi's activist view of man is paralleled by an activist conception of God. Human activity

---

8. See 1,67; 1,83; 1,89; 5,14.

acquires its most significant meaning as a response to the Divine call; as we have seen, it can also be viewed as a sequel to Divine activity. Activity by the human collective is the fullest expression of this continuity. This is the source of the superiority in principle of the collective over individuals.

The dependence on human experience of the meaning of God as phenomenon is cumulative and adds a dynamic dimension to God's identity. Just as the history of the Jewish people is marked by Divine revelations, the meaning of God as phenomenon is dominated by the history of the Jewish people. The Jews' unique status as the nation that received the Torah is rooted in their recognition of the God who took them out of Egypt. Were acceptance of the yoke of Torah rooted in recognition of God as Creator, "the white and the black man would be equally bound by it, since He created them all" (1,27 [21/47]). For Halevi, the discovery of this significance of God is the necessary culmination of the program of Creation. Only after God reveals Himself to Adam does he first appear in Genesis as "the Lord God": "This the Sages express in the words: A 'full name over a full universe' (Gen. Rabba 11). The world was completed only with the creation of man, who constitutes the kernel of all that was created before him" (4,15 [244/220]).

Because God's identity depends on repeated human experiences, it can never be conceptually exhausted. His identity is not an exhaustive definition of the God made manifest. Hence not only does God derive His meaning for man from His past and present epiphanies, He continues to draw His meaning from future revelations.

6. Anthropomorphisms in the Later Thought

The later thought's favorable attitude toward anthropomorphisms is a strong expression of the change that occurred in Halevi's ideas about man, God, and the relationship between them and of his consequent disavowal of the Aristotelian position. This sanction of anthropomorphisms derives from his integrated conception of man, whose essence includes imagination, the senses, and emotions—the faculties through which human beings make connection with God and with which they are called to serve Him. Halevi's attitude toward anthropomorphisms also derived from the nature of the components of the Divine identity. God, as grasped through sensible revelation, is necessarily perceived in physical images, because the prophets "without doubt saw the divine world with the inner eye; they beheld a sight that harmonized with their natural imagination. They described them as if they had seen them in corporeal form. These descriptions are true as far as regards what is sought by inspiration, imagination, and feeling; they are untrue as regards the reality which is sought by the intellect" (4,3 [228/208]).[9]

On no other topic are there such profound differences between Halevi's later thought and Aristotelianism as on anthropomorphisms. Whereas the Philosopher is interested mainly in defending the precise theoretical meaning of the concept of God in his doctrine, and this defense is itself a precondition for the relationship between man and God, Halevi was interested in preserving the intrinsic religious authenticity of the Divine pole itself.

The Philosopher venerates a God who is immanent in the world and highlights the transcendent significance of the Prime Cause qua prime. Halevi, for his part, wanted to guarantee the immanence of the transcendent God Whose essence cannot be known. This immanence is embodied in God's spontaneous activity in the world, especially in His revelations to human beings.

The Philosopher would eliminate anthropomorphic images of God because they blur the ontological distance between the essence of God, as the principle of form, and material existence. Halevi's attempt to preserve the authenticity of the two-way relationship between God and human beings led him to preserve, to the extent possible, the full content and vitality of the

---

9. Halevi's view on this point has much in common with that of Franz Rosenzweig. See Franz Rosenzweig, "Zum zweiter Band der *Encyclopaedia Judaica*, mit einer anmerkung über Anthropomorphismus," *Kleinere Schriften* (Berlin, 1937).

"moment" of this revelation. The best way to capture this moment is to use anthropomorphic images of God that are rooted in the moment itself.

The Philosopher underscores the ontological polarity of human existence and would use this polarity as the ground for the relationship between man and God. (This polarity in and of itself makes anthropomorphisms wholly untenable.) Halevi highlighted the integration of the human experience, an integration compatible both with the content of the revelation, including its concrete embodiments, and with the nature of the relationship that underlies the revelation.

Halevi held that the profound contradiction between the conceptions of God and the relationship to Him held by Judaism and other doctrines does not lie in the distinction between monotheism and polytheism nor in the distinction between God as spiritual versus God as corporeal. For him, the real opposition is between the God of Abraham and the God of Aristotle (4,16).

7. Summary

The *Kuzari* is unified in two senses. The first involves the relation among the various stages in the evolution of Halevi's thought, such that the later stage attempts to resolve the internal problems of the earlier stages. In the second sense, the book is unified by the correlations between the stages of his thought. All stages in his thought, including the Philosopher's method, are set in the broad context of recognition of the validity of these correlations. Hence we can view these stages in the evolution of his thought as different postulates advanced within a network of possibilities grounded in these correlations.

22

FORM AND CONTENT IN THE *KUZARI*

There are many aspects to the literary form of the *Kuzari*. Here we shall consider them from the perspective of their interaction with the philosophy expounded in the book. As we shall see, this interaction clearly reflects Halevi's own later thought and his beliefs at the time of his final revision of the book. We shall also address the relationship between the formal unity of the book and its dialectic and conceptual unity.

The literary genre to which the *Kuzari* belongs is narrative fiction. There are four reflections of this affiliation in the book: (1) the main tale, which begins with the King's conversion and ends with the Rabbi's emigration to Eretz Israel; (2) the brief frame story—the personal history of the narrator, Judah Halevi; (3) the episodic tales incorporated into the dialogue; (4) the dialogue that runs through the entire book. This dialogue is a direct continuation of the main tale, with the action restricted and the ideological underpinnings expanded. From the formal and narrative perspective, the dialogue moves the story forward with regard to the development of the plot[1] as well as with

---

1. The dialogue form can be traced back to the very beginning of the story, in the angel's repeated challenge to the King and the King's intermittent attempts to find an appropriate answer to the challenge in his deeds—worshipping in his pagan temple.

regard to the dramatic and descriptive elements woven into it. What is more, only the course of the dialogue makes explicit the full seriousness of the problems raised by the beginning of the main tale.[2] This exposition opens a way for dealing with these problems in a fruitful manner.

The dialogue is an integral part of the story from the conceptual angle as well: The main tale and the dialogue present an identical message; and the theoretical conclusion of the doctrine is that the problems raised by the story can be dealt with only in the context of an authentic dialogue. Accordingly, at the very start of the book the narrator deliberately creates a certain distance between himself and the Rabbi, noting that he has certain reservations about the latter's opinions (1,1). These reservations alert readers that they should pay attention, not only to the content of the Rabbi's discourse, but also to its context—its place in the dialogue. Not only does the location of the Rabbi's remarks in the course of the dialogue serve as a road sign indicating their affiliation to one or another stage in the development of Halevi's thought; in the dialogue the Rabbi takes account both of abstract truth and of his interlocutor's ability to attain that truth.

1. The Story in Aristotelian Philosophy

The Aristotelian philosopher's doctrine of human existence rests on a metaphysics of mutable reality. The primary ontological polarity between Divine existence, which is totally inward-directed and immutable, and material existence, which is variable and transient, is seen through the lens of human existence as an ontological dichotomy between the human intellect and

---

2. Before the King hears the Philosopher's presentation, his problem is that he knows that actions pleasing to God must exist. After listening to the Philosopher he understands that he must first deal with the fundamental problem; namely, the very possibility of God's speaking to human beings—the problem of the authenticity of his dream. Hence the plot emerges from the bipolarity in the King's soul generated by his dual confrontation with the angel and with the Philosopher.

the nonintellectual aspects of human existence. This dichotomy implies a basic demand that the human intellect focus inward. It follows that the biography of individuals, progressively constructed by the unique sensory experiences of their lives, is secondary to their essence as intellect. In keeping with this, the Philosopher brackets his own personality. Stylistically, this is expressed by his meticulous avoidance of the first person and presentation of his ideas chiefly in the third person (1,1)—in sharp contrast to the speeches of the representatives of the revealed religions.[3] As we have seen, this difference between the Philosopher and the spokesmen of the revealed religions is rooted in their fundamental disagreement about the status of Divine revelation to human beings and the meaning given to it by the revealed religions as a one-time event not available to voluntary experience.

Just as an individual life story has no importance, there is no basic importance to the narrative of history; human beings actualize their goal through an intentional detachment from their unique historical affiliations. Intellectual knowledge can nullify the distance between epochs and civilizations. So far as the Philosopher is concerned, the King can engage in intellectual communion with the great philosophers of ancient Greece (1,1).

2. The Story in the Earlier Thought

As we have seen, the earlier Halevi was in substantial agreement with the contention of the Aristotelian philosopher that the perfect human being, one who has managed to actualize his or her intellect, has no cause to be involved in collective life, to display interest in human history, or to be meticulous in the observance of particular disciplines. Nevertheless, Halevi parted company with the Philosopher and believed that, in the actual circumstances of history, the degree of human perfection is unattain-

---

3. The Philosopher's apathy to concrete lived experience and historical experience finds poignant literary expression in his general, ironic, and noncommittal response to the King's extremely personal and emotional request, based on biographical and historical experience (1,2).

able (3,1). Hence the capacity of individuals to liberate themselves from dependence on their biographical and historical circumstances depends, paradoxically, on defined historical circumstances. Indeed, actualizing the ideal of the pious individual, attainable even in the conditions of Halevi's present, depends on a recognition of the fundamental importance of human history (individual and collective) and, in parallel, on meticulous observance of the Torah commandments with the particular meaning attributed to them by tradition (3,24).[4]

Hence, while the Philosopher's stance regarding human history is unambiguous, the earlier Halevi has a fundamentally ambivalent position on the issue. Nevertheless, because the earlier thought relegates the philosophic ideal of the perfect human being to the realm of utopia, and in practice only the ideal of the pious individual remains as attainable in the present age, we can say that even at this stage in the development of his thought human history had acquired a central place for Halevi. But the earlier thought still does not require that the conceptual content be expressed in story and dialogue. Hence it is plausible that Halevi selected the literary form best suited to expressing his earlier thought not out of abstract doctrinal considerations, but for didactic and polemical reasons associated with the chief bent of the sections that express this thought: the dispute with Karaism.[5]

---

4. Already in the first section of Part III the reader is intentionally put on notice that the Philosopher's ideal of human perfection is irrelevant in the present. This irrelevancy grounds Halevi's subsequent contention that the only ideal that can be achieved by his generation is that of the pious individual (3,2). This ideal requires the adoption of an unambiguous position on three central and interrelated topics. Presenting the pious individual as the exclusive ideal for his contemporaries serves as an opening for Halevi's attack on Karaism, an attack that relies heavily on these very topics: (1) the meaning of the Torah commandments (3,23; 3,41); (2) the reliability of tradition (3,35); and (3) preserving the unity of the Jewish people (3,49).

5. It seems likely that in this dispute he took advantage of the historical fact that the real-life pagan king of the Khazars, an objective and sincere onlooker, adopted Rabbanite rather than Karaite Judaism. See Chapter 7, note 2.

3. The Dramatic Dimensions and the Story in the Later Thought

Unlike the Philosopher, the later Halevi believed that the intrinsic spiritual status of individuals or groups is determined by their actual biographies. These life stories include the aggregate of personal experiences, reactions to them, education, and general and historical circumstances. Halevi explained the philosophers' error against a historical background—their lack of contact with the tradition of revelation. The King renders a favorable judgment of the Christian and Muslim, taking into account their education and mother tongues. The process whereby human beings (individuals or nations) draw near to Judaism is not an immanent one, all of whose stages necessarily flow from the previous one. In the life of individuals, the process moves forward as a result of traumatic and immediate experiences: prophetic revelation, a dream, the prophet's outward appearance while prophesying (4,3). In the history of the Jewish people, it progresses because of their immediate experience of certain great moments. For humanity as a whole, it advances when they contemplate the miraculous presence of the Jewish people among the nations. Still, as we have seen, it is not just on the epistemological and didactic plane that these experiences possess intrinsic importance for human beings. Only thanks to these experiences can human beings serve God as enjoined.

Just as an individual's personality is progressively constructed through the events—the experiences and actions—of his or her life, so too God's significance for man is consolidated by repeated human experiences that are recounted in tales of His miraculous deeds. Just as the annals of the Jewish people are marked by Divine revelation, God's image is shaped by the history of the Jewish people. These events, including the central figures who take part in them, are constitutive elements that cannot be replaced by a mere definition of God's identity.[6]

---

6. As stated, this dynamic dimension to the development of God's significance for human beings makes this meaning inexhaustible and open to further enrichment in the future. This openness is anchored in the

This multifaceted drama, characteristic of Halevi's later thought, finds literary expression in the story and dialogue. The very first section of the book includes the elements of the human drama envisioned by the later thought—the drama expressed in man's unending efforts to draw nearer to God. The Divine initiative embodied in an unanticipated event—a dream—works a revolution in the soul of the king who experiences it: he finds himself enjoined to adopt a new way of life, responds to this demand with a fundamental willingness to abandon the rituals of his ancestors, and at the same time launches a vigorous campaign to identify the deeds that are pleasing in themselves.[7] The continuation of this story—the dialogue—describes these efforts and explains them conceptually. Hence the descriptions of these one-time events are interwoven in the dialogue with the conceptual explanations of their meaning. Through the dialogue, the reader learns that personal experience alone can work the revolution and that there are limits to dreams, because they are only dreams. The image of God cannot be distinguished from the manner in which He appears at the horizon of human knowledge, nor the identity of the human being addressed by God from man's obligation to observe the Divine commandments. Finally, one must not distinguish the image of man from the way in which God appears to human beings.

---

empiricist and inductive trends that dominate Halevi's later thought. Hence we should see Halevi's thought itself as a system open to the future. His doctrinal openness is reflected in the plot, which also remains open: When the King completes his conversion, the Rabbi "goes up" to Eretz Israel—an ascent that symbolizes the future ascent of the Jewish people when they conclude their mission in the exile. This ending is itself a new beginning—a beginning that stands under the sign of hope for the new spiritual awakening possible only in Eretz Israel (5,23).

7. As we have already seen, for the later Halevi these elements of the human drama and the order in which it evolves appear in all tracks of human development: the individual, the nation, and mankind as a whole.

4. Dialogue and Immediate Presence in the Later Thought

Not only is the literary genre appropriate to the content of the religious experience; it is also appropriate to the way in which human beings are supposed to participate in experience. As we have seen, Halevi accords great importance to immediate sensory experience, especially visual experience. Through vision, human beings become suddenly aware of the singular fullness of the object of experience. Just as this openness has epistemological and intellectual significance, emotional significance, and practical significance, it also has implications for interpersonal communication. The expression on his face is a necessary input for "transmitting the idea of the speaker into the soul of the hearer" (2,72 [125/126]). The weight accorded to vision entails a number of fundamental problems, such as the status of communication through the written word. Here too, Halevi coped with the problem, to some extent, by means of narrative and dialogue.[8] They enable him to present concrete situations to his readers, with characters whose activity and thought grow out of their identity and historical affiliations, as well as out of their unique biographical experiences.[9] The stylistic differences among

---

[8]. As we have seen, though, Halevi also tackled the problem with his theory about the unique nature of the Hebrew language.

[9]. From this perspective it is interesting to trace the sequence of topics as the book progresses. Their appearance at a particular juncture depends in large measure on the internal logic of the plot (which acquires its theoretical basis only through the course of the discussion). For example, the discussion about the Jewish people and Judaism emerges against the background of the problems and beliefs of non-Jews. At the beginning of his quest the King decides not to call in the Jews, because "I am satisfied they are of low station, few in number, and generally despised" (1,4 [12/40]). His perspective on the Jews and Judaism changes after he hears the Christian's discourse. The Christian representative notes that the uniqueness of the Jewish people is inherent in their status as the chosen people in the past. From the Muslim's remarks the King learns that Judaism plays a constitutive role even in the present, and finds that he has no choice but to summon the Rabbi. The Rabbi's initial presentation introduces the problem of the relationship between the particularistic and universalistic

the various sections of the book are noteworthy in this regard. These are manifested both in the polite tone of the debate and the large measure of agreement that each disputant evinces with the positions of his interlocutor,[10] as well as in the vicissitudes in the dramatic tension in the course of the dialogue.[11] Halevi exploits these differences to address his readers directly and implicate them in the vivid life of the dialogue.

5. Narrative, Dialogue, and the Unity of the Book

Halevi selected dialogue as the literary genre best suited to his later thought not only because of the dramatic element of this thought and not only because of the importance of interpersonal, dialectic relations for his philosophy, but also to stress the dialectic unity of the book—a unity constituted by the very multiplicity of contrasting outlooks included in it. Narrative and dialogue are well suited to describing a unity of contraries as the unity of a temporal process.

From this angle the tale can be seen as a comprehensive description of a single process: the spiritual development of a human being from paganism to Judaism, beginning in the private domain—in a dream—and concluding in the public domain—in the spotlight of human history. The Rabbi remains in exile as long as he is performing his task of guiding the King on

---

aspects of Judaism and the problem of the relationship between the status of the Jewish people as the chosen people and their actual destiny in the present. The relationship between the particularistic and universalistic aspects of Judaism is the crux of the rest of Part I and much of Part II. Halevi's fidelity to the inner logic of the narrative, while expounding the theoretical problems, in and of itself teaches us about the reciprocal relationship between form and content in the *Kuzari*.

10. Compare the King's polite response to the Philosopher's address, which includes a measure of agreement (1,2), with his response to the Rabbi (1,12 [17]). And compare this latter response with his cold cordiality (1,14) as well as with his severe disappointment (1,28).

11. Schweid, *Taʿam ve-haqqashah*, pp. 68–73; idem, "He-ḥaver ke-meḥannekh be-sefer ha-kuzari" (The rabbi as educator in the *Kuzari*), in *Mishnato he-hagutit shel R. Yehudah Halevi* (The philosophical doctrine of R. Judah Halevi), (Jerusalem, 1978), pp. 33–40.

his road to Judaism. After completing his mission, however, he emigrates to Eretz Israel. In parallel, it is incumbent upon the Jewish people to live among the nations as long as they are fulfilling their universal mission as a light to the Gentiles, guiding them along their historical progress towards Judaism. When this mission has been completed, the Jews are bound to "ascend" to Eretz Israel.

Dialogue can be seen as a literary expression of the relations among the various stages in this process of human evolution—relations that merge the various world-views into a single dialectic body of thought, on the theoretical plane, and, on the interpersonal level, forge the various stages in the spiritual evolution of humanity, individual or collective, into the unity of the biographical or historical process in which human beings draw ever nearer to God.

APPENDIX: THE GIVING OF THE TORAH AND COMMANDMENTS AS A PROCESS

Already in his earlier thought Halevi advocated the original and unconventional idea that human beings can bring down totally new commandments from heaven—commandments that were not given at Sinai.[1] Such commandments are incumbent upon the Jews, throughout the generations, by virtue of the original Divine revelation that has been transmitted by faithful emissaries—prophets or sages, who were favored with heavenly assistance and "inspiration." One recites a blessing before fulfilling them, just as for the commandments given by Moses (3,39 [183/171]). Diverging from the conventional approach, Halevi

---

1. This concept has been discussed in the following articles: E. E. Urbach, "Halakhah u-nevu'ah" (Halakhah and prophecy), *Tarbiẓ* 18 (1947): 21; D. Rappel, "Ha-bissus ha-filosofi shel mesoret ha-halakhah le-shittat RYHL" (The philosophical basis of the halakhic tradition in the doctrine of Judah Halevi), *Hagut ve-halakhah* (Philosophy and halakhah) (Jerusalem, 1973), pp. 33–41; N. Arieli, "Tefisat ha-halakhah eẓel RYHL" (Judah Halevi's concept of halakhah), *Daʿat* 1 (Winter 1977–1978): 43–52.

understood that the commandment against adding new commandments applies only to the "masses," who may not "conjecture and theorize and contrive laws according to their own conception, as the Karaites do" (3,41 [185/173]). Although one can find support for this idea among the talmudic sages,[2] Halevi evidently accepted it for reasons connected with his thought: in his earlier thought, for its polemic value; in his later thought, from internal considerations associated with the main points of his positive thought.

In the earlier thought the concept appears in the overall context of the dispute with Karaism. On the one hand, it underlies his contention that Karaism is inferior to Rabbanism, because the former ignores the innovations of these emissaries—innovations that are included in the rabbinic tradition and are an inseparable part of God's commandments (3,35; 3,49; 3,53). On the other hand, its acceptance frees Halevi of the obligation to interpret Scripture exclusively in accordance with halakhic prescriptions. For example, he is willing to agree in principle with the Karaites that, according to the plain sense of the words, the verses "on the morrow of the Sabbath" (Lev. 23:15) and "until the morrow of the Sabbath" (ibid., 16) refer to Sunday; nevertheless, he can still argue that the rabbinic halakhah (which understands "Sabbath" as referring here to the first festival day of Passover) rests on prophetic knowledge (3,41).[3]

Note that in both the earlier and later thought the recognition of the unqualified halakhic validity of non-Sinaitic revelations of God's will entails a diminution in the disparity between Moses and the other emissaries. According to Halevi, they too

---

2. Maimonides adopted the antithetical view. See Urbach, "Halakhah u-nevu'ah."

3. He took a similar approach with regard to the "strong drink" mentioned in the laws of the Nazirite (3,49). Nevertheless, in the context of Judaism's dispute with Christianity and Islam, this principle is inconvenient; see pp. 287–288. Historically and doctrinally, this problem is taken up next in Joseph Albo's *Sefer ha-'iqqarim*, and thereafter at great length; compare Maimonides' *Epistle to Yemen*.

are infallible (3,41).[4] This is the source of the Rabbanites' confidence in the reliability of their tradition (3,50; 3,53). What is more, the status of the new commandments can be deduced from a verse: "I will raise up a prophet for them among their own people, like yourself: I will put My words in his mouth and he will speak to them all that I command him" (Deut. 18:18) (3,41). This verse grounds the duty to obey the prophet who is equal in rank to Moses.[5]

In the later thought, this concept rests on weighty doctrinal considerations. It reflects the logical consequences of Halevi's theory of God and the essence of the commandments. His emphasis on the voluntary aspect of divinity, with the corollary accent on the centrality of the inexhaustible Divine activity[6] that is embodied in His guidance—his imperatives and commandments[7]—ipso facto entails understanding the giving of the

---

4. So too in his later thought: "Prophets and pious sages ... are original instruments of the divine will" (4,3 [224/204]). See also Ibn Ezra on Daniel 9:2, citing Halevi.

5. The later Halevi, too, stressed that Moses' rank can be attained by the elders (4,11). Similarly, at Sinai all the people heard all of the Ten Commandments, which are "the source and foundation of the law" (1,87 [41/61]). What is more, he seems to hold that the Patriarchs were superior to Moses; for example, Moses was received in the "palace" through he merit of the Patriarchs (1,109) and attained what he attained for "the descendants of Abraham, Isaac, and Jacob" (2,56 [113/117]). In light of what we have seen, this is precisely what he means. Compare 1,95. It is no accident that Halevi described the typical manifestations of prophetic life with reference to Moses. This description too hints that Moses' rank is merely that of any prophet who has actualized his potential. Moses is distinguished by his primacy (which in the later thought seems to be merely relative). He is "the first traveller" (1,109 [60/77]) or "first leader" (4,11 [240/217]). On this question, too—Moses' rank among the prophets—Maimonides was totally at odds with Halevi.

6. By contrast, the internal logic of a theory of the commandments that rests on eternal unchangeable states or on the absolute validity of some scale of values entails that the Torah was given once and for all time. Hence in the earlier thought the idea that the giving of the commandments is an ongoing process cannot be derived from the theory of commandments incorporated in this thought; it must be explained by differences in the degrees of those who receive it; see pp. 126 and 143ff.

7. See p. 275.

commandments as a process that can never be complete. This inexhaustibility is not merely an expression of the limitations of those who receive the commandments. It also reflects the internal logic of a will that determines itself without restrictions or boundaries, a will that does "what, how, and when it desires" (5,2).[8] What is more, God's will to guide concrete human existence, in all its particulars and vicissitudes, requires an ever-changing relationship with it.[9]

It follows that in his later thought Halevi dated the start of the process of the giving of the Torah to Adam and Noah.[10] At Sinai Moses did not abrogate any of these commands, but only added to them (1,83). Thus Halevi took a clear stand on this controversial question.[11]

    8. See pp. 190, 218–219, 256, 290, 327–328.
    9. See p. 278.
    10. This extension in the past is clearly out of place in the earlier thought, where Halevi's focus was on the dispute with Karaism. In the later thought, however, it was inevitable.
    11. See E. E. Urbach, *The Sages: Their Concepts and Beliefs*, trans. I. Abrahams (Jerusalem, 1975), vol. 1, pp. 335–336; *Enziklopediya talmudit* (Talmudic encyclopedia), 3:359, s.v. בן נח, subheading מצוות שנשנו ושלא נשנו בסיני; ibid., 6:2, s.v. גיד הנשה.

BIBLIOGRAPHY

Editions of the *Kuzari*

Arabic Original

1. *Al-Kitāb al-Khazari* (The book of the Khazars [or of the king of the Khazars]), the Arabic original with the Hebrew translation by R. Judah Ibn Tibbon. Critical edition, ed. Hartwig Hirschfeld. Leipzig, 1887.

1a. Idem, reprinted Jerusalem, 1970, with supplementary articles on the text of the *Kuzari*.

2. *Kitāb al-radd wa-ʾl dalīl fi ʾl-dīn* (The book of refutation and proof on the despised faith). Critical edition, ed. D. Z. Baneth. Jerusalem, 1977.

Hebrew

3. *Sefer Hakuzari*, trans. Judah Ibn Tibbon. With the commentaries *Qol Yehudah* and *Oẓar Neḥmad*. Warsaw, 1880.

4. *Sefer Hakuzari*, trans. Judah Ibn Tibbon, German trans. and commentary David Cassel. Leipzig, 1889.

5. *Sefer Hakuzari*, trans. Judah Ibn Tibbon, ed. and commentary A. Zifroni. Tel Aviv, 1967.

6. *Sefer Hakuzari*, trans. Yehudah Even-Shmuel. Tel Aviv, 1972.

English

7. *The Kuzari: An Argument for the Faith of Israel*, trans. Hartwig Hirschfeld, introduction H. Slominsky. New York, 1964; originally published 1905.

8. *Kuzari: The Book of Proof and Argument* [Revision of Hirschfeld translation], abridged ed., introduction and commentary Isaak Heinemann. Oxford, 1947.

Other Works by Judah Halevi

9. *Diwan, ve-hu kolel kol sifrei avir ha-meshorerim Yehudah ben Shemuel* (Complete poetry of Judah Halevi), ed. Hayyim Brody. Berlin, 1894–1930.

10. Selected Poems of Judah Halevi, ed. Heinrich Brody. Bilingual edition. English translation Nina Salaman. Philadelphia, 1924 (repr. New York, 1973).

Short Titles

The following short titles are used for works and authors frequently cited in the notes.

Baneth, "Halevi and al-Ghazali": D. Z. Baneth, "R. Yehudah Halevi ve-al-Ghazali." *Keneset* 7 (1942): 311–328.

Brody: No. 9 above.

Cassel: The German translation and commentary by David Cassel, No. 4 above.

Davidson, "The Active Intellect": H. Davidson, "The Active Intellect in the Cuzari and Hallevi's Theory of Causality." *Revue des Etudes Juives* 131 (1973): 351–395.

Efros, *Doctrines*: I. Efros, *Ha-filosofiya ha-yehudit bi-ymei ha-beinayyim: Shittot ve-sugiyyot* (Medieval Jewish philosophy: Doctrines and topics). Jerusalem, 1965.

Efros, *Terms*: I. Efros, *Ha-filosofiya ha-yehudit bi-ymei ha-beinayyim: Munaḥim u-musagim* (Medieval Jewish philosophy: Terms and concepts). Jerusalem, 1968.

Heinemann, "Philosopher-Poet": Y. Heinemann, "Ha-filosof ha-meshorer: Biʾur le-mivḥar piyyutim shel R. Yehudah Halevi" (The philosopher-poet: An interpretation of several liturgical poems by R. Judah Halevi), in Zemora, *R. Yehudah Halevi* (see below), pp. 166–235.

Hirschfeld, *Sefer Hakuzari* (1970): No. 1a above.

Komem, "Poetry and Prophecy": A. Komem, "Bein shirah li-nevuah" (Between poetry and prophecy), *Molad* 25 (1969): 676–697.

Moscato: Judah Moscato, *Qol Yehudah*, a commentary on *The Kuzari*. Included in No. 3 above.

Pines, "Shīʾite Terms": S. Pines, "Shīʾite Terms and Conceptions in Judah Halevi's *Kuzari*." *Jerusalem Studies in Arabic and Islam* 2 (1980): 165–251.

Schweid, *Taʿam ve-haqqashah*: Eliezer Schweid, *Taʿam ve-haqqashah* (Reason and analogy). Ramat Gan, 1970.

Wolfson, "Hallevi on Design": H. A. Wolfson, "Hallevi and Maimonides on Design, Chance and Necessity." *Proceedings of the American Academy for Jewish Research* 11 (1941): 105–163.

Zemora, *R. Yehudah Halevi*: Israel Zemora, ed., *R. Yehudah Halevi: Qovez meḥqarim ve-haʿarakhot* (R. Judah Halevi: A collection of studies and assessments). Tel Aviv, 1964.

INDEX OF TOPICS AND NAMES

A
Aaron (the high priest), 102n, 231
Abel, 266
Abraham (patriarch), 6, 10, 96n, 102n, 125n, 130, 150n, 156n, 176n, 194n, 200, 201, 206, 207n, 218, 219, 222, 224n, 231, 238, 239, 245, 246, 260, 285, 302n, 343n
Abraham bar Ḥiyya, 221n
Abramson, S., 9n, 153n, 210n
Action, deeds, 69n, 78–84, 94, 95, 97–106, 112, 130, 136, 141, 144, 145, 149, 152, 157, 160, 163, 170, 176, 187, 188, 194, 218, 229, 230–232, 236n, 237, 238, 244, 251, 254, 268–275, 280, 282, 284, 287, 300, 302, 303, 312, 325
Active Intellect, 18, 21n, 27, 33n, 36, 38n, 39, 41–46, 52, 53n, 54–72, 79, 81, 83n, 84, 85, 89, 93n, 94, 99, 100, 105, 127, 128, 134, 197n, 272, 317, 322
Activism, 231, 269, 270
Activity, contemplative, 39, 42, 251, 282. *See also* Contemplation.

Actuality, 12, 23, 52, 57, 318
Adam, 6, 32n, 56n, 91n, 94, 130n, 149, 150, 176n, 190, 214n, 219n, 221, 224, 225, 238, 239, 242, 267, 288, 294, 295, 299, 301, 328, 344
Akiva, R., 284, 285n
Albo, Joseph, 35n, 342n
Aliya, 102n, 115n, 153, 154, 155n, 157, 158, 231, 264, 269, 270n, 279n, 303, 331, 335n, 339
Allegory, 188
Aloni, Nehemiah, 114n, 115n, 295n
Altmann, A. A., 54n, 55n, 133n, 294n
Angels, 16n, 19, 20, 38, 42, 43, 91, 124, 131, 134, 137, 144, 188, 193n, 202n, 204, 205, 206n, 214, 235, 236n, 291, 298, 299, 301, 320, 323n
Anthropomorphisms, personification, 188, 226, 246–247, 328, 329, 330
Arieli, N., 341n
Aristotelian philosophy, Aristotelianism, 3, 4, 5, 9n, 10, 13, 15, 109, 110, 113, 114, 115,

349

Aristotelian philosophy (continued), 119, 125n, 129, 130, 153n, 162, 163, 169, 170, 171, 174, 177, 183, 217, 226, 239, 242, 251, 289, 290, 291, 297, 300, 303, 305n, 306, 311, 312, 315, 318, 321, 324, 327, 329, 332
Aristotle, 4, 16n, 17n, 19, 21n, 22n, 23, 34, 37n, 39, 40, 42, 44n, 55, 66n, 75n, 81, 82n, 113, 114n
Ascetics, ascetism, 97, 98, 104n, 139n, 233
Ashariya school, 29
Ashtor, E., 110
Assaf, S., 154n
Atoms, atomic theory, 17–18, 89n
Avicenna, 5n, 11, 17n, 20n, 25, 26n, 27, 31, 34, 35n, 42, 43n, 45n, 55n, 56n, 59, 64n, 72n, 128n, 133n

B
Baer, Y., 119n, 153n, 229n, 241n, 262n
Baḥya Ibn Paquda, 139n
Baneth, D. Z., 114n, 115n, 116, 117, 118n, 124n, 132n, 135n, 179n, 198n, 204n, 211n, 223n, 242n, 302n, 303n, 305n
Baron, Salo W., 9n, 110, 153n
Beauty, 249, 250, 294
Ben Sasson, H. H., 154n, 232n, 233n, 249n, 262n
Berman, A. Z., 63, 65n
Bible, Holy Scriptures, Scripture, 60n, 205, 174n, 179n, 342
Body, 18, 33n, 55, 56, 63, 70n, 72n, 99, 101, 105, 131–133, 138, 155n, 158n, 161n, 228, 229, 233–234, 250, 317, 319, 325
Bonfils, Joseph, 126n
Buber, M., 234n

C
Cain, 266
Cassel, D., 18n, 26n, 29n, 44n, 56n, 82n, 85n
Cause (Cause of Causes, Final Cause, First Cause, Prime Cause). *See under* God.
Change, mutability, 16, 20, 22, 25–30, 46, 48, 49, 51–53, 88, 141, 161, 217, 218, 223, 227, 317, 319
Choice, free choice, 300, 302
Christians, Christianity, 8, 66n, 83, 85, 110, 115, 143, 144, 171, 174, 177, 184, 225n, 261n, 262n, 264, 266n, 270, 283, 284, 287, 303, 342n
Cognition, 58, 62, 64, 67, 79, 101, 216, 237, 317
Collective, human collective, 6, 128, 137, 138, 139, 140, 150, 152, 157, 170, 181, 183, 212, 220, 230, 254–261, 269n, 272, 273, 276, 285, 300, 320, 323–325, 328, 333, 334, 339
Commandments, 66n, 81, 82n, 111, 122, 130, 135, 140n, 145–152, 154n, 155n, 157, 163, 164n, 165n, 170, 183, 188, 194n, 216, 227, 232, 233, 234n, 252, 275–286, 290, 291, 292, 296, 298, 302, 306, 320, 321, 327, 334, 336, 341–343. *See also* Torah.
 as guidelines, 146, 149, 151, 164, 275, 276, 280, 320
 as imperatives, 145n, 146, 149, 151, 219, 276, 277, 278, 280, 285
Communion, union, rapprochement between man and God, 10, 34, 36n, 42, 44n, 54–68, 71, 72, 75n, 76, 79n, 83n, 99, 105, 128, 130–136, 146, 147, 188, 199n, 201n, 206, 209, 213, 214, 233,

INDEX OF TOPICS AND NAMES

267, 276, 278–280, 292n, 296, 298n, 317, 320, 339
Contemplation, 65, 97, 155n, 157, 173, 231, 235n, 254, 272, 300, 302, 303, 312, 321
Contingency, 22–28, 32, 44n, 48, 217
Conversion (to or from Judaism), 88n, 110, 119n, 149, 189n, 240, 263, 271, 302, 331. *See also* Proselytes.
Creation, 11n, 25n, 33, 103n, 125, 130n, 145n, 165, 185n, 190, 215, 219, 218–226, 232, 256, 282, 291, 295, 319, 328
  ex nihilo, 47n, 129, 130, 180, 195n, 196n, 206n, 215, 218, 219, 222, 223n, 224, 236, 303, 304, 326, 327
  ex rebus, 180, 218, 220n, 223, 224n, 225, 304
Crescas, Hasdai, 46n
Crusades, 109, 171, 267n, 282. *See also* Holy wars; Reconquista.

D

Dan, J., 139n, 204n, 205n, 210n
David, king of Israel, 207n, 255
Davidson, H., 11n, 19, 38n, 55n, 92n, 98n, 197n, 198n, 199n, 202n, 206n, 209n, 211n
De Witt, K. W., 94n
Death, 5, 132, 133, 137n, 140, 234, 235, 245, 265
Decalogue. *See* Ten Commandments.
Democritus, 18n, 30n
Descartes, René, 36n
Determinism, determinist, 29
Diaspora, 267n. *See also* Exile.
Dinur, B. Z., 155n, 262n
Divine .... *See also under* God.
  Divine essence, 13, 20, 21, 35, 36, 37, 39, 42, 84, 106, 112, 119, 121, 122, 124, 130, 146, 163, 187, 188, 197, 198, 199, 200, 203, 212, 215, 225, 289, 315, 316, 318, 319, 322, 329
  Divine Glory, 210n, 214n
  Divine initiative, 75n, 150, 181, 217, 225, 287, 288, 336
  Divine Light, 76n, 97, 134, 149, 150, 162, 196, 206, 207n, 270, 280n, 320
  Divine Order, 124, 125, 126, 127, 130, 133, 135, 136, 141, 150, 151, 160, 162, 171, 184, 185n, 191n, 194n, 196, 197, 198, 199, 200, 201, 202, 203, 205n, 206, 207, 209, 210, 213, 214, 219, 233, 238, 244, 245, 246, 263, 267, 277, 278, 279, 280, 292, 293n, 296, 298n, 319, 321
  Divine Presence, 161, 173, 185n, 196, 205, 206n, 229n, 246, 250, 292, 293, 296. *See also* Shekhinah.
  Divine Providence, 21, 25n, 85n, 128, 130, 145n, 162, 171, 208, 219, 268n, 319
  Divine reality, 124
  Divine revelation. *See* Revelation.
  Divine sovereignty, 210, 215, 304
  Divine speech, 7n, 60n, 161n, 198n, 214n, 217, 249, 280n
  Divine will, 6, 11n, 47n, 53, 54, 81, 103, 112, 124, 125, 127n, 130, 149, 151, 160, 161, 165, 180n, 181, 194n, 200, 206n, 208n, 210, 211, 212, 214, 215, 217, 218, 219, 221, 222, 223, 252, 271, 273, 277, 278, 279n, 285, 290, 291, 295, 298, 299n, 300, 301, 319, 327, 342, 343n, 344
Divinity, 5, 15, 119, 170, 195, 198, 202, 208, 316, 319. *See also* God.

351

Dreams, dreaming, 60, 62, 95, 111, 112, 130, 162n, 171, 174, 176n, 217, 225, 228n, 246, 257, 259n, 271n, 322n, 335, 336, 338
  Khazar king's dream, 54n, 61n, 63n, 78n, 85, 95, 103n, 106, 111n, 120n, 126n, 164n, 174, 228, 230, 237, 240, 257, 258, 270, 277
Dualism, 45, 77, 101, 251, 325

E
Efros, I., 18n, 43n, 46, 57n, 58n, 59n, 126n, 127n, 140n, 151n, 198n, 199n, 204n, 238n, 278n, 301n
Egypt, 86, 123, 184, 186, 189, 241n, 247, 294n, 328
  Exodus from Egypt, 8n, 165, 185n, 202n, 259n
Election, 276
  of Eretz Israel, 162, 253, 294n
  of the Hebrew language, 253
  of Israel/the Jewish people, 151, 152, 156, 162, 183, 220, 227, 240, 241, 253, 256, 261, 276, 285, 287, 288, 304
Elijah (the prophet), 137, 207n
Elisha ben Abuya, 81, 82n, 144n
Emanations, theory of emanations, 16n, 20, 38, 42, 46, 57, 79, 91n, 125, 127, 128n, 163, 193n, 195, 197, 208, 209, 215, 297, 316
  Divine, 13, 17n, 18, 20, 21, 22, 24, 33, 39, 44, 45, 46, 59, 124, 125, 126, 161, 206n, 208, 235n, 317
Emotion, emotions, 187, 228, 229, 232, 242, 244, 245, 322, 325, 329
Enoch, 137, 207n
Epicurus, Epicurean, Epicureanism, 17n, 66n, 74n, 89n, 93, 94, 96, 99n

Eretz Israel, Land of Israel, 115n, 153, 154, 155, 156, 157, 158, 160, 161, 179, 200, 202n, 231, 241, 248n, 262n, 264, 266, 267, 269, 292, 293, 294, 295, 296, 298, 299n, 303, 331, 335n, 339. *See also* Holy Land.
  election of, 102n, 120, 162, 179, 207n, 253, 294n, 296, 302n
Esau, 267
Essence
  divine, 13, 20, 21, 35, 36, 37, 39, 42, 84, 106, 112, 119, 121, 122, 124, 130, 146, 163, 187, 188, 197–200, 203, 212, 215, 225, 289, 315, 316, 318, 319, 322, 329
  human, 5, 89, 110, 133, 137, 152, 164, 189, 228, 251, 252, 263, 272, 278, 280n, 316–319, 321, 324, 325, 328
Eve, 91n, 94, 130n, 224, 238
Even-Shmuel, Yehuda, 74n, 127n, 187n, 189n, 200n, 201n, 213n, 234n, 235n, 278n, 323n
Exile, 141, 153, 154, 155, 157, 261, 262, 263, 264, 267, 268, 269, 281, 284, 335n, 338. *See also* Diaspora.
Existence, reality
  Divine, 204, 332
  Human, 204, 332
  non-Divine, 13, 16, 17n, 18, 20, 22, 25, 26n, 39, 41, 48, 54n, 73n, 75, 125, 136, 146, 147, 162, 170, 193, 195, 196, 197, 198, 204, 207, 208–212, 252, 272, 289, 290, 294, 301n, 316, 319
Existence whose source is God, 15–21
Exodus from Egypt, 8n, 165, 185n, 202n, 259n

INDEX OF TOPICS AND NAMES

Experience
  collective, 259
  human, 143, 170, 173, 183, 187, 189, 190, 197, 200, 211, 212, 216, 220, 226, 227, 229, 327, 328, 330, 335
  immediate, 9, 32, 164, 180, 193, 256, 335
  personal, private, 258–259, 286
  prophetic, 6, 8, 9, 113, 176, 178, 179, 210, 216, 218, 246, 285, 304
  sensory, 24, 29, 31, 42, 170–176, 179, 180, 186n, 204, 226, 238n, 241–243, 245, 247, 248n, 324, 333, 337
Eye, inner eye, 185n, 188, 202n, 203, 207n, 329

F
Faith, 58, 58n, 185
Fancy, 59–61. *See also* imagination.
Farabi, al-, 5n, 11, 20n, 25n, 35n, 42, 43n, 55n, 59n, 100n
Fear, 68, 96, 170, 212, 244, 245, 278, 281
Festivals, 292, 293, 295n, 296. *See also* Sabbath.
  Day of Atonement, 144
  Passover, 342
  Simhat Torah (Rejoicing of the Law), 191
Fool, parable of the, 280
Form, 19, 23, 24, 31, 32, 34, 40, 42–48, 57, 68, 71, 77, 87, 94, 97, 138, 145–147, 160, 161, 195n, 212, 213, 216, 222, 243, 251, 299n, 305
Freedom, 27n, 29, 48n, 52n, 242, 279, 300–301, 319

G
Galen, 90n, 236

Gentiles, non-Jews, nations, 8, 149, 162, 185, 186, 200, 262n, 263, 264, 293, 295n, 337n, 339
Gerondi, R. Nissim, 180n
Ghazali, al-, 5n, 19n, 38n, 45n, 124n, 245n
Goal, telos, teleology, 39, 40, 51, 52, 53, 54, 59, 63, 64, 65, 71, 77, 80, 82, 83n, 84, 86n, 96, 97, 98, 99, 103, 104, 130, 131, 133, 135, 136, 137, 138, 179, 217, 254, 272, 273, 278, 280, 281, 284, 297, 298, 300, 312, 317, 333
God
  addresses, calls to, speaks, or holds intercourse or dialogue with human beings, 8, 61n, 75n, 111, 112, 175, 179, 218, 225, 226, 228, 232, 243, 257, 258, 321, 322, 323, 324, 325, 327, 328. *See also* Divine speech.
  as Cause of Causes, 15, 17, 33, 37n, 39, 42, 60, 67n, 71, 72, 73, 75n, 317n. *See also* as Prime Cause.
  As Final Cause, 39 42, 47, 51, 52, 53
  Glory of God, 162, 196, 202n, 203, 204, 205, 206n, 213n, 216
  God of Abraham, 122, 190, 200, 201, 206, 216, 330
  God of Abraham, Isaac, and Jacob, 183n, 189, 199, 201, 255
  God of Aristotle, 122, 163, 164, 187, 209, 216, 326, 330
  God of Israel, 190, 200, 243
  God of the Land, 200
  God of the philosophers, 122, 123, 184, 196n
  as intelligible, 183, 216
  made manifest, 177, 178, 180, 183, 190, 191, 193n, 238, 328

353

Gods (continued)
  names of God
    Adonai, Lord, 35n, 212
    Adonai Elohim, Lord God, 190, 328
    ehyeh, 178, 190, 198, 216
    Elohim, 6, 32, 35n, 70, 121, 123, 176, 190, 199, 200n, 214, 326
    Tetragrammaton (YHWH), 121, 178, 190, 216, 326
  as Prime Cause, 7, 16, 19, 20, 21n, 24n, 25n, 27n, 29n, 33, 34, 35, 36n, 37, 39, 42, 55, 61n, 64, 66, 71, 73, 83n, 121n, 122, 170, 184, 218, 225, 316, 317, 329
  as visible, 216
Goitein, S. D., 110n, 114, 115n, 116, 117, 118n
Golden Calf, 102n, 213, 231, 247, 268
Goldziher, Y., 66n
Guide for the Perplexed, 18n, 21n, 36n, 59n, 60n, 63n, 64n, 68n, 73n, 79n, 90n
Guttmann, J., 67n, 211n, 293n

H
Halevy, Yisrael, 38n. *See also* Ozar Nehmad.
Harmony, 8, 21, 79, 94, 165, 299. *See also* Order.
Hatred, 244–245
Hearing, 98, 229, 244, 249. *See also* Sight.
Hebrew, Hebrew language, 90n, 91n, 94, 120, 124, 161n, 179, 241n, 250, 292–296, 297n, 299n, 337n
  election of, 253
Heinemann, I., 7n, 10n, 124, 153n, 185n, 187n, 192n, 194n, 209n, 211n, 230n, 232n, 242n, 258n, 261n, 294n, 304n
Heredity, 149–150
Heresy, heretics, 5n, 9, 25n, 66n, 80, 135, 140
Hierarchy, hierarchies, hierarchical existence, hierarchical order, 33, 34n, 39, 41, 44, 48, 49, 54n, 54, 55, 70, 72, 73, 77, 84, 101, 128, 148, 161n, 162, 163, 179, 181, 212, 253, 254, 256, 275, 287–300, 305
Hirschfeld, H., 74n, 123, 124, 235n, 258n, 261n, 323n
History, historical processes, 7n, 76n, 137–139, 153, 164, 177, 212, 215, 216, 241, 253, 255–258, 265, 268, 269, 271, 272, 276, 293, 313, 328, 333, 334, 338, 339
  Jewish, 162
Holy Land, 156, 177, 201, 270, 298. *See also* Eretz Israel.
Holy Scriptures. *See* Bible.
Holy wars, wars of religion, 80, 109n, 110, 258, 259n, 270, 282–283. *See also* Crusades; Jihad; Reconquista.
Horovitz, S., 17n, 175n
Hume, David, 41n
Husik, I., 60n
Hyman, A., 46n

I
Ibn Bajja, 11, 27, 54n, 55n, 63n, 65n, 98n, 100n, 133n
Ibn Ezra, Abraham, 18n, 25n, 55, 59, 60n, 74n, 123, 125, 126n, 128n, 129n, 131n, 133, 137n, 144n, 185n, 188n, 190n, 210n, 213n, 214n, 243n, 250n, 292n, 299n, 305n
Ibn Ezra, Moses, 127n, 250n

INDEX OF TOPICS AND NAMES

Ibn Gabirol, Solomon, 7n, 35n
Ibn Sadik, Joseph, 17n
Ibn Tibbon, Judah, 74n, 123, 124, 200n, 201n, 203n, 238n, 258n, 278n, 323n
Imagination, 33n, 59, 61, 62, 185n, 188, 202n, 203, 228, 229, 246, 257, 259n, 325, 329. *See also* Fancy.
Immanenance, Divine immanence, 36, 75, 191, 193, 194, 196, 197n, 198, 199, 208–215, 304, 329. *See also* Transcendence.
Immortality, personal, 235. *See also under* Soul.
Individual
  and the collective, 212, 258, 260
Individuation, 15, 16, 21, 23, 32, 33, 42n, 44, 45, 54n, 128n
Infinity, 20n, 25n, 35
Intellect, intellects, 6, 22, 23, 26n, 27, 33, 35, 36n, 42n, 52, 53, 54n, 55n, 56n, 58, 59, 64–70, 72, 73n, 76, 80, 85, 91, 92, 97, 101–106, 119, 121, 123, 124, 127, 129, 130, 133–135, 139, 141n, 152, 156, 157, 164, 170, 173, 187, 188, 207n, 213, 214, 228n, 229, 232, 239n, 251, 272, 318, 319, 320n, 325, 329. *See also* Mind; Soul.
  actual, 36, 38–42, 46, 52n, 55, 57–60, 63n, 70n, 92n
  Divine, 26, 36, 37, 42, 104, 122, 129, 319, 321
  human, 55, 56, 63, 75, 77, 78, 79, 84, 86, 96, 100, 101, 104, 105, 113, 122, 134, 136, 155n, 317, 319, 321, 332, 333
  nondivine, 38
  passive, 36, 53, 58, 100
  potential, 57
  superlunar, 54, 55, 56, 75n, 79

survival after death, 63, 72
Intellection, 40, 41, 42, 56, 61
Intention, intentionality, 15, 24n, 27, 53n, 53, 60n, 69n, 73, 93, 94, 95, 100, 102–106, 135, 217, 219, 229, 231, 233, 254, 270, 279n, 283, 284, 285n, 290, 300, 303
  Divine, 26, 42, 152
Intuition, 5, 16, 25n, 55, 58
Isaac (patriarch), 245, 246, 260, 267, 285, 343n
  Binding of, 207n, 231, 302n
Ishmael, 267
Islam, Muslims, 8, 29, 66n, 85, 110, 115, 143, 144, 171, 177, 184, 238, 255n, 264, 266n, 270, 283, 284, 287, 303, 342n
Israel, Israelites. *See* Jewish people.
Israel, Land of. *See* Eretz Israel.

J

Jacob (patriarch), 150, 199n, 241, 260, 267, 343n
Jacobus, A., 9n
Jerusalem, 109, 202n, 241, 256, 270
Jesus, 265
Jewish people, Jews, Israel, Israelites, 6, 7n, 74n, 76n, 86, 109, 110, 113, 116, 120, 127, 130n, 135n, 140, 148, 149, 151–153, 156, 161n, 162, 165, 171, 177–180, 183, 184, 187, 189, 190, 200, 201, 206n, 210, 213, 215, 216, 218–220, 224n, 227, 229, 239, 240, 241, 243, 247, 249, 250, 253, 255, 256, 260–269, 270, 275, 276, 278, 281, 283–288, 291–298, 304, 305, 320, 321, 328, 335, 337n, 339, 341
  election of, 151, 152, 156, 162, 183, 220, 227, 240, 241, 253, 256, 261, 276, 285, 287, 288, 304

Jewish people (continued)
  history, historical experience of, 10, 189, 318, 328, 335
Jihad, 282. *See also* Holy wars.
Joy, 150, 154, 155, 230, 233, 279, 281
Judaism, 7, 9n, 11, 66n, 83, 85, 88n, 110, 115, 117, 120n, 129, 149, 151, 162, 169, 171, 176, 177, 185, 186, 211n, 217, 220, 226, 234n, 240, 242, 255n, 263, 264, 265, 269n, 271, 277, 283, 287, 304, 320, 330, 335, 338, 339, 342n. *See also* Karaites, Karaism.

K
Kabbalah, 188n, 204n, 264n
Kalam, Mutakallimun, 17, 18n, 29, 35n, 124, 145n, 219n, 303, 306n, 307n
Kant, Immanuel, 41n, 45n, 53n
  Kantian ethics, 52n, 68n
Karaites, Karaism, 17, 114, 115n, 115–117, 119n, 135, 140, 154, 162, 164n, 204n, 267n, 306, 311, 334, 342, 344n
Kaufmann, D., 9n, 110n, 175n, 210n, 222n, 243n
King of India, parable of the, 74n, 85, 93n, 174, 228, 229, 258, 259, 277n, 278n, 280
Knowledge
  adequate, 61, 123, 157, 160, 181, 186, 187, 190
  Divine, 15, 25, 26, 27
  philosophical, 6, 7, 113
  prophetic, 8, 121, 342
  self-knowledge
    Divine, 21, 38, 39
    intellects, 23, 38
  sensory, 8, 121, 187, 204
Komem, A., 9n, 111n, 153n, 171n, 246n

Koran, 60n, 240, 265
Kuzari
  earlier stratum, first edition/version, 116–118, 119n, 159
  later stratum, second edition/version, 117, 118n, 120n, 160, 161n, 165, 302, 312
  literary form, 331–334
  title, 114, 264
  unity of, 311, 313, 315, 330, 338

L
Language, languages, 60n, 69n, 89–94, 105n, 111, 144, 164, 179, 241n, 253, 292, 294, 295. *See also* Hebrew.
Law, Divine, 81–83, 86, 88n, 96, 186, 239n, 266, 291, 292. *See also* Torah.
Lazaroff, A., 139n
Leibniz, 18n, 36n
Leucippus, 18n
Levinger, Yaakov, 120n, 245n, 286n, 302n
Levites, 234, 250
Love, 68, 70, 96, 97, 127, 170, 175, 206n, 212, 244, 245, 260, 279, 281, 291
Luzzatto, Moshe I. Iayyim, 138n

M
Maimonides, 21, 60n, 63n, 68n, 90n, 92n, 342n, 343n
Man
  as individuum, 227, 252
  as rational being, 5, 36n, 52, 82n, 151
Matter, 16n, 23, 24, 28, 31, 34, 40, 42, 44, 46, 48, 56, 57, 60n, 77, 87, 94, 97, 101, 104, 105n, 126, 128n, 130, 145, 146, 147, 150, 156, 160, 161, 195n, 210, 222, 228, 251, 305

INDEX OF TOPICS AND NAMES

primordial/first/hylic, 28, 31, 32, 41n, 45, 47, 48, 130, 205n, 221–223, 225
Mediation, mediators, mediating agents, 43, 57, 71, 74n, 195, 196, 198, 201, 204, 207, 208, 210–215, 304
Messiah, 261n, 271
Mind, 37, 41, 56, 57, 58, 61, 63n, 64, 72n, 157n, 216, 228, 258, 285n. *See also* Intellect; Soul.
  emanated, 39
  human 44n, 53n
  mind of God, 36
  nondivine, 37
Miracles, 76n, 125, 165, 279n, 180n, 189, 201, 214, 216, 218, 224, 225, 241, 248, 257, 268, 278, 298, 304n, 319, 327
Monotheism, monotheistic religions, 75, 78n, 78, 149, 190n, 265, 330. *See also* Revealed religions.
Moriah, Mr., 207n, 246
Moscato, Judah, 5n, 18n, 26n, 33n, 35n, 36n, 46n, 56n, 58n, 74n, 80n, 85n, 100n, 123, 134n, 148n, 151n, 155n, 189n, 203n, 205n, 206n, 234n, 261n, 263n, 315n
Moses, 6, 59n, 61n, 74n, 91n, 156n, 178, 180n, 187n, 198, 200, 213, 234n, 247, 248, 260, 271, 280, 341, 342, 343n, 344
Motzkin, L., 115n
Multiplicity, 9, 16, 19, 20, 25, 28, 29, 33, 38, 45–49, 127n, 225, 275, 290, 291
Music, 234, 249–250

N
Nachmanides, 138n
Nahaondi, Benjamin, 204n
Narboni, Moshe, 65n
Natural law, laws of nature, 113, 165, 212, 215, 256, 287, 327

Nature, 44n, 165, 209
Neoplatonism, Neoplatonists, 31, 36n, 42
Neumark, D., 6n, 9n, 125n, 126n, 222n
Nissim, R., of Kairouan, 175n, 176n, 209, 210n
Noah, 221, 296n, 344

O
Order, 21, 33, 34, 40, 41, 45, 46, 48, 58, 74, 79, 92, 125, 128, 151, 152, 173, 198, 203, 222, 276, 277, 289, 293, 299. *See also* Hierarchy.
  political, 94
  social, 87
Otto, R., 73n
Oẓar Neḥmad 38n, 151n

P
Pagans, paganism, 6, 33, 74, 78, 240, 302, 338
Patriarchs, 121n, 200, 201, 206n, 207n, 343n. *See also* Abraham; Isaac; Jacob.
Perceptions, 6, 36n, 37–38, 40, 55, 57, 58, 61, 62, 63n, 67, 70n, 71, 72, 75, 79, 91, 226, 229, 232, 239n, 247n, 306, 322, 324. *See also* Experience, sensory; Knowledge, sensory; Senses.
  Divine self-perception, 38
  objects of, 37, 58
  self-perception, 38, 41, 55, 63n, 91n
Pharoah, 74n, 187n, 200
Pines, Shlomo, 11n, 18n, 36n, 59n, 64n, 74n, 99n, 117, 124, 199n, 230n, 233n, 242n
Pious individual, pious man, 7n, 82, 110, 111, 126n, 128n, 138n, 139–141, 144, 145n, 155n, 160, 165n, 199, 201n, 207n, 209, 229,

357

Pious individual (continued), 232n, 239n, 246, 277n, 278, 292n, 297n, 322, 334
Plato, 21n, 24n, 75n, 76n, 80n, 221n
Polytheism, 9, 190n, 330
Potentiality, 12, 22, 23, 25n, 48, 49, 52, 54, 86, 88, 217, 318
Poznansky, S. A., 175n, 210n
Prayer, 90, 122, 126n, 129n, 135, 138, 139, 141, 144, 232, 270. See also Worship.
Productivity, Divine Productivity, 42, 43, 46
Prophets, prophecy, prophetic degree, 5, 8, 9, 25n, 56n, 58, 59n, 60n, 62, 63, 66n, 76n, 87n, 111n, 133, 135, 137n, 138, 140n, 148n, 154n, 155, 156, 161, 162, 176, 179, 180, 188, 189, 191n, 196, 199, 201n, 203–205, 209, 214–216, 225, 229, 234, 235n, 238, 241, 243, 245–249, 257, 260n, 261, 262, 266, 277, 278, 280n, 288, 291, 292, 294, 296–301, 320, 322n, 329, 335, 341, 343. See also under Experience; Knowledge.
Proselytes, 285. See also Conversion.
Providence, Divine providence, 21, 25n, 85n, 128, 130, 145n, 162, 171, 208, 219, 268n, 319
Pythagoreans, 22n

R
Rappel, D., 341n,
Ratzhabi, Y., 281n
Rawidowicz, S., 68n, 119n, 294n
Reason, laws of, 82, 83n, 84
Reconquista, 109, 171. See also Holy wars.
Redemption, 155, 268, 269, 272
Revealed religions, historical religions, 5, 6, 9n, 12, 53, 62, 63, 78n, 80, 81, 109n, 143, 169, 170, 184, 217, 231, 240, 265, 270, 282, 283, 316, 333. See also Monotheism.
Revelation, 6, 8, 9n, 56, 62, 85, 91n, 102n, 103, 104, 105n, 112, 114, 116, 123, 143–148, 150n, 161, 164, 170, 175, 177–180, 185n, 188–190, 218n, 225, 227, 238–241, 244, 253, 282, 285, 294n, 305n, 323, 328–330, 333, 335, 341
at Sanai, 8n, 126, 219, 246, 247, 248n
Reward, reward and punishment, 5, 96, 122, 179n, 234n, 235n, 277n, 280n, 281n, 283, 286n, 301
Rituals, 82, 84, 336
Rosenthal, E. I. J., 100n, 119n
Rosenzweig, Franz, 329n
Rotenstreich, Natan, 36n
Rules of behavior/conduct, 80–87, 94, 96, 98

S
Saadia Gaon, 35n, 111n, 188n, 204, 205n, 209, 222n, 232n, 294n, 300, 301, 301n
Sabbath, 134, 141, 231, 293, 295n, 296, 342. See also Festivals.
Sabbatical year, 302n
Sages, 81n, 180n, 214, 278, 306, 328, 341, 342, 343n
Saturnus, 19
Schirman, Hayyim (Jefim), 110n, 153n
Schlanger, J., 291n
Scholem, Gershom, 138n, 204n, 206n, 221n, 222n
Schweid, Eliezer, 7n, 111n, 117, 139n, 228n, 237n, 238n, 255n, 266n, 295n, 296n, 301n, 338n
Scripture. See Bible.

INDEX OF TOPICS AND NAMES

Sefer Yetzirah, 6, 21, 23, 35n, 91n, 92n, 124–127, 129, 150n, 163n, 176n, 205n, 206n, 222, 223, 292n, 303n, 305n, 307n
Self sacrifice, 282–284
Senses, 28, 31, 57, 187, 190n, 227, 229, 234, 243, 250, 325, 329. *See also* Experience, sensory; Hearing; Knowledge, sensory; Perception; Sight.
Shekhinah, 126n, 138, 139, 155n, 156n, 196, 203, 204, 205, 206, 207n, 213n, 215n, 248n. *See also* Divine Presence.
Shem Tov, Joseph ibn, 60n
Sight, vision, 185n, 219n, 243, 244n, 244, 245, 246, 248, 337. *See also* Hearing.
Simon, Uriel, 243n, 250n, 292n
Sinai, Mt., 6, 7n, 91n, 234n, 247, 268, 341, 343n, 344
revelation at, 8n, 126, 219, 246, 247, 248n
Skepticism, 10, 32n,
Socrates, 76, 100, 105, 113, 114n, 135, 138
Solitude, 97, 99, 100
Solomon, king of Israel, 245, 255
Soul, 6, 9, 27, 28, 33, 38, 40, 41, 44n, 52, 57, 63, 66, 70n, 72, 98, 127n, 131–135, 138, 155n, 158n, 160, 171, 184, 209, 213, 228, 233, 234, 235, 245, 320n, 322, 324, 325, 326. *See also* Intellect; Mind.
human, 68
immortality of, survival after death, 27, 72n, 122, 127n, 131–133, 235, 248n, 320n, 320, 326
intellectual, 55
rational, 33n, 44, 59, 131n, 132, 133, 202n

Spain, 231n
Speculation, 6, 17n, 35n, 69n, 70, 76n, 122, 148, 174, 176n, 187, 190n, 194n, 208n, 245, 255
Sphere, spheres, 18–23, 38, 41, 45n, 46, 47, 52, 194n
lunar, 18, 40, 43, 45, 47
of Saturn, 19
uppermost, 20, 28
Spinoza, Benedict, 33n, 35n
Strauss, Leo, 9n, 80n, 82n, 83n, 84n, 99n, 103n, 111n, 115n, 301n
Sublunar existence, sublunar world, sublunar sphere, 22–25, 28, 29, 31, 32, 39, 41, 43, 44, 48, 49, 52, 53n, 57, 71, 75, 77, 79, 85, 87, 93, 99, 100, 104, 126–128, 151, 195, 204, 206n, 291, 292n, 316
Superlunar existence, superlunar world, 22–23, 25, 41, 43, 48, 49, 52, 91, 126, 128
Syllogism, syllogistic method, 9, 10n, 57, 69, 75, 220, 239, 317, 326

T

Temple (in Jerusalem), 138, 139, 155, 193, 202n, 241, 246, 248n, 256, 294n
First, 161
Second, 156
Ten Commandments, 6, 122, 125, 343n
First Commandment, 122, 123, 186, 187n, 318
Ten Plagues, 125n, 198n, 291n

W

Wars of religion, holy wars, 80, 109n, 110, 258, 259n, 270, 282, 283

Waxman, M., 125n, 127n, 185n, 198n, 199n, 202n, 207n, 209n, 211n, 222n

Wolfson, H. A., 5n, 19n, 25n, 28n, 29n, 46n, 56n, 57, 59n, 82n, 89n, 125, 127n, 197n, 198n, 199n, 204n, 205n, 207n, 208n, 213n, 218n, 221n, 223n

World to come, 5, 128n, 133, 134, 234n, 235n, 249n, 277n, 279n, 280, 280n

Worship, 66, 70, 75n, 83n, 96n, 143, 184, 186n, 187, 200, 212, 230n, 233, 238n, 247, 279, 292, 322. *See also* Prayer.

Z

Zifroni, 18n, 85n, 175n, 223n, 235n

Ẓafenat Paneaḥ, 61n, 126n, 128n, 144n

INDEX OF PASSAGES CITED

Kuzari

Part 1

1	3, 15, 16, 17, 25, 26, 27, 29n, 33, 34, 35, 36, 39, 42, 43, 48, 49, 53, 55n, 56, 58, 60, 62, 63n, 64, 65, 66, 68, 69n, 70n, 71, 79, 80n, 81, 82, 83, 84, 86, 87n, 88, 90, 91n, 95, 99, 100, 110, 115, 126n, 127n, 134, 135, 176, 218, 256, 270, 277, 302, 307, 317, 332, 333
2	5, 78, 80, 95, 102, 103n, 113n, 258, 259n, 283, 333n, 338n
3	106, 109n
4	7, 24n, 61n, 85, 104n, 122, 126n, 127n, 170, 184, 225, 228n, 265, 267, 270n, 316, 322, 337n
5	174, 175, 208n, 240, 304n
8–9	238
8	8, 8n, 174, 186n, 195n, 218, 219, 224n, 258, 327
9	258, 265
10	266
11–43	143
11	189, 220, 281n, 286
12	144, 184, 322, 338n
13	81n, 323

14	338n
15	175, 185
19–20	174
19	74n, 93n
20	74
21–24	258
21–25	174
21	85, 185n, 228, 229, 277n, 278n, 280
22	75n, 85n, 229, 259, 278n, 285
23	189
24	185, 189
25	184, 186, 201, 286
26	75n, 86, 229, 286, 288
27	86, 144, 185, 189, 214n, 220, 277, 286, 328
28	338n
30–43	5
35	82n, 148n
38	61n
39	147, 288
41	248, 293n
42	64, 299n
43	180, 225n, 248
44	179n
47	199n
49	6, 74n
54	89, 91
55	90
57	92
59	92
60–67	220
62	4
63	6
67	130, 176, 221, 224
68	21n
69	74n
73	18n, 44n

INDEX OF PASSAGES CITED

76	44n
77	147
78	147
79	148n, 280
80	87, 88
81	56n, 81, 84, 88, 102, 256, 291
83–84	198n
83	291n, 344
86	293
87	59, 60, 91n, 197n, 198n, 207n, 249, 320n, 327, 343n
88	9, 186, 198n, 248n
89	176n, 185n, 198n, 217, 248n, 249, 256
91	130n, 185n, 219
95	6, 56n, 61n, 151, 214, 238, 266, 288, 292, 294, 295, 296n, 298n, 299n
96	301
97	33n, 102n, 213, 231, 247, 256, 269n, 304n
98	7n, 102, 120n, 210, 259n, 277, 292
99	18n, 213
100	88n, 241n
101	91n
102	288
103	180, 234n, 235n, 248n, 249n, 280n, 288, 299n
105	248n
106	234, 235n, 248n
107	235n, 245
108	234, 234n
109	180n, 185, 206n, 229n, 234, 235, 248, 260, 268n, 269n, 277n, 278, 280, 287, 293, 298, 323n, 343n
110	69n
111	5, 122n, 265
112–113	265
112	265
113	284
115	140n, 284

Part 2

1–7	119n
1	88n, 120, 121
2	121, 124, 163, 216n, 318
6	17n, 124, 319
7	213n
8–24	156
8	162, 207
9	160
10	155n, 160
11	266n
12	154n, 296
13	156n
14	161n, 193n, 199, 207n, 209, 239, 241, 267, 279n, 294n, 299n
16	292, 293, 298
18–20	296
18	302n
20	248n, 267, 294, 295
22	241n
23–24	267n
23	263n, 269
24	155, 156, 209, 269
26	9n, 131n, 161, 202n, 250, 319
30	90n
32	268, 287
34	210, 233n, 261n, 263n, 267n, 268, 278
35	263
44	140n, 161n, 262n, 263, 264
48	66n, 210n, 292, 301n
49	83, 283
50–56	261
50	161n, 162, 201, 202n, 206, 208, 232, 233, 241n, 261, 279, 280, 281, 291, 292n, 297
51–55	161n
51	233n
53	180n, 201, 261

INDEX OF PASSAGES CITED

54	5, 17, 25n, 27n, 73, 76n, 162, 180, 187, 219, 220, 223, 224n, 249, 255, 261, 263, 268n, 297n, 315n
56	161n, 260, 263n, 281, 343n
58	281n
62	215n, 250
64	234, 250
65	249, 250
66	6
68	91n, 94, 161n, 296, 297
72–73	295
72	90n, 91n, 249, 337
73	297n
80	241n, 250, 294

Part 3

1	64, 65, 83n, 97, 98, 100, 105, 134, 135, 137, 138, 139, 155n, 207n, 232n, 280n, 321, 334
2	334n
5	7n, 139, 140, 141, 144, 229, 239n, 246, 277n, 293n, 320n
7	164n
8	139, 165n
9	148
11	105n, 110, 111, 114, 122, 126n, 128n, 138n, 140, 145n, 154, 165, 186, 199n, 206n, 232n, 244n, 279n, 292n, 318
12	141, 154
13–15	155
17	73, 122, 124n, 125, 126, 129, 135, 138, 140, 150, 206n, 230n, 235n, 294n, 318, 320, 321
19	128, 135, 140, 144, 319, 320
20	133, 319, 320n
21	122, 155
23	44n, 126n, 138n, 145, 147n, 148, 155n, 164n, 334n
24	334
35	334n, 342

39	341
41	342, 343
43	131, 132, 320
49	18, 140, 267n, 334n, 342n
50	343
53	111, 132, 145, 155
54	7n
65	81, 135, 138, 144, 155n, 284, 306
73	9n, 125, 151n, 165, 185n, 319, 320n
79	148

Part 4

1	32, 178, 190, 230n, 315n, 326
2	190
3	5, 6, 8, 9, 25n, 32, 33, 35, 61, 66n, 69, 73n, 79, 130n, 138n, 151n, 176, 178, 180n, 185n, 186, 187, 188, 190, 191, 199, 200n, 201n, 203, 204, 205, 207n, 208n, 212, 214, 216, 217, 219n, 224, 236n, 238, 240n, 241, 243, 246, 247, 248, 257, 278, 287, 291n, 292, 294, 296n, 298, 299, 323n, 326, 329, 335, 343n
4	68
5	32n, 56n, 61, 68, 92, 144n, 185n, 232, 243, 245, 323
6	92n, 244, 245n
7–9	293n
8–9	296n
8	157n
9	207, 291, 292
10	264n
11	87n, 200n, 247, 264n, 270, 343n
13	16, 33, 35, 64, 65, 66n, 67, 71, 76, 81, 96, 114, 123n, 187, 213n, 219n, 255, 280
14	248n
15–17	96
15	9, 15, 32, 35n, 66, 68, 69, 70, 72, 73, 74n, 83n, 175, 190, 214, 245, 282, 285, 328
16–19	96

INDEX OF PASSAGES CITED

16	66n, 69n, 70, 81, 83, 122, 238n, 283, 330
17	6, 81, 130, 158n, 194n, 200, 219, 238, 241, 245, 266, 285, 292n, 293, 305n, 307n
19	33n, 36, 64, 68, 79, 82n, 83n, 84, 94, 97, 98, 133, 281n, 318
20	110n
21	267
22	284
23	66n, 219, 242n, 261, 262n, 264, 267, 268, 271, 282, 284, 288, 292
24	150n, 306n
25	16, 18, 20, 21, 23, 33, 35, 37n, 38, 42, 55, 90n, 91n, 124n, 126, 130, 163n, 205n, 222, 292, 294, 299n
26–27	224n
26	130, 150n, 218, 222, 291, 303n
27	6, 92n, 125n, 129n, 130, 150n, 176n, 218, 222
28	303n
37	6

Part 5

1	11
2–4	45
2	9, 23, 24, 28, 29n, 31, 41, 47, 124n, 211, 222, 223, 319, 327, 344
3	28
4	19, 23, 43, 127n
6	179n
7	20
8	17n, 74n, 89n
10	15, 17, 33n, 36, 40, 41, 44, 46, 52, 53, 64, 72, 127n, 134, 199
12	11, 21, 22, 23n, 24, 26, 28, 36, 37, 40, 43, 44, 55, 56, 57, 58, 59, 60n, 61, 62, 63, 65, 99, 141n, 317, 320n
14	21n, 22, 25, 27n, 34, 36n, 38, 56, 63n, 68, 69, 72n, 76n, 83n, 98, 129n, 132, 176, 193n, 220, 225, 236, 305n, 326

16–18	303
16	306n, 307n
18	26n, 35n, 121n, 124n, 219n, 230n
20	29, 66n, 89n, 102n, 121n, 145n, 178, 212, 214n, 223n, 231, 262n, 278, 292n, 298, 302, 304n
21	21n, 23n, 34, 35n, 36, 39, 43, 52n, 71, 183n, 185n, 187, 188, 195, 196n, 197, 217, 218, 223, 224n, 236n, 252, 255, 317, 323n
22	157, 285n
23	102n, 154n, 155n, 248n, 264, 266, 269, 285n, 296, 336n
24	158
25	115n, 279
26	285n
27	102n, 155, 156, 158n, 231, 241, 262n, 266, 269, 270, 286n

Poems of Judah Halevi

ʿAvdei zeman ʿavdei ʿavadim hem (Brody 2:300) 279n
Devarekha be-mor ʿover reqoḥim (Brody 2:164), 155n
Elohai mishkenotekha yedidut (Brody 2:160), 246n
Liqrat ḥallal ḥeshqekha (Brody 2:34), 281n
Lord, Where Shall I Find Thee? (Yah, ana emzaʾekha) (Brody 3:150), 191–194
Meʾaz maʿon ha-ahavah hayita (Brody 4:232), 281n
Le-miẓrayyim ʿalei kol shir tehilah (Brody 2:180), 294n
Shuvi nafshi li-mnuḥaikhi (Brody 3:54), 194n
Yam suf ve-sinai limmeduni (Brody 4:212), 154n
Yeshʿakha yazkiru ʿam bekha yakhtiru (Brody 3:13), 230n
Yona nasata ʿal kanfei nesharim, 110n

Rabbinic Literature

BT Shabbat 156a	194n
Genesis Rabba 52,5	111n
Leviticus Rabba 1,13	111n

INDEX OF PASSAGES CITED

Abraham Ibn Ezra
Bible Commentary

Genesis (*FR* = First Recesion)
1:1	129n, 299n
1:2 (*FR*)	190n
1:3	60n
1:26	131n, 188n, 236n, 299n
1:26 (*FR*)	132n, 299n
4:22 (*FR*)	137n
6:2 (*FR*)	214, 299n

Exodus (*s* = short commentary)
3:15	132n, 137n
7:1	59n
8:18 (*s*)	294n
13:21 (*s*)	185n
Ch. 20 (*s*)	74n
20:1	123
20:20 (*s*)	126n
20:20	126n
23:20 (*s*)	85n, 188, 299n
24:5	126n
25:40 (*s*)	299n
31:18	213n
33:12	129n
33:21 (*s*)	127n
33:21	55n, 129n
33:22 (*s*)	55n
33:23 (*s*)	61n
43:23 (*s*)	61n

Deuteronomy
6:5	65n
21:20	66n
26:17	190n
32:39	144n

Ecclesiastes
Preface   132n
7:16   232n

Psalms
21:2   137n
49:21   133
73:24   137n
119:3   125n

Daniel
2:11   131n
9:2   343n
10:21   132n
12:7   33

Yesod Mora

§7   137n
§9   293n

www.ingramcontent.com/pod-product-compliance
Lightning Source LLC
Chambersburg PA
CBHW030126240426
43672CB00005B/33